1995

Changing to National Health Care

ETHICS IN A CHANGING WORLD
is a series that responds to issues dealing with
the ethical implications of developments in science and technology.
Publications in this series present technically reliable accounts of
such development and an extended examination
of the ethical issues they raise.

VOLUME 4 • ETHICS IN A CHANGING WORLD

Changing to National Health Care
Ethical and Policy Issues

Robert P. Huefner
Margaret P. Battin
Editors

University of Utah Press
Salt Lake City
1992

∞ The paper in this book meets the standards for permanence and durability established by the Committee on Production Guidelines for Book Longevity of the Council on Library Resources

ETHICS IN A CHANGING WORLD
Margaret P. Battin and Leslie P. Francis, Editors

Library of Congress Cataloging-in-Publication Data

Changing to national health care : ethical and policy issues / Robert
   P. Huefner, Margaret P. Battin, editors.
      p.   cm. — (Ethics in a changing world ; v. 4)
   Based on the Seventh Annual Utah Ethics and Health Conference in
Jan., 1991 held at the University of Utah; sponsored by a number of
University of Utah programs and departments.
   Includes bibliographical references and index.
   ISBN 0-87480-389-6 (alk. paper)
   1. Medicine, State—United States—Congresses. 2. Medical policy—
United States—Congresses. 3. Medical policy—United States—Moral
and ethical aspects—Congresses. 4. Health planning—United States—
Congresses. I. Huefner, Robert P., 1936–   . II. Battin, M.
Pabst. III. University of Utah. IV. Utah Ethics and Health
Conference (7th : 1991 : University of Utah) V. Series.
   [DNLM: 1. Delivery of Health Care—United States—congresses.
2. Ethics, Medical—congresses. 3. Health Policy—United States—
congresses. 4. State Medicine—United States—congresses.   W225
C456 1991]
RA412.5.U6C43   1992
362.1'0973—dc20
DNLM/DLC
for Library of Congress   91-40041
                                                                       CIP

Contents

IV. ETHICS AND THE DESIGN OF NATIONAL HEALTH CARE

V. PROVIDERS AND PATIENTS UNDER NATIONAL HEALTH CARE

Ethics in a Changing World

This book is the fourth volume in a series addressed to ethical issues posed by new developments in science, policy, and technology. Each volume presents both a sustained, technically reliable account of the specific development in question and extended examination of the ethical issues raised by that development. Ethical problems are often empirically complex, and much of the applied-ethics discussion of specific developments in science, policy, and technology suffers from the fact that partisans in these discussions are often not very well informed. By presenting *both* the science or subject material and the philosophic discussion which sophisticated inquiry requires, this series aims to alleviate this deficiency and thus to promote responsible discussion of the ethical issues.

Each of the volumes in this series treats a specific area of scientific or technological research, or concerns itself with a specific policy or group of policy proposals. Each includes detailed, reliable accounts of the relevant scientific or technological background, or of policy proposals, with particular attention to those empirical facts or claims which are relevant to the ethical issues raised. The first volume, a prelude to the series, addressed background issues of ethical theory and their relationship to applied ethics. The second, a volume on AIDS testing and privacy written by a doctor, a lawyer, and a philosopher, provides a detailed review of the medical, legal, and policy proposal backgrounds before examining current philosophical issues in privacy. Volume 3, in which a physiologist and a philosopher examine controversial methods of contraception, provides an extended examination of human reproductive physiology and endocrinology, an account of contemporary contraceptive technologies for women (and future prospects for men), and a comprehensive review of mutagenesis and teratogenesis as they affect the ethical issues these matters raise. This fourth volume, the product of a conference designed to fit the demands of this series, likewise provides as comprehensive a background as possible in the space available about the policy proposals concerning national health care before examining the ethical issues they raise. Future volumes will address a wide range of similar issues.

Margaret P. Battin and Leslie P. Francis

Preface

As national health care has become a topic of increasing public urgency, moving rapidly onto the political agenda, there has been much debate about whether the United States should or should not create a national system. A great deal of attention has been paid to the failings of the current partly private, partly public system, which incorporates both privately insured or funded medical care and care insured or provided under such programs as Medicare, Medicaid, and the Department of Veterans Affairs (the VA). Much of this attention has involved discussion of the ethical dilemmas which arise under this mixed system. But no sustained look has been given to the distinctive ethical dilemmas that would arise if the country were to move to a national system; it is to such dilemmas that this volume is devoted. Thus, it poses a hypothetical question: what if we had national health care? The question is not *whether* we should move to a national health system, away from our current partly private, partly public system, but what ethical issues would arise were we to do so. After all, our current system generates many ethical issues, including those associated with problems of funding and access and with the nature of medicine in a market system; but we can also consider what different ethical issues would arise in a national system providing coverage for all—whether that is a program of private health insurance, government health insurance, direct government health services, or some comprehensive combination of insurance and direct services.

Of course, it might be argued that this study of ethics is futile, even silly: that issues of ethics have little or no place in a major social transformation like the move from a largely private system to a program with centralized features. Ethics, on this view, is mere window dressing; it is the subject of a current but misguided fad. Political feasibility is the really central issue in the design and adoption of a national health system, and here, ethical considerations have no role. It is economic considerations that drive matters here: how a system can be shaped to be economically viable, what financing mechanisms are feasible, what obligations the voters as taxpayers are willing to support, and what advantage or damage to their own careers politicians foresee in supporting one or another sort of health program. Ethics, on this view, is merely the little province of that motley, growing tribe of bioethicists who hang around hospitals and serve on ethics committees—a useful group when their plug-pulling decisions help to keep costs down, but a nuisance in many other contexts.

Furthermore, this argument might be continued, it is a mistake to speak of the current pressures for national health care in ethical terms at all. These pressures are not ethical; they are pressures resulting from two new phenomena: many physicians are shifting to support it, and many large industries are supporting it too. On this view, there is nothing *moral* here; rather, physicians are seeing their incomes squeezed by, among other things, low Medicaid reimbursement rates, insurance practices discouraging specialist treatment, health maintenance organizations (HMOs) paying lower salaries and providing less attractive practice conditions, and, by no means least, the continuing aggravation of the paperwork involved in seeking reimbursement from a huge array of payers. Major industry is beginning to support a national health program too, as it observes escalating insurance costs to be representing a larger and larger share of the costs of manufactured items; it argues that covering health insurance costs as a benefit to workers is rendering American products less competitive with foreign ones. Voters, alarmed by journalistic accounts of the vulnerability of their current health insurance, are increasingly likely to say they support a national health program—though they say they are not yet willing to pay for it. These pressures, not ethical considerations, increase the likelihood that the United States will pass national health legislation—if not immediately, then sometime within the next decade or so.

And further still, it might be argued, political opportunism will ensure that the issue of national health continues to be increasingly conspicuous. While the incumbent president and the Republican party have been remarkably quiet on issues of national health, leaving such issues to a series of conservative surgeons general, candidates from the Democratic party are badly in need of a conspicuous, popular, public issue which addresses differences in basic philosophy between the two parties. National health is a natural for this role, and some commentators believe it will be central in the coming elections. Not only are the Democrats likely to promote a national health program, but the Republicans will be forced to respond either with a program of their own or at least a persuasive excuse for not inaugurating one. Some of the same considerations may also be true at the state level.

Thus, we may well get national health care, or a state-by-state patchwork of programs. But, the argument insists, this has nothing to do with ethics. If ethics is involved at all, it will be involved in a peripheral way at best, as, for example, in ranking the conditions to be covered or excluded under Oregon's overtly rationing Medicaid plan. Ethics, however, has nothing to do with the plan itself, which is dictated by political necessity, and it will have nothing to do with the adoption or rejection of a national health plan. After all, this may seem to be the message of the two essays with which the present volume addresses the question of why the United States does not already have health care: one of them documents the "surge and retreat" pattern in which political factors interfere with attempts to introduce national health care, and the other describes a political climate of self-interested choice in which national health care is pursued not for reasons having to do with the welfare of the populace but rather in attempts by one powerful group to shift costs onto another. If political conditions alter the cost incentives and there are no interfering factors, national health care will occur, but only for these reasons and not for ethical ones.

Is this argument—that national health care is not an ethical issue but a political and economic one—persuasive? We think not. On the contrary, we think the issue of national health care is one which raises profound ethical issues and which demands sustained ethical reflection, issues which no decent society ought to ignore. Of course, national health care could be allowed to function as a merely political and economic matter if these issues were brushed aside, but this is not a defensible course of action: there are ethical issues here far too important to ignore, and it is the purpose of this volume to begin to raise these issues in a way forceful enough that this cannot occur.

In order to begin this process, an extended seminar was convened at the University of Utah to commission essays on a range of topics;

the seminar met over a period of nearly a year to discuss and critique these essays. Comment was invited from a number of outside sources, and the resulting essays were presented at the Seventh Utah Ethics and Health Conference in January 1991. In addition to receiving major support from the FHP Foundation, the conference was also supported by a wide range of organizations—including the Salt Lake Veterans Administration Center, the Utah Medical Association, the Utah Hospital Association, the Utah Health Insurance Association, and the Utah Public Health Association—and sponsored by a number of University of Utah programs and departments, including the College of Health, the College of Humanities, the College of Law, the School of Medicine, the College of Nursing, the Department of Philosophy, the Department of Political Science, and the FHP Center for Health Care Studies.

The chapters in this book show the value of using an ethical lens to view the matters of how a national health care program might be shaped. This ethical lens identifies conflicts which need to be addressed and understood in the current political discussion, such as the issue of whether health care is a right, or the relative importance of economic interest and cultural values in shaping the impetus for and purpose of a national program. But although this book is primarily concerned with issues of ethics, it is also attentive to providing a reliable factual basis for discussion of these issues. For instance, it reveals facts which may surprise many participants in the debate about national health programs—for example, that the United States already has a national health service, the VA, which is as fully governmental as the British system, and that the experience of this system offers some of the most important insights available for fashioning a system which realistically reflects the American situation. Throughout the essays in this volume, effort has been made to provide extensive factual material as a basis for the responsible discussion of ethical issues—both current ethical issues and the projected future ones it is the particular concern of this volume to explore.

Following an introductory section introducing the issues at hand, the volume is divided into five principal parts, of which the first, a discussion of why the United States does not already have national health care, explores the underlying historical, political, and ethical issues; the second addresses issues of international comparison; and the third, on the VA, explores a form of national health care already in place in the United States—one with extensive morally relevant experience—but virtually always ignored. Part 4 considers the foundational ethical issues involved in the design of a national health system, and Part 5 looks at ethical issues in provider/ patient relationships in a functioning system. The remainder of this Preface follows these divisions.

INTRODUCTION: AN OVERVIEW OF THE ISSUES

What would be distinctive about an American national health system, and what specific issues would it raise? Philosopher Daniel I. Wikler's opening remarks provide a broad overview of the territory to be covered. Some of the ethical issues of a national system would not be very different from those we face in the present health care delivery system, though the context, and perhaps the likelihood of seeing and the ability to grapple with the issues, could change. He begins with a challenge to the whole idea of the book itself: could the discussion of the "what if" questions be used to delay the very adjustments most needed in the system? (This issue surfaces again later, in a somewhat different form, when Frank Thompson asks how much truth telling can be expected and afforded in our pluralistic democracy.) Moving to the explicit task of the book, Wikler walks us briskly through the daunting issues of who controls, how resources are allocated (through a single or tiered system, to what types of care, and with how much of total national production being given to health rather than education, consumer disposable income, etc.), patient and/or physician choice, privacy, and so on, with reflections on how the context of these issues changes if there is a comprehensive national health program. And he helps reveal the complexity of the choices by laying out some of the conflicts between presumed goods; for example, fairness in the allocation of care can inhibit innovation and the eventual quality of care.

Alan Nelson, M.D., past president of the American Medical Association and president-elect of the World Medical Association, recounts some of the evidence of breakdown in the current system, impelling us to change. He links the ethics of the physician, the society, and our politics with the question of whether medicine is a business or a profession. It has become evident that the design of either a national health program or incremental reforms in the present system will shape the balance between business and profession. Nelson believes significant change, not just tinkering, would be desirable and describes the way the professional qualities of medicine should be viewed and supported in light of such change.

Perhaps the most vivid account of the impetus for a national health system, however, appeared in the remarks made at the conference by Ann Marie Boyden, the executive director of the Benefit Insurance Trust for the American Institute of Architects in Washington, D.C., and former owner of an advertising and marketing firm in Salt Lake City. She said:

> When I sold my Utah business in 1988, the health insurance premiums for our employees had surpassed the cost of rent and utilities and, after salaries, were the second largest expense in our company. Today, according to Foster Higgins, for many small businesses the cost of health insurance can be the greatest payroll line item cost, exceeding both the cost of workers compensation and general liability insurance. Simply put, for many small employers and their employees access and cost are the same thing. For others, the fragmentation of the market and "actuarially fair" underwriting practices have effectively cut off from health care those who make their living in small business. These problems are brought home to me almost every day as I talk to members of the American Institute of Architects.

> There was a man who left his position on the faculty of a major university to go into private practice. He had been protected under the Consolidated Omnibus Budget Reconciliation Act of 1985, which requires that insurance coverage for many discharged employees be temporarily renewable by the employee, but his COBRA benefits were about to run out and he was looking for coverage for his family, including an eight-year-old diabetic daughter. He told me he expected coverage of her diabetes to be waived for a period of time, but he was concerned about other things. She was an active young girl, attending school and playing youth soccer. He could find no coverage for her at all.

> There was a firm where a single principal, whose name the firm bears, was the only person left on a Blue Cross-Blue Shield indemnity plan, and now Blue Cross-Blue Shield is insisting on a hundred percent participation from the firm. The other twelve people in the firm were all enrolled in an HMO, and they paid their own premiums, which were, of course, considerably less than those for the indemnity plan. The principal is sixty years old, has had open heart surgery, and is now uninsurable, according to the insurers—although he is working every day designing buildings.

> People over fifty-five are paying unbelievably high premiums, and upon reaching sixty-five the paperwork and red tape associated with Medicare and Medicare supplements is a health hazard in and of itself. When the AIA Benefit Insurance Trust offered a new improved plan to members, it took almost a year for each and every state, moving at their own speeds and with no sense of urgency either from the states or the

insurance carrier, to grant approval so that we could sell the product to our members.

As it stands today, our American system, as Dr. Alan Nelson describes it [in the essay following in this book], allows for an avalanche of cost shifting. Governments, through Medicare and Medicaid, use market leverage to keep payments at or below expenses, leading providers to raise rates for business. Larger employers, in turn, use their purchasing power to negotiate discounts. All of this increases the medical expenses paid by smaller companies to which providers shift costs. As Princeton University economist Uwe Reinhardt pointed out to an audience of more than 1,200 benefits managers at Benefits Expo '90, big government shoves it down the throat of big business, and big business shoves it down the throat of small entrepreneurs. In this regard, the homage paid to small business, to the entrepreneurs in our society, is purely lip service. The design of any national health care system must address this inequity to small employers. Professionals in practice and small employers fear, perhaps with justification, that these are habits which will be impossible to break.

Most people don't lay the problem of health care costs at the feet of their doctors. The reforms most Americans see as required are in who pays for what. The question businesses, large and small, ask is, Who's going to pay for it and how? It is conceivable, and in fact probable, that the same cost shifting to small, middle-income entrepreneurs will continue. No wonder the National Federation of Independent Business and other conservative small business associations continue to fight any and all mandates. NFIB says that they are caught in the clash between values and reality. Small business owners believe that every American has a right to health care, yet the NFIB, in accordance with member surveys, works to avoid regulation of any kind and for the repeal of COBRA and state mandates regarding insurance coverage. As economic considerations prevail, free enterprise becomes the battle cry. But, one must ask, free enterprise for whom?

Physician Arnold Relman, former editor of the *New England Journal of Medicine,* has said that health care is not an economic commodity, and if one tries to make it a commodity the result is what we have now: people who can't afford health care being excluded from the market, rising costs as everybody wants to get their share of the profits and distortions of the country's needs. Would any of this change under a national plan? The fear is that nothing but the banker would change.

PART I: WHY DOESN'T THE UNITED STATES ALREADY HAVE NATIONAL HEALTH CARE?

Of the developed industrial nations, only the United States and South Africa do not have national health care systems, and many much less developed nations do have national health care. Why is the

United States such an anomaly? In a pair of interestingly complementary papers, both historian Harold Bauman and economist Paul
J. Feldstein seek to explain why the United States does not have
national health care. Though their explanations are quite different,
both discuss the rhetoric of American individualism, raising questions as to whether the motives are liberty or the self-interest of
established groups.

Bauman surveys what he describes as a pattern of "surge and
retreat" characterizing the periodic drives toward national health
care: a pattern in which pressure builds up for national health care
and then is interrupted by some political force or event. The United
States came close to adopting a national program between 1910 and
1920, during the Progressive Era; World War I stopped this first wave.
The second wave began with the Social Security Act of 1935, buoyed
by the New Deal and the Fair Deal, and led to Truman's determined
effort in 1950 to enact comprehensive health care legislation; it was a
casualty of the cold war. The third wave began in 1965 with the
enactment of Medicare and Medicaid but foundered by 1980 in a sea
of rising costs and the aftermath of the Vietnam War. A fourth wave is
beginning now; and the question is whether this wave will ultimately
result in a national program or whether it too will be defeated by
political events.

Paul J. Feldstein also offers an account that explains the lack of
national health care in political terms. He rejects the thesis that the
objective of a national health program is the ethical one of serving
the poor or increasing efficiency—for we would have agreed long ago
on the means for accomplishing this—and argues instead that it is
meant to serve self-interested rather than altruistic goals. National
health is, he claims, an attempt by the powerful classes to shift their
costs onto others and can only be understood in these terms. It is for
political rather than principled reasons that we do not have a
comprehensive national health program.

Suzanne Dandoy, M.D., who has directed both the Arizona and
the Utah departments of health and is the immediate past president
of the Association of State and Territorial Health Officials and
president of the American College of Preventive Medicine, comments upon these essays by assessing the politics of federalism in this
country. Here she too finds polemics being used to mask self-interest:
that recent federal policy, for example, is less a search for comprehensive care than for mechanisms to avoid the burdens, and even the
responsibilities, of costs.

At a luncheon talk at the conference, David Sundwall, M.D., Vice-President and Medical Director of the American Health Care System Institute, previously an assistant surgeon general and, prior to that, director of the health staff for the Senate's Committee on Labor and Human Resources, described recent developments in Washington and, in the course of this, took issue with the many complaints about inadequate progress.

"Congress isn't idle," he said, as he offered a long list of congressional and administrative actions which, although incremental at best, represent much effort and political risk. He pointed to reductions in infant mortality, reductions in accidental deaths, and other improvements in healthiness and access to care to argue that there indeed has been progress. He provided a different perspective about the constraints and possibilities of political and administrative capacity by which the chapters of this section may be viewed:

> When the federal government was first formed, and with the first Congress of 1789, it didn't have any role in health except to provide for the health of merchant seamen and being authorized to build maritime hospitals at seaports. Other than that specified responsibility and some very primitive efforts in public health related to quarantines and the control of infectious diseases, it didn't do much until the turn of this century when it got into the business of regulating food, drugs, biologics, and—through some cooperation with local and state governments to collaborate on air, water, and garbage control—sanitation. That was pretty much the federal role and it did that very well, and all of our health is better because of it. But the presence of the federal government in our general health care delivery system, to any significant degree—and I apologize to the VA, which is a major effort created after World War I, and a few other important developments—didn't occur until 1965, when Medicare and Medicaid were passed. That was the first time our government at the national level had had a vested interest in the health care system per se, when it chose to care for the elderly and the poor, at least in part.
>
> Therefore, when I hear all this carping and complaining and aggravation and disappointment about what we're doing and what we're doing badly, I want to remind people that we're relatively new at this, and we're learning from mistakes made, and from promises made that weren't delivered upon. I don't think it's altogether fair to expect that what happened, which we all know was a compromise not based upon sound policy, was any more than a compromise in proposals that were extant at the time when we created Medicare and Medicaid. But we're learning from that. I like to remind people that what might hold true in many other policy areas—that is, the saying on the National Archives Building on Pennsylvania Avenue that "the past is pro-

logue"—is not true in health care in the United States: we're charting new territory and new ground.

PART II: COMPARING NATIONAL HEALTH SYSTEMS

How can we compare health care in the United States with national systems elsewhere? John G. Francis, a political scientist, and Norman J. Waitzman, an economist, both reflect on the difficulties posed by such comparisons. Still, both urge comparative analysis as a primary means of increasing our sensitivity to the ethical issues in the problems and opportunities for changes in the U.S. health care delivery system.

Francis looks at two clusters of ethical concerns: whether or not national governments should provide health care to their populations, and how they should approach cost containment. He considers in detail the systems of four countries with national health care: Britain, France, Canada, and Germany. He is particularly concerned about whether the ethical presumptions behind a national health care program make any significant difference. In other words, if there is a national health care program, does it matter whether it is primarily justified on the basis of rights, utility, or desert (i.e., serving those who particularly deserve service, such as, say, veterans)? This might lead us to consider, for example, whether a utilitarian justification, and guidance in implementation, results in more central control than a desert justification. Or does a utilitarian justification result in more aggressive and flexible mechanisms of cost control than does a rights justification?

Waitzman analyzes the relationships between health expenditures and health outcomes for these and four additional countries in the Organization for Economic Cooperation and Development (OECD) and poses a specific, troubling question, Why is the United States doing so poorly? Is the apparent fact that some significant health outcomes in the United States are inferior to those in other countries, even though we spend more, an artifact of the way international comparisons are made, or is the United States really doing poorly—much worse on many counts than countries with national health plans? Francis and Waitzman agree that the latter is the case: health care in the United States, despite the national myth that it is the best in the world, provides both less adequate and more expensive health care than that provided in many other places. What this may say is that whether or not there is major change in the health care delivery system, and whether the system is justified by rights, utility, or desert, there ought to be more aggressive questioning of the system's success.

Lawrence D. Brown, also a political scientist, seems to use the Francis and Waitzman chapters to take issue with the view of Feldstein, the economist, that special interests are the explanation of health policy. It is the nation's culture and its related political structures and processes which represent our values and explain much of our policy. It can even be the case that the "moral" standards of the culture are the matters which particularly threaten the equity and fairness of its programs. For example, is U.S. policy largely justified by a desert mentality which results in a categorization of recipients; does that in turn cause much of the inequity and inefficiency of the present system?

PART III: THE VA AS NATIONAL HEALTH CARE

What form of partial national health care do we already have? In the mixed private/public health care picture the United States now has, there are also several systems which function, much like the British National Health Service, as health providers rather than health insurance systems. In health provider systems, health care is dispensed in government facilities by physicians and other personnel who are government employees; it is supported directly by government funds; and it is subject to government regulation. The largest such system is the Department of Veterans Affairs (VA) medical system; others include the Indian Health Service and various smaller programs.

Mark W. Wolcott, M.D., and Charles B. Smith, M.D., both senior VA physicians, provide a portrait of the much-misunderstood, often ignored VA system and the changes it has undergone since the turn of the century. They challenge the conventional wisdom that attributes inefficiency and poor quality to the VA, and the related American presumptions about any bureaucratically operated and politically controlled program. They point to an impressive quality record in some areas, though they freely acknowledge the strains of recent severe budget cuts, and they reinforce observations that VA health care is one of the most cost-effective systems functioning in the United States today. With this as background to the situation and their view of it, they then take advantage of the opportunity which the VA provides to identify the ethical issues likely to arise in any national health program, whether a program of national health insurance or of national health care service. They particularly argue that the VA's recent history of severe budget cutbacks, forcing it to ration care, offer an American experience with distributive ethical dilemmas which is crucial to any discussion of national health programs.

J. William Hollingsworth, M.D., also a long-time practitioner in and student of the VA, extends this analysis, focusing upon the problem of rationing. He, like Brown, finds problems in the American inclination to ration according to "desert," but he finds difficulty with other forms of rationing. Yet rationing will be necessary, in any national health program, and if proof is needed it is provided by the history of the VA. He addresses not only the ways to approach rationing but offers valuable insights to related questions: can the VA bureaucracy reasonably represent the nation in allocation decisions, and what are the inclinations for (and the ethics of) the political institutions to avoid the basic issues—for example, to make incremental extensions of coverage in order to hold off major reform or rebellion?

David Wilsford, a political scientist, uses his extensive comparative studies of health care politics in the industrialized nations to reflect upon the importance of the VA experience. He believes that there is a fiscal imperative for major change in the U.S. system of health care. But the nature of the reform will reflect the arena in which it is carried out. He suggests that with all the problems of special interests, and incrementalism, government still offers the most promising arena for a comprehensive perspective for reform. The VA itself offers an interesting opportunity for experimentation because it more clearly accepts the public responsibility for health care, which presumably would be the basis for any national health care program. Wilsford is raising the question, similar to the apparent difference between Feldstein and Brown, of whether it is the force of basic interests which decides ethics or ethics which decides the basic forces. If it is the former, is it then important to select the arena for the contest, inasmuch as the balance of forces is different in, say, the VA than in a marketplace of competitive and profit-oriented providers?

PART IV: ETHICS AND THE DESIGN OF
NATIONAL HEALTH CARE

How should a national health care system be designed? Many of the ethical issues in national health care, especially those concerned with equality of access and differences in levels of care, focus around a single, central issue: whether health care is a right, or whether, instead, it is simply something a nation may or may not choose to offer its citizens. A physician-philosopher team, gastroenterologist Kenneth Buchi and philosopher Bruce M. Landesman, argue vigorously for the view that health care is a right—and, indeed, a fundamental right—of all persons. The positive right to a decent—though not lavish—level of health care for all persons, they argue, should be recognized and enacted in public policy.

The U.S. health care system, if it can be called by this term at all, is a mixed private/public system. The bulk of U.S. health care is provided under private insurance, in private hospitals, and by privately employed physicians. In addition to public provider programs like the VA, however, there are several large public insurance programs, notably Medicare, covering the elderly, and Medicaid, covering the poor. In an extended discussion of the relationship between the private and public components of a health system, philosopher Allen Buchanan considers whether it is the responsibility of government to fill in "gaps" between programs and to extend coverage to those not included in private programs; he rejects this claim, and argues that in a mixed system of this sort the private insurers and providers also bear some ethical obligation to construct their programs so that persons are not left without care. Private insurers, in particular, have a responsibility to help solve or at least not worsen problems of access to health care in the United States. This includes exerting pressures on the federal government to fulfill its own basic responsibilities— which it is not now doing—and to hold themselves accountable as well. To put it more plainly, experience-rating to shed high-risk clients, in the absence of other care for them, is not morally justified.

Introducing a national health system which will augment or replace the current private/public mixed system, however, will involve some changes in what is available to individuals. Some individuals will get more than they are accustomed to—the uninsured, for example—but a cost-controlled system may provide less to some others. Philosopher-lawyer Leslie Pickering Francis reflects on the nature of antecedent expectations developed under previous systems and raises ethical issues about when and whether these expectations must be satisfied. Does the fact that some Americans have been receiving health care at very high levels, and, accordingly, have developed expectations about the future which allow them to plan their lives in certain ways, mean that any ethically defensible national health plan would have to continue to meet these expectations? Need expectations that one will be able to continue receiving treatment from the same provider, for instance, or seek referral to a specialist, be met under a national health system? Or can some expectations be disappointed, and if so, which ones? Francis's discussion of such expectations raises many issues which would emerge in any transition to a national health program.

But there are other issues as well in the design of a national health system. In a search for these issues, political scientist Robert P. Huefner catalogues thirty different proposals and quasi-proposals now on the table in the public discussion of national health care, and assesses these with reference to the ethical issues each treats as central. Some plans emphasize access to care, intending to ensure that every individual will receive care; other plans emphasize the control of health care costs. Very few plans emphasize quality of care. Identifying the central concern of the various plans proposed is crucial in anticipating the ethical dilemmas each would raise if it were to be adopted as the basis for a national program. Huefner's analysis examines the structural and political problems of the present situation and uses them to assess further the nature of future change. He argues that three ethical issues deserve priority attention to help inform the design and implementation of a national health program: rights, fairness, and truth telling. His analysis also attempts to incorporate some beginnings of two crucial points raised by those assigned the task of commenting on this essay: the first is the matter raised by Allen Buchanan of who is responsible for ensuring that all have access, and the second is a concern raised by Frank Thompson about the problems of implementation.

In his comments on the Francis and Huefner chapters, political scientist Frank Thompson takes the opportunity to emphasize the importance of implementation, raising several crucial issues. One is that administrative capacity places limits upon available options and that understanding these constraints is crucial to mapping out the realistic choices, and hence in understanding the nature and real difficulties of the ethical issues in making these choices. A second issue is that implementation itself is a further evolution of policy and hence shares in the choices and the ethical issues of these choices. Thompson also raises another kind of issue by wondering how much of the truthfulness discussed by Francis and Huefner is possible in our democratic setting and processes: might open and specific policy debate aggravate the problems of expectations, and/or is vagueness or even some duplicity the stuff of the political compromise necessary for effective policy development in our pluralist society?

PART V: PROVIDERS AND PATIENTS UNDER NATIONAL HEALTH CARE

What would the relationship between providers and patients be in a national health care system? In the final section, the chapters examine the kinds of changes which might occur in the physician/patient relationship if a national health program were to be instituted.

Philosopher Margaret P. Battin, working under the assumption that a national health program would involve universal coverage in a noncompeting system, conjectures that the goal of such a system would be achieving maximal efficiency in providing health care: she imagines a system which provides "best-buy" rather than "best" health care, and, drawing on the poet Rilke's image of the poor of Paris dying "in 559 beds" in the charity hospital, reflects on whether this is appropriate in end-of-life care as well as other situations. Her answer is no: care of the dying cannot be subjected to the same measures of efficiency as other health care, since the end-point of care—death—cannot be the objective of treatment in the same way that cure or the control of a chronic condition can be.

Leonard J. Haas, a psychologist, and Peter C. Appleby, a philosopher, consider the ethical and interpersonal dilemmas that would arise for physicians and patients in a managed health care system, as a national health program would most likely be. The dilemmas they address focus on the issue of loyalty: is the physician's primary loyalty to the patient, or is it to the institution or system in which he or she is employed? Haas and Appleby foresee increasing pressures for cost control in a national health system: ought the physician give primary attention to these, in making treatment decisions for the patient, or does giving primary allegiance to the patient and hence bending institutional rules on behalf of that patient inevitably involve the physician in a posture of disloyalty to the health care system, which after all provides care for the patient? This is a problem in any managed care system but is likely to be particularly acute in national health care.

Philosopher Dan W. Brock, in the final commentary, again finds help in looking at the experiences of others to explore the conflicts between presumed goods. Does the pursuit of what Battin calls "best buys," a pursuit presumably of efficiency, conflict with informed consent and the related interest in moving away from the historical paternalism in the physician-patient relationship? The British experience says that it does. It is again an example of how the purposes, including the ethics, of our health care delivery system depend upon our capacity to act as intelligent participants in the political processes as well as in the provider-patient relationship. The conflict between efficiency and informed consent will be lessened by an increase in economic realism by patients, physicians, and politicians. Such an increase is possible. But the transition in programs and thinking are likely to be difficult; that will make for slow progress in matters of both efficiency and informed consent.

Robert P. Huefner
Margaret P. Battin

An Overview of the Issues

Ethical Issues in National Health Insurance

Daniel Wikler

What ethical issues would we face if the United States were to adopt a national health program? As with any large-scale reform, there can be no full answer to this question before the fact. But our own present experience and that of other nations which have had national health programs for many years indicate that a national health program would transform rather than resolve many of the ethical dilemmas we face in today's largely privatized system. What follows is a sketch of this moral terrain.

I must state at the outset, as I will repeat at the end, that none of the issues I will discuss is more important than the current lack of insurance provision for a seventh of our population. Our most pressing ethical problem, in other words, is that we do not have a national health program. There could conceivably be a risk, therefore, in pointing out difficulties which would arise in adopting this reform, for this modest list might be used by opponents of a national program to argue against its adoption, or it might convince those on the fence that the vision would create more problems than it would solve. I hope that this brief disclaimer will head off any such assumption.

WHAT KIND OF NATIONAL HEALTH PROGRAM?

It goes without saying that one cannot begin to speculate on what kind of problems would arise in a national health program without having some idea of what that program would entail. Indeed, a conservative approach to national health insurance, by which I mean one which changed the present system as little as possible while providing some kind of comprehensive insurance program, would

3

give rise to relatively fewer new ethical quandaries. The fact is that we *have* national health insurance already, in the form of Medicare (and we have a national health service: the Veterans Administration system; to which we can add military hospitals and clinics, and the Indian Health Service). Although Medicare has an age cutoff, so that it covers only one age group, the United States has had a quarter century's experience with a national health program. We could achieve full national health insurance simply by dropping the age requirement. Not that we should, but we could. Assuming that changing the age-related eligibility rule would not drastically alter the way Medicare works—though it might need a different kind of financing—we can say that adoption of a national health program need not raise ethical questions with which we are not already familiar. Indeed, these are largely the ethical issues arising in the health care system as a whole; by and large, patients covered by Medicare get the same kind of treatment that other insured patients get. This reflects a general truth about American medicine, that it is fairly homogeneous. Government, in Medicare, basically buys into the private health care sector, and what it gets for its insured is close to the same product that other payers get. This homogeneity extends even to many hospitals owned and run by the government, particularly university teaching hospitals, which participate in the same health care market environment that nonprofit and for-profit private hospitals do. Unless a public hospital has taken on the burden of providing care to the uninsured, it is generally difficult to tell which kind of hospital one is being treated in.

Therefore, if national health insurance were brought about in the most conservative way, we might not encounter many genuinely new ethical issues. For example, something which might qualify as a "national health program"—it would anyway be a national health *policy*, which we have also lacked heretofore—would cover all Americans in this way: those who have insurance would keep it; employers would be mandated to insure their uninsured workers; and Medicaid would cover the rest. This would resemble the present system in almost every respect, except of course that there would not be thirty-seven million uninsured citizens. Even the more ambitious proposal of the Physicians for a National Health Program (PNHP), which is modeled on Canada's system, would retain many of the features of the present system, including reliance on private, nonprofit hospitals, and the option of fee-for-service payment to physicians.[1]

But proposals for a national health program need not be so

conservative—though the more reform they propose, the less likely they are of being adopted. The United States could use the occasion of the institution of a national health program to change the system for the better, to tinker and experiment, even to redefine the mission of the system as a whole. Critics and reformers have, for example, proposed any number of radical changes:

> The democratization of American health care, with the policies of each hospital, clinic, and practice governed by a board of consumers chosen to be representative of the population served
>
> The demystification of medicine in this country, which would include the involvement of patients in their own care, and the transfer of decision making from physicians to patients
>
> The rationalization of the system, with public authorities having much more extensive control over the mix of physician residence training programs, with comprehensive regionalization, and with a radically increased program of empirical clinical research on the effectiveness of new and existing therapies
>
> The reconceptualization of the system as a whole as a *health* care system, as opposed to the present *medical* care system. This would involve primary emphasis on the nonmedical determinants of health, which many observers have held to be far more powerful than health care, at least in the aggregate; it would emphasize public health and would attend more fully to the nonmedical side of disability and chronic illness, including long-term care.

We need not extend this list to conclude that a highly revisionist, reforming, idealistic approach to national health insurance would introduce a great number of ethical questions, involving the profoundest reconsideration of what health care is and what it is for.

In this brief survey of potential issues of ethical concern in a national health program, I will steer a middle course. This cannot be the occasion to discuss in turn each of the radical proposals just listed, but neither ought the discussion simply assume that in national health insurance everything will be business as usual. Governed by a sense of what is politically feasible, I will assume that any reform movement powerful enough to enact a national health insurance program would aspire to make some use of the powers of national health planning which it might place in policymakers' hands. Still, it must be kept in mind that any ethical quandaries that arise will do so in the context of the particular system we adopt; the point of this essay, of course, is to add to the debate over adoption of a national health program a consideration of the kinds of moral questions each alternative might pose.

THREE ISSUES OF ALLOCATION

A national health program is a system of allocating health care resources. Accordingly, the first topics I will mention all touch on the core issue of allocation. I will divide these into three groups. The first have to do with the question of universality: are we to have one system of care for all? The second involves allocation decisions within that one system. Finally, I will mention the dilemma of deciding how to allocate resources among the many pressing social needs.

All Together Now?

The Canadian system of care provides medical services to nearly every Canadian citizen. Citizens may opt out, but only at great cost. The British National Health Service (NHS) offers care to everyone, but a significant minority decline its benefits and secure care in the private sector for many of the same kinds of services that the NHS purports to offer. An American national health program would need to decide between these alternatives and others.

Universality could be justified from either of two quite distinct moral positions. An egalitarian might argue that health care ought to be provided purely on the basis of need; that we are physiologically more or less equal, however different we are in other ways, and that in responding to our health needs the health care system should accordingly treat us as equals. The point of a universal system would be to ensure this kind of similar and equal treatment. In this view, the government has a positive obligation to ensure that this equality will prevail, and this moral goal necessitates a government-backed universal system.

The other position is agnostic on egalitarianism as a moral principle but endorses an egalitarian policy for strategic political reasons. One can make this argument even if one believes that the government ought generally to stay out of the business of providing for the needs of those who can afford to protect themselves. It does, however, assign to the government a welfare function of providing for the needy. Universality, in this view, may be a political necessity if the government is to meet this obligation, for it is a commonplace that universal programs, such as Medicare and Social Security, provide much more reliably for the worst-off than do programs, such as Medicaid, which are limited to serving those whose income is below a certain level ("means-tested" programs). The universal entitlement programs are supported by citizens with political clout, since they are regarded as "their" programs—never mind the advice of economists that government intervention in these markets surely produces inefficiency.

One problem with a fully universal plan, however, is that it channels all expenditures through the national treasury, burdening the governmental balance sheet. All over the world, countries with universal plans are looking into the possibility of partial privatization, shedding the expenditures which it could induce nonpoor citizens, or their employers, into taking on from their personal budgets. The commitment to universality, therefore, carries an economic and political price. True, proponents of national health insurance on the Canadian model argue that the feature of universality actually saves money, since it eliminates costly overhead which burdens the balkanized private insurance system of the United States. But I suspect that Canada's commitment for across-the-board universality is based on commitment to egalitarian principle as much as it is to economic efficiency, for the Canadians have chosen to offer a very complete package of services to all, one which is so lavish that few would choose to seek out care in the private sector.

It is often said that America's nearly unique refusal to enact national health insurance results from an enduring native individualism, and that we would have to change our basic values before a national health program could be accepted. I regard the enactment and enormous popularity of Medicare as an unanswerable rebuttal to this argument. As I said, Medicare *is* national health insurance, it covers nearly everyone in its age group, and politicians know better than to tamper with it. So there may be nothing in the American character which would demand a nonuniversal plan. But Medicare's cost is enormous, and the price tag for a non-age-restricted national health insurance system based on Medicare could put heavy pressure on a principled commitment to universality.

The alternative, however, would introduce its own moral problems. As the public-support argument suggests, the problem with mean-tested programs is that political support can flag, leading to cutbacks which eventually reach indefensible levels. The Oregon state government's rationing program, which will deny to Medicaid recipients health care benefits which middle-class insureds take for granted, is a case in point. In cities across the country, inner-city public hospitals, even if staffed by the most dedicated health care workers, find themselves providing substandard care as they face increasing demands and fewer resources.

Even when a national health care system offers care to all, toleration of a parallel private system poses special moral problems. The better the private system is relative to the public one, the greater the flight away from the public system, thereby exacerbating its problems. When individual doctors are permitted to offer services more readily in the private system to the same patients they treat in the public one, the incentives introduced yield practices which invite comparison to extortion and bribery: the doctor profits from denying care in the public system, while the patient can jump the public system's queue by making an offer the doctor will be loathe to refuse.

Those who favor a mix of public and private may do so in the name of freedom of choice. And, certainly, patients who can opt for private treatment have this one choice that patients in an all-public universal system lack. But they may not be better off. It depends on whether what they get from a single-sector system is good enough to eliminate the patient's motive for looking for alternatives. In Manitoba, for example, millionaires spend their declining years in state nursing homes. They could afford a private one, of course, but the public ones are so good that they see no reason to spend the extra money. To the extent that restricting choice is a necessary step to achieving this level of quality in the single-sector system, as the Canadians believe it is, then providing the extra choice of an extensive parallel private system reduces the value of the choices which would otherwise be made available. This factor—how munificent the public provision would be—colors a number of the ethical issues we might face in a national health program, a point I will return to shortly.

"You're Entitled . . . ": Choosing among People

Within the system of national health insurance, needs will inevitably be greater than the resources available. The choices which must be made constitute ethical dilemmas of excruciating difficulty. These so-called micro-allocation problems, however, are familiar ones. What special dilemmas would be posed by a national health program?

The answer could be none, if the government decided to cede authority for allocation to individual providers. In our present system, allocation decisions are made at multiple levels, in a complex, unorganized way, and it might be possible for decision makers to avoid taking the heat for any picking and choosing by perpetuating this pattern.

The institution of national health insurance, however, would provide the opportunity for a more orderly approach. Policymakers might hope that by making allocation decisions on rational grounds, the system would be both more efficient and more fair. More efficient, because resources would be concentrated on therapies which work and conditions which most need remedy; more fair, because in a rationalized system arbitrariness and inconsistency could be reduced.

In light of these considerations, and because in the end choices do have to be made by someone, it may be difficult to imagine that a commitment to rationalized allocation could be the source of ethical difficulty. But it can. Oregon's experience is once again a suitable example. In its attempt to make the dollars in its Medicaid budget stretch as far, and as broadly, as possible, Oregon's government has attempted to devise a formula of setting priorities which would reflect the values and preferences of the people in the state. This effort has not been a notable success. As Norman Daniels has noted, the process faltered in its attempt to take notice of the public's values, relying on public hearings attended mostly by health care providers, and using a definition of "values" which mixed apples and oranges.[2] Others have pointed out that the entire effort was premised on the availability of data on relative cost and benefit which have only begun to collect. It has not an accident that among the very highest priorities designated by this formula was treatment for thumb sucking.

Even when the choices are not absurd, the attempt to allocate rationally and explicitly leads to trouble, as Oregon's example has again showed. As Guido Calebresi and Philip Bobbitt noted in their book, *Tragic Choices*, the fact that difficult decisions must unavoidably be made does not mean that the public will accept any of the available resolutions.[3] Disharmony can be avoided in many of these contexts only by masking the decision, so that no one seems to have been intentionally left out. But this approach also raises ethical questions.

Any system of allocation will involve decision making by human agents; a computer cannot do the job. This poses a dilemma found also in private, fixed-budget clinical situations: if an administrator makes the choices, he or she is interfering with the physician's professional responsibility. But if the task is assigned to the physician, we are putting the doctor in a bind, demanding both dedication to the patient and also guardianship of the commons against the patient. One outcome of this double bind, spotted in the United Kingdom by Henry J. Aaron and William B. Schwartz in their book *The Painful Prescription*, can be deception: the physician denies a patient care which would be of benefit but tells the patient that the treatment is not medically indicated.[4]

Any number of serious difficulties will attend an effort to allocate care rationally and fairly within a national health program. The use of co-payments to reduce inappropriate use, or to raise revenues, inevitably tilts the system in favor of the better off. Even if fees are waived for the poor, the bias remains among the diverse income levels of the nonpoor. Similarly, patients of different social classes and educational levels vary greatly in their ability to "work the system," which is one reason that class differentials in health care utilization have not been erased in the British National Health Service, as they had been expected to be. Indeed, people vary in the likelihood of discovering that they have a condition needing treatment, or of being motivated to seek medical attention for it. This results in a pattern of care which answers to demand rather than to need, a pervasive area of unfairness. Yet a national health program which attempted to compensate for all these sources of inequity might have to rely on draconian measures to restrain the favorably endowed and to reach out to the others. This could cost the system the support of the former, who are the same individuals with political clout.

Illness, Homelessness, and Ignorance:
Choosing among Social Needs

The third kind of allocation-related ethical dilemma in a national health insurance program involves the decision to allocate public funds to health care, as opposed to filling other social needs. A national health program would post this ever-present dilemma in an especially troubling way, because responsibility for this macro-allocation is presently so diffused. The decisions of millions of providers, payers, suppliers, and patients now aggregate to determine that health care spending will be, say, 12 percent of the gross national product. But in a national health insurance program, the money might all come from the same pot, one which, moreover, is asked to supply the funds for housing, education, and other worthy social programs.

We face this dilemma now, of course, since government funds account for so large a share of health care financing. A national health care program would make the dilemma more acute. The tension would be further exacerbated by the fact that the United States spends a greater share of its national wealth on health care than does any other country, which, unless you subscribe to the theory that health care spending makes the economy grow, is to say that this nation diverts more of its funds away from other uses. The effect of this tension could be to raise anew the ethical question of the value of health care, and even of health, in relation to other social needs; in particular, to challenge the tendency to act as if each procedure in the heterogeneous collection of services we call medical care, varying so much in goal, effectiveness, and urgency, is covered under the same entitlement, effectively trumping nonmedical services which may contribute more to overall welfare.

If this ethical issue is resolved by ratcheting down the level of provision of health care service, however, in the manner of the British government's alleged financial strangulation of the National Health Service, it would be much more difficult to resolve the dilemmas in the first two categories of allocation decisions. Universality would be in greater jeopardy: given the great disparity of wealth and income in this country, the better-off are unlikely to accept stringent limits on health care provision which a reduced health care budget would require. They would press for the freedom to spend above the ration, presumably bolstering a parallel private system and creating widely spaced tiers of service.

The situation with the problems of choosing among competing needs within the public plan is similar. It is a truism in health policy that rationing is inevitable, a matter not of "whether" but of "how." But the key factor, in my view, is "how much." A lavish provision of care, whether through additional spending or through more efficient use of existing resources, makes the choosing easier. We can provide more for everyone, and the needs which must remain unmet will be less pressing ones. The United States spends more than twice per capita than does Britain's National Health Service; if the NHS budget were doubled tomorrow, doctors would have to recruit patients. Conversely, if America's budget were halved, draconian rationing would be in order.

In sum, the three categories of ethical issues regarding allocation which I have mentioned are interactive. Most difficult of all would be to achieve a simultaneous solution.

SOCIAL VALUES AND NATIONAL HEALTH CARE

Most of the standard arguments against a national health program leave me completely unmoved—that Americans are too individualistic ever to accept a government plan, for example, an argument refuted by the popularity of Medicare; or that we cannot afford it, which ignores the fact that the national health program of every other nation is cheaper than ours. One argument, however, has occasionally given me pause: that given the structure of the political process in this country, a national health program would inject an intolerable political dimension into health care delivery. Our society is replete with groups of activists pressing single issues, whether they be animal rights, opposition to abortion, or any number of others; whatever their success in the marketplace of ideas, or in winning over a majority of the voters, skilled leaders can often tie up agencies and legislatures until their demands are met. To take but one example, albeit one which I have found most to amaze foreign colleagues: as I understand the story, right-to-life forces successfully prodded the federal government into issuing a regulation which barred research on embryos unless the research had been approved by a special agency, an Ethics Advisory Board; they then engineered the destruction of the board, which put the kibosh on federally sponsored embryo research.

One might be concerned, therefore, that by making the provision, or even the financing, of health care primarily a government function, we would open up the range of emotionally charged clinical issues—be they questions of life, death, reproduction, or others—to political meddling. The risk would be that individual choice would be reduced and that the viewpoint of a strident minority would be imposed on the nation as a whole. As long as the health care system remains disorganized and atomistic, this kind of political pressure is ineffective. A centralized, federalized national health program could be more vulnerable.

This is a concern, but not a certainty. After all, it has not occurred under Medicare. Even in government-owned hospitals, the ethics of clinical care are more or less the same as those that prevail in the private sector. Physicians still hold most of the authority. The opportunity would be there, however. This presents an ethical dilemma, for what is called "politicization" by one person may be termed "democratic control" by another. Moreover, we have begun to see a legislative hand in medical ethics in the recent bill requiring hospitals to inform patients about opportunities to give, in advance, instructions as regards their wishes on the use of life supports. This action may be wholly benign, but the precedent it sets could stimulate concerns over whether the Congress could resist the chance to cater to interest groups bent on shaping clinical practices in a national health program.

A more subtle, but perhaps more unsettling, interaction of politics and medical ethics which could come about in a national health program stems from the direct economic stake which nationalization of health care financing would bring. Even those who first proposed the concept of mixing insurance and health care delivery functions in the same organization—health maintenance organizations, or HMOs—recognized that this created incentives to underserve. In the form of rationing, or straightforward budget limitations, these incentives can be recognized and dealt with, whether in an HMO or in a government-funded health insurance program. But when the government also intrudes on ethical standards, the challenge will be to keep the budget and the ethics from becoming a combustible mixture.

Consider this anecdote from the private sector: a nursing-home administrator attended a medical ethics conference and heard for the first time about living wills and other advance directives. Returning home, she called a staff meeting and directed the nurses to poll every resident about their preferences—not with the goal of increasing patient self-determination but to realize the savings that care foregone would bring. "I'm looking for sixty percent compliance," she was said to have told her staff, effectively setting quotas for each nurse.

When the decision maker simultaneously holding the purse strings and setting the ethical standards is the federal government, the potential cause for concern is of course much greater than in this isolated example. It is comforting that no such tendency has emerged, to my knowledge, under Medicare (though there are said to have been proposals by legislators to make certain insurance benefits conditional upon agreeing to nontreatment *in extremis*, on the theory that great savings could be achieved). But since a national health program would provide a greater budgetary strain than Medicare does, the incentive for leakage between financing and medical ethics

increases. Soviet bioethicists have taken an absolutist line on euthanasia issues, in part, they have told me, because they fear that the
budgetary motive would overpower moral judgment were their physicians free to contemplate this option. With our more ample budget,
and our tradition of individual rights, we should be able to resist this
tendency, but we should be aware of the possibility.

DR. BIG BROTHER

For many decades, the American Medical Association (AMA) successfully fought off the prospect of a national health program, despite the
documented popularity of the notion, under the banner of "freedom
of choice." The AMA's incessant message was that under any sort of
national health program, patients would see a physician of the
government's choosing, regardless of the patient's own preferences.
That this would be so was, and remains, dubious; whether in a
national health service, as in the United Kingdom, or in a publicly
financed private system, as in Canada, patients have a choice of
doctor. Ironically, freedom of choice is more restricted for many
Americans than for patients in the other countries' national health
programs, because of the balkanization of the market in the form of
preferred provider organizations (PPOS) and HMOS.

Nevertheless, the advent of a national health program has the
potential for restricting choice. Not everyone can see the most popular
doctors, and whether by waiting list or by some kind of eligibility rule,
patients will have to be channeled into available slots. National health
insurance is compatible with some degree of competition, however,
and in addition to the efficiencies which competition would bring,
the value of free choice would thereby be upheld were this built into
any national health program.

Might physicians have more to complain about on this score? I
am not sympathetic to the frequently voiced view that doctors have a
right—whether natural, moral, or constitutional—to practice medicine under conditions of their own choosing. As Dan W. Brock
pointed out in a report written for the President's Commission, the
work of many categories of workers is restricted by government,
without their freedoms being thereby trampled; and of course no
one is forced to be a doctor.[5] In any case, even the Canadians permit
physicians who do not wish to take part in the national health
insurance program to opt out. They make it difficult—doctors are
not permitted to participate in both sectors at the same time—but

the private option is there. Most patients prefer to accept the excellent care offered at no charge in the national system, but this, once again, does not violate doctors' liberties, any more than the liberties of academics are violated by the fact that they cannot make a living in private practice and must find a university willing to employ them.

Nevertheless, devisers of a national health program would be tempted to interfere with physicians' control over the manner and location of work. Under the current regime, patients who are left in the cold because they cannot find a physician willing to work in a remote rural location, or in the inner city, or whose physician refuses to accept low Medicaid payments, simply joins the millions of the underserved. A national health program would be committed to providing care to all, and this would, or should, entail resource development and mandatory assignment so that "access to care" is not merely a formal entitlement. Unless the government is willing to spend lavishly to lure practitioners to these locations—and the notion of extra spending on behalf of the rural and urban poor is an unlikely one—a stick would have to supplement the carrot. The government could, for example, make these assignments a condition of accepting medical school loans, in the manner of the National Health Service Corps, or it could restrict the number of doctors in more desirable areas. Whether these practices would create an injustice is questionable, in my view, but those affected could resent them.

More ominous would be a potential threat to privacy. We are at the threshold of an era in which medical confidentiality will greatly increase in importance. As genetic and diagnostic information increases in predictive utility, a person's employability and social acceptance, and even basic liberties such as freedom of travel, could depend on the security of the medical record. In a national health program, the government could be the repository of all these records, just as in our current, private system the health insurance companies pool their data on millions of patients in the Medical Information Bureau. Would the privacy of this information be respected? Would it be used for security checks, government employment screening, and other state concerns? The record of abuse of supposedly inviolable confidences provided by the Internal Revenue Service, which occurred under past administrations, gives one pause.

Again, the ethical concern derives from the interaction between medical ethics and national policy objectives when medical care

becomes national policy. It takes little imagination to come up with
other potential examples. A national health service which assisted
welfare mothers in overcoming infertility might draw criticism, as in
fact at least one local welfare program has done. Indeed, sterilizations
were carried out in the Progressive Era in the name of the common
good; a new eugenics would not be so crude, but its scope could be
wider.

LEVELING

I will conclude this parade of worries with a paradoxical complaint:
that a national health program might suffer from too much fairness.
The basis of this concern is not really with fairness per se, but with the
way concern for fairness has to play out in public policy. Apart from
the judiciary, which is equipped for the task, subtle weighings of
incommensurables are best avoided in public administration, where
fairness is required; bright lines and public rules are better assurances. But though these prevent abuses, they require that opportunities and benefits be forgone.

    For example, pressure to conform to a single standard of care
could put innovation at risk. As Lester C. Thurow has remarked,
Americans tend to accept both the desirability of every person's
trying to get the best health care possible and the moral requirement
that whatever is available to anyone be made available to everyone.[6]
This is a costly conjunction of beliefs. In a largely private system like
ours, individuals can seek out the innovative and the expensive, and
the rest of the system then tries to keep pace. If egalitarianism were to
rule in a national health program—unlikely in this country, I must
emphasize—the peaks could disappear along with the valleys. The
Canadian system, for example, is charged with lagging in innovation
and with being parasitic on the private American system for improvements in technology.

    Too much fairness could be a drawback in a national health
program also in regard to employment practices; the safeguards of
the civil service prompt the fear that the health care system could
come to resemble the postal service. The gloomy atmosphere prevail-
ing in some government hospitals, be they Indian Health Service or
some Veterans Administration facilities, is a case in point. The fact
that many of America's finest health care facilities, such as university
hospitals, are government-owned shows that there is no necessary

connection between state employment practices and mediocrity, but the tendency may be a real one.

THE GOOD NEWS

This has been a dreary recitation, or so it may appear to those who basically favor the prospect of a national health program for the United States. The good news is that I have presented only half the story. There is more good news than bad.

As the academics in the Physicians for a National Health Program have pointed out, for example, the efficiencies achievable in a Canadian-style program would free up funds, if we retain our current spending levels, which could make most of the trade-offs I have talked about less painful. The efficiencies stem from lower overhead, from the superior bargaining position of the single payer, and from the more efficient deployment of resources which could result from a truly national health care policy.

Moreover, the integrity of doctors and of clinical judgment could be maintained in a government system just as they are now in our premier public services. Decentralization and peer review, on the academic model, could stimulate competition for distinction.

And we must not lose sight of the primary reason for moving to a national health care system, the provision of care to the millions unable to afford it on their own, and the security provided to the presently insured who worry about expulsion from the system should they lose their jobs, become diagnosed as having an expensive disease, or run afoul of a change in the eligibility rules of a public program. Providers and insurers have discovered that the easier way to prosper in a competitive system is not by providing a superior, efficient service but by weeding out the high-risk, low-income patients. Increasingly, ours is a health care system for the well. If you are sick, and not rich, the system does not want you. The most significant ethical problems of a national health care service are the ones we would leave behind.

NOTES

1. The proposal put forward by Physicians for a National Health Program is presented in David U. Himmelstein and Steffie Woolhandler et al., "A National Health Program for the United States," *New England Journal of Medicine* 320 (January 12, 1989):102–8; and in K. Brumbach, T. Bodenheimer, D. Himmelstein, and S. Woolhandler, "Liberal Benefits,

Conservative Spending," *Journal of the American Medical Association* 265, No. 19 (May 15, 1991):2549–2954.

2. Norman Daniels, "Is the Oregon Rationing Plan Fair?" *Journal of the American Medical Association* 265, no. 17 (1991):232–35.

3. Guido Calabresi and Philip Bobbitt, *Tragic Choices* (New York: Norton, 1978).

4. Henry J. Aaron and William B. Schwartz, *The Painful Prescription: Rationing Hospital Care* (Washington, D.C.: The Brookings Institution, 1984).

5. Dan W. Brock, "Distribution of Health Care and Individual Liberty," in *Securing Access to Health Care*, vol. 2, Report of the President's Commission for the Study of Ethical Problems in Medicine and Biomedical and Behavioral Research (Washington, D.C.: Government Printing Office, 1983).

6. Lester C. Thurow, "Learning to Say 'No,'" *New England Journal of Medicine* 314 (December 13, 1984): 1569–72.

Notes from a Medical Perspective

Alan R. Nelson, M.D.

There are four assumptions concerning medical care in the United States with which, I think, most of us would agree. First, at its best, medical care in the United States is unsurpassed. Patients throughout the world come to our centers of excellence. Students from other countries would come here to study medicine if they could. Few of us, if we had a choice, would choose to have a serious illness in some other country. Second, the fact that thirty-one million people lack adequate health insurance is a disgrace for a nation as rich as ours. No woman should complete her pregnancy without prenatal care. Everyone should be immunized. Everyone should have cost-effective disease prevention screening. Third, health costs in this country cannot continue escalating at their present rate. And fourth, significant change—not just tinkering, but significant change—in the health care system in this country is not only necessary but desirable.

Almost everyone is unhappy with the way things are, yet even the most basic steps to fix them seem to be stymied, and the increasing levels of administrative hassles seem almost to be smothering us. Let me illustrate this discontent with some results of a survey taken by the American Medical Association (AMA) in 1990. When physicians were asked, "If a high school or college student asked your advice about becoming a physician, would you recommend medicine as a career choice?" 38 percent said no, 5 percent were unsure; 42 percent of these cited outside interference and regulation as the reason. One-third of the physicians in this country expect to be sued in the next twelve months. In the AMA Survey of Public Opinion on Health Care Issues, 1991, 73 percent of the public do not believe that the high quality of care justifies the high costs. Only 25 percent think that doctors' fees are usually fair. Fifty-one percent believe that doctors do

19

not care as much about people as they used to. Almost two-thirds think that we are too interested in making money. Still, 85 percent were satisfied overall with their most recent visit to a doctor. And the most frequent cause for dissatisfaction was the length of time they had to wait for an appointment. The vast majority of Americans would like to have free care, but would like to pay no more than $125 annually in tax increases to fund such a program.

Four trends in the medical environment appear to be governing the direction—the action and inaction—of health care evolution in this country. First, we are a media-driven society. The thirst for health-related information seems unquenchable. The PDR (*Physicians' Desk Reference*) is a best seller. The *Journal of the American Medical Association* changes its day of publication to use better the week's time frame for coverage. My patients find out about a gene-related osteo-arthritis before the information is published in peer-review litera-ture, and the story is misreported in the print and electronic media in a way that misleads my patients' expectations. Miracles are her-alded but never with a fiscal note. A child has a successful second liver transplant, and this is reported as a medical miracle. The family sues the hospital because it is unable to find a donor for a third liver transplant, and this is reported as an interesting ethical case. But nowhere does anyone talk about the cost of these procedures. Bone density screening for all women to determine osteoporosis risk or bone marrow transplants as a possible cure for AIDS are tossed on the nightly news with no consideration of what it would cost us as a nation to make these technologies broadly available to everyone. And as people hear more about health-related information, as they hear conflicting recommendations about, for example, mammogram screening or estrogen use, as they hear information that is downright wrong from quacks on radio talk shows, as they hear about inaccurate PAP smear screening or hospital resident doctors impaired by fatigue, they become simultaneously enamored on the one hand and distrust-ful on the other of the technology that we provide. Nonetheless, they want the miracles; they often self-refer; they pick from the health care menu one from column A, two from column B; they want the best, and they want it now. Columnist George Will said at a meeting I attended, "What do the people want? They want it all, and they want to pay for nothing."

Second, competition in the 1980s has put the buffet of health care services right out where we can partake of it easily, and it has been a feast for most. We have marketed our disease of the month;

our clinics have outreach (which sometimes I call "outgrab") programs; our helicopters have raced each other to the patient; our
hospital and clinic lobbies rival the Ritz Carlton; and we as a
profession have entrepreneured ourselves to the point where our
patients are wondering whether what we order is for our benefit or
theirs. And armies of allowed health professionals have created their
own demand for services. Drop-in clinics are becoming mobile so
that our patients do not even have to go to a shopping center to
receive care. Health fairs guarantee a steady supply of patients
coming to me armed with their cholesterol results to find out if their
oat bran is working. Is it any wonder that the volume of services is
going up? Does not cost equal price times volume? Wendy's entry into
the hamburger market might have kept the cost of the Big Mac steady,
but does anybody believe that that increase in marketing competition resulted in fewer dollars for hamburgers in this country? Why
did business and government think competition would control costs
in the 1980s? To challenge that assumption is to be met with looks of
disbelief.

Third, our government is budget-driven and intimidated by
special interests to such a degree that it seems incapable of confronting long-term responsibility. Were you not sobered by the legislative
anarchy that we saw surrounding the budget debate in the last session
of Congress? Has the read-my-lips willingness to continue disproportionate cuts for social programs softened beyond the syntax of
revenue enhancement? And how long will the militant elderly stone-
wall on the transfer of debt to the young worker? How different is
lawmaking, if you can call it that, from the legislative process that you
and I learned about in civics class?

The fourth trend is by no means new: physicians are having
difficulty sorting out the question, Is medicine a business or a
profession? That is not a new phenomenon. According to Henry
Burdette, over half the hospitals in the United States were owned by
physicians at the turn of the century. Nonetheless, contemporary
opportunities for joint ventures and entrepreneurialism make the
potential for conflict of interest greater than it has ever been and
raises again the question of whether medicine is an economic good
or a social good.

Fundamental change in our health care system is necessary and
desirable. The key question is, What kind of change, and how do we
achieve it? A good deal of attention has been given to systems that
have developed in other industrialized countries, and speculation

about their suitability in the United States continues. Should we attempt to implement the Canadian or the Swedish or the German systems, for instance? I believe it's undesirable to copy any system, but more important, it is not feasible. Americans are uniquely American; they have different expectations; they have a different relationship with their government. We are not likely to increase taxes enough to adopt the Canadian model—up to $330 billion in taxes.

Americans do not like to stand in line: they'll sue before they'll queue. Experience with Medicare should warn us that any assumption that government can do it more simply is not well founded. If we have a government-based single-payer system, the Medicare data system would probably be expanded rather than dismantled. And not only would the tax burden of a single-payer system, free at the point of entry, be unacceptable, but demand, and therefore costs, would increase if everything were free.

We Americans must suggest mechanisms to deal with the faults in our system, the faults that we all know exist. We must find rational, doable solutions that permit incremental implementation with highest priority problems addressed first; solutions that retain the strengths of our current system, our centers of excellence. We must deal with the access problem, with the AMA's proposal, Health Access America, or something like it. The elements of the Pepper Commission report are not far off.

First, the Medicaid program should be expanded to cover everyone below the regional poverty level with a package of benefits that is uniform across the country. Second, two-thirds of the thirty-one million to thirty-three million uninsured working people should be covered where they work. We must phase in such coverage gradually, however, in a way that provides tax incentives and tax credits to small business. We do not help workers by providing them with health insurance if in the process their employer goes out of business. Third, risk pools should be set in place to cover the uninsurable. Utah is a state that is well along the way to that with its legislative agenda. Fourth, catastrophic coverage and basic preventive services should be part of any minimum benefit package. And fifth, innovative approaches should be established to provide long-term care. These may include, for instance, provisions for asset protection, such as those proposed by Congressman Barbara Kennelly (D-Conn). Tax law changes to permit individual retirement accounts (IRAs) for health that could be used for long-term care, and if not used could go to the estate, and tax deductibility for premiums for long-term-care insurance.

Cost containment dominates our thinking, and it should. Here are some strategies that should be supported.

1. Appropriate cost sharing for those who can afford to pay a portion of their care. That is the most rational approach to the demand problem. The data are ample in showing that those who participate in paying some portion of their care are more prudent purchasers. They are more likely to ask the physician or health provider who is making a recommendation, "Why must I have this; why should I have this test or procedure?" if they are paying for it themselves.

2. Full implementation of the physician-patient reform legislation that Congress passed last year. And inequities in physician payment should be corrected by a defensible system based on resource costs.

3. Reduction of administrative costs. There are many ways to reduce such costs. We should eliminate utilization management that does not work. Conditions of participation for hospitals should be revised and such nonproductive items as co-signatures on the record and make-work committees eliminated. We should examine every administrative action against tests of relevance and cost-effectiveness. We must cut defensive medicine costs. As a physician, I do not set out each day to increase costs. I do not go to my office and say, "Well, I think I'll drive up volume today." But if I am worried about failure-to-diagnose liability, cost consciousness goes out the window, and I order what I would need to support my clinical decision in a court of law. We must get the Justice Department and the Federal Trade Commission to permit physicians to adjudicate complaints about fees. Business people all over the country say, "Why don't you deal with your bad apples?" When I tell them that local county societies have peer-review committees that would be more than willing to adjudicate complaints about excessive fees but are prohibited from doing so because of antitrust considerations, they find it unbelievable and so do I. We should support effectiveness research and get a better understanding of geographic variations. We know these variations exist; we do not know why, and we do not know where the optimal point within this range lies. We need practice parameters or strategies to assist physicians in better and most cost-effective care. Some of them will decrease unnecessary care if incorporated as part of a continuous improvement process; here, we can learn

something from Japanese industry. Then practice parameters should assist in ensuring quality. We must work toward better use of nursing resources in the hospital. As health workers and as a nation we must invest in and place more emphasis on health promotion and disease prevention, including better patient education, and beginning with health education in the schools, including sex education at the right time.

To summarize, our system has serious problems along with admirable strengths. It serves 87 percent of the people pretty well. We must confront and correct the problems that exist. We must set our priorities, fulfill our promise to the poor, increase coverage at the workplace. It will require money to accomplish these goals but nowhere near as much money as it would cost to replace our system with a foreign system free at the point of access with a single payer. And now is the time to do it. Now is the time to get it done.

The continuing confidence that the public has in a health care system and our ability to continue to attract bright, gifted young people into the medical profession depend on how we answer the question, Is medicine a business or a profession? and on whether we can maintain a balance between our art and our science. To hold to what I consider the correct answer to the question—that medicine is a profession—requires that we remember the three essential elements of professionalism: (1) a commitment to a continuous education process that never ends, (2) a commitment to peer review to ensure the quality of the services we provide, and (3) a commitment to place the welfare of our patient above our own economic self-interest. To maintain a balance between art and science, we must remember that we are perceived as being technicians rather than healers too often. Our science is speeding into the future, and it makes it more necessary than ever for us to teach, to measure, and to serve as exemplars of physicians who maintain such a balance. The art of medicine includes humanism, with its qualities of compassion and understanding; diligence, traditionally meaning not fleeing the plagues of the time but today meaning that patients with AIDS should have access to medical care; ethics, because without ethics our art would permit us to deceive, as did the medicine-show quacks and hucksters; altruism, which means putting the patient's welfare above our own interests; and, a special sense that represents the exchange between patient and physician. The last element forms much of the basis for the art of medicine and permits a distinction in the mind of the patient about whether a physician is a mediocre physician or a good physician. It is educated palpation; it takes a keen antenna; it is that sense about something about to happen that prepares a surgeon for the unexpected, or maybe it is that flash of insight that comes to a physician in the middle of the night if he or she is worrying about a patient. We must learn to measure that special sense and learn to teach it better. And if we are able, then, to put forth our professionalism and our humanity as well as our science, I think that the miracles of the future will be realized.

PART I

Why Doesn't the United States Already Have National Health Care?

Verging on National Health Insurance since 1910

Harold Bauman

Senator John D. Rockefeller IV, chairman of the bipartisan Pepper Commission, appointed by Congress in 1988 to recommend national legislation for health issues, last year sounded an alarm which is spreading across the land: "The American health care system is in total crisis." He added an apocalyptic warning: "We're plunging ahead in this country toward a health care catastrophe."[1]

In order to rescue our threatened health care system, reformers are once again urging the enactment of national health insurance. One such reformer, Barbara Ehrenreich, made the following appeal: "National health insurance is an idea whose time has come . . . and gone . . . and come again. . . . Today, with the health-care situation moving rapidly beyond crisis to near catastrophe, the age-old and obvious solution has the tone of a desperate whine: Why can't we have national health insurance—like just about everybody else in the civilized world, *please*?"[2] Ehrenreich's complaint is typical of the frustration of millions of Americans who have waited for decades for federal legislation to solve what is perhaps the most persistent social problem of the twentieth century, namely, the provision of adequate health insurance under federal supervision.

Why the "age-old and obvious solution" has not been adopted is a question that may be unanswerable. It is not for lack of effort, knowledge, imagination, and enthusiasm on the part of advocates that the plans and model bills for comprehensive national health insurance proposed or introduced into Congress since World War I have been rejected or allowed to fade into oblivion. The reason for the current chaotic and costly mix of insurance programs that cover the needs of some but not those of millions of others, no doubt lies in the traditional values of Americans, in the pattern of American

politics, and in the ragged sequence of events since the idea entered
the arena of public debate about eighty years ago.

When we review those eighty years we become aware of periods of
advance and near success followed by retrenchment and a regroup-
ing of forces. A pattern of surge and retreat characterizes the
periodic drives to achieve some form of equitable distribution and
financing of health care under national sponsorship. Every surge has
broken against the barrier of opposition from insurance companies,
organized medicine, pharmaceutical companies, patriotic and civic
organizations, ideological passions, the reluctance of the public to
pay, and the diversions created by America's involvement in devastating wars.

The surge-and-retreat pattern falls into four waves. The first
wave, about 1910 to 1920, coincided with the later stages of the
Progressive Era, a time when the idea was introduced and debated.
World War I stopped this first wave. The second wave, 1935–50,
coinciding with the New Deal and the Fair Deal, began with the Social
Security Act of 1935 and ended with a determined effort to enact
comprehensive health care legislation, supported by President Harry
S Truman. The proposed legislation became a casualty of the cold
war. The third wave, 1965–80, coincided with Lyndon Johnson's Great
Society, the costly Vietnam War, and its aftermath. Enacted in 1965,
Medicare and Medicaid constituted a watershed in the long campaign for national health insurance, but those programs covered only
the elderly and needy. The time seemed ripe to follow that partial
success by providing health insurance coverage for every citizen, and
the presidents of the 1970s, Richard M. Nixon, Gerald Ford, and
Jimmy Carter, supported plans to do that. But this wave of reform
foundered and ebbed away in a morass of rising costs, the consequences in great part of the Vietnam War. The Reagan administration's faith in reprivatization to solve health care problems in the
1980s has failed, and that failure has inspired a fourth wave, the
current agitation for national action to solve what is now perceived to
be a deep health care crisis. Whether or not the Persian Gulf war will
dissipate what appears to be a gathering wave, remains to be determined.

Health insurance, a feature of industrialized societies, began for
the modern industrial world with Chancellor Bismarck's scheme of
social insurance for working men in Germany in 1883. His plan
provided sickness insurance together with funeral benefits and covered three-fourths of the employees, or about 31 percent of the

population. Employees paid two-thirds of the cost, employers one-third. Although Bismarck's motives were to wean the workers away from socialism, it was the success of his initiative in raising the health level of workers that inspired other nations to follow suit. By World War I, ten European nations had adopted some form of compulsory health insurance. After Lloyd George returned to England from a visit to Germany in 1908 he pushed through the British Parliament a National Insurance Act in 1911 to raise the standard of living of workers. It enrolled all employed persons between sixteen and seventy.[3]

The period around the beginning of World War I, the peak of the Progressive Era, was a propitious time for enacting compulsory health insurance in the United States. The moralistic, evangelistic mentality of middle-class reformers, combined with the pragmatism and drive for efficiency characteristic of the young industrial giant nation, encouraged social experimentation and created some receptivity to the idea of national compulsory health insurance. The American Association for Labor Legislation, founded in 1906, created a standard health insurance bill based on the German model that was introduced into legislative debate in three states by 1915, and twelve states by 1917. In 1912, Theodore Roosevelt's Progressive party contained a plank on health insurance in its platform. The medical profession was mildly interested at first, partly because health insurance promised guaranteed payments for many physicians with marginal incomes.[4] Social workers believed that health insurance would prevent the impoverishment of working-class families and would thereby eliminate the poverty and disease that threatened social progress, efficiency, and vitality. Most labor unions supported health insurance legislation, but Samuel Gompers of the American Federation of Labor opposed it because he believed his union should gain its benefits through union power alone rather than through legislation, which he regarded as paternalistic.[5]

Entry into World War I in the spring of 1917 put an end to the euphoric mood of the Progressive Era. Cooperation between the various parties interested in health insurance proved to be fragile and broke down. Distrust between physicians and hospitals grew over misunderstandings about payments for care. The big insurance companies, led by Prudential Life Insurance Company, and Metropolitan Life Insurance Company, opposed the idea and contended that the European systems were not successful anyway. A. E. Forrest, president of the Health and Accident Underwriters Conference, asserted in June 1917 that the reformers "would impose on labor a compulsory, communistic system that is repugnant to American minds and destructive of American initiative and individuality."[6] The medical profession turned against the idea by the end of 1916 and charged compulsory health insurance with being pro-German and therefore un-American. Already in May 1916 a conferee at the Ohio Hospital Association meeting got rousing applause when he remarked that health insurance would mean the "Germanizing" of American medical care.[7] In February 1917 a spokesman for the Chamber of Commerce of the state of New York, John Franklin Crowell, argued, according to *The Survey* editor, that "poverty and exploitation of the weakest among laboring forces, with resulting widespread sickness, do not exist in this country and . . . European insurance systems based on such conditions are, therefore, not needed here."[8] In 1920, when the Davenport bill requiring compulsory health insurance coverage for employees died in committee in the New York Assembly, the end of the first phase in the campaign for health insurance had come.

While the Progressive Era produced no legislative results on the national level for health insurance, it was nevertheless a crucial era for defining many of the issues that entered into the debates about health insurance in the future. It also revealed some of the major cultural values, conflicts, and political alignments that to some extent have determined the legislative history of health insurance. The male working class was the target population for health insurance just as it was in the European countries. The working men were the people who earned enough money to pay for the premiums and they were also the class that needed to be kept on the job in a healthy condition for national efficiency and prosperity. Loss of working days through illness meant a serious loss of income with consequent family distress. Because of the limited goals during this early stage of health insurance the complexity of the problems involved in providing insurance was poorly understood, the range of data required was insufficient, and the form that insurance programs should take was not clear.[9] Furthermore, the public was ill informed and therefore hardly capable of participating in any debates about health insurance.

The experience of the Progressive Era also highlighted values so deeply embedded in the American psyche that they have often obstructed rational policies. Voluntarism is one such American value. It was often cited in the literature of medical and insurance organizations after 1917. "The voluntary way is the American way," was the general formula. The dominant value in American society is the freedom of the individual. Since freedom means the capacity and right to choose, any coercion is anathema. Already in the Progressive Era the charge of compulsion in health insurance aroused fears of the loss of individual freedom. American "rugged individualism" augmented the idea of the free individual. Dependency was a sign of weakness, and weakness was seen to be sustained by public health insurance in the minds of many of its opponents. For example, in 1916 a California physician commenting on health insurance stated, "Misconceived sympathies are being extravagantly squandered upon the undeserving, wasteful, and improvident."[10] The American love of experimentation, innovation, and solving problems as they arise also seemed threatened by a compulsory insurance system. The values of voluntarism, freedom, individualism, and pragmatism seemed not to be consistent with mandated health insurance.

The Progressive Era also identified the main protagonists in the long struggle that lay ahead. Social scientists, humanitarians, social workers, labor unions, and a small group of reform-minded physicians kept the idea of national health insurance alive and often dedicated their lives to its realization. The groups most actively opposed were the insurance companies, organized medicine, pharmaceutical houses, patriotic organizations, and groups that stood to gain from a continuation of voluntary and fee-for-service health care. The position of the hospitals was ambivalent; they could swing to either side. There was a strong Manichaean element in the debates. Proponents saw the adoption of public health insurance as a manifestation of social progress and as an aid to a healthier and happier society. They interpreted the ethical dimensions of health insurance in terms of social harmony, economic welfare, personal efficiency, and productivity. Opponents believed that such insurance would weaken the moral fiber of the nation and perpetuate the degenerate. They saw ethical issues in terms of freedom and self-reliance. For that reason the physicians were loath to give up their individualistic ideal of fees-for-service.

While the second wave of the drive for national health insurance began in earnest in 1935 with the Social Security Act, an important event leading to that moment began in 1927 when President Calvin Coolidge appointed a committee of fifty individuals, including seventeen medical doctors in private practice, to an independent group funded by eight foundations to study economic problems associated with illness. The committee, calling itself the Committee on the Costs of Medical Care (CCMC), prepared twenty-seven research reports, the final one in November 1932. That report concluded that *no one* was getting enough medical care, even some of those in the highest income groups. "The amount of care which people need is far greater than that which they are aware of needing, and greater than that for which they are able to pay under present conditions."[11] The CCMC felt that the nation could divert a much greater percentage of its gross national product (GNP) into the health arena.

The CCMC was badly divided and the reaction to the majority and minority reports from the American Medical Association (AMA) was extreme.[12] The AMA would not accept the recommendation for group practice organizations and group payment. Of course the reports rejected compulsory health insurance, but low-income individuals were to be assisted. The term "socialized medicine" began to be widely used because of the example of the Soviet Union.

After the CCMC had reported that health care and insurance coverage had to be expanded, the election of Franklin Delano Roosevelt promised action on that report. The result was the Social Security Act of 1935. Originally, it was supposed to include a provision for compulsory health insurance, but in the hearings, chaired by Secretary of Labor Frances Perkins, the representatives of the AMA and the American College of Surgeons (ACS), including the influential Harvey Cushing, made so strident a case against compulsory health insurance that Roosevelt and Perkins abandoned the plan for fear the inclusion of medical insurance would jeopardize the rest of the act.[13] Roosevelt indicated that the medical problem could be taken up later. This he did with the creation in 1937 of the Interdepartmental Committee to Coordinate Health and Welfare Activities, whose duty it was to describe the health needs of the nation and to formulate a national health program. The work of the committee led Roosevelt to call a conference in 1938 in Washington, D.C., to discuss such a program. This National Health Conference, held in July 1938, brought together more than 150 representatives of labor, farmers, and the health professions, who endorsed a broad program including compulsory health insurance with enthusiasm. Roosevelt was so gratified by favorable public response to the committee's work that he wanted to make the national health program an issue in the 1938 election campaign. "Then," reports Daniel Hirshfield, "without any explanation, he suddenly said that he thought that it would be better if the National Health Program were not made a political issue until the 1940 presidential election."[14] A conservative reaction set in with the election of 1938 and Roosevelt turned his attention to the crises looming in Europe and Asia.

In February 1939 Senator Robert F. Wagner of New York introduced a bill that incorporated the recommendations of the conference, but Roosevelt refused to support the bill. Organized pressures seemed too strong and the gathering war clouds engrossed Roosevelt's attention. He indicated that when the war was over he would press for health insurance. He urged Congress in 1944 to endorse an "economic bill of rights" which would include the right to adequate medical care.

The most important development to emerge from the National Health Conference was a series of four health insurance bills sponsored by Senators Robert F. Wagner (D-N.Y.) and James E. Murray (D-Mont.), and Congressman John D. Dingell, Sr. (D-Mich.), the Wagner-Murray-Dingell bills. The first, introduced in June 1943, called for centralized, federal direction and supervision of compulsory, universal health care. The timing was good. A Gallup Poll of 1943 showed that 59 percent of the American people were in favor of government low-cost health insurance. The Beveridge Plan in England had been endorsed and introduced into Parliament for the action that would lead to a National Health Service five years later.[15] By 1943, millions of American servicemen were receiving the finest medical attention, and they recognized the convenience of free health care. Interim reports of Congress that revealed an ominous number of young men found to be physically unfit for the draft, and the low state of health in America because of inadequate sanitation, nutrition, and medical care, served to fuel the growing demand in the nation in 1944 and early 1945 for congressional action on health insurance. But tragedy stopped the momentum. With the death of President Roosevelt on April 12, 1945, the most powerful voice available in the country for national health insurance was silenced. When Senator Wagner and Congressman Dingell introduced new versions of the Wagner-Murray-Dingell bill on May 24, 1945, the committees to which they were referred failed to report the bills out. At that moment, the future of compulsory health insurance was bleak.[16]

Meanwhile, a line of historical development had opened in 1929 with group insurance and private insurance that helped to thwart government-sponsored health insurance. Group prepayment insurance plans began in 1929 when a Baylor University Hospital administrator enrolled the Dallas schoolteachers—1,250 teachers at fifty cents per month—in the first Blue Cross plan. To protect the income of the hospital, it offered protection to patients and potential patients. This idea caught on and the number of insurance sub-scribers, roughly half of them covered by Blue Cross, rapidly expanded (see table).

Year	Number of individuals with insurance[17]
1941	12,300,000
1946	32,100,000
1948	53,000,000
1951	77,000,000

It was federal economic wartime policies that made such growth possible, for it created the employer-employee structure of financing operations that has continued in health care to our time. Because employers could make health insurance contributions on behalf of employees a "cost of doing business," they could deduct the amount of their contributions from what would otherwise have been profits. The result was a considerable reduction in taxes for the employer. For their part, employees did not pay income tax on the contributions their employers made for them, as they did on their own wages. Consequently, employers' contributions to health insurance reduced their federal income taxes but did not increase employees' taxes, and both groups benefited. That fact created a great incentive to buy health insurance. An additional demand for insurance occurred when the veterans returned from World War II, for they had had a taste of free medical care in the service and they wanted it to continue.[18] Another reason why this tax incentive is important is that it was the first time since 1913 that tax preferences had much value.

Furthermore, the decisions of the National Labor Relations Board in the years after the war forced employers to provide health insurance for employees. If employers did not provide health insur-ance coverage they could be charged with unfair labor practice. Employers could no longer claim that health insurance represented a gratuity subject to modification or removal. The result was that by 1950 more workers were covered.[19]

These developments changed the national picture but did not eliminate the need for a broad program of health insurance, because in spite of the expansion of insurance—private and group—most of the population by the end of the war was not insured, and most of the insurance plans sold provided only limited coverage anyway. Old people, the unemployed, and those unable to afford insurance were left out. There was an authentic need to continue the effort to provide broad health insurance coverage.

President Truman picked up where President Roosevelt had left off when the war ended. He proved to be a most able and committed proponent of universal compulsory health insurance. He told the National Health Assembly in May 1948 how he had become vitally interested in health matters as an official in his home county in Missouri twenty years before when he found that only the very rich and the very poor could have access to adequate medical and hospital care.[20] In November 1945 he asked Congress to pass a national program that would give everyone the right to economic protection against illness as well as adequate access to medical care. He was very much committed to a single health insurance plan that would include everyone, even those not covered by Social Security. His plan also called for expansion of hospitals, support of public health, and for federal aid for research and education. After his victory in the election of 1948, he felt that the time had come to enact his health plan.

The appropriate measure, Senate Bill 1679, was introduced on April 25, 1949, sponsored by Senators Elbert Thomas (D-Utah), James E. Murray (D-Mont.), Glenn H. Taylor (D-Ida.), Dennis Chavez (D-N.M.), Hubert Humphrey (D-Minn.), James H. McGrath (D-R.I.), Robert F. Wagner (D-N.Y.), and Claude Pepper (D-Fla.), certainly a powerful legislative team. Senator Thomas was chairman of the Committee on Labor and Public Welfare which held hearings on the bill. Seven titles covered and proposed to integrate the health care needs of the nation: I, Education; II, Research; III, Hospital Construction; IV, Aid to Rural and Shortage Areas; V, Grants to States for Local Health Work; VI, Grants to States for Maternal and Child Health and Crippled Children's Services; and VII, Prepaid Personal Health Insurance Benefits. A similar bill was introduced into the House of Representatives on the same day by Congressman Dingell of Michigan and was referred to the Committee on Interstate and Foreign Commerce. These were strategically chosen committees to give maximum opportunity for favorable action, since they did not demand the most exacting financial details.

The plan was to be financed by payroll taxes from employers, employees (3 percent), and self-employed persons. The states were to play a key role in distributing benefits, organizing the physicians, hospitals, and auxiliaries. The plan allowed considerable flexibility, such as free choice of physicians and the right of a physician to accept or reject a patient. In fact, the plan did not introduce anything new into the primary relationship of doctor and patient except for the manner of payment and for the fact of universal access.[21]

Many substitute health bills were subsequently introduced. Congressman Richard Nixon (R-Calif.) and Congressman Jacob Javits (R-N.Y.) offered a compromise—a government-subsidized but locally controlled nonprofit insurance system. Bernard Baruch's compromise plan called for voluntary health insurance to be purchased by high-income groups and compulsory health insurance for the poor to be provided under Social Security. It was clear that Truman's comprehensive plan was being challenged and that it was in trouble. Congressional opposition, however, was not as violent as the public outcry, which had been stimulated in part by the AMA's vendetta against the plan, carried out by the public relations firm of Whitaker and Baxter in the most expensive lobbying campaign in U.S. history up to that point. Support for the plan as measured by public opinion polls declined from 58 percent in 1945 to 36 percent by 1949.

Whitaker and Baxter played on the prevalent fears of the cold-war era—fear of socialism, fear of communism, fear of something alien, fear of the loss of freedom of choice, fear of degradation of the quality of medical care. Misrepresentation of what the bills said, and of what was happening in England where the National Health Service had come into being on July 5, 1948, was very effective in eroding support for Truman's plan. Prominent British physicians hostile to the National Health Service were brought to the United States by the AMA and sent around the country to lecture about the frightening destruction of health care in England under its "socialized medicine."[22]

The debates concerning this health plan, so disingenuously labeled "socialized medicine," spread throughout the length and breadth of the country, and, in the public mind, became a battleground upon which the future of civilization was fought out. So deep were the divisions created by the debates that rational discourse proved almost impossible. It was as if two different languages with different meanings assigned to key terms had developed, the most provocative being the use of the word "socialized" in the term "socialized medicine," which acted on the people as a red flag. In the hearings of May 5, 1949, Senator Pepper appealed to the witness, Dr. Lowell S. Goin, "to quit calling us the advocates of socialized medicine."

Dr. Goin: Well, Senator, there we get into an exercise in semantics, just what socialized medicine is. It is a nice, convenient name, and people know what it means.

Senator Pepper: The unfortunate connotation of it is that it suggests, and a lot of people charge, that anybody who advocates what they call socialized medicine is open to doubt as to whether they are good Americans or whether they are trying to import communism or something else into this country.

I think it would clarify the atmosphere a good deal if we could discuss this on the merits of it. As I said to a medical society in Jacksonville when I spoke to them, I will not accuse you of being selfish and acting out of pecuniary motives if you will not accuse me of being a socialist and acting out of sheer political merits.[23]

The main opposition came from the AMA on the grounds that the plan, according to the editorial in the *Journal of the American Medical Association* on May 7, 1949, represented an "Old World Scourge" spreading into the New World, "the discredited system of decadent nations," a system which would "regiment doctors and patients alike under a vast bureaucracy of political administrators, clerks, book keepers and lay committees."[24] In June the president of the AMA, Ernest E. Irons, argued in *JAMA* that freedom could not be compromised. "Our thirty years' war in behalf of this freedom for American medicine has reached the time of decision. . . . We have a right to resent the imposition on a virile nation of technics devised for those that are decadent." He continued by warning that "politically controlled medical care supported by a compulsory tax is an early but essential part of the development of a socialized nation, the forerunner of various forms of collectivism. This fight is not that of medicine alone; it is the fight of all America."[25]

The language used here is not that of civil disagreement; it plunges us into the pathological preoccupations of social Darwinism, which had long since been discredited. Apparently these physicians believed themselves to be promoters of civilization, freedom, and the higher destinies of nations. Furthermore, the Machiavellian use of propaganda by the AMA to inflame the public mind was a cynical method for bringing about the defeat of Truman's health plan. Anti-socialized-medicine propaganda appealed to volatile instincts of hatred, fear of the unknown and the different. Such passions often translate into invincible short-term political power, as was the case during the McCarthy era. This irrational power was summoned to rescue American medicine, and with it, American civilization, by exorcising what appeared to be an alien and destructive ideology.

Thus, the second wave in America's great surge to enact comprehensive health insurance broke against the barrier of the cold war and retreated. As a consolation, President Truman in December 1951 appointed a study group, the Commission on the Health Care Needs of the Nation, which was asked to issue a report at the end of 1952. The president of the AMA, John W. Cline, immediately stigmatized the commission "as an instrument of practical politics, to relieve President Truman from an embarrassing position as an unsuccessful advocate of compulsory health insurance." With exaggerated apprehensiveness, Dr. Cline declared the commission to be "the latest maneuver in President Truman's campaign to socialize the medical profession."[26] When the director of the Bureau of Medical Economic Research reviewed volumes 1, 4, and 5 of the commission's projected five-volume report he concluded his extensive critique with the recommendation that "this report should be filed away in the archives marked, 'Creeping Socialism.' "[27] Of the nearly 100 recommendations made by the commission, the recommendation urging attention to the health needs of the aged, a primary object of Truman's concern, most probably became the germ of the Medicare plan enacted thirteen years later.

We must not suppose that in the midst of so much conflict the government was either delinquent or retarded in its attention to health matters, for it still represented a nation for which health was a great preoccupation. The Truman era demonstrated a commitment to medical research and the construction of medical facilities. The Hill-Burton Hospital Construction Act of 1946, an important part of Truman's national program, enabled the country to gain the hospitals that it needed. Amendments that extended and liberalized the Hospital Construction Act met little opposition. Congressional support for medical research, particularly after the organization of the National Institutes of Health, was so generous throughout the 1950s, that on several occasions unused funds had to be returned to the treasury.[28] The effect of these liberalities, which augmented existing magnificent private hospitals and research institutions (such as the Rockefeller Institute, Mayo Clinic, Johns Hopkins Medical School, and big pharmaceutical houses), transformed the United States medical establishment into the most renowned and productive in the world. The creation of a cabinet post, Health, Education and Welfare (HEW), in 1953 also demonstrates a growing commitment to the nation's health. The fact that the nation rejected national health insurance is not contradictory to its record of largesse in construction and research. It is consistent with the American ethos of putting money where it will be wisely and rationally used.[29] Furthermore, it would be a mistake to argue that the United States was far behind other advanced industrial nations in providing health care for its citizens. In the forty years from the beginning of interest in national health insurance to the creation of HEW, the United States kept pace with European nations in health policies. Had Truman's health insurance plan succeeded, which it most likely would have had it not been for the cold war, the United States would have been virtually abreast of the socially advanced European nations in providing access to health care. Truman's plan was often confused with the British National Health Service and other European socialized systems of health care, a confusion in the public mind that was encouraged by opponents to discredit the plan.[30]

The Eisenhower years were sunny years for opponents of National Health Insurance, just as the 1920s were. Voluntarism had its best chances. Nevertheless, the third wave of the surge toward national health insurance had its inception in the Eisenhower era. There was a shift away from a comprehensive total health measure to plans limited to vulnerable parts of the population. President Eisenhower was sympathetic to the needs of an aging population. An old-age insurance bill, drafted by elderly reformers and supported by the AFL-CIO and holdover Truman Democrats such as Murray and Dingell, was introduced in 1957 by Congressman Aime Forand of New Jersey.

The Forand bill marked the beginning of an eight-year effort to enact a medical and hospital bill for senior citizens. It was strongly endorsed and supported by both Presidents Kennedy and Johnson and with considerable changes was finally passed as Medicare and Medicaid by an overwhelming vote on July 27, 1965. This was a favorable moment for such legislation, for President Johnson had just achieved a landslide victory over Senator Barry Goldwater in 1964 and had a strong Democratic Congress to support him. He was not yet bogged down in the Vietnam War, and the economy was strong.

Perhaps a year earlier or a year later the outcome would have been different. The nation's physicians dropped their opposition as soon as they discovered that this kind of national program did not threaten their autonomy, and certainly not their income. One physician wrote, "I do not want to go back to the pre-Medicare days under any condition whatsoever. I would hate to face again the situation when we didn't give high quality care to our elderly citizens who couldn't afford medical care."[31]

With this victory behind them, the reformers' next step was to complete the structure of nationalized medical care.[32] Voluntarism had not succeeded in providing health care for all, nor in containing costs, despite the assurances of the AMA. The delivery system was uncontrolled and inefficient. The social changes rampant in American society in the late 1960s led to assertions that health care was a basic right and not merely a privilege. A great change also was coming over the medical profession as it began to lose its prestige and its organized power. Responding to this situation, Senator Edward Kennedy in 1969 introduced his Health Security bill. This bill envisaged a new framework which would consolidate all health plans into one federally designed and directed health insurance system. This would provide medical care free of charge, allow for prepaid group practice, and grant physicians their own payment preferences. It seemed that the moment had finally come to consummate the movement begun by Medicare and Medicaid to extend health insurance coverage to all Americans. But the Kennedy bill faced even more problems in Congress than the Truman plan had twenty years earlier. Senator Kennedy was not the president. His bill was not circulated widely for debate among the people; there was no crisis affecting the middle class; the bill seemed to threaten existing medical financial arrangements; and Medicare and Medicaid had already helped to relieve the pressure for millions of Americans. The bill did not come to a vote.

President Nixon also recognized that there was a crisis in the health care system, particularly because of rising costs. To hold down costs the administration embraced the idea put forward by Paul Elwood, a Minnesota physician, to expand health maintenance organizations (HMOs). Based on previous prepaid group practice experience, the HMO idea was not radical, and Nixon believed that federal grants to help HMOs get started would eventually lead to the enrollment of the vast majority of the population in HMOs, thus cutting down the role of the federal government in health care. Accordingly he signed a bill in December 1973 that set aside $375 million for a three-year period to help HMOs get started. In the end, the HMOs did not live up to Nixon's high expectations.

Meanwhile, the Nixon administration created the Comprehensive Health Insurance Plan (CHIP), which, it was widely believed, stood a very good chance of enactment. It provided federal insurance for the poor and for the unemployed, made Medicare and Medicaid comprehensive, placed an upper limit of $1,500 that the patients would have to pay out for catastrophic health care, and set standards for employer-provided insurance programs requiring employers to pay 75 percent of the cost. The destruction of Nixon's presidency, as a result of the Watergate scandal, put an end to CHIP.

Edward Kennedy's Health Security Act was reintroduced twice more in the decade in somewhat modified form, and a number of plans such as the Catastrophic Insurance Plan of Senators Long and Ribicoff were also studied in committee but did not come to a vote.[33]

President Carter's election owed something to his promise to support comprehensive health insurance. Early in his campaign Carter realized that he needed the support of organized labor, particularly that of the United Automobile Workers, to win the nomination. Labor leaders were already behind Kennedy's Health Security Plan and they expected Carter to endorse it if he hoped to gain their support. Carter did not want to be identified with Kennedy, but his statement to the platform committee of the Democratic party on June 12, 1976, moved him close to Kennedy's plan: "We need a national health insurance program financed by general tax revenues and employer/employee shared payroll tax which is universal and mandatory. Such a program must reduce barriers to preventive care, provide for uniform standards and reforms in the health care delivery system, and assure freedom of choice in the selection of physician and treatment centers."[34] Later in June at a press conference, Carter stated: "I say that we need a national health insurance program. I mean to do it. Nobody's ever done it."[35]

During his campaign, Carter gradually backed away from his commitment and stressed the necessity of controlling medical care costs. He affirmed that national health insurance would have to wait until the budget was balanced. True to his priorities, he spent most of his presidency attempting to design cost-containment programs. He wanted to see a good health delivery system using more paraprofessionals to give the primary care needed before enacting national health insurance legislation. When he finally introduced his health insurance plan in 1979, it was too late, for costs remained uncontrolled, and Congress did not wish to exacerbate inflationary costs. Carter's plan called for expanded aid to the aged and the poor, responsibility of employers for providing insurance benefits for their employees, and the creation of a federal agency to sell insurance. In

March 1980 the Senate Finance Committee worked diligently to create a politically viable measure. When the committee could not find a way to control health care costs, the bill died. With a worsening economy and a troubled reelection campaign facing him, Carter abandoned his national health insurance plan and concentrated on bringing the hostages back from Iran. The era of efforts to enact national health insurance legislation had come to an end.[36]

Perhaps any of the three major health plans of the 1970s— Kennedy's Health Security Plan, Nixon's CHIP, or Carter's health insurance plan—would have served the nation well. But events such as Watergate and an inability to control costs stopped their realization. So ended the third surge.

Although the administrations of Nixon, Ford, and Carter promoted national health insurance, the preoccupation of the 1970s with cost controls became paramount by 1980 and set the stage for the policies of the Reagan administration. The ideas of competition and privatization guided the health agenda of the Reagan years. An old American faith in the power of competition, market mechanisms, and consumer free choice to solve health financing problems gained considerable support after 1977. Three individuals who were representative of the new approach to health care financing were Alain Enthoven of Stanford University, Congressman David Stockman of Michigan, and Senator Richard Schweiker of Pennsylvania. Enthoven, who had in 1977 written a competition health plan for Secretary Joseph A. Califano, Jr., of HEW, urged employers to give their employees a choice of different insurance plans, including HMOs, on the grounds that competition would hold costs down. In 1980 Stockman introduced an amendment to offer incentives to consumers to seek the best insurance buy and to eliminate a number of federal regulatory programs that inhibited competition. Stockman believed that inefficiency could be eliminated by competition; hospitals that were not efficient should be allowed to go out of business. Schweiker had been a member of the health subcommittee of the Labor and Human Resources Committee and had experience in preparing health plans. Stockman became Reagan's director of the Office of Management and Budget, and Schweiker was Reagan's first secretary of the Department of Health and Human Services. Enthoven's book of 1980, *Health Plan: The Only Practical Solution to the Soaring Cost of Medical Care,* served as a guide for competition in the health sector. Terms such as "procompetition," "reprivatization," and "creeping incrementalism" (to fill gaps gradually), characterize the objectives of the Reagan administration to move the costs of health care out of the federal and into the private sector of the economy.

Reprivatization, creeping incrementalism, and procompetition have not solved old problems such as lack of access to health care, the existence of millions of uninsured, and skyrocketing costs, and they have created some new problems such as costly administrative duplication and the rationing of care in the interests of cost containment. Employers are finding it more and more difficult to pay the health insurance premiums of their employees, and their insurance providers are often unable to pay claims.[37] The optimistic faith of the Reagan administration in the capacity of the private sector of the economy to provide necessary services efficiently and economically and to reverse the trend of accelerating costs has proved to be another Utopian dream. In an afterword to a collection of scholarly articles assessing the results of competition in the ten years since 1977, when the Federal Trade Commission sponsored the conference "Competition in the Health Care Sector: Past, Present and Future," Lawrence D. Brown stated that while progress in enhancing competition was certainly made during those ten years, none of the authors of the study "shows—or even contends—that this progress has saved the system money." He continued, "Perhaps the real issue is not competition after all, but rather the fragmentation of financing. Perhaps the real solution is not enlarged competition (which aggravates that fragmentation) but rather firm, comprehensive budgetary controls, for which one looks not to the market but to government."[38]

Meanwhile, total national health expenditures continue to skyrocket. In 1965, the $41.9 billion spent on the nation's health care was 5.9 percent of the GNP. In 1978, $189 billion represented 8.4 percent of the GNP. In 1988, Reagan's last year in office, $554.6 billion spent on health care was 11.4 percent of the GNP, and in 1990, the nation spent over $680 billion, representing 12.3 percent of the GNP. Sober corporation medical analysts such as Kenneth S. Abramowitz of Sanford C. Bernstein and Company say that the nation's health care costs "are out of control." The chaotic arrangements for financing, access to care, eligibility, allocation of resources, and bureaucratic control may or may not be amenable to solution by any comprehensive national plan or the application of more rigorous rational decision making which the experts such as Abramowitz recommend.[39]

The alarming crisis in America's national health care system has inspired a fourth surge toward national health insurance. The demand for a national health plan is now more active than perhaps at any other time during the past eighty years. Our historical experience gives us no clear indication of the form that a successful health plan should take; new complexities continue to arise that were not foreseen in earlier models of comprehensive health plans. Pragmatic ingenuity guided by the ideal of social justice, which has remained a constant throughout these eighty years of American experience with health insurance, will perhaps lead to an acceptable solution in the 1990s.[40]

In a retrospective review we can state that in spite of its troubled health insurance system, the nation has tried in its recent history to provide for the health needs of its citizens in a reasonable and constructive though incomplete manner and has created a formidable medical and health establishment. It has not been the intransigence of opponents alone that has defeated health insurance plans. A series of fortuitous events also played a role. World War I stopped the first surge; the cold war stopped the second; and the intrusion of Watergate and massive inflation stopped the third. The fourth surge is expected to continue despite the recent Persian Gulf war. Hardly had that war ended when demands for a solution to the health care crisis became vociferous.

Acting as a constant inhibition through most of these eighty years has been the reluctance of the citizens to pay for national health insurance. A government less responsive to its people, less sensitive to public opinion, would no doubt have inaugurated compulsory national health insurance long ago. Democracy is inherently a difficult political form, and people are willing to suffer and pay a high price for it. In its continuing experiment with democracy, the United States has not found it easy to solve its health insurance problem, but it has never abandoned the effort to do so.

But perhaps we should let Barbara Ehrenreich have the last word. She concludes the article in *Time* mentioned at the beginning of this essay, saying, "With the largest-ever consensus behind it, national health care's time is surely here at last. Otherwise, let us bow our heads together and recite the old Episcopal prayer: 'We have left undone those things which we ought to have done . . . and there is no health in us.'"

NOTES

1. *New York Times*, March 3, 1990.
2. *Time*, December 10, 1990.

3. For these beginnings, see Ronald L. Numbers, *Almost Persuaded: American Physicians and Compulsory Health Insurance, 1912–1920* (Baltimore: Johns Hopkins University Press, 1978), pp. 10–13, and a comprehensive brief study, "Health Benefits," in Margaret S. Gordon, *Social Security Policies in Industrial Countries: A Comprehensive Analysis* (Cambridge: Cambridge University Press, 1988), pp. 197–225. The immediate resistance of the British physicians to Lloyd George's bill of 1911 is discussed with sorrow in "British Insurance Bill," *The Survey*, (July 15, 1911): 584–86; and Derek G. Gill, *The British National Health Service: A Sociologist's Perspective*, U.S. Department of Health and Human Services. NIH Publication no. 80-2054 (Washington, D.C.: Government Printing Office, 1980), pp. 1–93.

4. See three papers published in the September 30, 1916, issue of the *Journal of the American Medical Association* (hereafter *JAMA*: Emmet Rixford, M. D., "Surgical Aspects of Industrial Accident Insurance Illustrated from California Experience," pp. 1004–11; I. M. Rubinow, Ph.D., "Health Insurance in Its Relation to Public Health," pp. 1011–15; and B. S. Warren, M.D., "Health Insurance in Its Relation to the National Health," pp. 1015–17; all advocated national health insurance, with critical, opposing commentary, pp. 1018–19, evidence that the AMA at that point still considered the issue one to be debated.

5. An optimistic summary of where matters stood early in 1917 is given by I. M. Rubinow, "20,000 Miles Over the Land: A Survey of the Spreading Health Insurance Movement," *The Survey* 39 (March 3, 1917): 631–35. Also see "Labor Getting Behind Health Insurance," *The Survey* 39 (March 30, 1918): 708–9.

6. A. E. Forrest, "Compulsory Social Health Insurance," *Proceedings of the 44th National Conference of Social Work* (Chicago: National Conference of Social Work, 1917), p. 543.

7. James G. Burrow, *Organized Medicine in the Progressive Era. The Move Toward Monopoly* (Baltimore: Johns Hopkins University Press, 1977), p. 149.

8. "Business Men on Health Insurance," *The Survey* 37 (February 24, 1917): 606.

9. Attempts to probe complex issues involving insurance were undertaken by I. M. Rubinow, "Health Insurance," and Lee K. Frankel, "The Relation of Insurance to Poverty," both in *Proceedings of the National Conference of Charities and Correction* 43 (1916): 434–43 and 443–51. Also see Alice Hamilton, M.D., "Health and Labor: Fatigue, Efficiency, and Insurance Discussed by the American Public Health Association," *The Survey* 37 (November 11, 1916): 135–37.

10. Frankel, "Relation of Insurance to Poverty," 151.

11. Paul Starr, *The Social Transformation of American Medicine* (New York: Basic Books, 1982), p. 264.

12. See Daniel S. Hirshfield, *The Lost Reform: The Campaign for Compulsory Health Insurance in the United States from 1932 to 1943* (Cambridge, Mass.: Harvard University Press, 1970), pp. 32–33; and Rosemary Stevens, *In Sickness and in Wealth* (New York: Basic Books, 1989), pp. 154–56.

13. The hostility between the administration and the doctors was exacerbated by the condescending and rude behavior that Frances Perkins's Committee on Social Security apparently showed toward two veteran surgeons, George Washington Crile, founder of the Cleveland Clinic, and Harvey Cushing, the famous neurosurgeon. Mrs. Crile, in a letter to Isabelle Martin, wife of the Director of the ACS, declared: "I was furious that George should have spent five days in Washington, in a crowded room filled with smoke, when the only purpose seemed to be that of 'window dressing.' He came home with a full realization of just what the business men are up against.

"G.W.C. [George W. Crile] and Harvey Cushing represented medicine in Roosevelt's hope to socialize medicine. They were told they were there to listen and not comment. Not being allowed to speak in a meeting, they went early and delivered themselves before [the] meeting, then Harvey went to Roosevelt about it. They came home with a bunch of mss. as big as 2 N.Y. telephone books—But it was dropped for the time." ("It" was the inclusion of a health insurance component of the Social Security Act.) Mrs. Grace Crile to Isabelle Martin, Feb. 16, 1935, Crile Family Papers, MSS. 2806, Cont. 62, f. 77, Western Reserve Historical Society, Cleveland.)

14. Hirshfield, *The Lost Reform*, p. 115.

15. Gill, *The British National Health Service*, pp. 95–119.

16. Monte M. Poen, *Harry S Truman versus the Medical Lobby* (Columbus: University of Missouri Press, 1979), p. 60.

17. Figures taken from Rashi Fein, *Medical Care, Medical Costs: The Search for a Health Insurance Policy* (Cambridge, Mass.: Harvard University Press, 1989), p. 23.

18. Ibid., pp. 21–22.

19. Ibid., p. 24.

20. *Public Papers of the Presidents. Harry S Truman.* January 1 to December 31, 1948 (Washington, D.C.: Government Printing Office, 1964), p. 240.

21. "The President's New National Health Bill," *JAMA* 140 (May 7, 1949): 114–17.

22. See Poen, *Harry S Truman versus the Medical Lobby*, pp. 140–53; and Steven M. Spencer, "Do You Really Want Socialized Medicine?" *Saturday Evening Post*, May 28, 1949; Spencer, "How Britain Likes Socialized Medicine," *Saturday Evening Post*, May 14, 1949; and Spencer, "How British Doctors Like Socialized Medicine," *Saturday Evening Post*, May 21, 1949.

23. "Hearings on Health Insurance," *JAMA* 140 (May 25, 1949): 893.

24. "Statement on Truman Health Plan," *JAMA* 140 (May 7, 1949): 114.

25. Ernest E. Irons, M.D., "The Time of Decision," *JAMA* 140 (June 11, 1949): 505.

26. John W. Cline, M.D., "The President's Page, a Special Message," *JAMA* 148 (January 19, 1952): 208.

27. Frank G. Dickinson, "What We Get for What We Spend for Medical Care," *JAMA* 151 (March 21, 1953): 1037.

28. Carol Ann Boyer, *Government Health Spending in the American State,*

1929–1981: A Socio-Historical Analysis. (Ph.D. diss., Yale University, 1986), p. 136.

29. For comprehensive data on the extent of America's medical establishment, see *Health Services in the United States.* 2d ed., ed. Florence Wilson and Duncan Neuhauser (Cambridge, Mass.: Ballinger, 1987).

30. For information on European health systems see Marshall W. Raffel, ed., *Comparative Health Systems* (University Park: Pennsylvania State University Press, 1984).

31. Fein, *Medical Care, Medical Costs,* p. 92.

32. This discussion about the 1970s is based on Jonas Morris, *Searching for a Cure: National Health Policy Considered* (New York: Pica Press, 1984), pp. 50–171.

33. Summaries of various health insurance proposals including the AMA "Medicredit" Plan, the Long-Ribicoff-Wagner Catastrophic Protection Plan, and the Kennedy-Mills bill are included in Kenneth Friedman and Stuart Rakoff, *Toward a National Health Policy* (Lexington, Mass.: D. C. Heath, 1977), pp. 164–69.

34. Quoted in Morris, *Searching for a Cure,* p. 95.

35. Ibid.

36. Ibid., pp. 168–71.

37. Thomas G. Donlan, "MEWA Mischief: These Health Plans Are Not What the Doctor Ordered," *Barron's,* March 19, 1990.

38. Lawrence D. Brown, "Afterword," in *Competition in the Health Care Sector: Ten Years Later,* ed. Warren Greenberg (Durham, N.C.: Duke University Press, 1988), p. 140.

39. This paragraph is based on Kathryn M. Welling, "The Sickening Spiral: Health-Care Costs Continue to Grow at an Alarming Rate," *Barron's,* June 11, 1990. Also Jonas Morris, "The Reagan Years and Beyond," in *Searching for a Cure,* pp. 172–207.

40. For good discussions of the values that may serve as guides to medical policy studies, see Charles Lockhart, *Gaining Ground: Tailoring Social Programs to American Values* (Berkeley: University of California Press, 1989), and Roger J. Bulger, *Technology, Bureaucracy, and Healing in America: A Postmodern Paradigm* (Iowa City: University of Iowa Press, 1988). Prospects for congressional legislative action in 1991 on selected problem areas such as long-term care and supplying health care insurance to the thirty-five million uninsured are considered good. See, for example, Ray Stephens, "Closing the Gaps: Mitchell to Move on Health Care," *AARP Bulletin,* January 1991.

Why the United States Has Not Had National Health Insurance

Paul J. Feldstein

National health insurance (NHI) means different things to different people. To some it means established budgets for hospitals and physicians with expenditure limits; to others it means tax credits and vouchers. In some versions there is a great deal of government regulation and control over provider fees, capital investment, and access to medical technology. Other versions have competition among health maintenance organizations (HMOs) for enrollees, with a great deal of flexibility on payments to hospitals and physicians and on capital investment. Proposals as to how NHI should be financed also vary greatly, from excise taxes to income taxes to some combination of both. Each of these aspects and versions of NHI has implications as to how equitable and efficient NHI is likely to be, as well as how rapidly medical expenditures are likely to increase.

The debate over these various design features actually represents the controversy over the underlying objective that is to be achieved by NHI. Discussing the possible goals of NHI therefore clarifies the selection of the design features of different NHI proposals; discussion of NHI goals also provides insights as to why this country has not had NHI.

There are several possible goals that NHI can achieve. These goals are not often explicitly stated, and when they are the intent may be more to mislead than to inform. For example, providing medical services to those with low incomes and increased efficiency in the delivery of medical services are two possible NHI objectives. Enabling politically powerful groups to shift their medical costs to those who are less politically powerful is also a possible NHI objective. Few persons are explicit regarding this latter, selfish, objective, preferring instead to claim more noble objectives, such as helping the poor or increasing efficiency. Only by examining the design features of different proposals is it possible to determine their underlying objective.

I propose that if the objective of NHI was simply to help the poor or increase efficiency in the delivery of medical services, we would have arrived at consensus on these issues and implemented NHI long ago. Instead, I argue, NHI is meant to serve self-interest rather than altruistic goals. My underlying assumption is that NHI is an attempt by politically powerful groups to use the power of government to achieve what they could not otherwise achieve.

The conflict over who is to benefit and who can be made to bear the costs has worsened both equity in financing and efficiency in delivery of services. Until recently, the middle class has been insulated from the costs of medical care by employer-paid premiums and the tax-free status of those premiums. As the middle class develops a concentrated interest in holding down its rising medical costs, it is likely to favor certain types of financing and a certain structure of NHI. Under NHI, both the financing and delivery of medical services, I believe, will reflect an attempt by the middle class to shift their costs to others. The resulting outcome is likely to be an inequitable financing scheme and a less efficient delivery system.

Whether or not the goals of NHI are altruistic or based on self-interest provides competing hypotheses as to why we have not had NHI, the conditions necessary before NHI can be enacted, and the likely design of its financing and delivery system.

THE GOALS OF NATIONAL HEALTH INSURANCE

Increased Medical Services for the Poor

Individuals who favor increased medical care to the poor favor government intervention to help them achieve their goal. If such individuals alone were to contribute voluntarily, the amount provided would be less than they would like the poor to receive. Further, others who do not contribute benefit by knowing that the poor are receiving care; they receive a "free ride," they benefit without bearing their share of the cost. The power of government is necessary to levy taxes on all those who benefit from knowing that the poor are provided with an appropriate level of medical services.

While many individuals certainly support increased services to the poor, this is not, nor has it ever been, in my opinion, the driving force behind NHI. Medicaid is NHI for the poor. To use the power of government to achieve one's objectives requires political power. The structure and funding of Medicaid is indicative of the limited political power of the poor and their advocates. Medicaid's extensive inadequacies are not the actions of a few miserly bureaucrats or legislators but is instead reflective of th̶e̶ resources that society—the middle class—is willing to devote to it. The states vary in their generosity and in the ... ining eligibility for Medic... ...vel in determining Medic... ...25 percent of the fede... ...ally provide more be... ...r than states with lo... ...or are willing to spe... ...poor themselves have, ...nonpoor, and on how m...

Sin... ...to determine the alle... ...me that the inadequa... ...or desire among th... ...funding for the poor... ...Medicaid, why would the... ...r the poor?

Increased Eff... ...m

Another possible objective or ... to improve efficiency, thereby freeing up sufficient resources to provide the same services for less or to be able to provide more services to all. (An efficiency goal is different from the objective of limiting expenditure increases. While greater efficiency is likely to reduce the rate of increase in medical expenditures, an expenditure limit by itself is unlikely to achieve efficiency or the appropriate rate of increase in expenditures.) Often-cited examples of inefficiency in the U.S. medical care system are the lower administrative expenses for medical services in Canada and the numerous unnecessary procedures and duplication of costly equipment and services among hospitals in this country. A nationalized system, it is claimed, can cut the waste without harm to the public. The power of government is needed, under this scenario, since physicians and hospitals, whose incomes are the waste in the system, would not voluntarily permit these efficiencies to occur.

Few people would argue with the premise that there is waste in the medical system. Use of services varies widely among physicians as does the appropriateness of care. And administrative costs in Canada are lower than in the United States. Still, why is it necessary to use the power of government to force a presumably more efficient system on the public?

The underlying premise of a competitive market is that if there is a sufficient demand for a particular product, someone will supply it. Presumably, if there were a sufficient number of consumers that wanted a more efficient health insurance plan, it would be made available. Until 1982, however, there were many anticompetitive restrictions in the health field that limited the growth and development of more efficient health plans. In addition, health providers could not advertise, medical societies could boycott health insurers, and medical staffs excluded competitors and participants in HMOs. In 1982 the U.S. Supreme Court ruled that the antitrust laws applied to the health field. Since then, a number of successful lawsuits have been brought against providers engaging in anticompetitive behavior. Currently, few restrictions inhibit the development of efficient health plans. Therefore, why is government legislation required to enhance efficiency?

There are obvious differences between the medical services market and traditional competitive markets. Inadequate information among all the participants in the market is the major difference. And competitive markets do not evolve immediately. Still, is government nationalization really needed to improve efficiency? The most efficient health insurance product on the market today appears to be managed care, that is, HMOs and preferred provider organizations (PPOs). The rates of hospital use in managed care organizations are lower than in other health insurance plans, as are their premiums. And other countries, such as Canada, are trying to start HMOs. The closest comparison to the Canadian health system is the current Medicare program. Under both systems, the beneficiary has free choice of provider. The costs of both programs are restrained by the government's use of its power to fix prices and limit expenditure increases. Incentives for the use of innovative delivery systems, such as HMOs and PPOs, are limited in both Canada and in Medicare as are incentives for alternative cost-containment approaches that are used in the non-Medicare market, such as prior authorization for admission and case management for catastrophic illnesses.

The Canadian health system and the U.S. Medicare program have lower administrative costs than the private health insurance market. When everyone is enrolled in a single system and the subscribers have no need to choose among health plans and consumers do not have to be informed of the differences in their choice of health plans, then marketing costs can be greatly reduced.[1] Thus even an efficient plan, such as an HMO, will still require high marketing costs in the United States, since it has to compete not only with indemnity plans but also against other HMOs.

There is a trade-off between the lower administrative costs of having a single nationalized plan and the more efficient delivery systems that result when managed-care plans compete with one another and subscribers have an incentive to choose the most efficient plan. Thus it is debatable whether a nationalized health system will improve efficiency.

The efficiency issue also depends upon whether this country should permit a multiplicity of health plan choices or require a standardized nationalized plan for everyone. As long as the public is willing to pay the price of having a multiplicity of choices, then they should be able to do so. To attempt to remove this choice would not only be undemocratic and paternalistic, it would also be politically unwise. (It is economically inefficient to prevent someone from purchasing a medical plan at the cost of providing it).

The public is not yet willing to give up their choice of health plans. Unions have gone on strike over their health benefits. They want unrestricted choice of provider and a comprehensive set of benefits without cost sharing. Attempts by employers to restrict their employees' choices have not been very successful with unions whose members have had relatively generous benefits, such as the United Auto Workers (UAW) and the "baby Bells." If these groups are unwilling voluntarily to choose more restrictive health plans in union negotiations, why would they be expected to vote for government to impose on them what they voluntarily did not accept?

Neither the search for greater efficiency nor the desire to increase services to the poor are, in my opinion, the motivating factors behind the discussion of NHI.[2] Instead, one has to examine the objectives of those with sufficient power to bring about government action; namely the nonpoor.

The Use of Government to Benefit Politically Powerful Groups

If the major reasons for NHI are not to increase resources to the poor nor to achieve greater efficiency, what does NHI represent? And why is it necessary to use the power of government to implement NHI? Since government responds to those with political power, politically powerful groups must be demanding from government what they could not otherwise receive from the marketplace.

Politically influential groups are those who have a "concentrated" interest in a particular issue and who are able to organize themselves so as to provide legislators with political support, that is, campaign contributions, votes, and/or volunteer time.[3] A group is said to have a concentrated interest when some regulation or legislation has a sufficiently large effect on that group to make it worthwhile for it to invest resources either to forestall or to promote that effect. The potential legislative benefits are greater than the group's costs of organizing and providing political support to achieve its legislative objectives.

Implicit in this discussion of concentrated interests is the assumption that legislators respond to political support, since their objective is to be reelected. Legislators, similar to the other participants in the policy process, are assumed to be rational; they undertake cost/benefit calculations of their actions. The costs and benefits of their legislative decisions, however, are not the legislation's effect on society but instead are the political support gained and lost by the legislators' actions.

In the health field, physicians and hospitals were initially the major groups with a concentrated interest in health legislation. Payment systems under both public and private insurance systems had a large effect on their revenues. Subsidies to increase the demand by those with low incomes also increased hospital and physician revenues. The availability of competitors, such as HMOs, PPOs, outpatient surgery centers, foreign-trained physicians, and so on, also affected hospital and physician revenues. Given their financial interest in issues affecting their demand for services, methods of pricing, the availability of substitutes for their services, and their overall supply, physician and hospital associations represented their concentrated interests before both state and federal legislatures. The defeat of President Truman's proposed NHI plan by the American Medical Association (AMA) was a demonstration of the AMA's political power and showed legislators that the AMA was a force to be reckoned with at election time for those legislators that were opposed to its economic interests.

The consequences of these legislative actions by physician and hospital associations were neither very obvious nor initially very costly to consumers of medical services. Medical prices were higher than they would otherwise have been and fewer alternatives were available to the fee-for-services system, such as HMOs and PPOs, but these costs were not sufficiently large to make it worthwhile for consumers to organize, represent their interests before legislatures, and offer political support to those legislators favorable to their interests.

The concentrated interests of medical providers and the consequent diffuse costs imposed on consumers explains much of the legislative history of the financing and delivery of medical services until the early 1960s. Payment systems for physicians and hospitals and the structure of the medical services delivery system were a direct result of economic benefits gained by medical providers as a result of government legislation.

The American Federation of Labor and Congress of Industrial Organizations (AFL-CIO) had a concentrated interest in their retirees' medical costs which placed them in opposition to the AMA throughout the 1950s and early 1960s. Employers that funded union retirees' medical costs had not prefunded these liabilities; instead they were paid as part of current labor expenses. If union retirees' medical expenses could be shifted away from the employer, then those same funds would be available to be paid as higher wages to union employees. The union's attempt to shift these costs onto others became the basis of the debate over Medicare.

To ensure that their retirees would be eligible for Medicare, the unions insisted on Social Security financing.[4] The AMA was willing to have government assistance go only to those unable to afford medical services, which was the approach being used by the states. (Physicians benefited by the increase in demand for their services when those with low incomes had their medical care subsidized.) Thus the AMA favored an income-related program that was funded by general tax revenues. The AMA was concerned that a program that subsidized the nonpoor would not increase their demand but would instead substitute government payment for private payment. Such a program would cost too much, leading to controls on physicians' fees.

Thus the real fight over Medicare was over Social Security financing.

With the landslide victory of President Lyndon B. Johnson in 1964, the unions were able to achieve their objective of Social Security financing. Once Social Security financing was used to determine eligibility for Medicare, Part B, a program for the government to pay for physician services, was added, which was financed by general tax revenues.

Although the unions won on the financing mechanism, Congress acceded to the demands of the medical and hospital associations on all other aspects of the legislation. A payment system to hospitals and physicians was implemented that promoted inefficiency (cost-plus payments to hospitals), and restrictions were placed on alternative delivery systems that limited competition. The outcome of this historic conflict in medical care between opposing concentrated interests left them both victorious. To fund these benefits to the aged and the payments to medical providers required a diffuse cost to be imposed on the working population. The working population paid for Medicare in terms of higher Social Security taxes, higher general taxes (for financing Part B and Medicaid), and in higher prices for their own medical services.

The power of government was used to benefit politically important groups. As a result of Medicare, a massive redistribution of wealth occurred in society. The beneficiaries were the aged and medical providers; the working population paid the bill. Medicare and Medicaid were designed to be both inefficient and inequitable because it was in the economic interests of those with concentrated interests.

This brief discussion of Medicare illustrates the real purpose of NHI. It is to redistribute wealth, that is, to increase benefits to politically powerful groups without having them pay the full costs of those benefits or, similarly, to shift costs from those who are politically powerful to those who are less so.

GROUPS WITH A CONCENTRATED INTEREST IN CHANGE

An important reason why health policies change is that groups that previously had a diffuse interest develop a concentrated interest in the policy's outcome. For example, physicians and hospitals initially were the only organized groups having a concentrated interest in the financing and delivery of medical services. The potential benefits to unions of having their retiree's health benefits shifted from the employer to the government (via the taxpayer) under Medicare became great enough to provide them with a concentrated interest in this issue. Thus groups that have a diffuse interest may develop a concentrated interest as the potential benefits or costs to their members increase. As diffuse costs become "concentrated" there is greater incentive for a group to organize and represent its interests.

Many more groups today have a concentrated interest in health legislation and they have organized to represent their interests. Chiropractors, for example, lobby to have their services included under public programs. Podiatrists are seeking to change state Practice Acts to extend their scope of practice beyond the foot to the leg. To understand the conflicting forces pressuring for change and NHI, however, one has to examine the objectives of several of the more important groups having a concentrated interest.

The Federal Government

Since Medicare and Medicaid were enacted in 1965, every adminis- tration has been faced with the problem of rapidly rising Medicare and Medicaid expenditures. As expenditures greatly exceeded pro- jected expenditures, an initial diffuse cost became a concentrated cost to successive administrations. Each administration faced choices that were politically costly. To prevent the Medicare Trust Fund from going bankrupt, the administration could reduce benefits to the aged, increase Social Security taxes, or pay hospitals less. It was considered to be more politically costly to the administration if they reduced benefits to the aged. Thus the only remaining choices were to increase Social Security taxes and to place limits on how much hospitals were to be paid. Although both policies are politically costly, they are less so than reducing benefits to the aged.

To continue funding rapidly rising Medicaid expenditures, which are funded from general tax revenues, the states could reduce other politically popular programs or increase taxes. Instead, the states chose to limit Medicaid eligibility and reduced their payments to health providers. (The distribution of Medicaid benefits also began to shift away from adults and children toward the aged, who represent a relatively small percent of those eligible for benefits.) The percent of the poor served by Medicaid declined as did the participa- tion of physicians and hospitals.

Medicare Part B is also funded by general tax revenues, which contributes to the federal budget deficit. As these expenditures began to increase, the administration's interest in controlling them similarly increased. Again the federal choices were quite limited; an increase in taxes or a larger deficit are both politically costly to the administration; increasing the aged's contribution (they currently pay 25 percent of the premium) is also politically costly; the only alternative was to pay physicians less and place them under an expenditure limit, which was enacted as part of the new physician payment system (relative-value scales) in 1989.

Administrations at both the federal and state levels developed a concentrated interest in holding down the rise in government expenditures, which placed them in conflict with hospital and physician organizations. Currently, federal and state health policy appears to be primarily concerned with limiting the rise in Medicare and Medicaid expenditures. And the least politically costly approach is to pay providers less. Only under Medicaid are the politically weak beneficiaries also adversely affected.

Employers

Employers are interested in reducing the rise in the cost of their employees' medical benefits. Rising employee medical expenses became a concern to employers in the 1980s because of more intense import competition. High labor costs, of which the fastest increasing component was medical benefits, caused employers to raise their prices, which in turn reduced their international competitiveness.

More important, the stimulus for several large corporations, such as Chrysler, promoting national health insurance has been a recent ruling by the Financial Accounting Standards Board (FASB). The FASB ruling requires employers who provide their retirees with medical benefits to add that liability to their balance sheet starting in 1993. This liability would have to include not only the full estimate of their retirees' future medical expenses, but it would also have to include the estimated retiree benefit liability for their current employees. Currently, retiree medical benefits are an unfunded liability to those large corporations that provide such benefits. The employer pays retiree medical costs as they occur; they are thus treated as a current expense. To place this entire liability on the balance sheet will reduce the net worth of many major corporations by a significant amount. Their equity per share will drop substantially. In addition, corporate earnings will decline, since a portion of this retiree liability for medical benefits (for both retirees as well as current employees) will have to be expensed annually.

Any NHI plan that restricts the growth of medical expenditures will provide a direct economic benefit to large corporations by limiting the size of their retirees' unfunded medical liabilities and by limiting the rise in their employees' medical costs, thereby improving their international competitiveness.

Unions

The percentage of the working population that is unionized has been declining. Currently, only 14.5 percent of employees are unionized; this is down from 25 percent in 1972.[5] The wages earned and medical benefits received by union members vary widely from those engaged in manufacturing to those employed in the retail and construction businesses. Because unions are organized, several of the larger unions have been able to provide legislators with sufficient political support to exercise political influence that is greatly in excess of their numbers as a proportion of the total working population.

The economic interests of the major unions, such as the UAW, have not changed since the enactment of Medicare. At that time they were successful in shifting part of the cost of their retirees onto the general working population. Since that time they have been trying to do the same for the medical benefits of their working members. Medical benefits for UAW members are among the most expensive of all employees. If the unions can retain those benefits while shifting part of their costs to others—for example, having them financed by an increase in the Social Security tax—the savings could go toward increased wages.

Physicians and Hospitals

As other groups with a concentrated interest in limiting medical expenditures (particularly the federal and state governments) developed, the influence of physician and hospital associations declined. Also adding to their loss of political influence was the inability of their national organizations to represent the interests of their diverse constituencies. As long as the pie was expanding rapidly, all provider groups benefited; the diverse constituencies within each association did not need to compete with one another. When expenditure choices under public programs had to be made between these constituencies (urban versus rural hospitals, teaching versus nonteaching hospitals, surgical specialties versus primary-care physicians, and so on), however, these provider coalitions split apart, each trying to gain at the expense of the other.

Hospital and medical associations representing narrow constituencies no longer rely on their national organizations to represent their interests before the legislature. And as these separate associations provide political support to further their own interests, the political influence of their national associations has declined. In the legislative conflict between purchaser groups with a concentrated interest, provider associations have been greatly weakened.

The years of excessive provider payments are over. Hospitals and physicians are striving to limit further deterioration of their financial well-being. Their objective, as opposed to that of the federal and state governments and employers, is increased medical expenditures. Hospitals form the strongest lobbying group for financing medical care to the poor today, since it is in their own economic interests; they stand to gain additional revenues.

The Aged

The aged have NHI for acute care (Medicare). While the aged would like lower out-of-pocket payments for their medical expenses, the most pressing concern of the middle- and high-income aged is for protection from the costs of long-term care. An extended stay in a nursing home will deplete the assets of many of the aged. Medicare does not cover long-term care or nursing-home care unrelated to an acute illness. Those aged with low incomes have to rely on Medicaid for their long-term care. If an aged person's assets exceed the Medicaid limit, they must "spend down" those assets to qualify for Medicaid. Government-subsidized long-term-care insurance is a means whereby the aged can protect their assets. Rather than purchasing such asset protection in the marketplace, the aged prefer government legislation whereby they can shift part of their costs to other population groups.

To the extent that the aged are successful in achieving government-subsidized long-term care, a tax would be imposed on the nonaged to finance those benefits. A long-term-care tax on the working population would be substantial and could preempt tax revenues that might otherwise be used to provide NHI for the poor. Thus legislation subsidizing the aged's long-term care is somewhat substitutable with NHI in terms of funding sources.

The Middle Class

The middle class (those in the middle-income group) have a disproportionate amount of political power, since they are the median voters; it is difficult to form a majority of voters without those in the middle. If national health insurance were a highly visible issue and strongly supported by the middle class, legislators would respond to the political support that would be forthcoming from the middle class. It is instructive therefore to consider why the middle class has not been a strong supporter of NHI.

Rapidly rising medical costs have, until recently, been a diffuse cost to the middle class. Tax-free health insurance and employer-paid insurance premiums insulated employees and their families from the rising costs of medical care. For example, a thousand-dollar increase in income is worth more to the employee if it is not first reduced by federal, state, and Social Security taxes. High rates of inflation, which pushed employees into high marginal tax brackets during the 1970s, provided employees with an incentive to increase their insurance coverage rather than pay their dental, vision, and other medical out-of-pocket expenses with after-tax dollars. Until the last several years, employees have had unlimited choice of providers, limited cost sharing, and small, if any, co-premiums. According to a 1989 survey conducted by the Bureau of Labor Statistics, 53 percent of medium and large employers still pay the full health insurance premium for their employees and 34 percent still pay for families.[6] Tax-free employer-paid health insurance has been a form of NHI for middle- and high-income groups; the forgone tax revenue of employer-paid health insurance premiums is currently estimated to be $58 billion. Although employer-paid insurance premiums are a part of the employees' total compensation, the effect of increased employer-paid premiums on their wages is not very visible. And given the significant tax advantages of employer-paid premiums, rising insurance premiums have been a relatively small cost to employees.

Since employees have been relatively immune from rapidly rising medical care costs, NHI has not been an important financial issue. Employees have probably been at greater financial risk for the long-term-care needs of their aged parents than for their own acute-care needs. Further, according to numerous polls, employees and their families are satisfied with the care they receive from their physicians and hospitals; they are not concerned with how much is spent on health care in the United States; and employees enjoy their free choice of physicians and hospitals.[7]

Public opinion polls have come up with some surprising and seemingly contradictory findings. For example, 89 percent of Americans surveyed see the need for fundamental reform of the U.S. health care system. This is a much higher sense of dissatisfaction and call for change than expressed by Canadians or those living in England. Of those who are dissatisfied and prefer the Canadian system, however, a larger portion are black, earn low wages, and are disabled—individuals who are likely to have little or no employer-paid health insurance. Higher-income groups have also responded favorably to a Canadian health system; unfortunately, it is not clear that those favoring the Canadian system fully understand the implications of such a system. For example, respondents were asked:

> In the Canadian system of national health insurance, the government pays most of the cost of health care out of taxes and the government sets all fees charged by doctors and hospitals. Under the Canadian system—which costs the taxpayer less than the American system—people can choose their own doctors and hospitals. On balance, would you prefer the Canadian system or the system we have here in the United States?

Even though I am actually opposed to the Canadian system, if I had had only the facts as stated in that question I would have answered that I would prefer it. It promises everything for less money: unrestricted choice of provider, no limits on access to services or technology, and at a lower total cost. Sounds ideal.

Another survey (1989) asked whether the person would favor a comprehensive national health plan that would cover everyone and be paid for by federal tax revenues; 67 percent of the public said yes.[8]

However, Blendon and Donelan state, "the level of public support for the adoption of a tax-funded program of national health insurance declines in proportion to the size of the proposed increase in taxes."[9]

Based on exit polls from the last presidential election, 74 percent of the voting public endorsed Governor Michael Dukakis's proposal that employers be responsible for their employees' health insurance. This received more support than a proposal to replace the U.S. system with the Canadian health care system.

What can one conclude from these surveys? The public was not asked to make any trade-offs when comparing health systems in different countries. They were led to believe they could have the best of the current system at a lower cost. When they were asked whether they were willing to pay more, their support for a comprehensive national health system declined. Basically, the public would like someone else, either government or employers, to pay for their health care.

It is not possible to have a comprehensive national health plan for everyone without paying increased taxes. It is not possible to shift these costs to the government or employers, since to do so means either increased taxes, lower wages, unemployment, and/or increased prices for goods and services.

The middle class is not yet ready to make the necessary trade-offs in terms of taxes, access to care or technology, restricted choice of providers, higher co-payments, or lower wages to have a national health plan. The dissatisfaction of those in the middle class with our current system is increasing because their out-of-pocket payments are increasing and they are being forced into more restrictive health plans. There is, however, currently no consensus as to the type of trade-offs they are willing to accept.

When one examines those groups having a concentrated interest in health policy, it becomes clear why there has not been (nor is there currently) consensus on national health insurance. The federal and state governments, as well as large employers, want to limit the rate of increase in medical expenditures. The previously politically powerful physician and hospital associations want increased medical expenditures. The aged, who have national health insurance, want a new long-term-care program whose costs would be borne by the working population. The unions and the middle class want no less than what they have now but at a lower cost, presumably by shifting those costs to others, either different population groups or to the providers by paying them less. These conflicting objectives by powerful interest groups explain why there is no consensus as to what NHI should attempt to achieve.

THE LIKELY STRUCTURE AND FINANCING OF NATIONAL HEALTH INSURANCE

The pressure by the members of the middle class for NHI will increase when they realize that they must make trade-offs with regard to their medical care. Continually rising medical expenditures are causing employers to shift part of these increased costs to their employees. Employees are being required to pay an increasing portion of their health insurance premiums; their insurance plans have larger deductibles and cost sharing; and they are facing greater restrictions in their choice of medical provider, as when their employer chooses more restrictive health plans, such as HMOs, PPOs, and EPOs (Exclusive

Provider Organizations), and more stringent cost-containment approaches.

As out-of-pocket costs for both medical insurance and medical services increase and as the choice of provider is reduced, the costs of medical care will no longer be diffuse; the middle class will develop a concentrated interest in holding down its medical costs while retaining the free choice of provider. Many of the middle class have not yet arrived at this situation. (Remember, 34 percent of medium and large employers still pay the entire health insurance premium for their employees and families.) When the costs of medical care become concentrated to a greater portion of the middle class, NHI will then become a visible political issue for which the middle class would be willing to provide its political support.[10]

When those in the middle class are finally willing to provide political support for NHI, what is it that they are likely to want? If NHI is to benefit them, then they must receive benefits in excess of their costs; that is, to pay less for their medical care. How can the powers of government be used to provide the middle class with medical care for less than full price? There are several possibilities.

First, a tax could be imposed that essentially causes other population groups to pay more than their share. For example, if those in the middle class use more medical services than those with lower incomes and they each pay approximately the same size of tax, then there would be a net subsidy to the middle class.[11] Such a scheme could be implemented by imposing a diffuse tax, such as a sales or an excise tax. (Such a tax would be regressive, in that those with lower incomes would pay a greater portion of their income on such a tax.) This was the approach used to finance Medicare. Not only did it cause intergenerational inequity but it was also regressive. Social Security taxes have now become such a large portion of income (in excess of 15 percent), however, there is political pressure to reduce such taxes. A different excise tax would therefore have to be used. An excise tax to fund a comprehensive NHI is not likely, since it would have to replace the approximately $350 billion a year currently being spent on medical care in the private sector (approximately one-half being private insurance expenditures). It would involve too great an increase in taxes.

A second approach that has been suggested is mandated employer health insurance (MEHI). There is currently a great deal of interest in mandating employers to provide their employees with health insurance or else pay a per-worker tax. (Most employees without health insurance earn low wages and work in small firms, less than twenty-five employees.) The main opposition to this legislation comes from small employers who employ low-wage labor and who would be most affected by this approach. There is, however, a great deal of support for such legislation. State governments favor this approach, since it would shift medical costs off the Medicaid budget onto small employers and their low-wage employees. Hospital and physician associations also favor this approach, since it would increase the demand for their services without disrupting the current practice of medicine or payment systems. Many large employers and their unions also support employer mandates because it would increase the labor costs of low-cost competitors, possibly reduce "cost shifting," while not placing any additional burdens on their own employees' medical costs. The middle class is unlikely to oppose MEHI, since it is a means of providing medical care to those with low incomes without explicitly increasing the middle class's taxes; it would appear to be a means of shifting the cost onto employers, even though the burden would fall mostly on the employee.[12]

Mandated employer health insurance, while politically feasible, is, however, not NHI. It does nothing to limit the increase in medical expenditures, which is a major objective of the federal and state governments and large employers. More important, MEHI does not provide the middle class with any visible net benefits, nor would it reduce their rising out-of-pocket expenditures, which would be the basis for their support for NHI. Mandated employer health insurance is therefore likely to be combined with another, politically popular, approach.

The powers of government could be used to fix prices and place expenditure limits on hospitals and physicians. No new taxes would be required. Health insurance premiums and out-of-pocket expenses of the middle class would rise less rapidly; part of the costs of its care would be borne by the providers. In this manner, middle class members could be assured of their choice of provider at lower prices. This would be similar to the Medicare system. Placing price and expenditure limits on providers would achieve consensus among those in the middle class, since they could still have their choice of provider but at lower prices; they would not be required to make any sacrifices. Expenditure caps on providers would serve the interests of employers and the federal and state governments (who are already using this approach). Insurance companies would not be opposed, as long as their role is not eliminated. The main opposition from such an approach would be from physicians and hospitals, who would receive lower payments.

Combining mandated employer health insurance with expenditure limits on physicians and hospitals would, in my opinion, be the most likely political route to NHI. Most of the uninsured, particularly low-income employees, can be provided insurance by requiring their employer to pay the premium. Those in the middle class would not be required to make any sacrifices; they would be relieved to know that the problems of the uninsured are resolved, without its being obvious that the low-wage employee is in fact being taxed to bear most of the burden of his or her own insurance. The middle class also receives the visible benefits of lower out-of-pocket expenditures with the belief that its rising medical costs are shifted back to physicians and hospitals. Large employers and unions would benefit, as would the federal and state governments, as a portion of their Medicaid costs are shifted onto small employers and their employees. (Since this approach would minimize the need for new taxes, a new—regressive—excise tax could be enacted to provide long-term care for all the aged.)

Any long-term-care program for the aged is likely to provide net subsidies to all the aged, regardless of their income or assets. The repeal of the Medicare Catastrophic Insurance legislation is illustrative of this reasoning. The aged were initially provided with a new benefit for which they had to pay the full costs themselves. The legislation represented a net cost to the higher-income aged, since their new benefits were worth less than the additional taxes required to fund those benefits. This legislation was a first in that the aged's benefits were not subsidizied by the non-aged. While the financing mechanism was equitable (higher-income aged subsidized low-income aged), the aged were not interested in being required by government to be more charitable to their lower-income members. To receive the political support of the aged, all of the aged, including those with higher incomes, had to receive net benefits. The bill was therefore repealed.

The repeal of the Medicare Catastrophic Insurance law also provides an indication as to the likelihood of eliminating the tax-free status of employer-paid health insurance premiums. The fifty-six billion dollars in lost tax revenues could be a source of new revenues for providing increased medical care to those with low incomes. The likelihood of middle- and upper-income groups taxing themselves to provide new revenues to support medical services to the poor (however equitable it may be) is unlikely.

The structure and financing of national health insurance becomes a *consequence* of the economic interests of politically powerful groups. To forecast the likely financing methods and structure of the delivery system does not require an understanding of which methods of taxation are more equitable, what their effects are on employment, which delivery systems are more efficient, and so on. Instead it is more important to understand the political feasibility of different alternatives.

National health insurance could be achieved by using a price-competitive market; managed-care plans could compete for subscribers, some of whom have subsidized health insurance premiums (vouchers). A market approach, however, is unlikely to be used as part of any NHI plan. The reason for this has nothing to do with issues of market efficiency or market imperfections. If vouchers and competing managed-care plans were used, then the middle class would presumably not benefit, since they would not receive any net subsidies. If the middle class did receive subsidies, then the financial costs of NHI would become much greater and an explicit tax would have to be imposed on some population group to provide those subsidies to the middle class.

To provide the poor with subsidies to join managed-care plans and receive the same care as the middle class would require the government to pay the market price charged by HMOs and other such plans. This would be too large an expenditure for the government to make without increased taxes.

Instead, a nonmarket approach is likely to be used because it makes it easier to shift the costs from the purchasers, the middle class, employers, and government to providers. For example, the annual limit on Medicare hospital expenditures—through the diagnosis-related group (DRG) price updates—shifts costs off the federal Medicare budget onto hospitals; they are paid less; eventually they will have to reduce services to the aged. Expenditure limits represent a diffuse cost imposed on future beneficiaries, however, since they will have less access to services.

The same approach is being used with the new Medicare physician-payment system. A relative-value scale, which is basically a national fee schedule (similar in concept to uniform prices per admission under DRGs), has been enacted. An overall expenditure cap will then be used to limit physician volume and fee increases (again, similar to the DRG annual update factors).

There is, of course, a trade-off in using expenditure limits. There are legitimate reasons why the costs of medical care are increasing. There have been costly advances in technology, such as transplants and care of low-birthweight babies; the population is aging and there are unmet needs for care among the poor, causing increased demands for acute care; the highly trained labor supply working in health care is not increasing as rapidly, requiring greater wage increases; there are new diseases, such as AIDS; and the economy-wide inflation rate necessitates increased prices for supplies and wages. If the government limits expenditure increases to a rate that is insufficient to meet the above expenditure requirements, then which of the above are to be sacrificed?

The consequences of insufficient medical expenditures, however, will not be felt for some time. Until the middle class is affected by lower access to services and technology, the costs of such a policy will not be obvious.

NOTES

1. The higher insurance costs among small employers associated with adverse selection, high employee turnover, and preexisting conditions can be handled in ways which do not require a standardized nationalized plan for everyone.

2. Even if one were to assume that savings could be achieved by greater government intervention in the delivery of medical services, which is contrary to empirical evidence in the health field, it is doubtful that these savings would be used to subsidize the poor and uninsured. The likelihood of subsidies to the poor was discussed earlier as an objective of NHI.

3. For a more complete discussion of the economic theory of regulation applied to the medical sector, see Paul J. Feldstein, *The Politics of Health Legislation: An Economic Perspective* (Ann Arbor, Mich.: Health Administration Press, 1988).

4. Union members had some of the most generous (and more costly) health benefits. Substituting a small Social Security tax on current union members would still provide union employees with a large savings on their retirees' benefits.

5. U.S. Bureau of the Census, *Statistical Abstract of the United States*, (Washington, D.C.: U.S. Government Printing Office, 1975 and 1990), pp. 343, 371 (1975 ed.) and pp. 418–19 (1990 ed.).

6. U.S. Department of Labor, Bureau of Labor Statistics, *Employee Benefits in Medium and Large Firms, 1989*, Bulletin 2363, June 1990, p. 124.

7. See the following for surveys on the public's view on health care:

Cindy Jajich-Toth and Burns Roper, "Americans' Views on Health Care," *Health Affairs* 9 (Winter 1990): 149–57; Robert J. Blendon and Humphrey Taylor, "Views on Health Care: Public Opinion in Three Nations," *Health Affairs* 8 (Spring 1989): 149–57; Robert J. Blendon and Karen Donelan, "The 1988 Election: How Important Was Health?" *Health Affairs* 8 (Fall 1989): 3–15; Robert J. Blendon et al., "Satisfaction with Health Systems in Ten Nations," *Health Affairs* 9 (Summer 1990): 185–92.

8. Blendon and Donelan, "The 1988 Election."

9. Ibid., p. 9.

10. Making employer-paid health insurance premiums taxable would not only hasten the time when the costs of medical care become concentrated and visible to middle- and high-income groups, but it would also improve equity; the vast majority of the $56 billion in forgone taxes benefit those in the highest income groups.

11. Even if medical care were made free to all, higher-income groups could have higher use of medical services because they might be located more closely to such providers and/or their attitudes toward use of services might be different. As long as their tax was not proportionate to their use, they would receive net subsidies.

12. Mandated employer health insurance is an inequitable approach for providing low-wage employees with health insurance. Statutorily imposing the cost of such coverage on the employer does not mean that the employer actually bears the burden of that tax. Similar to the Social Security tax, one-half of which is imposed on the employer, studies indicate that most of the employer share is borne by the employee. The portion not borne by the employee is shifted forward in a competitive industry to the consumer in the form of higher prices for goods and services, which again is a regressive tax (John A. Brittain, "The Incidence of Social Security Payroll Taxes," *American Economic Review* 61 [March 1971]: 110–25. Also see the comment on that article by Martin S. Feldstein and the reply by Brittain in the September 1972 issue of the *American Economic Review*, pp. 735–42.

Insurance or Access?

Suzanne Dandoy, M.D.

In his essay "Verging on National Health Insurance since 1910," Dr. Harold Bauman presents a very thoughtful summary of why we have had so many fits, starts, and stops with respect to national health insurance in the United States. I would question, however, his definition of what he describes as "the most persistent social problem of the twentieth century, namely, the provision of adequate health insurance under federal supervision." I would prefer to define the problem as "the provision of equal and adequate access to health care." Having insurance does not ensure access to care, especially if you live in rural America, or if you are a member of an ethnic minority, or if you have AIDS. You need a payment mechanism but you also need the presence of medical care professionals who are willing, able, and available to provide you with services. National health insurance is only one mechanism to achieve increased access to care. We must never assume that national health insurance is the panacea for all the problems of the U.S. medical care system. While it may be the "age old and obvious solution" to some, it is not so to all.

"Disarray" must be the current "in" word. In 1988 the Institute of Medicine issued a report indicating that the public health system in this country was in disarray.[1] Dr. Bauman has suggested that the U.S. health insurance system is in disarray. While I may argue with that description of the public health system, I wholeheartedly agree with the characterization of the health insurance system as duplicative, administratively inefficient, more bureaucratic than is government, and more concerned with how to *avoid* financing the delivery of care than in *insuring health*, which is what the words "health insurance" imply. In his essay, Dr. Paul J. Feldstein points out that if citizens wanted more efficiency in health insurance, they could demand and get it in a competitive system. Obviously, the middle class is satisfied with the disarray.

Both Dr. Bauman and Dr. Feldstein lay responsibility for why we do not have national health insurance on middle-class citizens, who either do not see the need and/or are unwilling to pay the costs. Polls throughout the United States have indicated that the majority of citizens believe that everyone should have access to basic medical care but that others, usually employers, should pay for it. The amount of tax increase people are willing to pay to expand coverage for the poor is inadequate to do the job.

Dr. Feldstein is correct that the nonpoor have the political power to determine the allocation of resources to the poor. Usually that power is given to legislative bodies or other elected officials. While middle-class citizens are not yet ready to make trade-offs for their own care, such as increased co-payments, higher deductibles, restricted choice of providers, waiting periods, and lack of coverage for expensive procedures, they are comfortable having such decisions made for the poor by elected officials.

David M. Eddy from Duke University has suggested a form of rationing by patient choice.[2] He proposes that we let a group of patients, both those currently receiving care as well as those not yet in need of care, decide which health services are worth the cost and which cost too much. These decisions would be implemented in the financing mechanism, with no exceptions permitted except what individuals can purchase with their own funds. Thus, those who pay for services, either through their taxes, out-of-pocket, or through a deduction from their wages, would be the ones to decide the value of specific health care services. This idea puts medical care really into the marketplace, where people decide if the value is worth the cost, that is, those procedures that may appear important when thought to be free may become unattractive when costs are assigned. The middle class would make decisions about its own care, rather than having those decisions made by employers, insurers, or government.

Dr. Feldstein suggests that a combination of mandated employer-purchased health insurance with expenditure limits on physicians and hospitals would be the most likely political route to national health insurance. All routes to national health insurance step on someone's toes. That is one reason we do not have national health insurance in this country; people scream loudly when their toes are stepped on. Dr. Feldstein is probably correct in his analysis because that route steps on the toes only of those whom the middle class—

that is, the bulk of the voters—think can most afford the pain of being stepped on. Most citizens believe that employers and health care providers can absorb such changes without screaming loudly or affecting the average citizen's care or pocketbook.

I also want to comment on how the remarks by Drs. Bauman and Feldstein relate to the Medicaid program. Dr. Bauman quoted a 1949 editorial from the *Journal of the American Medical Association,* which described a proposed national health plan as a system which would "regiment doctors and patients alike under a vast bureaucracy of political administrators, clerks, book keepers, and lay committees." I would guess that many recipients and service providers believe that statement could be used to describe the Medicaid program today.

Dr. Feldstein's statement that higher-income states provide more Medicaid benefits and cover a greater portion of the poor than do states with lower per capita income is no longer accurate. Congressional mandates expanding coverage of pregnant women and children are rapidly erasing differences between states on eligibility and service delivery, at least for these two population groups which comprise the majority of the Medicaid population. This use of federal mandates to expand Medicaid is an example of the creeping incrementalism mentioned by Dr. Bauman. The federal government has not proposed any definitive strategy to solve the health care access problem, but Congress is using Medicaid as a way to tackle the need in progressive stages. While the mandates have served to provide financial coverage for services to greater numbers of women and children, these same mandates may actually interfere with access for other potential Medicaid recipients because the state money to expand coverage has been made available at the expense of adequate reimbursement for the providers of care. Many states may reach the point of having insufficient numbers of providers willing to care for the increasing number of Medicaid clients. Once again, the issue may not be one of financing but of availability of services.

Can we tackle national health insurance or some other plan to provide universal access without considering costs? Of course not. Many states have created health data organizations to provide information that may be used to educate health care providers and consumers regarding cost issues. Concern over access, however, does seem to have replaced costs as the primary topic of conversation among state legislators, governors, business leaders, associations of health care providers, and citizen groups. While national health insurance or some other federal initiative might solve the problem of financing, it is the states that must find ways to lower all the barriers to access and to ensure the quality of care that is delivered.

NOTES

1. Institute of Medicine, *The Future of Public Health* (Washington, D.C.: National Academy Press, 1988).
2. David M. Eddy, "Rationing by Patient Choice," *Journal of the American Medical Association* 265, no. 1 (1991): 105–8.

PART II

Comparing National Health Systems

Lessons from Abroad in Assessing National Health Care Systems: Ethics and Decision Making

John G. Francis

Reform of the health care system is very much on the agenda of American politics, and it has generated a good deal of interest in the health care systems of other nations. This interest in other systems is motivated by a range of concerns that embrace both ethical and budgetary imperatives. Some Americans look to other countries to survey systems that realize the goal of universal access to health care for the population. But other Americans are looking for a system that supplies health care for less money than is currently expended in the United States. This search for lessons from abroad provides the focus of this chapter on the location of institutional decision making in health care allocation and its implications for access and cost containment. An important caveat in searching for lessons from abroad is the recognition that the interplay of ethical justifications and institutional structures goes a long way towards shaping a health care system and the strategies needed for reform.

Over the course of this century, European health care systems have moved toward universality of coverage while increasing what is included in that coverage. But during the past two decades these same European states have confronted intensifying budgetary pressures that have resulted in the search for cost-containment strategies. In both strategies—expansion and containment—a central question is how to determine institutional responsibility and accountability. In these systems, there are often divisions between actual responsibility for health care decision making and the institutions at more distant locations that are ultimately held accountable. The pertinent issues in health care system decision making include how open or insulated decision making should be from political currents and what the appropriate level of involvement of consumers, practitioners, payers, and policymakers is in health care decision making.

This essay compares health care delivery systems and costs in four selected advanced industrial nations—Britain, Canada, France, and Germany. It begins with an account of the principal ethical justifications associated with the introduction of national health care systems in these societies. Second, it provides a brief account of the politics of health care reform in the United States that has promoted interest in the health care systems of other nations. Third, the paper offers an analysis of national health care systems that includes how they work, what ethical justifications have been employed in their defense, and where decision making about health care resource allocation is located. It argues that the interplay of political values and institutional structures is critical to the success of health care reform.

THE ETHICAL BACKGROUND

This section develops two clusters of ethical concerns that have recurred in policy debates over the prospects for a national health care system. This discussion should not be understood as exhaustive of the ethical issues in health care. Rather, the aim is to lay out two recurring clusters of questions that have framed ethical debates about introducing national health care systems, both in the United States and in other advanced industrial nations. First, should access to the health care system be privately arranged or publicly assured and, if the latter, on what basis? Second, what are the ethical consequences of the introduction of cost-containment goals in the provision of health care?

Health is universally regarded as an important human value. Good health not only is regarded as a value in its own right but is judged to be a necessary condition for the performance of a vast number of human endeavors. The critical importance of professional health care is, therefore, found in the claim that such care can restore a patient to good health or prevent a deterioration of a person's health. Once this claim for effectiveness of professional health care became widely accepted over the course of this century, the burden of justification fell on both medical practitioners and political leaderships to explain why there should be significant financial barriers to health care access throughout their respective societies. Arguments for making health care universally available to a nation's population have been frequently justified on grounds of human rights, utilitarianism, and desert.

The importance and distinctiveness of these justificatory traditions is apparent in the public discourse about health care that is found in the United States and Germany in comparison to the nature of the discourse found in Britain. In Britain, justifications for the National Health Service have been largely utilitarian (Halper, 1989). The claim most frequently advanced in British politics is that universal health care is justified not only because it is a strong popular preference but also because it is of considerable benefit to the great majority of the population. In Germany, universal health care was originally justified in terms of desert for the working classes. In the United States, the debate over establishing a universal health care system is often defended in the language of rights (see the essay by Kenneth N. Buchi and Bruce M. Landesman in this volume). But American political practice has been to establish health care programs based on desert, for example, that veterans should have access to health care because of their service to their country, or that the elderly should not find cost a barrier to health care because of their long years of productive labor. Over time, however, this argument for desert appears to shift to the language of rights as veterans or the elderly come to regard entitlement programs as creating rights.

The desert argument appears historically to have been a point of origin for many health care systems. But the argument from desert suggests selectivity, not universality, in who should receive access. Gradually, however, demands for a universal system gain force and arguments shift to utilitarian and rights justifications with shared presumptive standards of equality as the guiding principle for health care access. Equality of access is the standard that guides the comparative examination of health care systems in this essay.

On both rights and utilitarian approaches, there is a strong presumption of equality in access to the health care system. This presumption is not necessarily that every individual should receive all the ministration he or she may desire—an important point—but rather that he or she have substantive access to the health care system. The argument may be understood in terms of John Rawls's work (1971) on distributive justice. Rawls argues that a just society allows inequality to the extent that the least well off are benefited. The principle found in universal health care systems is that of solidarity— that is, the most healthy underwrite the care of the least healthy. All are included in the pool that finances the system. In private health insurance markets, by contrast, the guiding principle is to remove high-risk members from the pool in order to realize a profit or at least to avoid a loss on resources invested in the pool.

But the arguments of rights and utility, as well as desert, have been met over the past century with two recurring principal objections to the assumption by the state of responsibility for the provision of health care. The paramount objection is the concern that choice, both for the patient and for the physician, would be compromised by the imposition of state supervision. The second, and related, concern is whether the commitment and trust that should govern the physician-patient relationship would be compromised by the state's perceived inevitable erosion of professional autonomy. The medical professions in many countries, notably France and the United States, have stressed the centrality of the physician-patient relationship (Starr, 1982; Godt, 1989). This relationship was characterized as beginning with the patient's free choice of a physician. Once the physician was selected, a relationship of trust developed, with the patient coming to accept that the physician's paramount goal was restoring health. This goal drove the course of treatment, and other considerations receded. The physician, therefore, had to have complete autonomy in the exercise of his or her professional responsibilities.

Over the past century, a debate moved from country to country between physicians who claimed that if the state were to assume budgetary and general administrative responsibility for the provision of health care, the autonomy and choice that underpinned the physician-patient relationship would recede as the forces of budgetary constraint and organizational imperatives came increasingly into play. In short, opponents of the state's role in health care argued that quality of medical care would suffer as constraints came to be imposed on both patient choice and physician practice. It might be the case that anyone could visit a physician without paying a fee, but the state would restrict the components of quality of care, from the tools for diagnosis and treatment to sophisticated hospital equipment. The prediction was the introduction of assembly-line medicine, resulting in a loss of individuation in medical care (see the essay by Margaret P. Battin in this volume).

In recent years, the argument has been made that professional autonomy may indeed be challenged by state health care. Others have argued, however, that challenges to professional autonomy also may be a consequence of health care cost-containment strategies by the private sector. The existence of health maintenance organizations (HMOS) with their commitment to quality-control policies suggests that such strategies imposed clear limits on professional autonomy in light of criteria to manage the provision of health care within strict financial limits.

The second group of concerns focuses on the consequences of the introduction of cost-containment goals in the provision of health care. Cost containment—at least, constraining the rise in the rate of growth of health care expenditures—preoccupies many advanced industrial nations today (Culyer, 1989). The issue of cost containment draws attention to the challenges to the health system at a time of steady-state economies (Abel Smith, 1984). The ethical issues are complex in state-funded systems, for, of course, populations are not stable, disease is not a constant, and medical innovation is ongoing. The task becomes a search for strategies to restrict patient consumption of medical care, such as developing waiting lists, introducing co-payments, or imposing constraints on fees charged by health care professionals and hospitals. For example, how does a health care system handle a request to expand nursing-home care in an era of cost constraint? Should that decision be market driven or should the expansion be placed in the context of competing needs, such as health care for children or expectant mothers? Perhaps an advantage from an ethical viewpoint is that cost cutting or cost containment is understood in terms of trade-offs rather than seen as a distinct action isolated from the rest of the health care system.

In the context of nation-states seeking cost containment, it is useful to consider the framework of values that structure expectations of the population for health care. In systems that appeal to utilitarian arguments, it may be reasonably hypothesized that the state has greater flexibility in its justification for allocating health care. Allocative decisions that affect specific components of a population can be seen as trade-offs against decisions that affect other components. In contrast, a rights-based understanding of health care takes the individual as its operating assumption. Efforts to reduce or at least constrain health care utilization immediately confront the political challenge of taking away from the individual what, under a rights doctrine, is regarded as a legitimate expectation for the full measure of health care.

A point of controversy central to this comparative analysis is the frequent charge that state-managed systems, because they are conscious of budgetary constraints, seek to limit the numbers of physicians and hospital beds, the introduction of technology such as innovations in diagnostic tools, and the numbers of procedures. Taken together, these efforts by state managers would suggest the freezing of a health care system. This stabilization of a system may come to be characterized by strained quality, the use of waiting lists, or other tactics to discourage use that lead to care of questionable quality.

Cost containment has brought to the fore scrutiny of what is accomplished by the health care system for the resources spent (Culyer, 1989). Resources, access, and costs brought to the attention of policymakers the problem of effectiveness and efficiency in delivery and, most important, the consequences of medical intervention. Efforts have been made to create indicators of performance. The amount of time needed to perform and to recover from certain surgical procedures, which is presumably a statistical average, has been incorporated into American health care regulation of Medicare reimbursements by the establishment of diagnostic-related groups. Malpractice litigation in the United States is a blunt and costly mechanism to set standards of performance (Danzon, 1985). A critical issue is the extent to which efforts at adopting performance indicators have restricted professional autonomy and the extent to which that is a good or bad restriction.

An important objective of contemporary state-centered health systems is cost constraint. Managers of state health care systems are said to oppose any changes in the principal factors of health care services, such as the supply of health care professionals. New technologies are resisted as budget breaking. The criticism of such cost-conscious systems is that innovation in diagnosis and in treatment is discouraged. Indeed, constraint is likely to extend to holding steady the existing patterns of health care service use by the current population. These constraints can be a burden on individuals within the population who suffer from illnesses that are costly or on an aging population whose demands are likely to be far greater than those of younger age groups. Yet these concerns about increased burdens on health care systems have occurred at a time when most state-managed systems have increased the resources available to patients.

In general, in first-world countries the supply of health professionals, notably physicians but also nurses, has increased substantially over the past fifteen years. In some countries such as the United States and Australia, where there has been a steadily increasing population, it is not surprising to observe the increase in health care professionals. But the rate of increase in supply clearly outstrips the rate of population growth in these countries. What is more striking is the clear increase in health care professionals in countries that have remained stable in their respective population sizes (OECD Secretariat, 1989). This suggests an important concern in the control of costs: that the increase in the supply of health care professionals results in an increased use of health care services. Increased use increasingly consumes resources, thus threatening budgetary stability.

An important ethical consideration in developing cost-containment strategies has been their impact on the health care system as a whole. If cost containment were to be pursued in specific areas without consideration of other health care areas, then distortions in fairness may be the result. There may be cuts, for example, in health care for newborns while support is maintained for dialysis programs without a global consideration of the values that should underlie cost containment. Yet if we value health care as an important public good, then its allocation should be debated as a matter of public policy. Allocative decisions should not be hidden in the penumbra of a semiprivate/semipublic, fragmented health care system. A review of the ethical concerns stated above will suggest that on grounds of resource sufficiency, access/use, consequence/assessment, and cost, state-funded systems in Europe appear to offer more appealing options for care than the mixed public/private system found in the United States.

INSTITUTIONS AND HEALTH CARE DECISION MAKING

Locating institutional responsibility for decision making about health care allocation has significant implications for both the ethics of expanding health services and the ethics of cost containment. In periods of health care system expansion, it is not uncommon for political parties operating through legislatures to take the initiative and the credit for expanding coverage and the depth of care provided by the state.

In times of contraction—or at least in the present era, when states are committed to containing costs—the institutional question becomes where to locate decision-making authority to restrict resource use. It might, for example, be located in the office of a national health minister setting priorities for health care allocation. In other systems it may be located in the surgeries of the general practitioner determining who is to receive the attention of the specialist. In other systems it may be a quasi-autonomous insurance organization determining compensation for health care professionals for services performed. In a federal system, it may be a division of labor between central and subnational authorities. The federal authority may set a global budget leaving it to the subnational authority to determine how it is to be allocated.

The crucial point for an ethical as well as a political theorist is joining power with accountability. It is important that there be an identified institutional capacity to make critical allocative decisions about health care. There is a delicate balance between providing sufficient insulation to enable policymakers to make hard choices and still enabling democratic accountability.

THE UNITED STATES: THE CURRENT ISSUES

American health care faces a dilemma: a combination of rising costs and an often strikingly uneven distribution in access and utilization of health care. Various efforts have been made over the past decade by both private and public health care payers to contain costs. These efforts at cost containment will be the focal point for comparison between the United States and other advanced industrial nations.

A survey of health care expenditures from 1960 to 1987 in selected advanced industrial societies suggests two quite distinct trends (Schieber, 1990). Among the seven leading industrial nations, there has been continuing growth in dollars adjusted for inflation spent per capita on health care. In 1960, per capita health expenditures ranged from $26 in Japan to $149 in the United States. By 1987, the ratio of six to one in expenditures had changed to a ratio of less than three to one. The range was from $746 in the United Kingdom to $2,051 in the United States. In the United States, Germany, and the United Kingdom, the annual rate of growth in expenditure per capita has remained the same since: a compounded rate of 3.9 percent per year. In Canada the rate of increase has been less, growing at 3.6 percent. The rates of growth were much higher in France, Italy, and Japan. But at the end of day the United States in inflation-adjusted dollars spends the highest amount of dollars per capita, and the gap in per capita expenditure is widening between it and the other countries. An important factor in the analysis of health care expenditure and the widening gap between the United States and the other industrial powers is the relatively slow rate of growth in the American economy. Our spending rates have continued to climb, but our income continues to grow at a slower rate than in other nations.

Many specialists in health care budgets have concluded that the volume and intensity of health care services provided on a per capita basis are greater in the United States than in the other industrialized countries (Jonsson, 1989). Yet dividing health care expenditure by the population as a whole is not particularly helpful in understanding the actual distribution of health care services. Such calculations convey neither what health care services are available to the citizens in affordable terms nor what use the citizens make of the system.

Approximately 16 percent of the U.S. population is without health insurance (Davis and Rowland, 1990). Many of these individuals work for firms that do not provide health insurance benefits, and their income is too modest to enable them to purchase adequate insurance on the private market. At the same time, their income is sufficiently high to exclude them from federal and state programs designed to provide health insurance to the poor and/or the elderly (see the essay by Norman J. Waitzman in this volume for a full account of the American health care dilemma).

A recent compilation of health care surveys of the fifty American states reveals remarkable and often disconcerting inequalities (Northwestern National Life Insurance Company, 1990). Striking inequalities are apparent in access to physicians, the receipt of prenatal care, and the provision of public insurance. The reasonable inference is that the intensity and volume of medical services consumed in the United States would be better understood as applying only to a subset of the population rather than as being enjoyed by the population as a whole.

American politics is schizophrenic about health care. On the one hand, in the context of the American debate among policymakers and business community leaders, the paramount issue is cost containment. On the other hand, the issue for lower-income advocates and for significant sectors of the American political leadership is universal access to the health care system. What is often striking about American politics is the extent to which these two critical aspects of the provision of health care are rarely linked in American public-policy debate.

Consider the activity throughout the past decade to devise

strategies to contain health care costs. Congress began in the 1970s to promote health maintenance organizations (HMOS). Encouragement also has been given to the creation of preferred provider organizations (PPOS), which, like HMOS, permit both employers and prospective patients to choose among competing organizations for services at presumably competitive rates. Another strategy is adoption by federal health care authorities of diagnosis-related groups (DRGS) as a strategy for standardizing reimbursement schedules for hospital services. As James A. Morone (1990) reminds us, such cost-containment strategies are often billed as technical changes outside the political sphere. Cost-containment strategies adopted by the federal program administrators of Medicare and Medicaid have, if anything, intensified pressures on private-sector payers to respond to rising costs by such exclusionary methods as eliminating coverage for employee families or not including recent employees in firm-provided health care policies. Such efforts at reducing coverage in a nation where many groups have long lacked access add to the challenge of universal access. The solution to the problem that is often proposed is some sort of employer-mandated health care coverage. But this is a complicated strategy for securing universal health care in a sector increasingly preoccupied with reducing inclusiveness. Nonetheless, mandatory employer-based health insurance appears to meet the seeming American political requirement to avoid direct federal involvement in the provision of health care.

The lament of American proponents of universal health care is that the fragmented, antistate political culture of American politics obfuscates not only the connection between the issues of cost containment and universality but the fundamental importance of the state in the provision of health care. In European parliamentary politics, with the tradition of responsibility that fuses executive and legislative powers in societies, there is less ambiguity over the central role of the state, and the debate over the provision of health care is fundamentally a political debate.

So before discussing cost-containment policies in other nations, it is important to reflect on the implications of what is often described as the problem of American exceptionalism. Do the fragmentation of power and ambiguity in which state action is held in American society present insurmountable challenges toward regarding other countries as possessing experience that can be instructive for American health policy?

In dealing with the issue of American exceptionalism, it must be recognized that other nations are often drawn to examine the consequences of American experimentation. Health maintenance organizations have been discussed in Canada and Britain. Diagnosis-related groups have drawn considerable interest in Germany and France. Both Germany and France have maintained sickness funds and insurance associations, respectively, to realize the state's objectives of health care cost containment. Why keep these organizations that are largely the servants of the state? The answer is that European states have the obverse problem of American politics. If American politics is characterized by fragmentation and ambiguity toward state action, European state action is systematically interpreted as the pursuit of partisan advantage. Parties in power will find their attempts at cost containment scrutinized as partisan while opposition parties will look to assess state action as the pursuit of votes or ideology.

The competition for power in some European states may lead to the neglect of reform in health care in order to avoid partisan attack or to radical oscillation in policies for the health care sector as parties compete for support among various constituencies. Consequently there is increasing reliance on institutions that are one step removed from direct political accountability but are nonetheless responsible for implementing cost-containment strategies, such as fees paid by the consumers of medical services, shifts in health care services to the private sector, or constraints on compensation for health care professionals.

Perhaps there is a certain symmetry in the relationship between American and European politics. Whereas the European nations seek to reduce the force of partisan politics in order to manage health policy reform, the United States faces the challenge of forcing the politicization of health care in order to place health care, broadly conceived, on the nation's agenda. If one of the main political parties adopts a broad policy commitment to some version of universal health care, the chances are likely that the rival party will adopt a different but related version of universal health care. The European aim is to introduce a measure of depoliticization in order to contain costs, whereas the aim in the United States is to politicize the issues related to universal health care. Common to both is the desire to strike a balance between political commitment and administrative independence—a balance of accountability and responsibility. To put the point in another way, a useful dialectical relationship between the two sides of the Atlantic may ultimately be needed to realize the ethical concerns of health care provision.

THE EXPERIENCE WITH NATIONAL HEALTH SYSTEMS IN WESTERN EUROPE AND CANADA

This section examines the health care systems in Germany, France, the United Kingdom, and Canada. These countries have had a range and variety of experiences with universal health care systems. They also illustrate the impact of differing political values and institutional structures. In some cases, these experiences have extended over a century and in others for a good thirty years. They are nations with advanced industrial economies and large populations. All these nations have records of sustained and often complex negotiations with medical associations, a necessary component not only of the formation of a national health system but, more to the point, of its capacity to continue. In drawing comparisons with the United States, accommodation to political institutions is obviously of considerable importance. None of the other systems possesses the American tradition of separation of powers, but we do find the relationship between central and subnational units. Canada and Germany are both federal systems; this factor enables us to consider the central role of subnational governments in the provision of health care.

Two goals are sought in the accounts of the health care systems below. The first is a descriptive account of how they work. Specific attention is given to the location of health care allocative decision making in these systems. The second is a discussion of the efforts at cost containment that have been undertaken by each of these countries since the late 1970s. In both the account of how the system works and the discussion of how the respective states have sought to contain costs, the interplay between ethical frameworks and political institutions is apparent.

Germany

Among the parallels between the German and the American health care systems is the high level of resources devoted to health care in each country. The aim of this discussion is an examination of the highly regulated private organizations, the sickness funds, in managing the costs of health care. The sickness funds as described below are the intermediaries for federal policymakers to use in containing health care costs. The importance of these sickness funds might parallel what could become the role of insurance firms in the United States.

The American experience may in some quite useful ways be compared with the German. Germany is a country of comparable per capita income. It has as well a federal system of government. It has a health care system that provides a wide range of services and enjoys wide deployment of high-technology medicine, large numbers of hospital beds, and a tradition of physician choice. It provides a wide range of medical services for the population (Drummond, 1987).

The German universal health care system is one of the oldest in Europe and has steadily evolved over the past century under a series of sharply different political regimes (Schulenburg, 1983). There are five principal components to the German health care system: the 1,200 sickness funds, the Länder (the German states), the federal government, the physicians, and the hospitals. The sickness funds are the most distinctive component of the system and will be the focus here. They are private organizations comparable to health care insurance firms in the United States. But there are quite serious limits to the comparison between the sickness funds and private insurance firms, for the sickness funds are strictly regulated. The funds are not-for-profit organizations that serve a specific geographical area or a particular industry or a certain sort of economic activity. Membership is compulsory up to a particular salary limit, above which membership is voluntary. A member's family is automatically covered by the fund. All Germans are allowed access to membership in the funds; 90 percent of the German population are members. Approximately three-quarters of these are compulsory members. The practice for Germans is to remain with a specific sickness fund or, if their income is at a high enough level, to opt for a private insurance carrier. Once with a private carrier, however, the German citizen cannot return to the sickness funds. The sickness funds may have received their impetus from Bismarckian prudence to secure the electoral support of the German working classes for the newly united Imperial German state, but the justification through the years has been desert: the rewarding of those who have toiled for the economy and the state.

The sickness funds are the payers in the system and they have the responsibility for negotiating with physician organizations over fee schedules. The funds negotiate hospitalization costs as well, although responsibility for hospital construction rests with the respective German states.

The system is financed out of the total compensation paid to employees regardless of family size or health conditions. Retired individuals have contributions taken as a percentage of their pensions. Nationally this contribution has averaged about 13 percent of income. The working population clearly subsidizes the health care costs of the elderly. It is estimated that the elderly contribute about 40 percent of their health care costs; the remainder comes from the employed community (Reinhardt, 1990).

In the 1950s and 1960s, the German federal government was responsible for enforcing the universality of the system but exercised little control over health care budgets. The sickness funds often competed with one another in the provision of services. Health care costs continued to climb as a percentage of gross national product and led to a growing debate over the imposition of cost containment.

In the early 1980s, with the fall of the Social Democratic government of Chancellor Helmut Schmidt and its replacement in 1982 by the Christian Democratic government, there was a good deal of discussion of a *Wende*—a turnaround—that was to result in sustained commitment to cost containment. Throughout the last decade a number of federal initiatives have been undertaken to restrain the rate of health care cost increases. The strategy of cost containment has been directed at the costs of pharmaceuticals, physician fees, hospital costs and construction, and to some extent at selected services such as spa cures.

In the mid-1980s, negotiations between the sickness funds and the physician associations brought about an agreement on capping physician reimbursement that, although originally seen as a temporary measure, appears now to be understood as a long-lasting one. In Uwe E. Reinhardt's judgment (1990), the cap has not reduced services but rather has increased the delivery of services.

German states have undertaken a number of cost-control measures. They have cut back hospital construction in order to reduce surplus. The number of hospital beds has been held constant. In 1983 the sickness funds under government impetus imposed a charge of ten marks a day for patients in convalescent homes and five marks a day for adults for the first two weeks in a hospital. In addition, the long-standing practice of assigning specialists in hospital care to the patient in contrast to allowing a patient to choose a general practitioner has to some extent held down costs. It should also be noted that the extension of coverage to centers noted for their curative waters has been reduced.

The sickness funds now negotiate with each hospital over charges. The strategy has been to limit the shifting of costs by examining budgets on a line-by-line basis. These efforts are significant against the background context of the duration of a patient's stay in a German hospital, often twice as long as in the United States.

In the area of pharmaceutical costs, the Germans seemed to be spending a good deal more than other advanced industrial countries. Until recently, the German sickness funds reimbursed fully the cost of medications. The government of Chancellor Helmut Kohl has shifted to reimbursing full price for the lowest-priced generic drug. If the doctor or patient wishes to opt for a higher-priced drug, the patient must pay the difference in cost.

Although many of these cost control initiatives have their origins in the federal government, nonetheless the responsibility for their implementation has been given to the sickness funds and the physicians' associations. During the 1950s and 1960s, the state sought to expand the range of health care services and now has found in the funds the effective indirect means to decentralize responsibility for cost containment. The efforts to contain costs suggest the strategic importance of the sickness funds and the physicians' organizations in making health care policy decisions. The concerted action strategy of the Federal German government is to integrate the state, sickness funds, physician organizations, employer associations, and trade unions in a consultative group with the stated objective of containing costs without reducing the quality of health care. But it would appear that this exercise in corporatist consultation has not resulted in the creation of a structure that has the capacity to implement a national plan to reduce costs. The allocative decisions remain located in the semiautonomous organizations of sickness funds and physicians' organizations.

France

There are some clear parallels between the German and French experiences in the justifications employed for the public provision of health care. In both countries, the health care system originated in the idea of rewarding workers. The French health care system was

initially established to provide mandatory health care insurance to
French workers. Over the course of the last sixty years, the state has
expanded health care coverage to other sectors of the population.

This discussion of the French health care system emphasizes
what is, of course, a crucial relationship in the provision of care and
prospects for effective cost containment: the working relationship
between physicians' associations and state health care administrators. The development of the French health care system has included
a high degree of physician autonomy, even as cost-control measures
have been introduced.

French health care is a system of reimbursement for services
performed by physicians and hospitals. State-established insurance
funds reimburse health care practitioners on a fee-for-service basis.
Fee schedules were negotiated ultimately between the French government and physicians' associations. French health care insurance is
financed by the contributions of workers. Contributions from the
employed have risen to finance the inclusion of the self-employed,
the retired, and the unemployed. The outcome is in practice if not in
structure one of universal health care. The French health care
structure formally places health care allocational decision making in
two semiautonomous organizations with the responsibilities of management of health care (De Ridder, 1989). But behind these state
insurance organizations are the national ministeries of Finance,
Social Security, and Health, which make critical decisions in determining budgeting, fee schedules, and hospital policy.

The funding of French health care insurance from time to time
appears to run the risk of exhausting employment taxes collected to
finance it (Freeman, 1990). It appears that the financial strains on the
system could be attributed to several factors: the willingness of the
French political leadership to expand coverage, the slowdown in the
economy that began in the early 1970s and has continued through
the past two decades, and the growing consumption of health care by
the French population.

There is a good deal of similarity between the French and
German health care experiences. Indeed, Alsace-Lorraine was under
German administration at the time of Chancellor Otto Bismarck's
introduction of the German health system. A contributing factor to
the change in the French political environment was the return of
Alsace-Lorraine to France after the First World War. With the return,
the French authorities had to determine what to do about the
German health care system of sickness funds that provided health

care insurance for a large portion of the population. The system was popular in Alsace-Lorraine, and the French authorities were left with the choice of either scrapping the system or extending it to the rest of France. In the 1920s, health care insurance was extended to the rest of France (Godt, 1989).

French medicine has long been characterized by organized physicians who stress the autonomy of French doctors. Physicians under this regime were understood to have rights to negotiate their own fees with their respective patients and to maintain confidentiality in their patient relationships. These principles and the relatively slow rate of industrialization constrained the state's role in health care. When the French state initiated health care insurance after the First World War, the state became the propelling force in the building and direct management of hospitals. This role in French health care has gradually declined as the private sector has grown, which suggests both the growth in the health care sector and the strategy of cost containment pursued by the national government.

The medical profession in France has continued to enjoy an important organizational position in negotiating conditions of employment and fee schedules. Nevertheless, it is quite clear that both the left and right governments of the Fifth Republic have first sought to provide care and now have moved to a strategy of cost containment. This strategy has embraced efforts to constrain the incomes of health care professionals and hospitals, as well as to restrict the numbers of graduates from hospitals and thereby limit demand on the part of the medical care consumer.

The rate of increase in health care costs became a source of mounting concern during the presidency of Valery Giscard d'Estaing in 1974–81. It took on a sense of urgency during the early years of Socialist government after the election of François Mitterrand in 1981. The power of the French state became apparent as a series of initiatives were undertaken to contain costs. The state moved to restrict the numbers of students graduating with medical educations. The working assumption was that if the supply of physicians was limited, medical use would in time be limited as well. The state also moved to restrict new hospital construction, although its ability to realize this goal was constrained by the fairly large number of privately owned clinics. The French state had long struggled with physicians over the acceptance of contract, or reimbursement, rates provided by the state. The agreement that had been struck was to divide physicians into three categories. These were, first, physicians who refused to accept contract rates and thus were outside the system except for occasional modest reimbursements; second, the overwhelming number of doctors who accepted contract rates; and, third, the 12 percent of doctors who because of their reputations were allowed the right of extra billing. In 1980 a fourth category was added: physicians who charged more than contract rates but as a result lost their pension rights. Another initiative was the introduction of user fees, with a charge of twenty francs a day to be paid by the patient for each day he or she spends in the hospital. The poor were exempted from the charges. By 1984 hospitals were placed on global budgets—that is, they were given a fixed amount of money for the year and left the task of allocating the funds on the assumption that no additional revenue would be forthcoming. The funds allocated were based on the hospital's patient-diagnostic mix for the previous hospital year (Godt, 1989).

Thus in France the institutional groundwork has been laid for health care cost containment. The divide-and-conquer strategy which separates physicians into those who must accept contract rates and those who may double bill represents a significant step in redefining the traditional autonomy of French physicians.

The origin of the French health care system in desert theory has facilitated the creation of semiautonomous insurance organizations that are responsible for mediating the relationship between the state and the population. To an important extent, the existence of semiautonomous organizations shields the state in making difficult cost-containment decisions. The desert-theory origins should not be overstated, for over the decades since the introduction of health care insurance, there has been an acceptance of health care insurance as a component of citizenship. French policymakers, therefore, show caution in cutting back on what is provided by insurance and in limiting users' fees.

Canada

In Canada, justifications for the introduction of a universal health care system are less clearly attributable to a specific ethical position but appear to be a blend of utilitarian and rights arguments that allow the system to be judged today as something of an aspect of Canadian citizenship.

The Canadian health care system provides a useful comparison with the United States because of the countries' many shared health care traditions. Most notably these common traditions are physician choice and a fee-for-service system of reimbursement. A less frequently noted but also critical point of comparison is the central role played by federal Canadian states in cost containment.

, The United Kingdom and Canada both have severed the linkage between health care insurance and work. Rather, these systems grant universal coverage on the basis of citizenship. The two systems diverge in several quite fundamental ways, however. Canada is a federal system and the role of the provincial governments as administrators of the program is essential. The Canadian system works on a fee-for-service basis with considerable latitude given to prospective patients.

Canadian national health care began in the province of Saskatchewan over a quarter of a century ago. The Saskatchewan plan was expanded to other provinces and ultimately adopted as a federal program. The system is guided by five principles, including universality in coverage and portability from province to province of both hospital and health care professional services. A complicated funding formula allocates federal funds to the ten provinces on the bases of population and some measure of redistribution of income from the wealthier to the poorer provinces. This formula has an important constraint in that it is a fixed amount that pays approximately half the cost of health care in a province. If a province spends more, the provincial government must find its own resources to pay for it. There is therefore no incentive for a province to spend "half" dollars compelling the federal government to match the spending level of the province in question (Falcone and Mishler, 1989).

There are waiting lists in Canada for some procedures, notably coronary bypass and hip replacement; however, even these procedures require no longer than four months in the queue. Research and teaching hospitals appear to provide a greater range of diagnostic and procedural possibilities than other hospitals within a province. In some cases, sophisticated care cannot be found within the province, which means that patients must travel to other provinces for services; their respective home provinces then reimburse the province providing the service.

There is little question that the level of technological adoption in Canada is lower than in the United States. The Canadian federal government has sought to monitor the introduction of new technologies. Provincial health care ministers have not encouraged the introduction of expensive services. The system perhaps more so than any other in this discussion has sought to maintain a totality of commitment to social insurance objectives. The general practitioner does perform something of a gatekeeping role in controlling the preferred route to specialist care. But this gatekeeping role is by no means as complete as it is in the United Kingdom. In Canada a patient can seek a specialist on his or her own, but if the specialist takes the case without a referral from a general practitioner, the fee for service is at the rate of reimbursement for a general practitioner rather than at the higher specialist rate. In 1984 the federal government moved to eliminate supplemental billing by physicians who judged that provincial reimbursement was insufficient for the service rendered. Later efforts of the medical societies to protest the banning of supplemental billing, including a strike in Ontario, revealed quite clearly the relative political isolation and ultimate futility of the medical associations in opposing what proved to be a very popular piece of legislation.

It is clear that the cost of health care is less in Canada than it is in the United States. The explanation is not to be found in the ratio of physicians to the population nor in a record of obviously poorer health care in Canada than is found in other nations. The converse is more likely the case. Rather, the explanation lies in lower hospital costs, lower fees to physicians, and much lower administrative costs (Evans, 1983).

The rate of increase in health care expenditures in Canada, while slower than in the United States, has nonetheless been a growing source of concern at both the provincial and the federal levels of government. Federal health officials have sought to restrain the introduction of capital-intensive health care technologies. Efforts have been made to distribute physicians more uniformly, in order to avoid oversupply in the urban areas and to reduce transportation costs in rural areas. Extension of the health care service for the elderly to include nursing-home care as a universal provision has not occurred and there are demands for private practice and for modest co-payments.

The Canadian system's health care costs continue to rise, as for that matter do health care costs everywhere. But one should not underestimate the institutional effectiveness of cost containment by fixed federal budgetary contributions. One also should not underestimate the importance of locating authority to contain cost by restricting reimbursement and services at the subnational, that is, the provincial, level. This key role of the provincial health care minister in setting budgetary limits illustrates the uses of a federal system in the provision of health care. Canada enjoys a division of responsibility in the location of decision making about health care allocation. Dividing the responsibility between officeholders at both the national and the subnational levels allows a measure of political influence and retains democratic accountability.

The United Kingdom

This account of the British health care system emphasizes first its reputation for cost containment and second the debate about the effectiveness of its health care system. Cost containment has been realized in part by centralized budgetary control and by a tradition of general practitioners maintaining high thresholds for their patients' use of specialists and certain expensive procedures. The debate over effectiveness is measured in the relative health records of occupational groups in the British population.

The United Kingdom has the most centralized health care system among the advanced industrial nations. It has employed a capitation method for physicians (that is, a flat payment amount per patient) and a user-fee system for specialists. The system has been universal from its inception in 1948, ranging from the services of visiting nurses, to general practitioner visits, through hospitalization. Great emphasis has been placed on geographical accessibility for patients to both general practitioners and hospitals. An impressive range of services can be found relatively locally. The general practitioner serves as a central actor in health care provision. He or she is an independent contractor with the National Health Service. The critical role played by the general practitioner is that of gatekeeper, that is, determining if the patient needs to see a specialist. British medicine has brought to health care decision making a social utilitarianism—that is, advice against certain procedures on grounds of the general good rather than the condition and desire of the patient. Older patients may be advised against major surgery on the grounds that they have relatively few productive years remaining, and younger patients might receive a specific procedure on grounds of greater social utility (Halper, 1989).

The British system came under challenge in the late 1970s with the Black Report (Black, 1982). The report argued that inequality had not been reduced in the three decades of the National Health Service. An examination of the rates of morbidity and mortality had revealed sharp differentials between the unskilled work force and those in professional and managerial occupations. These differentials had predated the Health Service but had not apparently changed under it. The report raised issues often found in social discussion of health care in societies—such as the extent to which health care can make a difference in the lives of the population and the extent to which middle-class patients because of their sophistication may realize more from their system than the less educated working classes. Recent studies suggest that while such differentials do indeed exist, they were overstated in the Black Report because it failed to grasp that occupational change in Britain has brought about a greatly enlarged, service-employed middle class and a much smaller and less educated unskilled working class. Access and use of British health care is now much greater than in the past, but by no means is it uniform in use or consequence (O'Donnell and Propper, 1990).

The success of the British in holding the percentage of gross national product (GNP) spent on national health care to approximately half of the GNP expenditure percentage in the United States can be attributed in part to utilitarian attitudes of British doctors and to the global budgeting of the government that fixes the budget at a certain amount. Fixed budgeting has contributed to long waiting lists for procedures which are not considered emergencies. But during the 1980s the government of Margaret Thatcher, as previous British governments had been, was concerned about rising health care costs in the context of an often uneven economy. The historical response to this tension had been to impose increased fees for certain services such as eyeglasses and dentures as well as prescription medicines. The Thatcher government instead sought to use internal markets to generate competition as a means to constrain costs (Le Grand, Winter, and Woolley, forthcoming).

One strategy of the Thatcher government was to encourage the private sector in health care, which, although always allowed, had not grown over the years. The Thatcher government sought to introduce internal markets by having hospitals compete in the provision of specific services and keep whatever income they derived from such ventures. Competitive bidding was introduced in areas as diverse as food service, flower stalls, linen, and medical testing. Performance indicators were established and global budgeting offered for general practitioners undertaking large practices.

The formidable scale of the Thatcher government's proposed reforms could not be realized. A broad coalition that included

Conservative backbenchers, physicians, and, according to opinion polls, a good deal of public opinion, combined to limit the extent of government reform. It was one of the few defeats of the Conservative government's major legislative initiatives. But the scaled-down version that did become law allows some hospitals and general practices of at least 9,000 patients to apply for self-management and contract with one another. The government of John Major has implemented the law, arguing that quasi-autonomous hospital and practitioner organizations may make tough decisions about staff size and provisions that cannot be achieved by direct state management. The popularity of the National Health Service may indeed not be what it once was, but changes being implemented by the Conservative government are perceived as threatening the state's commitment to universal care. The Labour Party opposition is using these changes in the management of British health care as a claim that the Conservative reforms threaten the very core values of the National Health Service.

Over the years concerns with the British National Health Service have involved what are judged to be serious waiting lists for procedures that if performed would contribute to quality of life, procedures such as hip replacements. Other criticisms have been directed to the apparent lack of interest in the heroic medical tradition that is said to have characterized British health care. Indeed critics have argued that general practitioners are rather stern gatekeepers who have been discriminating against less-productive members of society in receiving expensive specialist care if they are judged to be too old. The pervasive influence of utilitarian arguments on policymakers and physicians provides a powerful justification for constraining care and thereby containing costs more successfully than the other systems described.

CONCLUSION

By the most frequently employed measures of health care comparison, the United States spends a greater proportion of its gross national product on health care than other advanced industrial nations. This high level of expenditure is likely to increase, since the rate of American expenditure is growing faster than the rate of expenditure in other nations.

It also seems quite reasonable to conclude that while Americans spend more on health care than other nations and have more

expensive procedures performed, both absolutely and proportion-
ately, access to health care is not uniformly distributed throughout
the American population. The elderly, covered by Medicare, and the
middle classes, who either pay for appropriate health insurance
policies or who have employers who provide them, are the prime
recipients of American health care. Medicaid provides for certain
low-income groups and the large Veterans Administration hospital
system provides for the men and women who have served in the
armed forces. Private charities also provide a measure of health care.
But significant portions of the population either lack health care
insurance or possess quite limited coverage. We have, therefore, a
system that is quite generous to some but imposes parsimonious
barriers to entry to others.

In an age of transnational concern about health care costs,
sharply different approaches are found in the United States and
other nations to the issue of reducing or containing costs. Federal
programs in the United States are committed to introducing quality-
control measures such as DRGs and are willing to discourage expensive procedures and to impose caps on reimbursements. But in other
arenas of the health care system, employers concerned over maintaining competitive positions in international markets have sought
to reduce the expensive premiums required for covering their
employees and their families by excluding recent workers or families
from policies. Insurance carriers have sought to review their risk
pools and consider ways to exclude potentially high-risk patients who
have conditions, such as HIV disease, which incur expensive medical
bills. Moreover, efforts to contain health costs seem to contribute to
the high administrative costs associated with American health care.
It seems likely that the disparities in the provision of health care will
only become more apparent in the United States.

Health care everywhere in the first world is changing as states and
private institutions confront growing demands for additional care
compounded by aging populations and changing expectations.
Health care professionals are faced with demands to provide high
levels of service without new funds being made available. In addition,
health care professionals face new willingness on the part of both
state and private administrators to reconsider the content of health
care and scrutinize what professionalism is. This new era has clear
implications for both the health care professional and the patient.

A review of these four health care systems clearly suggests that
there are quite distinctive alternatives to the health care system

found in the United States. All four systems are inclusive of their respective populations and spend less of their respective national incomes than does the United States. But an account of these systems raises issues that are pertinent in the intensifying debate over reform of the system of health care delivery in the United States. The ethical justification can make a difference in the nature of the institutionalization of health care decision making. The German and French experiences of justifying health care systems on grounds of desert have led to the creation of semiautonomous organizations that mediate between the state and the insured population. These organizations insulate the state from criticism in making difficult cost-containment decisions, but they leave the state open to the charge that the institutional ambiguity of the decision-making authority lessens the accountability for those decisions.

In the United Kingdom the reliance on utilitarian justification has equipped the state with a powerful tool for constraining cost: the general view that health care is a social good rather than a right or desert. The utilitarian view may be efficient for the nation as a whole but does leave troubling questions about the individual's claim on care. The British state, even with this utilitarian justification, has nonetheless encountered criticism for directly containing costs in the face of rising expectations. The solution has been a move to global budgeting and encouraging some measure of privatization. This leaves physicians and hospital administrators with the task of allocating health care within increasingly stringent budgets.

In some respects, the ethical justificatory origins of health policy in these countries have come to play a role in the cost-containment strategies they employ. The origins of the German and French systems in occupational health care insurance left a heritage of quasi-state, quasi-private insurance funds to insulate the state to some extent from direct implementation of cost-containment measures. The managers of these funds have been given an increasingly important role in dealing with practitioners and consumers of medical care. It certainly appears that in the German system, with its long-established relationship of consultation among the components of German health care (notably, federal and state authorities, physician organizations, and sickness funds), policy change is slower than in other countries but that once a decision to change a policy has been reached there is a greater probability of successful implementation than in France, where the relationship between the state and physician organizations is more combative. Although Germany somewhat blurs the location of health care allocation decision making, it provides insulation from popular pressure in the implementation of plans.

The utilitarian tradition in the United Kingdom reduces the claims of individuals for the full measure of health care. Ethical justifications based on rights or desert tend to impose constraints on what policymakers believe they can choose in containing health care costs. The British utilitarian tradition facilitated the considerable latitude given to general practitioners to serve as quite powerful gatekeepers. But even this tradition, which has contributed to a remarkably low percentage of GNP going to health care, has not been sufficient for British policymakers. The British have moved to internal markets and limited privatization as strategies to insulate the British government to a certain extent from the location of allocative decisions.

In Canada, cost containment is constrained by federal structuring. The federal budget determines a provincial allocation but leaves the provincial health care minister with the task of either finding additional funds beyond a set matching federal grant or imposing constraints on reimbursement schedules for hospitals and physicians. The location of decision making is divided between federal and provincial elected officeholders. This division reduces to some extent pressure that would obtain if a single level of government were the repositor, but diminishes the clear identification of accountability for decisions made. Thus the argument can be made from the vantage point of the ethics of cost containment that the Canadian system with its shared location of decision making offers the United States an institutional arrangement that is consistent with American political traditions as well as a system that suggests a greater sensitivity to the ethical questions that center on the government's role in both providing and limiting access to health care.

REFERENCES

Abel Smith, Brian. (1984). *Cost Containment in Health Care: The Experience of Twelve European Countries, 1977–83.* Luxembourg: Commission of the European Communities.

Black, Sir D. (1982). *Inequalities in Health* (The Black Report). Harmondsworth: Penguin.

Culyer, A. J. (1989). "Cost Containment in Europe." *Health Care Financing Review, 1989 Annual Supplement,* 21–32.

Danzon, Patricia. (1985). *Medical Malpractice: Theory, Evidence and Public Policy.* Cambridge, Mass.: Harvard University Press.

Davis, Karen, and Diane Rowland. (1990). "Uninsured and Underserved: Inequities in Health Care in the United States." In *The Crisis in Health Care*, ed. Nancy McKenzie. New York: Meridian.

De Ridder, Marie Martine. (1989). "France." In *The Comparative Study of International Public Policy*, ed. Jack Paul DeSario. Westport, Conn.: Greenwood Press.

Drummond, M. F. (1987). "Economic Appraisal of Health Technology in the European Community: Future Directions." In *Economic Appraisals of Health Technology in the European Community*, ed. M. F. Drummond. Oxford: Oxford Medical Publications.

Evans, Robert G. (1983). "Health Care in Canada: Patterns of Funding and Regulation." *Journal of Health Politics, Policy and Law* 8:1–43.

Falcone, David J., and William Mishler. (1989). "Canada." In *The Comparative Study of International Public Policy*, ed. Jack Paul DeSario. Westport, Conn.: Greenwood Press.

Freeman, Gary P. (1990). "Financial Crisis and Policy Continuity in the Welfare State." In *Developments in French Politics*, ed. Peter A. Hall, Jack Hayward, and Howard Machin. New York: St. Martin's Press.

Godt, Paul. (1989). "Health Care: The Political Economy of Social Policy." In *Policy Making in France*, ed. Paul Godt. London: Pinter.

Halper, Thomas. (1989). *The Misfortunes of Others: End-Stage Renal Disease in the United Kingdom.* Cambridge: Cambridge University Press.

Jonsson, Bengt. (1989). "What Can Americans Learn from Europeans?" *Health Care Financing Review, 1989 Annual Supplement*, 79–110.

Le Grand, J., D. Winter, and F. Woolley. (Forthcoming). "Health: Safe in Government Hands." In *The State of Welfare: The Welfare State in Britain since 1974.* Oxford: Oxford University Press.

Marone, James A. (1990). "American Culture and the Search for Lessons from Abroad." *Journal of Health Politics, Policy and Law* 15:129–44.

Northwestern National Life Insurance Company. (1990). *The NWNL State Health Rankings.* Minneapolis: Northwestern National Life Insurance Company.

O'Donnell, Owen, and Carol Propper. (1989). "Equity and the Distribution of National Health Service Resources." Discussion paper WSP/45. London: Suntory Toyota International Centre for Economics and Related Disciplines.

OECD Secretariat. (1989). "Health Care Expenditures and Other Data: An International Compendium from the Organization for Economic Cooperation and Development." *Health Care Financing Review, 1989 Annual Supplement*, 111–94.

Rawls, John. (1971). *A Theory of Justice.* Cambridge, Mass.: Harvard University Press.

Reinhardt, Uwe E. (1990). "West Germany's Health-Care and Health-Insurance System: Combining Universal Access with Cost Control." In

A Call for Action, Pepper Commission Supplement to the Final Report. Washington, D.C.: Government Printing Office.

Schieber, George J. (1990). "Health Expenditures in Major Industrialized Countries, 1960–87." *Health Care Financing Review* 11:159–68.

Schulenberg, Graf J.-Mattias. (1983). "Report from Germany: Current Conditions and Controversies in the Health Care System." *Journal of Health Politics, Policy and Law* 8:320–51.

Starr, Paul. (1982). *The Social Transformation of American Medicine: The Rise of a Sovereign Profession and the Making of a Vast Industry.* New York: Basic Books.

Expenditure and Outcome in Eight National Health Systems: Why Is the U.S. Doing So Poorly?

Norman J. Waitzman*

The United States spends more on health care than other countries, so the question arises, how do the additional benefits measure up in terms of the extra costs? Efficiency and equity are often treated as separate issues and competing goals in economics (Okun, 1975) but, as discussed further below, there is reason to believe that the level of health achieved among populations is intimately bound up with and directly related to, the degree of equality of spending on health care. The distribution of health care therefore constitutes one component of the framework I have established for analyzing the global efficiency of health expenditures in terms of aggregate health outcomes.

Distributional issues are of concern in and of themselves, however, when considering standards of justice and fairness. Within a Rawlsian framework, primary goods are those that are important to the integrity of the individual and are therefore accorded special treatment in their distribution as a condition of justice (Rawls, 1971). Evidence presented here on the distribution of health and health resources therefore contain additional implications for justice and fairness if health were to be accorded the status of a primary good in a Rawlsian sense.

---

*In addition to participants associated with the Utah Ethics and Health Conference, the author would like to thank members of the Writing Seminar at the Institute for Health Policy Studies, San Francisco, for their valuable comments. Both the seminar and the author received partial support through the National Research Service Award THS00026 from the Agency for Health Care Policy and Research. The author would also like to acknowledge financial support through a 1990 summer faculty research grant from the Department of Economics, University of Utah.

COMPARATIVE OUTCOME-EXPENDITURE RELATION

Health outcomes are only one among several facets of health care systems that can be analyzed in terms of the efficiency of health expenditures. Values regarding choice of provider, the discretion exercised by health professionals, and several other dimensions of social organization are also important. Cross-country comparisons can be treacherous if there is a lack of sensitivity to these dimensions. Even so, there is sufficient similarity among other health systems and the problems with which they are grappling that a cross-country comparison can provide valuable lessons for the United States.

In this era of slack macroeconomic growth, for example, most industrialized countries are introducing fiscal restraints and wrestling with the problem of reining in the growth of health budgets. A variety of measures, some directed at consumers, others at suppliers, have been introduced in several countries to check the growth of health expenditures. From consideration of both efficiency and ethics, the objective is to cut expenditures with minimal adverse effects on health. Increasing the cost to consumers is likely to discourage some utilization. Lower utilization poses the danger of adversely affecting health outcomes. An important relationship to explore in this cost-containment environment, therefore, is that between health expenditures and health outcomes across countries.

Say there was a standard health service unit or bundle in which all health services could be expressed—an office visit, a hospital visit, a regimen of medicines, or some combination. Assume as well that this standard unit cost the same across nations. Total expenditures on health would then act as a proxy for utilization: the higher the expenditure, the greater the number of standard units consumed. Given a direct relationship between utilization and health, higher expenditures would be associated with better health.

This model of expenditure and outcome is admittedly an idealized and grossly simplified characterization, but it can act as a point of departure in systematically analyzing some of the important differences between characteristics of health systems. In particular, it draws immediate attention to the paradoxical situation in the United States, where health expenditures are greater and have been rising relative to other countries while its health performance, according to some indicators, has lagged.

Because health is multidimensional, no single summary measure can successfully capture the health status of a population. Tables 1

Table 1. Infant Mortality as a Percentage of Live Births

Country	1960	1970	1980	1987
Canada	2.73	1.88	1.04	0.79[a]
France	2.74	1.82	1.01	0.76
Germany	3.38	2.34	1.27	0.83
Italy	4.39	2.96	1.43	0.96
Japan	3.07	1.31	0.75	0.50
Sweden	1.66	1.10	0.69	0.61
United Kingdom	2.25	1.85	1.21	0.91
United States	2.60	2.00	1.26	1.00

Source: OECD, 1990, table 58.
[a]1986.

and 2 provide two measures of health outcomes, infant mortality and life expectancy, that are relatively independent of the age structure of the population. The World Health Organization considers infant mortality to be not just an indicator of infant health, but a good measure of overall health status and the effectiveness of a health system; "The infant mortality rate is a useful indicator of the health status not only of infants but also of whole populations and of the socioeconomic conditions under which they live. In addition, the infant mortality rate is a sensitive indicator of the availability, utilization, and effectiveness of health care, particularly prenatal care" (Jonsson, 1990).

Every country listed in table 1 logged significant reductions in infant mortality between 1960 and 1987, but the United States lagged significantly behind other countries in terms of its rate of improvement. While it ranked third in infant mortality among the eight

Table 2. Life Expectancy at Birth, Selected Years

Country	Males				Females			
	1960	1970	1980	1987	1960	1970	1980	1987
Canada[a]	68.4	69.3	71.9	73	74.3	76.4	78.9	79.8
France	67.0	68.6	70.2	72	73.6	76.1	78.4	80.3
Germany	66.5	67.3	69.7	71.8[b]	71.9	73.6	76.5	78.4[b]
Italy	66.8	68.6	70.7	71.6[c]	71.8	74.6	77.4	78.1[c]
Japan	65.4	69.3	73.3	75.6	70.3	74.7	78.7	81.4
Sweden	71.2	72.2	72.8	74.2	74.9	77.1	78.8	80.2
United Kingdom	68.3	68.8	70.2	71.9	74.2	75.2	75.9	77.6
United States	66.7	67.2	69.6	71.5	73.3	74.7	76.7	78.3

Source: OECD, 1990, tables 50–51.
[a]Years for Canada are 1961, 1971, 1981, and 1984; [b]1986; [c]1984.

countries listed in 1960, the United States ranked eighth by 1987. Data on life expectancy in table 2 show a less pronounced relative shortfall, but gains in life expectancy were generally greater in Western Europe, Canada, and Japan between 1960 and 1987 than in the United States. Furthermore, in terms of life expectancy, the United States ranks near or at the bottom in 1987 for both males and females.

Why has this country performed relatively poorly with respect to these health measures? From our simple model, we are steered first toward looking at health expenditures, a proxy for utilization. Tables 3 and 4 provide data showing not only that the United States generally spent more on health than other countries between 1960 and 1987 but that its rate of increase in expenditure exceeded that of the others, particularly between 1980 and 1987.

Some analysts have been critical of health expenditure data expressed as a percentage of gross domestic product (GDP), such as those in table 3, because economic growth in the United States is seen to have been slower than in some of the other countries, particularly Canada. But table 4 expresses health spending in terms of expenditure per capita, which does not rely on figures on national output. The conclusion is basically left unaltered. While the gap in per capita spending on health care in other countries as a percentage of U.S. spending closed a bit between 1970 and 1980, it grew much wider during the 1980s, as the percentage figures in table 3 would suggest. The Canadian case is an exception, where per capita spending remained nearly three-quarters that of the United States despite relatively slow growth in the proportion of GDP devoted to health. The other countries average about half the spending per capita on health as the United States, and the proportions are uniformly lower than in 1980.

POTENTIAL REASONS FOR POOR U.S. PERFORMANCE

Why this paradox between higher expenditure and worse health? Several assumptions underlying the simple model could be flawed, and each alone or several together could generate the above results. This study focuses on five potential reasons:

First, a "standard unit" of health services may be more costly in the United States than in other countries, and/or its cost may have risen at a faster rate. In that case, analyzing expenditures strictly in monetary terms will mask the true relationship between utilization

Table 3. Total Expenditures on Health as a Percentage of Gross Domestic Product, Selected Countries

Country	1960	1970	1980	1987
Canada	5.5	7.2	7.4	8.8
France	4.2	5.8	7.6	8.5
Germany	4.7	5.5	7.9	8.1
Italy	3.3	5.2	6.7	7.2
Japan	2.9	4.4	6.4	6.8
Sweden	4.7	7.2	9.5	9.2
United Kingdom	3.9	4.5	5.8	6.0
United States	5.2	7.4	9.2	11.2

Source: OECD, 1990, tables 1 and 63.

Table 4. Health Expenditures per capita in Selected Countries (Nominal $)

Country	1960	(% U.S.)	1970	(% U.S.)	1980	(% U.S.)	1987	(% U.S.)
Canada	117	(78)	282	(77)	819	(75)	1,515	(74)
France	66	(44)	189	(52)	663	(61)	1,090	(53)
Germany	84	(56)	189	(52)	704	(65)	1,073	(52)
Italy	46	(31)	146	(40)	528	(48)	884	(43)
Japan	26	(17)	128	(35)	522	(48)	917	(45)
Sweden	92	(62)	278	(76)	874	(80)	1,263	(62)
United Kingdom	77	(52)	149	(41)	455	(42)	751	(37)
United States	149		366		1,089		2,051	

Source: OECD, 1990, tables 1, 61, and 67.
Note: Dollar amounts expressed in terms of purchasing power parities.

and health outcomes. It would be fruitful to compare component costs and their rate of increase across countries. Alternatively, a comparison of the physical bundle of health resources across countries would provide an adjustment.

A second potential drawback with the naive model concerns the "standard unit" of health services. All doctors are not alike, nor are all hospitals nor accepted practices for like diagnoses. Qualitative differences in resources and practice, in other words, could account for differential health outcomes. This does not necessarily imply that other countries have superior health resources. Payment and utilization patterns in the United States could simply direct the health system to emphasize the development of some types of resources over others. This issue touches upon distribution of health resources, and is addressed more fully below.[1]

A third reason for the lack of correspondence between expenditure and outcome in the United States could be the existence of sheer waste. If there is greater inefficiency in the use of resources here than abroad, then higher expenditures will not result in better health outcomes.

A fourth rationale concerns distribution. The data provided above on health outcomes are averages for entire populations. Hidden by the average is the dispersion of infant mortality or life expectancy among the population. Two countries could have very similar averages while having vastly different dispersions or variances. The issue of distribution of health services and health outcomes is of interest in itself, but there is good reason to look to the distribution issue for insight into a lack of correspondence between overall health expenditure and average health indicators. It is likely that the more skewed the distribution of health services in a population toward those of higher socioeconomic status, the less an equally skewed added expenditure on health will increase overall life expectancy or infant survival. Such is the case if the effect of additional health resources on these measures of health is greatest for those with the least amount of resources. So if additional expenditures on health have been more skewed to those of higher socioeconomic status in the United States than in other countries, then average health outcomes would not have improved as markedly in the United States.

A fifth reason for a lack of association between health expenditures and health outcomes is that health services are only one factor among several that influence health. These factors include environmental, behavioral, cultural, and socioeconomic characteristics other than those directly incorporated into the health system. While such characteristics have independent effects on the health of a population, they also tend to establish infrastructural constraints on the potential contribution of medical measures to health.

A government task force, for example, has noted that homicide is the leading cause of death for black males of ages fifteen to forty-four and that black males of ages twenty-five to thirty-four were 7.8 times more likely to be victims of homicide than white males (U.S. Department of Health and Human Services, 1985b, p. 160). Environmental factors associated with violent death noted by the task force include low income, physical deterioration, welfare dependency, disrupted families, lack of social supports, low levels of education and vocational skills, high unemployment, overcrowded and substandard housing, and a society with a long tradition of discrimination against minorities, conditions hardly remediable by or attributable solely to the health system. Many of the same conditions were cited by the task force as etiological factors associated with low birthweight and high infant mortality (U.S. Department of Health and Human Services, 1985b, p. 174). Summary statistics presented below on health outcomes and the distribution of those statistics undoubtedly reflect, to a certain degree, the extent and distribution of such conditions in the United States vis-à-vis other industrialized nations.

Even within the health system, the relative merits of preventive and/or public health measures versus curative and/or individual measures are often debated in terms of their marginal contributions to health outcomes. Some medical historians have maintained that medicine played a relatively minor role in the reduction of morbidity and mortality through the early part of the twentieth century, but few would take issue with the fact that modern medicine has contributed significantly to health advances in the postwar era. The extent to which factors other than medical measures are responsible for a relative slowdown in the improvement of life expectancy or infant mortality in the United States either directly, or indirectly through reducing the potency of medical interventions, is beyond the purview of this comparative analysis. The conclusions that are drawn must therefore be considered tentative.

COMPARATIVE EVIDENCE ON COSTS, RESOURCES, UTILIZATION, WASTE, AND DISTRIBUTION

Component Costs

The exercise of comparing costs between countries poses a number of methodological problems. Using exchange rates may ignore important facets of purchasing power parity—the fact that relative prices of goods may differ significantly between countries. If time trends are analyzed, relative rates of inflation should be taken into account.

There is evidence that certain components of health services are more expensive and their costs have increased faster in the United States than abroad. The ratios of average physician salaries to average employee compensation in table 5 are derived from national currency units and therefore allow for internal comparisons over time. They show the relative performance of physicians to average employees within any specific country. Cross-country comparisons in any

Table 5. Ratio of Average Income of Physicians to Compensation per Employee by Country (in national currency units)

Country	1967	1977	1987
Canada	4.8	3.5	3.7
France	4.8[a]	3.6	—
Germany	6.6[b]	5.2	4.3[c]
Italy	1.4	1.0	1.1[d]
Japan	2.0	2.1	2.5[c]
Sweden	3.7[c]	2.2	1.5
United Kingdom	—	2.2	2.4
United States	5.0[f]	4.6	5.4

Source: OECD, 1990, tables 14 and 65.
Dashes indicate that data were not available.
[a]1966; [b]1968; [c]1986; [d]1981; [e]1970; [f]1969.

year are suspect because the data are not adjusted for purchasing power parities. Cross-country trends, however, are suggestive. Physician incomes in many of the countries listed in table 5 declined relative to average employee compensation in both decades, from 1967 to 1977, and again between 1977 and 1987. The rate of increase of the ratio in the United States between 1977 and 1987, however, was exceeded only by Japan. Changes in the composition of national work forces—their skills and work hours—can certainly affect the above ratio, as can the specialty distribution, hours, and practice patterns of physicians. The extent to which the increase of the ratio in the United States reflects a higher proportion of specialists underscores some of the problems with the concept of a "standard" unit of care discussed earlier.

In a recent cross-national study of physician incomes, Simone Sandier made adjustments for purchasing power parities and separated out general practitioners from all physicians (Sandier, 1990). Sandier found that compared with the average wage, net incomes of physicians were considerably higher in Japan and slightly higher in Germany than in the United States from about 1983 to 1985. The ratio of physician income to average income in the United States, in turn, was slightly higher than that in Canada and considerably higher than the ratios in France and Denmark. Direct comparison with figures in table 5 is not possible, but trend data reported by Sandier for periods that overlap are in general agreement with those in the table.

Victor R. Fuchs and J. S. Hahn (1990) analyzed 1985 data on expenditures for physician services in the United States and Canada (and Iowa and Manitoba) in an effort to isolate the components that made such expenditures 1.38 times higher per capita in the United States than in Canada. They found that the quantity of physician services delivered was not responsible for the difference; in fact, utilization per capita was actually much higher in Canada than in the United States. The major culprit for higher expenditures were physician fees for medical procedures, which were 3.34 times higher in the United States than in Canada. Only part of the higher fees were reflected in higher net incomes of physicians in the United States— one-third higher than in Canada after adjusting for differences in specialty mix. Most of the difference in fees was attributable instead to "the fact that Americans use more resources [more overhead, for example] to produce a given quantity of services" (Fuchs and Hahn, 1990, p. 887). The extent to which this reflects differences in quality of care versus efficiency requires further study.

Health Resources and Utilization Patterns

Comparison of physical resource data bypasses some of the complications that arise with comparison of cost data. Quality differences, however, can get lost in lack of refinement of measures. Employing what has come to be termed an "adjusted" needs-based approach in 1980, the U.S. Graduate Medical Education National Advisory Commission (GMENAC) developed a sophisticated model which projected physician requirements in the United States to the year 2000. Based upon estimates of disease patterns, demographic structure and changes, and several other factors, the GMENAC report estimated physician requirements that translated into a ratio of 190 physicians to every 100,000 population in 1990 (GMENAC, 1981). Figures in table 6 show that the United States had well surpassed this ratio by 1987 and faced the prospect of a surplus of physicians. While the GMENAC study generated controversy over several aspects of its methodology, few revisions and updates have projected shortages,[2] while several studies have corroborated the likely existence of surpluses through the year 2000 (Weiner, 1989).

Of course, the specialty and geographic distribution of physicians is a different matter, and the GMENAC report projected larger surpluses for some specialties than for others. Still, the United States does not suffer from an overall shortage of physician services, even if the population could benefit from a redistribution of those services. The fact that Sweden, Germany, and France surpassed the United

Table 6. Practicing (Active) Physicians, by Country
per 100,000 Population

Country	1967	1977	1987	% Change 67–87	% Change 77–87
Canada	135	178	223	65	25
France	119	172	250	110	45
Germany	149	204	281	89	38
Italy	58	94	111	91	18
Japan	105	116	157	50	35
Sweden	117	187	268	129	43
United Kingdom	—	116	137	—	18
United States	162	184	234	44	27

Source: OECD, 1990, tables 27 and 61.
Dashes indicate that data were not available.

Table 7. Population per Inpatient Bed, by Country

Country	1967	1977	1987
Canada	—	62 [a]	61 [b]
France	102	94	93 [b]
Germany	91	85	91
Italy	101	97	130
Japan	84	77	66
Sweden	70	69	79 [b]
United Kingdom	103	120	146
United States	119	157	188 [b]

Source: OECD, 1990, tables 25 and 61.
Dash indicates that data were not available.
[a] 1979; [b] 1986.

States in terms of the number of active physicians per 100,000 population in 1987 indicates little in terms of resource sufficiency. First, the percentage of elderly among these countries' populations is greater than that in the United States (Jonsson, 1990), and it is well known that older people utilize more care. Second, differences in practice patterns must be taken into account. For example, a general practitioner in the United States oversaw an average of 6,723 visits in 1985, whereas the comparable number in France in 1979 was 5,101. The average length of visits for general practitioners in Germany were less than that in the United States, but the average work week was also shorter (Sandier, 1990). Finally, other countries are grappling with surpluses of physicians themselves (Schroeder, 1984).

The absolute number of inpatient beds in the United States, as well as in several European countries, has declined during the course

Table 8. Use of Inpatient Care: Bed Days per Person, by Country

Country	1967	1977	1987
Canada	2.0	2.1	2.0[a]
France	3.0	3.5	3.3[b]
Germany	3.6	3.6	3.5
Italy	2.5	2.4	1.6
Japan	2.8	3.1	3.9[b]
Sweden	4.3	4.5	4.2
United Kingdom	3.1	2.5	2.1[b]
United States	2.5	1.8	1.7[c]

Source: OECD, 1990, table 20.
[a]1985; [b]1986; [c]1981.

of the last twenty years, also reflecting a surplus. A decline in hospital beds pushes the population-to-bed ratio higher (table 7). The surplus arose, to some extent, from a decline in the average length of stay in the hospital. With the notable exception of Japan, the average length of inpatient stay per person has remained stable or declined over the past twenty years (table 8).

The ratio of population to hospital bed (table 7) is substantially higher in the United States than in the other countries, which reflects in some part differences in medical practice or utilization patterns. Length of inpatient stay in general (table 8) and for specific diagnoses (tables 9–11) is significantly shorter in the United States than abroad. This reflects the often-cited higher "intensity" of medical practice in the United States.

The mean length of stay for inpatient care of breast cancer (table 9) is one week in the United States and France, about half of that in the United Kingdom, Sweden, and Canada. The average length of stay

Table 9. Mean Length of Stay for Breast Cancer, by Country (In Days)

Country	1980	1981	1982	1983	1984	1985	1986
Canada	15.9	17.0	15.5	15.1	15.7	14.5	—
France	9.0	8.0	8.0	7.0	—	7.1	7.0
Germany	25.2	—	—	—	—	—	—
Italy	18.0	—	—	—	—	—	—
Japan	—	—	—	—	—	—	—
Sweden	12.4	—	—	—	—	14.0	16.6
United Kingdom	13.2	12.5	11.7	12.2	13.0	12.0	—
United States	11.0	10.6	10.0	9.4	8.3	7.2	7.1

Source: OECD, 1990, tables 38–44.
Dashes indicate that data were not available.

Table 10. Mean Length of Stay for Complications of Pregnancy and Childbirth, by Country (In Days)

Country	1980	1981	1982	1983	1984	1985	1986
Canada	4.8	4.8	4.7	4.7	4.6	—	—
France	—	—	7.2	7.1	6.8	6.9	6.6
Germany	9.1	—	7.5	7.4	7.5	7.4	—
Italy	—	—	5.9	—	—	—	—
Japan	8.7	8.5	8.8	8.8	10.2	—	—
Sweden	5.9	5.8	5.7	5.6	—	5.3	5.1
United Kingdom	2.9	3.1	2.7	2.6	2.5	2.4	—
United States	2.5	2.5	2.5	2.5	2.6	2.5	2.5

Source: OECD, 1990, tables 31–37.
Dashes indicate that data were not available.

Table 11. Mean Length of Stay for Diabetes Mellitus, by Country (In Days)

Country	1980	1981	1982	1983	1984	1985	1986
Canada	19.4	20.0	17.9	15.9	15.9	17.2	—
France	16.0	15.0	15.0	14.0	—	12.9	12.6
Germany	15.4	—	—	—	—	—	—
Italy	18.0	—	—	—	—	—	—
Japan	63.8	67.3	66.3	62.3	71.0	—	—
Sweden	27.1	—	—	—	—	—	—
United Kingdom	18.2	16.8	20.7	18.0	17.8	17.9	—
United States	10.5	9.7	9.5	9.5	8.2	8.1	7.6

Source: OECD, 1990, tables 38–44.
Dashes indicate that data were not available.

in the United States and United Kingdom for childbirth and complications of pregnancy is about two and one-half days, generally one-half to one-third of the average for the other countries listed. For diabetes mellitus, there is a similar picture, with the average week-long stay in the United States about half of that in several other countries. As with most other diagnoses, Japan heads the list in terms of length of stay for diabetes mellitus with an average of over two months.

Are the traditionally lower hospital stays in the United States responsible for worse health outcomes for specific diagnoses? There is little evidence to support such a contention. The reduction in length of hospital stays for specific diagnoses in this country since 1984, however, undoubtedly bears some relation to the introduction of the prospective payment system (PPS) under Medicare and suggests a different story. Under prospective payment, hospitals are reim-

Table 12. Prevalence of Surgical Procedures about 1980 (Rates per 100,000 Population)

Country	Males				Females		
	CB[a]	AP[b]	PR[c]	DT[d]	CB[a]	HYS[e]	MAST[f]
Canada	44	155	229	1,210	10	470	145
Japan	1[g]	244[g]	—	—	1[g]	90	91
Sweden	25	165	48	—	20	145	—
United Kingdom	—	—	70	—	—	132	82
United States	99	134	308	2,143	25	556	88

Source: OECD, 1985, table E.8.
Dashes indicate that data were not available.
[a]Coronary bypass; [b]Appendectomy; [c]Prostatectomy; [d]Digestive tract; [e]Hysterectomy; [f]Mastectomy; [g]Males and females.

bursed up to the maximum allowed for a specific diagnosis-related group (DRG) by Medicare, and no more. This contrasts sharply with the previous fee-for-service method of payment. Results from a large study conducted by the Rand Corporation indicate that the introduction of PPS is likely responsible for an across-the-board increase in elderly patients discharged from the hospital in unstable condition for the five diagnoses analyzed. The associated rise in death rates might be as high as 0.5 to 0.9 percentage points, depending on how broadly "unstable condition" is defined. Evidence from the study also suggests that severity of sickness upon admission increased for several diagnoses with the introduction of PPS (Rogers et al., 1990). Cost-saving measures introduced into the health system, in other words, have had an effect on utilization patterns, which in turn have likely had an adverse effect on health outcomes.

Evidence that "high-intensity" medicine is a trademark of U.S. medical practice is suggested by statistics on the prevalence of various surgical procedures in table 12.[3] For routine surgical procedures, like appendectomies, the United States has an average rate. For coronary-bypass surgery, however, which is resource intensive, the rate is relatively high. The United States also has high rates for other surgical procedures, such as hysterectomies (table 12) and cesarean sections (table 13). Indeed, by 1985, nearly one of every four deliveries in the United States was by cesarean section, about twice the rate of most Western European countries and more than three times that of Japan (Notzon, 1990). Yet, the higher rate of this more resource-intensive procedure was not found to be significantly associated with measures of outcome (Notzon, 1990, p. 3287).

Table 13. Cesarean Section Rates per 100 Hospital Deliveries in Selected
Countries, 1985

Country	Rate
Canada	19[a]
England and Wales	10
Italy	13[b]
Japan	7
Sweden	12
United States	23

[a]1984 and 1985; [b]1982.
Source: Notzon, 1990.

Waste

Are the higher rates for certain surgical procedures in the United
States an appropriate or optimum use of resources? What physicians
consider to be appropriate may differ from what economists deem to
be optimum. If a procedure improves health, then the procedure is
medically appropriate. If using resources in an alternative manner
would improve health to a greater degree than its current usage then
the current usage from the vantage point of the economist is not
optimum.

Even in adopting the conservative standard of the medical profession, there is evidence of considerable waste under the medical
care system in the United States. One study estimates that among the
population sixty-five years of age and older, one-quarter of coronary
angiographies and upper gastrointestinal endoscopies and two-
thirds of carotid endarterectomies were performed for reasons that
were less than medically appropriate (Brook et al., 1990). The degree
to which the organization of the U.S. medical care system and which
specific features of it are responsible for such waste are difficult to
establish. Indeed, except for carotid endarterectomy, where the
likelihood of undergoing inappropriate surgery was higher among
patients whose physicians performed many rather than few such
procedures, the authors found that very little of the variability in
appropriateness of the above procedures could be attributed to
easily identified characteristics of patients, hospitals, or physicians.

Inefficiency and waste can take several different forms in a health
care system. There has not been much cross-national research on
system-wide inefficiency. However, in one widely cited comparative
study of the amount of resources devoted to administration in the
United States, Canada, and Great Britain it was estimated that

administrative waste in this country, arising predominantly from the need for coordination among a multitude of providers and payers, amounted to 8 percent of the total health care budget—$48 billion in 1988—when compared with the administrative structure of the Canadian system, and over 10 percent when compared with that of the National Health Service of Great Britain (Himmelstein and Woolhandler, 1986).

Distribution of Health and Health Services

Evidence presented thus far on component costs, utilization patterns, and inefficiency suggest that each may contribute to the perceived relationship between expenditure and health in the United States relative to other countries. What about the role of distribution of health and health resources? As with earlier data, the evidence presented in this section tends to be more suggestive than conclusive.

Averages of life expectancy were presented in table 2. In table 14 two summary statistics on the distribution of life expectancy (or age at death) among the populations of the same countries are given. To adjust for differences in the age distributions of the countries, the data are standardized to the age distribution of England and Wales. One statistic is the Absolute Mean Difference (AMD), indicating the average deviation of age of death from the mean age of death. The smaller the AMD, the less inequality in age of death. The computation of the other statistic, the Gini coefficient, is a little more complex.[4] It

Table 14. Aggregate Inequality in Age at Death (All Ages, Standardized)

Country	Year	Mean	AMD[a]	Gini Coefficient
Canada	1982	71.99	9.01	.125
England and Wales	1982	72.82	8.54	.117
France	1981	71.80	9.53	.133
Germany	1982	72.72	8.91	.123
Italy	1979	72.63	9.06	.125
Japan	1982	73.92	8.71	.118
Sweden	1981	73.63	8.53	.116
United States	1982	70.22	9.67	.138

Source: Le Grand, 1989.
Note: Standardized according to the age distribution of the population in England and Wales (England and Wales = 100).
[a]Absolute Mean Difference.

ranges between 0 and 1; the closer the coefficient is to 0 (1), the more equal (unequal) is a distribution. In general, a difference in the Gini coefficient of .01 between two distributions indicates a significant difference in inequality.

From both AMD and the Gini coefficient reported in table 14, the United States ranks at the bottom, indicating greater inequality in this health measure than among the other countries. Indeed, its performance is closer to that of Yugoslavia, Romania, and Poland (unreported in the table) than to France, the country that ranks next to the United States in the table.[5] Even when infant mortality is teased out of the statistics, the United States ranks barely and only above France in terms of AMD.[6]

An estimate of the extent to which these inequalities are attributable to differences in access to and utilization of health services is beyond the scope of this essay, but other evidence bears on this issue. Table 15, for example, presents data on the extent of statutory coverage of public health plans in several countries for hospital care, ambulatory care, and medical goods. Statutory access to care under public plans is close to 100 percent for most of the countries listed for most types of care. The United States, of course, is a major exception, covering 40 percent of hospital care and 24 percent of ambulatory care mainly through Medicare for the elderly and Medicaid for the poor. Estimates from the 1987 National Medical Expenditure Survey indicate that during some part of 1987, 47.8 million people lacked health insurance, with 34 to 36 million uninsured on any specific day, and 24.5 million uninsured for the entire year (Short, Monheit, and Beauregard, 1989; Short, 1990). The extent of the bill covered under public plans is also substantially higher abroad (table 16).

The greater comprehensiveness of public plans outside of the United States does not by itself indicate a greater equality of utilization and care per se, but it does suggest that the likelihood of inequality in utilization is lower. In several of these countries, there is an elite tier of service for people who opt out of the public plan, but this tier is relatively small because of the comprehensiveness of the public plan. A multitiered system is more entrenched in the United States where there are several plans, where coverage is largely contingent on employment status, and where the public plan is less comprehensive.[7]

Several country studies have shown that lower socioeconomic status is associated with worse health (Townsend and Davidson, 1988, and Whitehead, 1988 [England]; Fox, 1989 [Europe]; Kohler and

Table 15. Percent of Population Eligible for Public Health Insurance, by Type of Coverage, 1987

Country	Hospital Care	Ambulatory Care	Medical Goods
France	99	98	92
Germany	92	92	97
Italy	100	100	99
Sweden	100	100	100
United Kingdom	100	100	99
United States	40	25	—

Source: Jonsson, 1990.
Dash indicates that data were not available.

Table 16. Average Percentage of Bill Paid for by Public Insurance in Selected Countries, 1987, by Type of Benefit Received

Country	Hospital Care	Ambulatory Care	Medical Goods
France	92	62	58
Germany	97	85	56
Italy	99	65	63
Sweden	100	90	75
United Kingdom	99	88	93
United States	55	56	—

Source: Jonsson, 1990.
Dash indicates that data were not available.

Martin, 1985 [Scandinavia]; Wilkins, 1988; Wilkins and Adams, 1983 [Canada]; U.S. Dept. of Health, Education, and Welfare, 1979; U.S. Dept. of Health and Human Services, 1985a; Kitagawa and Hauser, 1973; Waitzman, 1988 [United States]). Evidence also points to less utilization of health services for a given degree of illness the lower one is situated on the economic ladder. Still, several reports on health inequalities in Britain (O'Donnell and Propper, 1989), in European countries (Fox, 1989), in Scandinavia (Kohler and Martin, 1985), and in Canada (Wilkins, Adams, and Brancker, 1990; Evans, 1984) have maintained that extension of national health insurance and public health services has reduced inequalities in utilization of health services and subsequent inequalities in health status. Inequalities in health and health care comprise a formal part of the agenda of the health systems in these countries.

A recent study of health care provisions in the United States, however, provides evidence that even when uninsured and Medicaid patients gain access to care for cardiac procedures, they receive significantly fewer services than those with private insurance (Wenneker, Weissman, and Epstein, 1990). Statutory access evidently does not by itself eliminate multitiered service.

CONCLUSION

This essay has provided a simple framework and some tabular data within that framework for drawing cross-national comparisons of the relationship between health expenditures and health outcomes.[8] Further study is required at the national and cross-national level on the distribution of health resources and relating those distributions to health indicators. Such analysis is important not just as part of the framework for assessing system-wide efficiency but for informing the debate over principles of justice and fairness and how they are to be applied in a health care system. The extent to which U.S. citizens consider health care to be a right is likely to hinge on their perception of the degree to which a certain level of health is important to the integrity of the individual and to his or her ability to realize life plans—that is, the extent to which health care is a primary good in the Rawlsian sense. Further confirmation of the disparate and loosely tied evidence provided above on distribution and health may present an ethical imperative for the United States to move toward a national health scheme.

NOTES

1. Along with this issue of the "standard unit" of health care is the lack of a "standard" measure of health outcome, mentioned briefly earlier in the text. While the two measures used have particular strengths, they are certainly not comprehensive. Particularly if U.S. resources are geared toward different utilization patterns, U.S. performance might appear better when yardsticks other than infant mortality and life expectancy are used. In any case, data on cross-country utilization patterns would provide valuable insight as to differences in "standard" care between countries.

2. The one major exception is Schwartz, Sloan, and Mendelson (1988).

3. Rates reported in table 12 are not age standardized, do not adjust for epidemiological differences between populations, and may reflect differences in country reporting. For more details of problems of intercountry comparison with this data, see OECD, 1985, pp. 101–3.

4. To calculate the Gini coefficient, the population is first sorted into quintiles from the lowest life expectancy to the highest. The bottom

quintile (20 percent) of the population, for example, would account for under 20 percent of the total years lived among the population, unless everyone lived an equal life span, in which case each 20 percent of the population would account for 20 percent of total years lived. The Gini coefficient measures how far the actual distribution departs from that of perfect equality. In more technical terms, this is the ratio of the area between the Lorenz Curve (which traces the actual distribution) and a 45-degree line divided by the triangular area bounded by the 45-degree line and the horizontal and vertical axes. The resultant Gini coefficient ranges from 0 (no departure, perfect equality) to 1 (gross inequality).

5. Based upon statistics reported by Le Grand (1989, p. 90).

6. Based on Le Grand, 1989, p. 91. Gini coefficients were not available for noninfant and adult age-at-death distributions.

7. See Reinhardt, 1990, pp. 110–11.

8. The extent to which the noted cross-national differences are attributable to specific organizational features of health systems (for example, globalized versus open-ended budgets, fee-for-service versus capitation or salaried methods of payment, use of primary physicians as gatekeepers, and so on) is behond the scope of this essay. The reader, however, is directed to the monographs in OECD (1990) and the essay by John G. Francis in this volume for a description and analysis of the role of some of these organizational features in several countries' health systems.

REFERENCES

Brook, Robert H., Rolla Edward Park, Mark R. Chassin, David H. Solomon, Joan Keesey, and Jacqueline Kosecoff. (1990). "Predicting the Appropriate Use of Carotid Endarterectomy, Upper Gastrointestinal Endoscopy, and Coronary Angiography," *New England Journal of Medicine* 323 (17): 1173–77.

Evans, Robert G. (1984). *Strained Mercy: The Economics of Canadian Health Care.* Toronto: Butterworth.

Fox, John, ed. (1989). *Health Inequalities in European Countries.* Brookfield, Ver.: Gower.

Fuchs, Victor R., and J. S. Hahn. (1990). "How Does Canada Do It? A Comparison of Expenditures for Physicians' Services in the United States and Canada," *New England Journal of Medicine* 323 (14): 884–90.

Graduate Medical Education National Advisory Committee (GMENAC) to the Secretary, U.S. Department of Health and Human Services. (1981). *Summary Report*, vol. 1, September 1980. GPO pub. no. 1980–0-721–748/266. Washington, D.C.: Government Printing Office.

Himmelstein, D. U., and S. Woolhandler. (1986). "Cost without Benefit: Administrative Waste in U.S. Health Care." *New England Journal of Medicine* 314 (7): 441–45.

126   *Norman J. Waitzman*

Jonsson, Bengt. (1990). "What Can Americans Learn from Europeans?" In OECD, 1990: 87–101.

Kitagawa, Evelyn M. and Philip M. Hauser. (1973). *Differential Mortality in the United States.* Cambridge: Harvard University Press.

Kohler, Lennart, and John Martin., eds. (1985). *Inequalities in Health and Health Care.* Stockholm: Nordic School of Public Health.

Le Grand, Julian. (1989). "An International Comparison of Distributions of Ages-at-Death." In Fox, 1989: 75–91.

Notzon, Francis C. (1990). "International Differences in the Use of Obstetric Interventions." *Journal of the American Medical Association* (June 29) 263:3286–91.

O'Donnell, Owen, and Carol Propper. (1989). "Equity and the Distribution of National Health Service Resources." Discussion paper WSP/45. London: Suntory Toyota International Centre for Economics and Related Disciplines.

Okun, Arthur M. (1975). *Equality and Efficiency, the Big Tradeoff.* Washington, D.C.: The Brookings Institution.

Organization for Economic Cooperation and Development (OECD). (1985). *Measuring Health Care, 1960–1983: Expenditure, Costs, and Performance.* Paris: OECD.

————. 1990. *Health Care Systems in Transition: The Search for Efficiency.* Paris: OECD.

Rawls, John. (1971). *A Theory of Justice.* Cambridge, Mass: Belknap Press of Harvard University Press.

Reinhardt, Uwe. Untitled commentary on Bengt Jonsson's essay. In OECD, 1990:105–12.

Rogers, William H., David Draper, Katherine L. Kahn, Emmett B. Keeler, Lisa V. Rubenstein, Jacqueline Kosecoff, Robert H. Brook. (1990). "Quality of Care before and after Implementation of the DRG-Based Prospective Payment System: A Summary of Effects," *Journal of the American Medical Association* 264 (October 17):1989–94.

Sandier, Simone. (1990). "Health Services Utilization Trends and Physician Income Trends." In OECD, 1990: 41–56.

Schroeder, S. A. (1984). "Western European Responses to Physician Oversupply." *Journal of the American Medical Association* 252:373–84.

Schwartz, William B., Frank A. Sloan, and Daniel N. Mendelson. (1988). "Why There Will Be Little or No Physician Surplus Between Now and the Year 2000." *New England Journal of Medicine* 318(14):892–97.

Short, P. F., Monheit, A., and Beauregard, K. (1989). National Medical Expenditure Survey: A Profile of Uninsured Americans: Research Findings 1. Rockville, Md: National Center for Health Services Research and Health Care Technology Assessment.

Short, P. F. (1990). National Medical Expenditure Survey: Estimates of the Uninsured Population, Calendar Year 1987: Data Summary 2. Rockville, Md: National Center for Health Services Research and Health Care Technology Assessment.

Townsend, P., and N. Davidson, eds. (1988). "The Black Report." In *Inequalities in Health*. London: Penguin, 1988.

U.S. Department of Health, Education, and Welfare. (1979). *Health Status of Minorities and Low Income Groups*. DHEW Publication no. (HRA) 79–627.

U.S. Department of Health and Human Services. (1985). *Health Status of Minorities and Low Income Groups*. DHHS Publication no. (HRSA) HRS-P-DV 85–1.

U.S. Department of Health and Human Services. (1985b). *Report of the Secretary's Task Force on Black and Minority Health*. Volume I: Executive Summary. Washington, D.C.: U.S. Government Printing Office: O-487–637 (QL 3).

Waitzman, Norman J. (1988). "The Occupational Determinants of Health: A Labor Market Segmentation Analysis" (unpublished Ph.D. dissertation). Washington, D.C.: American University.

Weiner, Jonathan P. (1989). "Forecasting Physician Supply: Recent Developments." *Health Affairs* 8 (Winter): 173–79.

Wenneker, M., Joel Weissman, and A. Epstein. (1990). "The Association of Payer with Utilization of Cardiac Procedures in Massachusetts." *Journal of the American Medical Association* (September 12) 264: 1255–60.

Whitehead, M. (1988). "The Health Divide." In *Inequalities in Health*. London: Penguin.

Wilkins, Russell. (1988). "Special Study on the Socially and Economically Disadvantaged." *Canada's Health Promotion Survey*. Technical Report. Ottawa: Minister of National Health and Welfare.

Wilkins, Russell, and Owen Adams. (1983). "Health Expectancy in Canada, Late 1970's: Demographic, Regional, and Social Dimensions." *American Journal of Public Health* 73 (September): 1073–79.

Wilkins, Russell, Owen Adams, and Anna Brancker. (1990). "Changes in Mortality by Income in Urban Canada from 1971 to 1986." *Health Reports* 1, no. 2: 137–74.

Why Americans Are Different

Lawrence D. Brown

The central virtue of the essays by John G. Francis, "Lessons from Abroad in Assessing National Health Care Systems," and Norman J. Waitzman, "Expenditure and Outcome in Eight National Health Systems," is that they drive home a point whose importance can hardly be overstated and yet is not widely understood. All other comparable Western democracies manage to reconcile universal coverage with relative stability in the rate of growth of health care costs. The United States has achieved neither objective. About 15 percent of our nonaged population has no health coverage at all and many more are inadequately insured. And the costs of our system, whether measured by percentage of gross national product (GNP) spent on health care (now about 12 percent) or per capita spending, stand far above those of our peers. (Waitzman, in his tables 3 and 4, shows that we spend 2–5 percent more of GNP per year than do comparable Western nations, and our per capita spending on health care is about 25 percent greater than Canada's, number two on the list, and twice that of France and Germany.)

The comparative record is, it seems to me, a corrosive commentary on U.S. health care policy, one that should inspire extensive cross-national research and debate. By and large, however, this is not occurring. The business community, physicians, the federal government, and most foundations seem to be skeptical about cross-national learning, adopting the view that that's them, and we're us, and who cares? An enormous intellectual and strategic provincialism and parochialism hamper the U.S. health policy debate. The Francis and Waitzman essays help broaden our field of vision, which is vitally important if we are ever to adopt and implement a sound plan for national health insurance.

What explains American exceptionalism? Why have we failed to achieve both universal coverage and stability in health care spending, and why are we so reluctant to ponder the legacies of other nations that have done so? One familiar explanation is plain politics: the U.S. system is extremely fragmented and therefore is both resistant to the effective assertion of unifying purposes and easily captured by single-purpose special interest groups. A classic pluralistic model pictures government umpiring a battle of social forces in which supportive and opposed groups mobilize their resources and clash. In this view the uninsured are too weak to win the struggle for universal coverage, while providers are too strong to lose the fight to contain the costs that constitute their incomes. Is this familiar image valid in today's health care politics? Yes and no. The roles and powers of interest groups and social forces are never to be discounted, but they are far from the whole story.

Consider, for example, the federal government's assault on health care costs. The early 1970s found no percolating social forces marching down Pennsylvania Avenue demanding health maintenance organizations. Few people knew what the acronym "HMO" meant when the government started pushing this cause. Few heavyweight lobbying groups fought hard for HMOs, and some very prominent interests—notably, the American Medical Association—opposed legislation that would promote them. The federal government backed HMOs anyway. The reason is that steadily growing billions of federal dollars were on the line in the health budget, and government was improvising solutions to salient problems of its own. In a sense government has become the most important "group" in the group struggle, a new and portentous pattern. This consistent built-in impetus to innovation means that the content of policymakers' values and preferences are an increasingly important political "resource" in policy-making.

To be sure, these state-centered politics better describe cost-containment policy than measures to expand benefits, which are still pretty well captured by a pluralist image. Yet even in the politics of problem solving for the uninsured, state autonomy may be gaining. Few strong groups, rhetoric notwithstanding, put new coverage for the uninsured at the top of their action agendas, and some powerful groups oppose initiatives that would increase their costs. Nevertheless some political leaders have agreed that the problem deserves a solution and have moved, albeit tentatively, to explore strategic options. Interests do not explain all political inputs and outcomes. Norms, values, those applied ethics that define political culture weigh heavily; indeed political culture seems to me to set the frame-work, the context of legitimacy, that governs the play of interests in the political process.

What value differences, then, explain American exceptionalism? I shall turn first to issues of coverage and the rights-based rationales that address them. Certainly American arrangements look very odd to Canadian and European observers, who wonder how we can tolerate a large, growing number of uninsured citizens, and how we can fail to see that we are thereby violating some kind of human right. The civic lethargy seems doubly perplexing because American politi-cal culture is, after all, very big on rights—civil rights, gay rights, rights for the disabled, rights of speech and religion, rights to bear arms, and on and on. We take rights very seriously, and we regularly resort to the legislature to codify them and to the judiciary to enforce them.

The key to the puzzle is that by and large we decline to extend our broad interpretation of citizenship rights into the sphere of policy entitlements. The sole exception—which proves the rule—is educa-tion. In the United States we grant everyone a free and (theoretically) equal public education, which means that the playing field is leveled. Everyone starts out fairly in the race of life, and what happens thereafter can be ascribed to merit or luck. If people end up with very different jobs, housing, incomes, or health care, these different outcomes ("inequalities") are normatively acceptable. Except for education, the linchpin of the cultural scheme, policy entitlements are a difficult notion for the U.S. system to swallow. Once political and civil rights have leveled the field in this highly competitive and individualistic society, no one is owed any particular policy outcome thereafter. The good things in life that policy can confer are viewed as legitimately up for grabs in the political economic system. When pollsters pose general questions inquiring whether the average per-son finds it acceptable that some citizens go without health coverage or care, many give the "right" answer. But if pressed (as they too seldom are) to address trade-offs and programmatic preferences, many deny that government should create new entitlements to coverage and raise taxes to enforce them. Solidaristic norms that Europeans take for granted are often remote from the American mindset.

Nor is it only the average citizen who is muddled about what a right to health coverage should mean concretely. Thoughtful policy-makers and proponents of broader coverage do not agree either.

Everyone knows that the American Medical Association (AMA) and private insurers have fought national health insurance, and some are content to end the story there. But, equally important, whenever a window of opportunity has opened, various advocates have urged cradle-to-grave coverage in a public system; others, catastrophic coverage and no more; others, employer mandates; others, coverage for the neediest group, perhaps children; and so forth. Proponents have routinely failed to form a coherent, cohesive political coalition, allowing opportunities to pass without action.

In European systems variations on parliamentary government bring policymakers together to bargain out their differences in private. They leave the bargaining table to articulate *the* position of *the* ruling party or coalition and then go forth and implement it. In the American system leadership by parties, committees, and presidents is generally too weak, and our separated powers too splintered, to create legislation in this way. Even if we could agree on the existence of a right to health care we would still face huge institutional difficulties in striking an agreement on what that right requires in practice.

What then of the utility rationale that Francis examines? Health care is good for people and so they ought to have it when they need it. This is not a very controversial proposition (except for Ivan Illich perhaps) and most Americans would probably endorse it. The catch is the corollary, which, in the U.S. belief system, comes out as "Yes, health care is important and we want a good system. If we get too much politics and government in it that will surely foul it up and make it worse." Utility is supposedly maximized in the private sector—those who like the Post Office will love national health insurance, and all that. These cultural tenets are part of the (polluted) political air we breathe. A deeply ingrained political distrust goes back to the founding of the nation. It is not of itself determinative—it can be neutralized as in the New Deal and Great Society or reinforced as in the Reagan years—but it is always a constraint to be reckoned with.

The situation is different in the four countries that Francis reviews. Citizens in Britain, Canada, Germany, and France may take issue with what the regime is doing, but this disaffection does not activate pervasive distrust of government in general. In these nations the civil service commands respect and may even be viewed as a noble embodiment of the public good. In the United States the charge that some innovation means entrusting large new powers to the federal bureaucracy can be the kiss of death. Moreover, political distrust doubtless conditions our attitudes toward health care access. Probably the average American would agree that health care is an important social good, that people who need it ought to have it, that those who lack health insurance should have coverage, and so on. But the average American probably also believes that those who lack health coverage can go to the emergency room of their community hospital and get care that is reasonably good and timely. With such safety valves in place, why get government into the act? Why raise taxes, empower the bureaucracy, activate command and control regulation, and trigger other such perverse follies?

Francis also mentions a third rationale for coverage: desert. As he notes, desert tends to fade over time in the health policy debates of other countries, absorbed by rights and utility-based justifications. But not here. In the United States, debates about desert in public programs remain lively, and explicit or implicit distinctions between the deserving and undeserving poor are remarkably tenacious. Our social policies are replete with categories of aid that reflect moral judgments about desert. We recoil to think that unworthy types may be getting public benefits at taxpayers' expense. In our welfare system, it is not enough that one is poor, that is, lacks a certain income. Rather we invent distinct categories for the blind, disabled, those with dependent children, and other pigeonholes that are forceful cultural declarations.

Our programmatic categories mirror moral judgments. Medicare, the one version of national health insurance that (as Daniel I. Wikler remarked) we have willingly embraced, is (again) the exception that proves the rule. The group deemed worthy of governmental support has a unique legitimacy by virtue of its obvious needs and equally obvious inability to get private health insurance on reasonable terms. Groups that fail to clear the moral thresholds have never been viewed as fit candidates for public coverage.

We Americans tend to be aggressively moralistic about the terms on which public entitlements should be created and extended. Our extensive social pluralism works against solidarism, and although the nations that John Francis examines are themselves growing more heterogeneous and pluralistic, one finds in them a historically entrenched and institutionalized solidarism preserved in social democratic thought and its programmatic legacy, all of which is largely lacking here. We Americans love America but often cannot stand our fellow Americans. There thus springs eternal the fear that the mythic prototypical recipient who uses his welfare benefits to buy a Cadillac or her food stamps for vodka is itching to charge the new government health insurance program for cosmetic surgery and such. And this social aggravation has grown over the past twenty-five years since government threw itself deeply and dramatically into social problem solving by means of the Great Society and the War on Poverty, with results that failed to impress many Americans.

In sum, political distrust checkmates expansionist arguments founded on the moral grounds of rights, utility, and desert. We start with a society innately suspicious of government, add a recent legacy of public activism with controversial consequences, stir in continuing tensions about race, crime, drugs, and the decline of moral standards, fold in a dollop of political demogoguery by politicians who promise voters that all will be well if only we cut taxes and shrink government, and end up with social divisiveness and governmental defensiveness. This, it seems to me, is the basic context in which the debate about national health insurance will (or will fail to) unfold. This basic context is political culture.

I want to turn briefly now to the issue of costs. The key lesson of the European and Canadian systems, demonstrated effectively in the Francis and Waitzman essays, is that it is indeed possible to extend broad health benefits and universal entitlements and yet stabilize costs with relative success. As former President Ronald Reagan liked to say, some solutions are simple, though not easy; a cross-national perspective highlights them. They include structured negotiations over physicians' fees, perhaps with ceilings set on rates of increase; firm controls on the diffusion of technology; planning that gives the state some significant say in how many hospitals and beds there are to be and where; global budgets for hospitals; careful, limited use of co-payments for certain services; and some queuing for some elective procedures. Even in 1991 most of these options continue to fall on deaf ears in the U.S. policy debate. Why? The opposition of provider and payer interests are of course one familiar and potent explanation. But, again, these interests are only part of the story. Providers are increasingly troubled by the growth of behavioral regulation—utilization review and other nitpicking interventions into clinical and managerial details—that does little to contain costs but generates extensive red tape and aggravation. Providers are increasingly open to new policy avenues.

Is the problem, then, a lack of governmental energy and capacity? Again, yes and no. In many ways the federal government has been a powerful leader for cost containment—witness the installation of the prospective payment system (PPS), resource-based relative-value scales, and more. But the rub is that these initiatives have come solely on behalf of the federal government's own financial interests, which means that from a societal standpoint we are talking cost containment but practicing cost shifting. And the prudent public purchaser has been content to channel costs to the private sector. In the 1990s, then, the cost-containment policy ball lies squarely in the business community's court. But alas, the corporate world remains poorly equipped to play the policy game because its members are imprisoned by their ideology and worldview. Interests are not the real issue. Business's interests would lead them to pursue cost controls fairly hard because they pay handsomely for employees' health coverage and have long loudly decried those expenses. The problem is that they do not believe in regulation, planning, global budgets, structured negotiations, and government itself. Their faith rests on competition, community forces, local coalitions, and voluntary schemes, which have achieved next to nothing in most places and probably can never succeed at curbing costs on a large scale. The corporate mindset in turn protects the interests of providers and payers because doctors, hospitals, insurers, and the whole vast voluntary sector that is the heart and soul of the U.S. health system preserve their autonomy as a consequence of payer fragmentation and confusion. The results are precisely what Francis and Waitzman document: higher costs and weaker coverage. The best antidote would be a vigorous public/private partnership concerting action between governmental and corporate payers, but this would require a 180-degree turn in the thinking of business leaders.

What, if anything, might produce a strategic reorientation? Interests alone evidently are not enough, given the lamentation and lassitude of the past decade. Perhaps what we most need are lucid examples and patient reiteration of the fundamental points driven home by Francis and Waitzman: costs can be stabilized. Other nations do it. They have perfectly decent health care systems. Life goes on. Their doctors practice good medicine. Patients put on their hospital gowns one arm at a time. We could begin emulating elements of foreign systems' success while maintaining American variations on their strategic themes.

PART III

The VA as National Health Care

Can We Learn from Our Own Experience? The VA as National Health Care

Mark W. Wolcott, M.D., and
Charles B. Smith, M.D.

The American public is increasingly frustrated and concerned with the status of the health care system.[1] The cost of health care in the United States is the highest in the world, and the rate of increase far exceeds that of our economy as a whole.[2] These expenditures, however, have failed to satisfy our perceived needs for quality of care and particularly our desires for more equity of access to care.[3] More than thirty-five million Americans now lack health insurance, and an additional fifty million are underinsured for serious medical illnesses.[4]

An interesting ambivalence exists within our society about the issue of equity of access to health care. On the one hand, over the past decade we have become less interested in an egalitarian redistribution of income, and the working poor in this country have lost ground in their ability to pay for health care.[5] Even with the recent increase in the minimum wage, the purchasing power of the working poor is 25 percent below the 1981 level, whereas the share of the nation's wealth owned by the top 10 percent of the households rose from 67.5 percent to 73.1 percent between 1979 and 1989. In recent years, the executive branch of the government and Congress have contributed to the problem of declining access of the poor to health care by decreasing the level of support for health care through Medicaid, Medicare, and the VA, formerly the Veterans Administration, now the Department of Veterans Affairs.

On the other hand, and possibly as a result of the perceived effects of these cuts in health care funding, the public is increasingly supportive of some form of a national health care program.[6] Currently almost 75 percent of Americans support some form of national health care insurance, a level of enthusiasm that is the

highest since World War II. The ambivalence, however, surfaces again
when the public is polled about its willingness to pay for a health care
system which provides care for all citizens. Seventy-two percent
indicate support for an increased tax, but only 22 percent indicate a
willingness to pay more than two hundred dollars per year.[7]

The long-standing opposition of physicians and the medical
establishment to a significant government role in solving the problems of access to care now appears to be weakening as the problems of
our current health care system become more evident. The American
Medical Association, traditionally opposed to government involvement in health care, has recently determined that we must "tear
down the Berlin Wall that is shutting out millions of Americans from
access to care." Its new proposal, Health Access America, represents a
major step in the direction of working with government to provide
care to needy Americans.[8] In a similiar fashion, the American College
of Physicians has recently strongly supported the need for a national
plan for insurance to provide universal access to health care in
America.[9]

Many plans have been proposed to address the need for improving equity of access to health care while maintaining quality and cost
containment.[10] The most centrally controlled is the National Health
Program, proposed by D. Himmelstein and S. Woolhandler.[11] It would
give the federal government total responsibility for administering a
single public insurance program that would pool resources from the
private insurance sector and both state and federal governments,
with the eventual goal of phasing out private health insurance. More
typical of the mixed plans which have been proposed is that of
A. Enthoven and R. Kronick, which would maintain existing funding through public Medicaid, Medicare, and VA programs, and
employer-based insurance programs.[12] Universal access would be
ensured by a tax on employers and an income tax on individuals to
provide the necessary funds. Care would be given by managed health
care plans that would compete for contracts with public and private
providers. These two plans are quite radical in that they would lead to
replacing the current fee-for-service system with a salaried system
for physicians. A different plan, which preserves our fee-for-service
tradition and most of the existing public and private structures for
funding but which would provide universal access at a basic level of
health care through broad-based taxes, has recently been proposed
by the National Leadership Commission on Health Care.[13] Most of

these recent proposals for expanded access to health care have preserved the current basic pluralistic system of national health care. The degrees of socialization of health care as seen in Great Britain do not appear to have much support, although less tightly controlled systems, such as the Canadian system, have received increasing attention.[14]

The United States remains the only industrialized country without some form of national health insurance. Recent surveys of other countries have shown a high degree of satisfaction with their health care systems, while the United States was largely dissatisfied with high out-of-pocket cost and to a lesser degree with the quality of care.[15] Eli Ginsberg is quite concerned that a

> society such as ours—which places a high value on pluralism, which is enthralled by technology, which resists domination by the federal government, which accepts the prevailing inequality of income and wealth, and which promotes the sovereignty of consumers—is not likely to opt for serious constraints on biomedical research and development or to favor the explicit rationing of proved health care services to the public. Its concerns are more likely to be focused on ensuring access for the entire population to an effective level of care and on finding ways of covering the health care costs of those who cannot pay their own way.[16]

He ends with the caveat that this may hold true until we approach the upper limit of acceptable health care costs.

In this essay we will explore the possible role of the Department of Veterans Affairs in some pluralistic approach to achieving universal access to health care. The VA health care system is the single largest health care system in the United States (and possibly in the world). It is a politicized anomaly in that it is a highly socialized health care system that resides in a nation that is highly committed to capitalism. The socialistic nature of the VA health care system has allowed it to function in an efficient manner in providing health care to veterans who are poor.[17] The close involvement of the government in managing the VA, however, has created problems for both providers and patients. Arguments that the VA should have an expanded role to play in the future evolution of health care are based on its size, its experience in caring for special populations, and most important, its experience in balancing the demands for quality of care with the constraints of a strong need for fiscal accountability.

THE HISTORY OF THE VA

Health care for veterans of our wars has been a concern of the public from the inception of this country.[18] The founding fathers of Plymouth Colony in 1636 decreed that soldiers injured in the line of duty should be cared for by the public. This care consisted mainly of pensions until fifty-seven Marine Hospitals, first established in 1801 for sick merchant marines, were taken over by the U.S. government in 1902 and named the Public Health Hospitals; they were transferred to the Veterans Bureau in 1922. The Veterans Bureau was the result of consolidation of the Bureau of War Risk Insurance established in 1914 to provide insurance for soldiers and sailors of World War I, and the Rehabilitation Division of the Federal Board of Vocational Education, established in 1917 to help returning veterans. The name Veterans Bureau continued until 1933, when it was changed to the Veterans Administration. In 1989 the name was changed to the Department of Veterans Affairs, when the organization attained presidential cabinet status headed by a secretary.

The year 1946 marked a significant change in the status of the health care division of the Veterans Administration with development of affiliation agreements with medical schools and the creation of a Department of Medicine and Surgery within the Veterans Administration. The quality of health care delivered to the veteran, which until 1946 was mediocre at best,[19] steadily improved because of the medical school affiliations, so that in the 1980s it was comparable to the best care in the nation. The VA has developed particularly strong programs for care of patients with spinal cord injuries, loss of limbs, and alcohol and drug abuse. It has clearly led the country in the development of modern care techniques and rehabilitation for the elderly.[20]

Since 1946, and increasingly over the past forty years, the VA's role in graduate medical education has increased. Over 100,000 individuals receive all or part of their training in VA hospitals annually. Approximately 50 percent of all physicians in graduate training receive part of their training in VA hospitals, often considered the best training ground.

Research in the VA hospitals has also made many important contributions to health care in this country. The VA has contributed to our knowledge about effective medical techniques by conducting numerous multihospital cooperative studies of therapy for tuberculosis, hypertension, psychoses, coronary artery heart disease, and drug and alcohol addiction. Research in the VA has resulted in two Nobel Prize recipients.

THE VA'S CURRENT ROLE IN U.S. HEALTH CARE

The VA health care budget in 1989/90 was $11.2 billion, representing about 2 percent of the total U.S. health care budget of $600 billion and about 5 percent of the federal portion of the health care budget.[21] In 1990, more than three million American veterans of the military service received their health care in the VA. This represents about 27 percent of the population of currently eligible veterans and more than 1 percent of the American population. In the past few years, because of fiscal constraints, access to VA health care has been limited to veterans with a service-connected illness or disability and to the financially needy. The current income level that determines eligibility for VA care is an annual income of less that $18,000 per year for an individual and $22,000 per year for a veteran with a spouse. This has been arbitrarily set at an income level of approximately 2.5 times the national poverty level.[22] These criteria currently entitle 40 percent, or eleven million of the nation's twenty-seven million veterans, to receive VA health care.

Health care benefits for eligible veterans now include full access to acute inpatient and ambulatory care, and all medications, including over-the-counter drugs. In 1988, Public Law 100–322 required the VA to provide ambulatory care to low-income veterans as well as to those with service-connected illnesses or disabilities.[23] Despite the high percentage of elderly individuals among the veteran population, Congress has not seen fit to mandate extended care to elderly veterans. To meet this increasing need, the VA is gradually increasing the number of beds available for extended care and is actively pursuing agreements with state and public nursing homes to provide extended care for veterans.

Care in the VA system is provided in 172 hospitals and 36 free-standing clinics distributed throughout the fifty states and Puerto Rico. These centers vary in size from 1,000-bed hospitals, which provide highly technical tertiary medical and surgical care, to 100-bed rural hospitals, which provide primary and custodial care for patients. Some of these hospitals have been built recently and match those of the private sector in pleasant ambience and availability of modern technical equipment. Many others are more than forty years old and less well equipped.

Figure 1

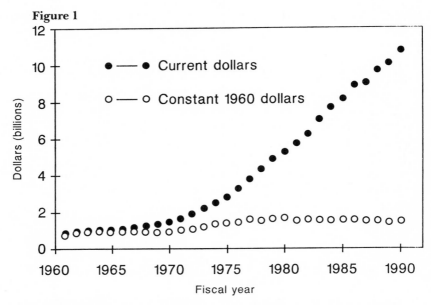

THE VA'S ETHICAL DILEMMA: QUALITY HEALTH CARE
WITH LIMITED FUNDS

A very important role the VA can play in the national health care
scene is to serve as a model for testing resolutions to the major issues
facing health care in the United States. The new chief medical
director of the VA stated, "We clearly have the capability to be the
nation's laboratory to develop and test innovations in health care.[24]
How do we achieve a balance between declining resources for health
care and the maintenance of an acceptable level of accessibility and
quality of care? It is our thesis that the VA's experience over the past
twenty years provides us examples, both successes and failures, that
can be helpful in guiding the national health care system in address-
ing the issues of increasing health care costs, access by the poor, and
maintenance of quality.

The fiscal constraints on VA health care in the past twenty years
have been much greater than those on the rest of the health care
system. Where the private sector has experienced an increase in costs
of health care of approximately 10 percent each year, the increase in
VA funding over this period has averaged about 2 percent per year,
resulting in essentially flat funding when adjusted for inflation (fig.
1).[25] This reduction in real dollar support for VA health care would
not have created a problem had the VA not at the same time been

Figure 2

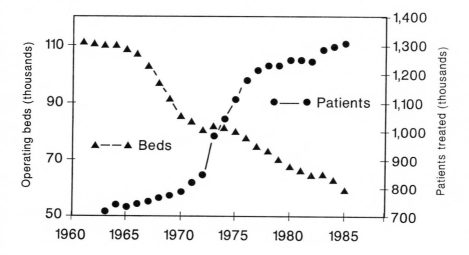

encouraged by the demands of its veterans' constituency and by congressional legislation to provide care for more individuals. As shown in figure 2, in the fifteen-year period 1970–85, when VA funding was held level in terms of real dollars, the number of inpatients treated by the VA increased 63 percent, from 800,000 to 1,300,000, and its outpatient care from 2.5 million to 22 million visits.[26] This same figure reveals that a significant number of beds are no longer used; this is a direct result of the marked reduction in the length of stay of patients. Two factors are important in this change: (1) authorization to care for patients on an ambulatory basis in 1985; (2) the implementation by the central administration of reimbursement by diagnosis-related groups (DRGs).

COST EFFICIENCY OF VA HEALTH CARE

The first response of the VA to the pressure of decreasing funding and the demand to provide more care has been to increase the efficiency of its health care system. The average length of stay of veterans in acute medical and surgical units has decreased over the past two decades from more than fourteen days to less than eight days. This change was brought about in a short period of time by administrative changes in the method of funding individual VA hospitals for the care provided. The previous system of paying for patient "bed days" actually encouraged extended lengths of stay, while the new resource-allocation model initiated in the mid-1980s adapted a system for funding that was based on patients' diagnoses (DRGs) that was similar to the system adapted nationally for Medicare patients. This system paid fixed amounts per episode of patient care and rewarded early discharge. The VA is the only hospital system in the United States to be entirely funded by this mechanism, and the lesson is clear that hospitals and clinicians can respond in a dramatic fashion to changes in the incentive system for funding. In non-VA hospitals only Medicare patients are funded by DRGs. The effect of this new funding mechanism, however, has been similar reductions in the average length of stay.

In addition, the VA has shown a remarkable ability to economize on the use of personnel to provide care. Comparisons between VA and community or university hospitals that provide similar levels of care indicate that total staffing in the VA is only one-half of that of the community hospitals. A study done four years ago compared three VA hospitals in Florida with their affiliated university hospitals, and found staff-to-patient ratios of between 3.6:1 and 4.6:1 in VA hospitals and 6:1 and 9.9:1 in the university hospitals. Nationally, in 1987, the American Hospital Association found an overall staff-to-patient ratio of 4.29:1 while the VA had an average staffing ratio of 3.2:1.[27] A recent survey conducted by Charles B. Smith indicated that nurse staffing levels on acute medical beds in six VA hospitals were less than 50 percent of those of comparable community and university hospitals. Even more striking was the finding that respiratory therapists in VA hospitals cover three times as many beds as do therapists in the community hospitals.

Physician services in the VA constitute only 9 percent of the total health care budget.[28] This percentage is remarkably smaller than the 19.5 percent calculated for the U.S. health care system as a whole and the 15.7 percent figure characteristic of the Canadian health care system.[29] The lower costs for physician services in the VA are due to a combination of lower salaries paid to physicians, particularly to surgeons and and other specialists oriented to expensive procedures, and to lower staffing levels in VA hospitals. A recent Institute Of Medicine unpublished study further supports this ratio of 2:1 in the staffing levels of physicians between university and VA hospitals.

A comparison of the less costly Canadian health care system with that of the United States concluded that higher expenditures for physician services in the United States can be entirely explained by higher physician fees in the U.S.[30] There is a particularly large difference in fees charged by different physician groups in the United States, the larger fees being charged by specialists and surgeons. In an attempt to control physician costs, the U.S. government, with the support of many physician groups, has recently adopted a relative-value scale to achieve a better balance between the very high fees charged by the specialists and the lower ones charged by primary-care physicians.[31] The VA has, in fact, been functioning with a remarkably flat relative-value scale for physicians for many years. Although the VA does allow for bonus payments to "scarce" physicians, such as radiologists and some surgeons, these bonuses do not generally bring their incomes up to the levels earned in the private sector, and, for the most part, specialists and generalists earn similar salaries in the VA. These salaries currently lag 33 percent or more behind national pay levels for physicians, and recent evidence that recruiting of physicians to the VA has become more difficult has led to legislation intended to narrow the gap.[32] The ability of the VA to stay in business with such a large non-competitive gap between the salaries it pays to physicians and other caregivers and the salaries in the private sector is in large part due to the strong affiliations that the majority of VA hospitals have established with medical schools. Academic physicians have traditionally been willing to work for lower salaries than are offered in the private sector; the rewards of being provided the time and resources to teach medical students and conduct research appear to provide the compensatory nonmonetary benefit.

In addition to the lower cost of physician services provided by the VA, the structure of the physician practice in the VA is designed to reduce the cost of medical care. A. S. Relman has argued that prepaid group practices provide more cost-effective care because there is less incentive for inappropriate use of specialists and expensive procedures.[33] Physicians working in the VA system have no financial incentive to perform inappropriate tests or procedures, a "socialistic" characteristic of the VA system that partially explains the relatively lower cost of care it provides. A recent study found that the use of special diagnostic procedures increases enormously when the physician has a special financial interest in the technology.[34]

The common opinion that government-managed systems are excessively costly because of high administrative overhead does not appear to be true for the health care system. Himmelstein and

Woolhandler estimated that the overall administrative costs of the U.S. health care system were 22 percent in 1986.[35] These included estimated administrative costs for hospitals of 18 percent and for physicians in private practice of 43 percent, mostly spent on the burdensome processing of insurance forms. More recently, the administrative costs of private insurance carriers have been estimated to vary between 10.5 percent and 40 percent.[36] In contrast, the administrative cost of the Canadian universal health insurance system has been estimated to be a paltry 2–3 percent and the U.S. Medicare system runs on an administrative overhead of only 4 percent.[37] The VA administrative costs in 1989 were calculated to be 7.7 percent of the total health care budget, a figure that is not as low as that of Medicare or the Canadian system, but one which is considerably less than that of the private sector. The higher administrative costs of private medicine today can in part be attributed to the costs of maintaining a competitive market-oriented system that spends money on advertising, marketing, and paying dividends to investors, all items that are clearly missing from the VA budget.

The bottom-line question then is, how efficient is the VA health care system compared with the private sector? Little public information is available that allows for direct comparisons of costs of health care within the VA and alternative systems. The illustrations we have just given of comparative staffing and overhead efficiencies of the VA system suggest that the VA may well be the most efficient system functioning in the United States today. J. K. Iglehart reported in 1985 that the Office of Management and the Budget during the Reagan administration considered the possibility of vouchering or mainstreaming VA health care through the private sector and concluded that it would be more costly than maintaining the current VA system.[38] J. P. Sanford reported that the Department of Defense currently provides direct health care at less than 60 percent of the cost of the CHAMPUS (Civilian Health and Medical Program Uniform Services) insurance system, which pays for the care of military retirees and dependents in the private health sector.[39] He advocated that the VA join the department in expanding what he believes to be the most cost-effective federal system to care for the uninsured.

QUALITY OF VA HEALTH CARE

The VA has been deeply concerned with quality of care as demand has increased and budgets have decreased. It has recently reorganized and expanded its quality management efforts both centrally and in the field, and VA administration is working even more closely with the Health Services Research and Development and the Cooperative Studies Programs in VA Research Service to further its ability to evaluate the quality of medical care.

Given the evidence that the VA currently provides health care at a comparable or lower cost than the private sector, the logical question arises, is the less costly care in the VA of lower quality?[40] J. Sunshine believes that the general public and non-VA physicians have a poor opinion of the VA, based on the comparatively Spartan appearance of many VA facilities and the "down and out" image of some of the VA patient population.[41] The tendency of the media to view the VA as a vested and bureaucratic government agency and to emphasize problems rather than successes in providing care has no doubt significantly influenced the public's perceptions.[42] Customer satisfaction is a telling measure of the quality of care, and as the fiscal squeeze on the VA has increased and rationing methods have been instituted, patients have increasingly complained about longer waits for clinic appointments and elective surgeries.

The Joint Commission on Accreditation of Health Care Organizations (JCAHO) is the major national assessor of quality of care in hospitals, and it routinely reviews VA hospitals using the same measures as those used to evaluate private-sector hospitals. Until recently, all VA hospitals were fully accredited.[43] In 1989, however, deficiencies in the structure (buildings, equipment, and organizational structure) and processes of care were found in some VA hospitals.[44] It is possible that the efficiencies associated with low staffing levels of nurses and respiratory technicians are partly responsible for the recent increased problems in structure and process that have been detected by the JCAHO. On the other hand, outcomes represent another important measure of the quality of care, and a recent report on morbidity and mortality following surgical procedures suggests that the VA is doing as well as, if not better than, the private sector.[45]

There is great need within the entire health care system for better information about the links between allocation of resources, and patient outcomes. The VA is positioned to become a major contributor of data for such analyses because of the outstanding and comprehensive medical information system that has been developed in the 172 VA hospitals. That system can potentially be linked to the military as well as the Indian Health Service. It is a highly flexible system and is an enormous potential source of critical health service data.

Our overall impression is that the VA is still able to maintain a level of quality of care comparable to that of the private sector but that persistent fiscal constraints are beginning to threaten that quality.

RATIONING OF HEALTH CARE IN THE VA

The alternative strategy to becoming more cost efficient in response to increasing fiscal constraints, and to avoiding the associated possibility of reductions in the quality of care, is to ration health care. For many years, Congress provided the VA with a fiscal and quality safety valve that allowed each hospital the option to exclude "low priority" veterans—with non-service-connected illnesses—from their clinics and hospitals when "sufficient funds" were not available. This system, which allowed each hospital arbitrarily to exclude some patients from the VA health care system, was difficult to manage and often led to disagreements between hospital administrators, who were responsible for balancing budgets, and clinicians, who were responsible for caring for patients. The local hospital safety valve was eliminated in 1988 with the passage of Public Law 100–322, which extended the responsibility of the VA to care for low-income veterans with non-service-connected ailments. It appears the lawmakers intended to protect the quality of care in the VA system by establishing a means test to limit access to health care to eligible veterans who were very needy. The net effect of the law, however, was greatly to increase the number of veterans the VA is mandated to care for (estimated at eleven million) without significantly increasing funding. The present concern is that the quality of care given by the VA will suffer as a result of the congressional mandate to care for more patients with resources that have been stationary for the past decade.[46]

This new law formalizes the VA policy of rationing care according to patient income. Unlike the private sector, which appears to give less care to those who are less able to pay for it, the VA has chosen to exclude those who are not clearly indigent.[47] As mentioned previously, the current threshold for eligibility for VA care is an annual income of $18,000 for single veterans and $22,000 for a veteran with a spouse, a level more than two times the national level for "poverty" and quite generous when compared to the thresholds for eligibility for Medicaid, the other federal safety net for providing care for the needy. In 1989, the average income threshold for a family of three to qualify for Medicaid assistance was $4,942, an income that was less that one-half the federally determined poverty level of $10,080.[48]

Even though the VA has been more generous to the poor by setting the threshold for access at more than twice that of the "official" poverty level, it can be argued that the VA threshold is still too low to provide an adequate health care safety net for low-income veterans, especially given that the veteran population is aging faster than the general population. Income and health insurance profiles of veterans who qualify for care according to the new thresholds established by the VA indicate that 71 percent have annual incomes of less that $15,000 and 23 percent have incomes of less than $5,000.[49] No private insurance is held by 76 percent of veterans with incomes of $5,000 to $10,000, 61 percent with incomes of $10,000 to $20,000 and 44 percent with incomes of $20,000 to $30,000 and 33 percent over $30,000. Of the veterans with non-service-connected illnesses using the VA system (70 percent of the current users), 68 percent have no insurance.[50] Users of the VA medical system are also eligible for other public health insurance programs. Forty-three percent of VA users are enrolled in Medicare Part A, the part which pays for hospital bills. This still leaves more than half of the overall population of veterans without any coverage, however, and many of those who are covered cannot afford the deductibles and co-payments.

Quality of health care is traditionally measured in systems where care is provided. Unfortunately, little attention has been given the quality of care, if any, that is received by individuals who are excluded by health care systems. S. D. Fihn and J. B. Wicher assessed the changes in health status of veterans who were discharged from VA outpatient clinics in 1983 because of budget shortfalls and found that 41 percent of the discharged veterans believed their health was much worse (versus 8 percent in a control group), 23 percent had seen no health care provider over the period of a year, 47 percent had reduced the use of prescribed medications, and in 41 percent of those who had been treated for hypertension the disease was determined to be out of control.[51] Their findings, similiar to those of N. Lurie et al., who found that several measures of health status declined when patients were excluded from Medicaid funding in California, indicate that the policy of rationing access to care by income in an attempt to maintain quality of care just shifts the problem from the hospitals to the streets, where it is more easily ignored.[52]

Some other methods for rationing care do not utilize income as the primary criterion. H. J. Aaron and W. B. Schwartz have pointed out that the British model for rationing expensive health care procedures by simply limiting availability suffers from being arbitrary and poorly linked with cost effectiveness and outcomes.[53] This approach is a potential problem for government-run health care systems where the budget for health care is determined by a capricious political process, and the VA health care system has begun to feel the influence of rationing by the limiting of resources over the past decade. The waiting time for hip-replacement surgery in the VA often exceeds a year or more, and patients' access to simple ambulatory care is often limited by the long distances they must travel to VA clinics and by waiting periods of many months for clinic appointments.

From the experience of most national health care systems, substituting rationing by queue for rationing by price, a move that occurs in the private sector, tends to delay the delivery of elective health care and procedures.[54] This phenomenon is well known to the VA hospitals. The reasons for rationing by queue are multiple. Lack of resources, both personnel and supplies, is probably the most important. It is, however, time for emergent care to be promptly available. Whether a national health care system could be so structured as to modify or avoid such queuing is a major question and one of considerable importance, given the expectations of this country's citizens of complete, immediate health care.

A more reasonable form of rationing care involves attention to the appropriateness of care.[55] Many expensive health care practices, however, are too poorly documented to assess the outcomes, and as much as 30 percent of the current cost of medical care has been attributed to inappropriate care.[56] These observations have led to an intensive new effort to develop "practice guidelines." On the positive side, the VA has made important contributions to our understanding of the value of common and expensive surgical procedures, such as coronary bypass surgery, and expanding VA programs for health services research and cooperative clinical studies have great potential for using the unique VA clinical data base to study issues of appropriateness of care.[57] The larger ethical issues of limiting the care given to elderly and terminally ill patients have become increasingly discussed in the VA as they have throughout our society, with no clear consensus as yet. The VA was among the first health care institutions to formalize "Do Not Resuscitate" (DNR) policies, and specific funding needs to be allocated to the VA to establish centers for research and development in medical ethics.

AN EXPANDED ROLE FOR THE VA IN A NATIONAL PLAN FOR UNIVERSAL ACCESS TO HEALTH CARE

Several roles have recently been proposed for the VA in meeting the challenge of expanding access to health care.[58]

1. All veterans could be provided their health care in the private sector, thereby permitting the closing of those VA hospitals and clinics where adequate community beds are available. In a highly critical article, D. S. Greenberg has suggested that the VA hospital system is a medical anachronism, underfunded and understaffed; a creaky empire of medical socialism.[59] His observations, while containing many inaccuracies, raise the issue of using a voucher system to allow veterans to purchase health insurance. The so-called voucher, or mainstream, system was supported for many years by physicians, who coveted the additional business the system would generate. In recent years, with the realization that government payments for medical care barely cover the costs, the AMA has pulled back from support of vouchering. In the present pluralistic system, vouchering would be enormously expensive. It would ignore the uninsured middle class, as the current system does, unless full privileges were restored to veterans with higher incomes. Still, it would extend care at times to veterans living long distances from a VA hospital. Lost in such a system would be the function of VA hospitals as backup facilities for military hospitals, a function acknowledged during the Iraq crisis to be an important one.

2. Another conservative approach would be to continue in the same mode, perhaps even with increased constraints on eligibility; limiting care only to veterans with service-connected disabilities who were injured directly as a result of combat, and to veterans (with or without service-connected ailments) who fit an indigence index perhaps lower than the current $18,000 maximum.[60] This approach would be consistent with the current administration's plans to have the health sector shoulder the major burden of reducing the deficit. Many veterans will argue that this approach is ethically unfair and is discriminatory against veterans with nonservice-connected illnesses who served as honorably as those who had service-connected injuries. The current income threshold of $18,000 per year, although considerably higher than the poverty lines for Medicaid, is arbitrary

and still leaves the uninsured "middle-class" veteran potentially unable to pay for catastrophic illnesses. Certainly a few thousand dollars' difference in annual salary is no significant protection against any major illness, and reducing the poverty level further would seem to be further denial of the government's responsibility to the veterans.

3. A modest expansion of the eligibility of veterans with non-service-connected illnesses would have the advantage of more efficiently utilizing the 30,000 unused beds in the VA system and of providing more care to those in the middle class who are underinsured. Public Law 99–722 (April 7, 1986) empowered the VA to recover the cost of caring for veterans with non-service-connected illnesses by charging these costs to private insurance carriers and state and other local public agencies. Implementation of this new law was surprisingly slow, and new legislation, passed in 1990 (Public Law 401–508), was designed further to encourage the VA to collect from insurance carriers by providing specific funds to establish a billing program. An extension of eligibility to include veterans who are middle class, and more likely to be insured, could be mostly financed by collections of their insurance benefits.

It needs to be recognized that the expansion of VA health care to other than veteran consumers has several political implications and would require that the prerogatives of the veterans be firmly maintained. A way of avoiding problems in this area would be to expand eligibility to those veterans with illnesses that are not service connected who have incomes above the current set cutoff point. This could be done by permitting the VA to collect from Medicare, Medicaid, CHAMPUS, and the Indian Health Service for the care of veterans covered by those agencies. Such a transfer of dollars is currently under investigation, an encouraging sign that the various providers of federal health care are beginning to talk to each other.

Because the VA has shown its leadership in developing and evaluating cost-effective methods of caring for and rehabilitating the elderly, the American College of Physicians has made a strong argument for expanding eligibility to all veterans who are over age sixty-five.[61] This expansion would require legislation to permit the VA to recover costs of care from Medicare and other government funds. The past lack of dialogue between the VA and other government providers regarding the development of efficient methods for sharing resources and responsibilities for caring for the aged is, in part, a result of the separation of planning and funding responsibilities for these programs in Congress and the executive branch, and is an example of bureaucratic and political territorialism that could be corrected by appropriate legislation.

4. The role of the VA could be expanded to care for families of eligible veterans.[62] This would take care of some of the uninsured or underinsured persons and, by broadening the patient profile to include women and children, would enhance medical education and aid in the retention of staff. Such an expansion would require legislative action and would increase the cost to the VA, since additional personnel and supplies would be needed. The bed capacity would probably be inadequate even if each current user had only one dependent, and it may well be that including spouses would encourage more veterans to use the VA facilities in the future and thus increase the need for beds. The distribution of VA hospitals nationally would present some inequities of access. The government would have to make arrangments to care adequately for the other noninsured poverty-level dependent persons in non-VA hospitals in order to forestall any complaints of discrimination. Using the VA in this way would be cost-effective, since VA care has been shown to be about 10–30 percent as costly as private-sector care.[63]

5. A national health care package administered by the central government could totally incorporate the VA health care system into its overall plan, using those VA hospitals and clinics in areas where health care is inadequate. The VA's long experience—more than seventy-five years—in delivering health care within fixed annual budgets and delivering a comprehensive type of care would seem to point to the VA as a means of putting together a pilot program of universal health care in a limited area. Such a pilot program, which could include all the poor and uninsured citizens in the area, might be a way of incrementally instituting a national health care program. A good number of the smaller VA hospitals are located in rural areas, which frequently are marginally supplied with health care facilities. A significant number of larger VA-affiliated hospitals are in the poorer sections of our cities and could bring care to these areas. Expanding VA medical services to cover nonveterans would be met with great concern by the veterans' lobby, which has a most paternalistic interest in VA hospitals. The public also would not be likely to accept such an extreme form of socialized medicine.

We believe that the VA should be an increasingly important partner in a pluralistic approach to expanding access to health care in the United States. The VA should continue to carry out its historic mission of providing health care to those who risked their lives and health by serving in the armed services. For many years, American veterans have expected this recognition of their contributions, and Congress will undoubtedly continue to support the expectations of veterans and maintain some form of a separate health care system dedicated to their special needs.

In addition to this special mission, however, we feel that the VA health care system has many positive attributes which should make it an attractive partner in planning for expanded access to health care. To recapitulate, these attributes include:

1. The VA is the largest health care delivery system in the United States. Its large size has provided the benefits of efficiencies in centralized purchasing and a large integrated data base which allows for standardization of policies and processes, and for assessing outcomes and quality of care.

2. The VA, following ten years of austere budgets, is now probably the most cost efficient of the large health care systems in the United States, as judged by comparative staffing levels and administrative costs.

3. The VA currently plays a disproportionately large role in filling the educational needs of students and trainees in all areas of health care. These needs are particularly well met by the VA, and as private hospitals become less welcoming to medical trainees the importance of the VA as an educational resource will increase.

4. The VA, because of its close affiliations with schools of medicine and other health care professions, has become an increasingly important partner in medical research in the United States, particularly for research that focuses on clinical problems and requires the cooperation of multiple hospitals.

5. Current reductions in funding for VA staff and supplies have led to the elimination of 20,000–30,000 beds. These are potentially available for use in expanding access to health care through sharing agreements with Medicaid, Medicare, the Department of Defense, CHAMPUS, the Indian Health Service, and the private sector.

The major problem with an expanded role for the VA in a national health care system is the control that government can have on such a system. Many years of experience in the VA indicates that political influence and micromanagement by legislators can interfere with the efficiency and goals of a health care system. By having total control of the budget, legislators can arbitrarily and swiftly disenfranchise large populations from access to health care, a concern that has been validated by the recent decisions by Congress and the administration to make disproportionate cuts in Medicare and Medicaid funding in the budget-balancing process. These concerns, however, apply to any government-funded plans for expanding health care access, and it is to be hoped that the painful lessons learned in the 1990 budget year will not be repeated.

SUMMARY

The VA health care system not only provides excellent health care to a segment of the population, many of whom are indigent, but is a critical part of the medical research and health care education system of this country. We suggest that the VA health care system has much to offer in the final solution to the pressing health care delivery and financing problem faced by the United States. Dr. Donald L. Custis, a former chief medical director of the VA, said it well, "If the current neglect of ethical and humanitarian imperatives in health care legislation is to be reversed, corrective intervention will require more circumspect political leadership backed by professional and informed societal demand. Veterans can and must be a potent segment of such a consortium."[64]

We feel that the most useful role of the VA in the short time frame would be to extend eligibility to the families of indigent veterans and in the long term to have the VA play an expanded role in caring for the poor, in a pluralistic universal health care system for all, at the same time recognizing in some significant way the special contribution of the veteran patients.

NOTES

1. A. S. Relman, "Assessment and Accountability: The Third Revolution in Medical Care," *New England Journal of Medicine* (hereafter *NEJM*) 319 (1988): 1220–22.

2. National Leadership Commission on Health Care, *For the Health of a Nation: A Shared Responsibility* (Ann Arbor, Mich.: Health Administration Press, 1989).

3. U.S. Congress, Office of Technology Assessment, *The Quality of Medical Care: Information for Consumers*, OTA-H-386 (Washington, D.C.: Government Printing Office, 1988); National Leadership Commission, *For the Health of a Nation*.

4. American College of Physicians, "Access to Health Care," *Annals of Internal Medicine* (hereafter *Ann. Int. Med.*) 112 (1990): 641–62.

5. E. J. Dionne, "The Idea of Equity Is Proving Unequal to the Demands of Today," *Washington Post,* national weekly edition, May 7, 1990; A. S. Relman, "Universal Health Insurance: Its Time Has Come," *NEJM* 320 (1989): 117–18.

6. R. J. Blendon and K. Donelan, "The Public and the Emerging Debate over National Health Insurance," *NEJM* 323 (1990): 208–12.

7. Ibid.

8. C. J. Tupper, "Dreams, Dollars, and Deeds: The Sacred Fire and Health Access America," *Journal of the American Medical Association* (hereafter *JAMA*) 264 (1990): 1150–52.

9. American College of Physicians, "Universal Access to Health Care in America: A Moral and Medical Imperative," *Ann. Int. Med.* 112 (1990): 637–61.

10. Relman, A. S., "Universal Health Insurance: Its Time has Come." Ed. *NEJM* 320 (1989): 117–18.

11. D. Himmelstein and S. Woolhandler, "A National Health Program for the United States," *NEJM* 320 (1989): 102–8.

12. A. Enthoven and R. Kronick, "A Consumer's-Choice Health Plan for the 1990's," parts 1 and 2, *NEJM* 320 (1989): 29–37, 94–101.

13. National Leadership Commission, *For the Health of a Nation.*

14. V. R. Fuchs and J. S. Hahn, "How Can Canada Do It? A Comparison of Expenditures for Physicians' Services in the United States and Canada," *NEJM* 320 (1990): 884–90; R. G. Evans, J. Lomas, M. L. Barer et al., "Controlling Health Care Expenditures: The Canadian Reality," *NEJM* 320 (1989): 1851–57; B. J. Percy, "Perspective on the Canadian Health Care System," *American College of Surgeons Bulletin* 75 (1990): 5–13.

15. "Which Countries Are Satisfied with Their Health Care?" *Medical Journal Bulletin in Health Letter,* August 1990, pp. 9–10; R. J. Blendon and H. Taylor, "Views on Health Care: Public Opinion in Three Nations," *Data Watch in Health Affairs,* Spring 1989, pp. 149–56.

16. E. Ginsberg, "A Hard Look at Cost Containment," *NEJM* 316 (1987): 1151–54.

17. J. W. Hollingsworth and P. K. Bondy, "The Role of Veterans Affairs Hospitals in the Health Care System," *NEJM* 322 (1990): 1851–57.

18. B. J. Lewis, *Veterans Administration Medical Program Relationship with Medical Schools in the United States,* 91st Cong., 2d sess., January 19, 1970, House Committee on Veterans' Affairs Print, no. 170.

19. Ibid.

20. L. Z. Rubenstein et al., "Effectiveness of a Geriatric Evaluation Unit," *NEJM* 311 (1984): 1664–70.

21. House Committee on Veterans Affairs, *Report to the Committee on Budget from the Committee on Veterans Affairs: Budget Proposal for FY 1991,* March 2, 1990, Print, p. 13.

22. Jonathan Sunshine, Capitol Comment: "Who Should Receive VA Health Care in the 1990's?" *VA Practitioner,* February 1990, p. 68.

23. T. J. Meyer, D. A. Nardone and A. Prochazka, "Congressional Impact on Ambulatory Care," *VA Practitioner,* August 1990, p. 26.

24. J. W. Holsinger, "New Directions for VHSRA" (Paper presented at Federal Day of the Annual Convention of the American Hospital Association, Washington, D.C., October 1990).

25. Hollingsworth and Bondy, "Role of Veterans Affairs," pp. 1851–57.

26. T. J. Meyer, et al., "Congressional Impact on Ambulatory Care," p. 75.

27. Malcolm Randall to author, concerning the VA staffing deficit, personal communication, 1987.

28. House Committee on Veterans Affairs, *Report to the Committee on Budget,* p. 13.

29. Fuchs and Hahn, "How Can Canada Do It?" pp. 884–90.

30. Ibid.

31. J. K. Iglehart, "The New Law on Medicare's Payments to Physicians," *NEJM* 322 (1990): 1247–52.

32. H. Schwartz, "Speaking Out: Doling Out the dollars," *VA Practitioner,* June 1991, pp. 28–29.

33. A. S. Relman, "Reforming the Health Care System," *NEJM* 322 (1990): 991–92.

34. B. J. Hillman et al., "Frequency and Costs of Diagnostic Imaging in Office Practice: A Comparison of Self-Referring and Radiologist Referring Physicians," *NEJM* 323 (1990): 1604–8.

35. D. U. Himmelstein and S. Woolhandler, "Cost without Benefit: Administrative Waste in U.S. Health Care," *NEJM* 314 (1986): 441–45; S. Woolhandler and D. U. Himmelstein, "The Deteriorating Administrative Efficiency of the U.S. Health Care System," *NEJM* 321 (1991): 1253–58.

36. American College of Physicians, "Access to Health Care," p. 648.

37. Evans et al., "Controlling Health Care Expenditures," pp. 571–77; Himmelstein and Woolhandler, "Cost without Benefit," pp. 441–45.

38. J. K. Iglehart, "Health Policy Report: The Veterans Administration Medical Care System Faces an Uncertain Future," *NEJM* 313 (1985): 1168–72.

39. J. P. Sanford, "Federal Facilities Seen 'Answer' to Uninsured," *U.S. Medicine,* April 1990, p. 35.

40. N. A. Graham, *Comparative Cost of Inpatient Hospital Care: The Veterans Administration and the Private Sector,* Allocation Development Service Department of Medicine and Surgery (Washington, D.C.: Veterans Administration Central Office, May 1986), p. 222.

41. J. Sunshine, "How Good Is VA Health Care?" *VA Practitioner,* January 1990, p. 103.

42. Iglehart, "Health Policy Report," pp. 1168–72.

43. Sunshine, "How Good Is VA Health Care?" p. 103.

44. "VA Officials Confident of Hospitals' Quality," *U.S. Medicine* 26 (1990): 1.

45. Department of Veterans Affairs, Veterans Health Services and Research Administration, *A Report on the Quality of Surgical Care in the Department of Veterans Affairs,* Phase II Report to the Congress of the United States under the provisions of Public Law 99–166, sec. 204 (Washington, D.C.: GPO, 1989).

46. Meyer et al., "Congressional Impact on Ambulatory Care," p. 26.

47. M. B. Wenneker, J. S. Weissman, and A. M. Epstein, "The Association of Payer with Utilization of Cardiac Procedures in Massachusetts," *JAMA* 264 (1990): 1255–60.

48. American College of Physicians, "Access to Health Care," pp. 641–62.

49. R. Pollack, "AHA Staff Study on Veterans Administration Health Care System" (Washington, D.C.: Executive Briefing Med Source Teleconference Network, April 22, 1986).

50. Department of Veterans Affairs, *Survey of Medical System Users,* (Washington, D.C.: Arawak Consulting Corporation, February 1990), p. 84.

51. S. D. Fihn and J. B. Wicher, "Withdrawing Routine Outpatient Medical Services: Effects on Access and Health," *Journal of General Internal Medicine* 3 (1988): 356–62.

52. N. Lurie, N. B. Ward, M. F. Shapiro, "Termination of Medi-Cal Benefits: A Follow-up Study One Year Later," *NEJM* 314 (1986): 1266–68.

53. H. J. Aaron and W. B. Schwartz, "Rationing Health Care: The Choice Before Us," *Science* 247 (1990): 418–22.

54. C. D. Naylor, A. Basinski, B. S. Baigrie, "Placing Patients in the Queue for Coronary Revascularization: Evidence for Practice Variations from an Expert Panel," *American Journal of Public Health* 80 (1990): 1246–52.

55. J. M. Eisenberg, *Doctors' Decisions and the Cost of Medical Care* (Ann Arbor, Mich.: Health Administration Press, 1986).

56. L. Leape, "Practice Guidelines and Standards: An Overview," *Quality Review Bulletin* 16 (1990): 42–49.

57. Takaro, T., et al., *Veterans Administration Cooperative Study of Medical vs. Surgical Treatment of Stable Angina,* Progress Report, sec. 1: "Historic Perspective," *in* Prog-Cardiovasc Disease (Washington, D.C.: Department of Veterans Affairs, November-December 1985) 28(3): 213–18; D. Deykin, "Federal Aid to Dependent Variables: Surveying the Health Services Research Landscape," *Health Services Research* 25 (1990): 149–57.

58. Hollingsworth and Bondy, "Role of Veterans Affairs Hospitals"; Sanford, "Federal Facilities"; D. S. Greenberg, "Washington Perspective," *Lancet* 335 (1990): 1391–92.

59. Greenberg, "Washington Perspective."

60. T. Jemison, "Theoretical Reforms Surface in White Papers," *U.S. Medicine* 26 (October 1990): 1.

61. American College of Physicians Board of Regents, *"The Role of the*

Department of Veterans Affairs in Geriatric Care." Available from American College of Physicians (Philadelphia, PA: 1991).

62. Hollingsworth and Bondy, "Role of Veterans Affairs Hospitals."

63. Iglehart, "Health Policy Report," pp. 1247–52.

64. Donald L. Custis, "The Challenge to the VA Health Care System," *Paraplegic News,* May 1985.

Lessons from the VA Experience as a National Health Care System

J. William Hollingsworth, M.D.

In their essay, "Can We Learn from Our Own Experience: The VA as National Health Care," Drs. Mark W. Wolcott and Charles B. Smith have provided a splendid description of the health care system provided by the Veterans Administration (now called the Department of Veterans Affairs [VA]), and its changes over the years. I have nothing radically different to add, but it seems to me that the VA experience offers cogent reasons why eventually (and not too far in the future) we must assure our citizens complete access to a health care system. Government and individual citizens alike want universal access to health care, but everyone is afraid of runaway costs which may cause any universal system to self-destruct. The VA certainly has some lessons to share in how to deliver medical care at prudent costs.

ACCESS TO VA CARE: A CHANGING MANDATE

Until a decade or so ago, almost any sick veteran could gain admission to a VA hospital if he presented himself or if his doctor referred him for hospitalization. In practice, many of these referrals occurred because some social service agency encountered a veteran and arranged for him to be evaluated for admission. Admission criteria were quite loose, and hospital diagnosis and care were performed at a highly deliberate pace. The VA quite properly deserved its reputation as a slovenly system. Drs. Walcott and Smith have described how funding cuts plus increased mandatory workload transformed the system.

Although those earlier years were characterized by essentially universal access to hospital care, continuing ambulatory care was not really an option on the VA menu. Indeed, pressure from the

American Medical Association (AMA) prohibited such activity. The prohibition against ambulatory care was circumvented to some extent by the VA's assertion that hospital care included ambulatory care "to prevent hospitalization" in some circumstances, and included "post-hospital follow-up." This interpretation of regulations permitted clinics for specific diseases—an excellent teaching and research device for subspecialists but a mechanism that only partially met the needs of the veteran clientele.

The access by veterans to ambulatory care was abruptly mandated by Congress in 1974, a move not anticipated by the VA. I have been intimately associated with VA hospitals in Lexington, Kentucky and San Diego, California, both new hospitals which opened in 1974. Neither hospital had any clinic space when it opened, and, in both, one of the first acts was to reconstruct space for ambulatory care. The entire VA system launched its program for ambulatory care in makeshift arrangements, and only a few recently completed hospitals were designed with proper clinic space.

The provision of ambulatory care plus hospital care proceeded comfortably together for only a few years. Costs were going up, congressional appropriations rose very little and more veterans were beginning to use their recently attained free access to clinics. The system was being swamped with patients, and the open access which generally had marked the VA before 1980 became no longer tenable. By the early 1980s, access was being curtailed—medical care was being rationed—by a variety of rules and regulations and also by the actual denial of services by the individual VA medical centers.

COMMENTS ON MORALITY OF THE VARIOUS SCHEMES OF RATIONING

Service-Connected Disabilities

From the very beginning, the VA had described its care as mandated for service-connected disabilities of its clients, with other patients being served "as capacity permitted." Each veteran was assigned a service-connected status based on medical evaluations. Those who were wounded seriously received 100 percent service-connected disability. Lesser wounds received lower ratings. These decisions were arbitrary, but with war wounds were, at least, sensibly debatable. But, would clients rated at 20 percent disability status have the same access as those rated at 100 percent? This argument emerged when access to ambulatory care was curtailed, or when intercurrent illness required hospital care. The young men with rheumatoid arthritis, asthma, or ulcerative colitis were fortunate, indeed, to contract the illness while they were in military service: the illnesses were deemed service-connected and carried high priority for care. The young men who developed a similar illness a year after leaving military service received no special status.

Mental illness, personality disorders, and stress syndromes are much harder to factor for "service-connectedness." My favorite example of that dilemma was exemplified by a television program in 1985 commemorating the fortieth anniversary of the end of World War II. Some veterans had returned after forty years to the tropical island of Iwo Jima, where 25 percent of the American invaders were killed or wounded. A television cameraman tracked a sixty-five-year-old man walking along the beach with Mount Suribachi in the background. The man glanced up at the towering mountain with a full moon shining down on it and said, "I have seen that mountain in my dreams every night for forty years."

The Vietnam War further strained the concept of service-connected illness. Many of our soldiers hoped for a war wound that would take them back home with honor. Widespread use of alcohol, marijuana, and cocaine generated part of the medical and social problems of the Vietnam veteran, and drug and alcohol abuse often continued or worsened in civilian life. Certainly, awarding degrees of disability related to military service is not a very exact science and presents philosophic nightmares.

Age and Eligibility for Care

As an inexpensive but effective and sentimentally popular political gesture, Congress has a habit of rewarding special status to very elderly veterans of our wars. I have watched all veterans of the Spanish-American War and of the Civil War receive special care, and then die off. Currently, World War I veterans are nonagenarians or older, reaping their special status as the end of a wartime grouping. Recently, Congress decided to use age as one criterion for VA eligibility and decreed those above age sixty-five as eligible. This grandiose gesture failed to take into account that veterans over age sixty-five already use about half of the VA system's medical care resources, and the mandate was withdrawn. Thus, age seems a poor criterion for defining eligibility.

Penury, Affluence, and Rationing Care

As money became more scarce in the Veterans Administration, Central Office finally began rationing by annual income of veterans. As Drs. Wolcott and Smith describe, poor veterans (defined as single veterans with annual incomes of less than $18,000 or married veterans with less than $22,000) were eligible, but those with more income were excluded or were expected to share the cost burden. This sort of rationing scheme favors the poor people (which makes sense) but pushes the lower middle class downward (which does not make sense). Basically, how much medical care can you buy today with the excess money of a $22,000 income?

Rationing by Queueing

Shortages of most goods are exemplified by long lines of people waiting to buy gasoline in this country during the gas crisis, to buy bread and meat in Russia, or to receive minimal subsistence in drought-stricken Africa. The VA has been forced to rely on the queue increasingly in the last three or four years. Patients wait hours to be seen in the emergency room, hours to get their prescriptions filled, days to get a CAT scan or an MRI, and weeks or months before getting a berth in a primary-care clinic or a consultation from a surgical specialist. Waiting—the queue—is the most irritating type of rationing for both patient and caregiver. The queue may not be a bad solution to inhibit overuse of facilities for trivial problems (if medical problems can be so defined), but it is a dreadfully immoral way to handle seriously ill people. Still, VA hospitals have survived fairly well in this era of queue-rationing because, somehow, we have mostly sorted out the worried from the ill.

THE VA LEARNS TO SHIFT COSTS TO OTHERS

The national scene is replete with schemes by one agency or sector to shift its medical costs to another. Within the VA, cost shifting is practiced internally by a variety of petty frauds related to the RAM (resource allocation models) allocation of funds to the individual hospitals. More serious, however, is the cost shifting related to patients with dual eligibility for Medicare and VA care. More and more, patients needing such procedures as coronary artery bypass grafts and hip replacements are being quietly told by their VA doctor to take the problem to the private sector, usually the affiliated university hospital. Often, the institution and the surgeon receiving the patient agree informally to waive the 20 percent co-payment, which is billed to patients under Medicare.

Shifting of patients from VA to other agencies is unofficial, and the amount of cost shifting is unknown. Most of us, however, suspect that the amount in dollars is substantial. The overall costs for the federal government are significantly greater than if the VA had been funded to do the work. This sort of cost shifting is foolish—disrupting care of the patient and increasing costs for care only because two federal bureaucracies cannot work together, either by law, regulations, or inclination.

HOW BAD IS THE VA BUREAUCRACY?

Any contemplation of a federally funded system for medical care brings nightmares of a "big brother" type of oppressive and depressing bureaucracy. Doctors see their autonomy and clinical decision-making capacity being usurped by bureaucrats and their computers. The nature of the various constraints on the VA are worth brief discussion.

First, Congress has in some circumstances been more despotic than any bureaucracy. Congressional power has largely dictated the placement of hospitals, and the VA has no authority to close a facility, no matter how redundant or anachronistic. The Secretary of Veterans Affairs now has a committee reviewing the system, but it is proscribed by Congress from recommending any hospital closure. At the same time, the congressional committees are helpful with legislative matters generally and their staff quite knowledgeable about veterans' affairs. Sometimes, Congress is plainly ambiguous, as in passing legislation to mandate ambulatory care and preventive care for veterans, without too many specifics attached but also without allocating money. Any federal system of health care must ensure congressional oversight while protecting itself against congressional micromanagement.

What is viewed as bureaucracy emanates from a building in downtown Washington known as the VA Central Office. Central Office, with its Chief Medical Director, interprets congressional legislation and executes medical policy, currently under the overall supervision of the Secretary of Veterans Affairs and his fairly extensive bureaucracy. Over the years, Central Office has variously decentralized itself through regions and districts. Central office functions primarily as a management adviser for a $12 billion HMO (health management organization)-type of health care system. It issues standards of care and educates individual hospitals on such problems as quality assurance and reporting and measuring workload for RAM. A huge system needs a central office even though central officers (the Chief Medical Director and now the Secretary of Veterans Affairs) come and go, creating varying turbulence in the bureaucratic pot.

Although on paper the Chief Medical Director has awesome power, it is worth commenting that no one could imagine Washington actually dictating patient care in detail. What sane central officer would want to dictate which brand of nonsteroidal drug patients in San Diego can take, or deny a bone-barrow or liver transplant to a worthy veteran in Temecula, California? In any national health service, such central authority would surely not be exercised. The VA Central Office can be slow and nonresponsive, but when it issues foolish directives, the local hospitals tend to treat them as foolish suggestions, not directives, and quietly lose the pertinent papers. It is worth recalling that VA bureaucrats represent a sampling of all of us, and in a national health care system the bureaucracy would be similarly constructed.

In each local VA hospital, the buck finally stops. Decisions have to be made, resources allocated, and patients treated. Theoretically, at the local level, the Hospital Director is a tinhorn dictator, and the Chief of Staff a nag. In practice, the Chief of Staff and the Director tend to learn to work together, and if either gets too far out of line the staff complains and in about two to four years the invisible bureaucracy replaces the misfit. Several rather key administrative groups (the Personnel Office is the most obvious) are deluded by their Washington counterpart that they are working for some primal force emanating from Foggy Bottom along the Potomac. This delusion tends to dissipate quietly in the give-and-take of the daily workings of the hospital.

Although a few people in VA hospitals spend a lot of their time in administration, the majority of staff doctors feel they are personally little involved and that their professional decisions in the VA are remarkably free. I greatly prefer practicing as a VA physician and having the VA in the form of my local colleagues tell me that certain drugs should be used because they are cheaper, than practicing in the private sector and worrying that a patient will not be able to fill the prescription at all, be it for the cheaper or the more expensive drug. This feeling, ultimately, is what keeps a lot of good doctors in the VA system and is, perhaps, one motivating force toward a national health care system. The VA's decentralized administration deserves a careful look by health care planners.

CONCLUDING THOUGHTS

The VA is a national health care system, used mostly by poor old men, and it is effective because it has learned how to provide more health care with less money. Basically the hospitals have a fixed budget and a large workload and the methods of achieving frugal medical care vary somewhat from hospital to hospital. My Aunt Alice said that she learned to be poor by not spending any money. That mechanism worked for her for many years, but when Aunt Alice died, we had to tear down her house because years of leaking roofs had literally rotted out the stanchions. The VA's roof is beginning to leak, and a national system should note that fact. The VA's attempt to ration care as a way to confine costs is not satisfactory. As H. J. Aaron and W. B. Schwartz (referred to in the Wolcott and Smith essay) point out, there are no really satisfactory ways to ration medical care. If and when we achieve some type of universal health insurance in this country, we must ensure that costs are acceptable to the American people by providing an adequate but frugal system.

The need for universal access to health care in the United States is becoming urgent. If the U.S. is to create the best system, we need steadily to decrease, over the next ten to fifteen years, the number of people with no access to care or with inadequate insurance. If we cannot achieve these changes by consensus, we risk having some sort of inadequate system imposed by a politically driven Congress. In the gradualism which will lead eventually to universal access, the modest expansion of the VA by the addition of dependents of veterans, or other groups specified by Congress, makes sense. The fiscal reimbursement to the VA should be fair but adequate. The VA as a stronger system can move into the final pluralistic health care solution with confidence in itself and with strongly supportive patients, and it can bring leadership to the final coalition which will, I believe, give us the strongest and most flexible federal system.

A Comparative Perspective on National Health Insurance: The VA as Example and Vehicle for Change in the United States

David Wilsford

The VA hospital system in the United States is striking, for it occupies an extraordinarily anomalous position compared with the rest of America's health system. In the midst of the most resolute "free enterprise" system in the developed world, the VA is socialized medicine, and a very successful example of it.[1] In this essay, I will discuss the ways in which the VA resembles the socialized and national health insurance systems of all the advanced industrial democracies—with the exception of the United States—and I will suggest some ways in which the VA is pointing to the future of health system reform in this country. These changes will in the end make American health care look more like the rest of the developed world, in short, more like the VA. Yet, because of the pluralist character of American politics and the fragmented character of the American health care system, these changes—while inevitable—will come slowly. And, unfortunately, these changes may not, in the end, necessarily amount to a more coherent, rational overall system.

My argument in this comment is built around four points. First, cost is a problem everywhere and it pushes all systems to change. I call this the "fiscal imperative" in health care. Second, the amount of money spent in a health care system is poorly correlated, if at all, with the health status of the population within that system. In other words, in health care one does not necessarily get more by paying more. This factor is responsible for the perception that cost is, in fact, a problem, for if one got more by paying more, then consumers or payers could choose the relevant trade-off between available resources and increments of health desired. Third, in the search for solutions to the cost of care and to the kind of access that a system should provide, the United States must look elsewhere at relevant

Figure 1. Public Expenditures as Percentage of
Total Health Expenditures, OECD 7

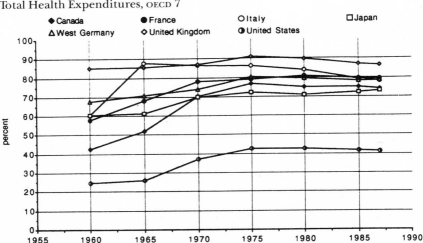

Data drawn from CREDES, *Eco-Santé* (Paris, 1989).

reference systems. These will be found in the rest of the developed world outside our borders, but they will also be found in the VA, a reference system within our borders. Finally, change will occur in the United States, but will it occur rapidly or slowly? All change is characterized by either acceleration or delay. For the United States, while change is inevitable, that change will occur more slowly than it would in other parts of the developed world.

In all of this, the VA will serve as an example for change, that is, a source of ideas and practices which the rest of the American health system will study and perhaps adopt. It will also serve as a vehicle for change. That is, the VA will increasingly be integrated into the mainstream health system. It already trains a large proportion of the American medical corps through its teaching hospitals. Adopting some VA practices will spill over into integrating additional VA functions into mainstream medicine, as well.

THE FISCAL IMPERATIVE IN HEALTH CARE

Each health system of the developed world has severe problems with cost. The entire postwar period is characterized by an increasingly large share of gross domestic product (GDP) being taken to pay for health care every year. Figure 2 shows that, while cross-sectionally

Figure 2. Health Expenditures as Percentage of GDP, OECD 7

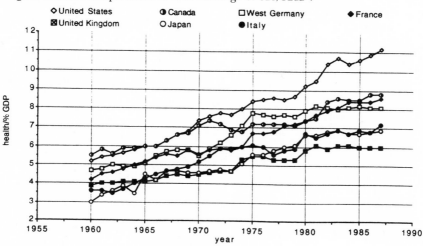

Data drawn from CREDES, *Eco-Santé* (Paris, 1989).

there are significant differences in the percentage of GDP devoted to health care, longitudinally each country of the OECD Group of Seven (G7) is faced with higher and higher costs every year. While the least expensive health system, the British, spent "merely" 6.0 percent of GDP on total health expenditures, this compares with "only" 3.9 percent of GDP in 1960. For the most expensive system of the G7, the American, 11.2 percent of GDP went to health care in 1987, compared with 5.1 percent in 1960. The point is surely not difficult to understand, but it is extraordinarily important nonetheless: in each of the advanced industrial democracies, the "fiscal imperative," that is, paying for the extensive delivery of sophisticated health care, has come to be a dominant concern for policymakers and other actors in the health system. As for the Americans, the rate of increase in the postwar period has been most rapid of all. While the cost of health care is clearly a problem for each of the seven countries, it is a problem most serious of all for the United States.

This point is only reinforced by figure 3. It presents expenditures on health care in terms of per capita OECD purchasing price parity units. This technique washes out any effect that size might have on the relationship between the seven countries. It also washes out the effects of volatile exchange-rate fluctuations. It is therefore a more reliable comparative indicator of the differences between countries and their evolution over time. If anything, figure 3 makes the United

Figure 3. Per Capita Health Expenditures in OECD Purchasing Price Parity
Units, OECD 7

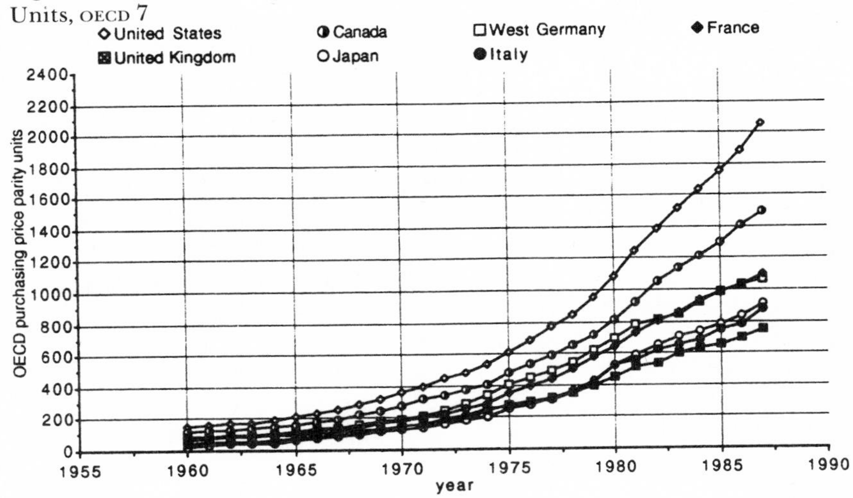

Data drawn from CREDES, *Eco-Santé* (Paris, 1989).

States look even worse because its rate of growth is notably more
rapid that those of its six counterparts and because the distance
between the highest spender, the United States, and all other spend-
ers is greater. Indeed, with the exception of Canada, the other G7
countries resemble each other closely in terms of levels of expenditures using per capita purchasing price parities.

However one may choose to display the data, they show that each
country has experienced increasingly pressing fiscal problems since
1960. What the data do not explicitly show but do implicitly suggest is
that the countries of the G7 with the flattest growth curves, and
especially those with the flattest curves through the 1980s, are those
countries which have taken the fiscal imperative most into account in
reforming the financing and delivery of health care in their system.
That is, flattening curves represent the effects of these countries'
policy responses to the fiscal imperative. It is no accident that the
sharpest curve, that for the United States, represents the system
characterized by the laxest policy response to the fiscal imperative.

COST VERSUS QUALITY IN THE DELIVERY OF HEALTH
CARE SERVICES

All health systems, indeed, all political systems, face scarcity. That is,
the resources available to pay for health care or any other good or

service are finite. Scarce resources imply that choices must be made. Each of the advanced, industrial democracies has a sophisticated, extensive health care system. Financing these systems is a major imperative facing public policymakers and private policy actors. The first choice facing these actors is how much to devote to the health care domain compared with other policy domains. Each political system and each society is a complex universe of many diverse demands for resources pressing in upon the state from societal actors. Given that all states face resource scarcity, the choices that are made to finance health care will inevitably lead to fewer resources being channeled to other policy domains in response to other societal demands. By the same token, restraining the cost of health care frees resources that may then be devoted to other needs or desires.

Likewise, within the health care domain, all states have decided, explicitly or by default, upon a certain level of expenditure—higher, as in the United States, or lower, as in Japan and the United Kingdom. But even in the American health care system—the most expensive one of all in terms of percentage of GDP devoted to it—$675.7 billion is not enough to pay for every medical good and service that could be supplied or that will certainly be demanded.[2] Therefore, within the health policy domain, choice must also come to the fore in channeling the available resources toward some and away from others. Cost will thus always be a central concern.

Yet one could more easily justify the choice to pay more if one clearly got more in return. Paying more for health care—in the aggregate—does not provide better health, however.[3] Of course, sometimes by spending more on an individual patient, better health is achieved. But even here, many expensive techniques are not more effective at the individual level than cheaper ones. The highest spender of the G7 countries, the United States, ranks sixth out of seven on two common indicators of aggregate health status, infant death rates, and life expectancy at birth (table 1). Of course, these are not the only possible indicators of health status. While most global measures focus on death rates, life expectancy, morbidity rates, and various other dysfunctions, these do not, unfortunately, always yield a coherent view of aggregate health status. For example, increased life expectancy may lead to increased dysfunctions. Nevertheless, the two indicators displayed in table 1 do provide a systematic comparative view of health status across the seven countries.

While the United States does badly on both indicators, one

Table 1. Total Health Expenditures and Health Status, 1987

	Total Health Expenditures		HEALTH STATUS			
	% of GDP	Ranking in Expenditures	Infant Death Rates[a]	Ranking in Infant Death Rates	Life Expectancy at Birth	Ranking in Life Expectancy
Canada	8.8	2	9.10	2	75.50	2
France	8.6	3	9.70	3	75.00	3
Germany	8.1	4	9.75	4	74.70	4
Italy	7.2	5	15.45	7	74.35	5
Japan	6.9	6	6.10	1	77.75	1
United Kingdom	6.0	7	10.80	5	74.30	7
United States	11.2	1	11.50	6	74.65	6

[a] Deaths per 1,000 live births.

Source: OECD, Financing and Delivering Health Care (Paris: OECD, 1987), pp. 33–36 for indicators of health status; and CREDES, *Eco-Santé* (Paris: CREDES, 1989), for health expenditures.

country that does comparatively quite well, Japan (the lowest infant death rate and the longest life expectancy), spends much, much less on health care. Japan ranks sixth in the OECD G7 on expenditures, spending just 6.9 percent of GDP on health. It is thus clear in the aggregate that the price-quality relationship in the American health care system is a very poor bargain indeed.

It is also a particularly poor bargain in the United States because access to health care is so severely restricted, compared with the other six countries, and in this respect, the United States is clearly exceptional. The question of cost versus quality thus takes on more urgency when one considers that thirty-five million Americans have no health care coverage whatsoever available to them, and that an estimated fifty million Americans are underinsured. That is, *there are more people living in the United States with no access to health care than live in all of Canada* (twenty-six million). The number of Americans without access to health care is *about the same as the population of Spain* (thirty-eight million). It is thus clear that spending 11.2 percent of American GDP on health care does not buy Americans a great deal of health. For many of them it buys none at all.

The cost-quality debate is only intensified by the fact that while modern medicine projects a hard scientific orientation, it is in reality only partly science and perhaps a rather small part, at that. Much of modern medicine is, rather, nonscientific: it is art and it is culture. Variations in practice patterns, which have been demonstrated across the countries of the OECD G7, as well as *within* countries, demonstrate this nonscientific element of modern medicine. There are significant variations in everything from incidence and types of surgery performed to types of treatments and drugs prescribed for a given condition to even the maladies that ail people across cultures. For example, Americans perform many cesarean sections (for which there is also very high variation across geographical regions of the United States), the French suffer from *crises de foie* (liver ailments), and the Japanese stay in the hospital an inordinate length of time. Suppositories and powders are popular in southern Europe; pills and capsules dominate northern Europe. None of these variations has much to do with science. Each of them has a great deal to do with idiosyncratic variation in culture and customs. Such nonscientific variation is pervasive in modern medicine. Should one therefore pay more in order to get better health? If so, pay more for what? Variation in practice patterns vitiates the ability to know what to buy because it is so difficult to know what works. This difficulty is based in seemingly arbitrary, nonscientific variations in diagnoses, treatments, and drugs. Cost does not, therefore, seem to equal quality very often.

REFERENCE SYSTEMS

It does not take a Nobel Prize winner to know that something is wrong with the American health care system. It is very expensive, and it ignores many citizens. Both scientific journals and the popular press have devoted increasing space to diagnoses of America's problem with health care and prognoses, usually quite pessimistic, about where America will go with health care. Yet part of the problem with this debate is that it usually occurs on exclusively American terms. That is, while Americans know that something is wrong with their system, they do not have very clear notions about possible alternatives. Americans, unlike the Japanese and perhaps other cultures, are not very good at seeking out *reference systems*. Yet such systems are a crucial source of ideas and alternatives in problem solving. The Japanese, for example, have aggressively sought out reference systems since the Meiji Restoration in the nineteenth century as they strove rapidly to modernize in the face of Western influence and competition. They sent delegations to Prussia, to cite one instance, to study the medical education system, then generally thought to be the most advanced in the world. They brought back the Prussian system and then *adapted it to their own purposes*, carefully studying and comparing all its features to their particular needs and capacities.

Seeking out reference systems does *not* constitute copying. Robert G. Evans (1986, p. 25) stated this point very well: "Nations do not borrow other nations' institutions. . . . The point is that by examining others' experience you can extend your range of perceptions of what is possible." Seeking out reference systems certainly *does* constitute a systematic search for plausible solutions and alternatives to one's own practices and it thus constitutes a way to avoid having to reinvent the wheel. Americans, unfortunately, have always been characterized by a rather self-satisfied faith in the individual and the market as the prime movers of innovation, efficiency, and justice. These attributes have not, however, been characteristic of America's rather poor contemporary efforts to reform a health care system that has clearly failed to reach important goals, such as cost containment and equitable access, much less those of innovation, efficiency, and justice.

Reference systems may exist within or without a particular overall system, like the American health care system. In this respect, one might and should look to the experiences in organizing and delivering health care in other countries that resemble the United States in important, relevant respects. These countries are usually referred to as the advanced, industrial democracies, as I have mentioned, and they resemble the United States in that they are each characterized by democratic politics, that is, the free play of social forces within the political system that compete for policy outcomes. They are also characterized by sophisticated, complex health care delivery systems, whose interests—such as providers—have long freely organized for political purposes. Finally, each country is characterized by what I have referred to as the "fiscal imperative." This is, on the one hand, the conjoining of great, ever-increasing demands for health care services with an ever-increasing technological and physical capacity to provide those services, in great confrontation, on the other hand, with increasingly finite resources to pay for health care. The fiscal imperative that arises from the relative scarcity of resources in the face of seemingly infinite demand pushes the actors in both the public and the private systems—providers, payers, consumers, and politicians—to struggle over reforms to system delivery and financing that define the very character of a health care system. This fiscal imperative, I have argued elsewhere, has pushed policymakers and payers everywhere to curb the autonomy of physician and patient to determine the kind of care that is delivered

(Wilsford, 1990a, 1990b, and 1991, pp. 272–91). It also pushes them to contain the incomes of providers.

The foregoing argument implies that the United States will have to seek out reference systems aggressively if its health care reform is to be at all successful in responding to the fiscal imperative. Like the Japanese, Americans will have to cultivate the outlook and skills necessary to import, examine, adopt selectively, and adapt aggressively the features which have enabled other, similar systems to deliver more quality health care to more people at lesser cost than we have been able to do. That is, as Evans has argued, we must seek alternatives by looking outside and then, not copying, but adapting. As Evans knows, politics is about policies that are possible at any one moment in a nation's history, given levels of resources, cultural and historical constraints, and the configuration of social and political forces. These factors change over time, of course, so that what may be impossible during one era may very well become plausible, even probable, in a future era as these variables change.

But while many good reference systems exist among the advanced, industrial democracies, there is also one very good reference system that exists within the United States. That system is the Department of Veterans Affairs. The VA represents a system wholly unlike the "free-enterprise" system of the rest of the United States that Roemer (1977) described. The VA, in fact, resembles the health care systems of our advanced, industrial, democratic counterparts far more than it resembles anything in the United States. What can one learn, then, from the VA?

In their essay "The Role of the Veterans Administration in a National Health Care System," Mark W. Wolcott and Charles B. Smith paint a very compelling portrait of the VA that highlights the ways in which it resembles these other socialized and national health insurance systems: The VA is centrally managed. It has low budgets. Providers are salaried. The VA stresses low-technology medical responses rather than high-technology ones. There are great economies of scale. Many comprehensive guidelines are centrally enforced. These work to lower costs. Treatments and referrals are strictly circumscribed by these guidelines. Hospital stays tend to be much shorter. Staffing is extremely lean, about half of the staff available in the comparable community hospital. Physician costs are much lower, as well, in part due to the salaried structure of the physician staff, in part due to the low differential between general practitioner and specialist salaries and in part because the incentive structure surrounding the VA physician works to limit physician-initiated charges, such as the number of tests performed and the types and number of drugs prescribed. And there is very low administrative overhead compared with the free-enterprise American system.

As to the quality and kind of care that the VA provides, one can readily see the similarities between it and other socialized and national health insurance systems. Unlike the free-enterprise-based American system, the VA does not provide ready access to high-technology, rescue medicine. It does not provide *unregulated* access to any procedure, test, or drug that might be therapeutically indicated or beneficial. What it does provide is ready access for its eligible patient pool to comprehensive, basic, low-technology care. Limitations on its budgets force the VA, like the British or other systems, to ration some kinds of more expensive care and to reduce costs in other ways. Financial constraints, given the priority assigned to the provision of comprehensive, basic care, lead to practices such as queuing (waiting lists) for nonemergency procedures and to the implementation of a host of practice guidelines such as those I have mentioned that circumscribe the physician's traditional clinical autonomy. In terms of basic care, the VA does much more with much less. In terms of rescue, miracle medicine, the VA does very little indeed.

For these reasons, the VA system is very cost-effective. In other words, for the amount of money the VA has to work with, it accomplishes a great deal. With a budget of $11.2 billion, or less than 2 percent of total expenditures in the United States on health care, the VA is responsible for treating eleven million eligible patients, or more than 4 percent of the American population. And while the increase in private-sector expenditures in the United States has averaged well over 10 percent a year for more than twenty years, the average increase in the VA's budget for the same period was less than 2 percent a year, far below the inflation rate. But the VA can be judged cost-effective according to this evidence only if one has chosen to trade access to basic care for all citizens for access to high-tech, glitzy care for some. Since both the eligible patient pool of the VA and that of the British National Health Service (NHS) are quite content with their systems, one may assume that this trade-off is in general supported by the patients.

DIFFICULTIES WITH HEALTH CARE REFORM

The VA and a host of other health care systems in the advanced, industrial democracies can serve as reference systems for reform of the American health care system. Further, one attractive feature of the VA as a reference system to Americans is that it is present in our own backyard.[4] That is, it is one that is culturally, politically, and economically imbedded within the vast, uncoordinated, private-enterprise-based nonsystem that is called health care in America. It may, therefore, serve as a focal source in our search for alternatives in managing and delivering modern health care services.

Yet I do not wish to suggest that reform is easy, even with a shining example in one's own yard. Change is difficult, especially in established systems which are characterized by enduring habits, unquestioned values, and entrenched interests. Each of these characterizes health care in America. And in any country, it is very difficult to start from scratch, wiping a slate clean and redesigning a system on a tabula rasa. I will momentarily suggest that nonincremental change is, in fact, more easily accomplished in some political systems than in others. In particular, state-led systems are more successful at starting over from scratch, as the British did with the NHS in 1948. But even in these systems, traditions weigh heavily and often constrain just how far one can go. Payment systems, for example, are often influenced by such traditions. The fee-for-service payment system in France, Canada, and Japan, is anchored in cultural habits; both physicians and patients cling to such habits and constrain state-led reforms in some important ways.

History also influences the character of organizational reform, and this influence may stretch far back into time. The contemporary character of the British, French, Canadian, German, and Japanese health care systems hearkens back to similar organizational forms that developed quite early on. For example, it is unlikely that the creation of the National Health Service would have been as successful or as rapid as it was without the historical foundations of the early friendly societies, the mutual aid associations that grew up at the close of the nineteenth century, or without the immediate historical influence of Britain's wartime medical services. In Japan, the extremely segmented character of the contemporary health system emerges out of a persistent but piecemeal effort by the Japanese state to cover more and more of the occupational categories of Japanese workers, beginning with the merchant seamen in Japan's early years of modernization. This segmentation is illustrated by Table 2.

The tabula rasa problem in reform is thus better recognized and incorporated into reform efforts than refuted or resisted. In other

Table 2. Organization of Health Insurance Funds in Japan

Employees Insurance	Type of Employees	# of insured persons (10,000s) (5–30-85)
Health insurance		
General employees		
Government-managed health insurance	Employees at workplaces (mainly small/medium enterprises) with no Health Insurance Society	3,234 (27.0%)
Society-managed health insurance	Employees at workplaces (mainly large enterprises) with a Health Insurance Society (KEMPOREN)	2,911 (24.3%)
Day laborers	Persons employed on a daily basis or for a set period within two months	36 (0.3%)
Seamen's Insurance	Seamen (on defined vessels)	60 (0.5%)
National Public Service Employees MAAs*	Public service employees and employees of Japan National Railways, Japan Monopoly Corp., Nippon Telephone & Telegraph	485 4.0%)
Local Public Service MAAs	Local public service employees	692 (5.7%)
Private School Teachers and Employees MAAs	Private school teachers and employees	68 (0.7%)
Regional Insurance		
National Health Insurance Municipalities and National Health Insurance Associations	Those not covered by employees insurance (e.g., farmers, self-employed, physicians and liberal professions, small business, artisans)	3,887 (32.5%) 349 (2.9%)
Municipalities	Retirees formerly covered by employees insurance (including dependents)	267 (2.2%)

Source: Japan International Cooperation Agency, *National Health Administration in Japan*, vol. 3 (Tokyo, [1988]), p. 195.
*Mutual Aid Association.

words, it is not realistic to expect that the VA or any other reference system can be copied, cut from whole cloth, and imposed upon the American health care system. A number of countries that have adopted forms of comprehensive national health insurance have done so by building upon and incorporating past practices and organizational forms. In Germany, both methods of payment and the organization of sickness funds grew out of the early history of the German health care system. The block-like structure of the Japanese health care system, seen in Table 2, is a result of the Japanese inclination to build the future upon the past, adding on ever more segments of society, without unduly disturbing older structures. Yet the structure hangs together, for the Japanese state has taken the lead in providing the design and the glue for an overall, comprehensive system.

The VA or other reference systems, as sources of ideas for reform in the United States, will not dictate all the features of a successful reform. Reformers will have to adopt ideas and practices selectively from these reference systems, and they will have to craft them on, little by little, to the existing system. Such a system may look segmented, like a structure made out of different colored blocks that are also of different shapes. But like the Japanese health care system, such a structure, if well designed, can hold together remarkably well and provide high-quality extensive care to many for a relatively low price.

ACCELERATION VERSUS DELAY OF REFORM

One way in which the United States differs from every other advanced industrial democracy is in the extreme pluralism of its health care politics. This is not to suggest that other systems are not characterized by a diversity of conflicting interests. Each system has its physicians, nurses, patients, hospital directors, pharmaceutical manufacturers, third-party payers, high-technology innovators, and so on. Some of these systems are segmented, like the Japanese, or decentralized, like the German, or relatively centralized, like the VA or the British. But these other systems also tend to be state-led, in contrast to the United States, thus exhibiting a greater coherence of public policy-making in the health care domain, a coherence given to policy by the state authorities, often in conjunction with societal actors. These systems also often exhibit greater speed in undertaking reform.

But, I have argued, the fiscal imperative *will* play out its effects

across all the health care systems of the advanced, industrial democracies, including the United States. The extreme pluralism of the
American system will permit well-organized interests within that
system significantly to resist the onset of reforms. But they will not be
able to delay reform forever.

We may indeed see in ten years or so that the liberal parenthesis
in modern American medicine has come to a close. That is, that the
glorious period of the solo practitioner especially characteristic of
much of the postwar history of American medicine was in fact a mere
parenthesis in the whole history of medicine. For decades and
centuries before the opening of this parenthesis, medicine was
artisanal and craft-based with little marginal advantage over other
competing dispensers of health, such as the witches, traveling medicine men, and other healers who plied the byways of the nation. The
rise and consolidation of modern orthodox medicine with the
advent of scientific advances constituted the early opening of the
liberal parenthesis. With the closing of that parenthesis, we will see a
decline of solo practice, a decline in incomes and prestige relative to
the rest of society, a gradual concentration of medical workers into
larger hierarchical organizations, a gradual "proletarianization" of
the medical work force, that is, providers, to borrow Charles Derber's
phrase (1982).

Change *has* occurred in the American health care system. Who
would have predicted the advent of diagnostic-related groups (DRGs),
especially under the Reagan administration, champion of free-market economics? Yet the fiscal imperative renders traditional ideological posturing irrelevant, and the Reagan and Bush administrations
have engaged in many reforms that have reduced providers' clinical
autonomy, as well as their incomes. And while the American system is
still a resolutely free-enterprise one compared with its OECD counterparts, these important reforms at the level of the federal government
have had and will continue to have important effects on the private
sector. Federal government reforms in the United States often carry
with them significant spillover effects insofar as they serve as bench-
marks for the private sector.

The difference is that *state-led systems can be reformed more comprehen-
sively and more rapidly than society-led systems*. The VA is, of course, the
equivalent of a state-led system. This is why the VA has been so
successful in reforming its structures and its practices in response to
the fiscal imperative. The rest of the American system is, by contrast,
society-led. This society-led system will neither quickly nor easily

adopt reforms from any of the state-led reference systems. It may well, in typical American fashion, adopt reforms piecemeal, disjointedly, without a clear plan for comprehensive change.

Two evolutionary changes in the United States, however, may augue more positively for a more hopeful long-term scenario. The first is the emergence of a business-government consensus that health costs too much. The advent and rise of HMOs constitute one early indication of how American health care may be evolving. HMOs are, after all, mini-socialized systems, much like a microscale VA or British NHS. The second is the increasing structural role of the VA in the mainstream American system. Wolcott and Smith point out very clearly how the VA has come to play an ever more important role in mainstream system functions, such as medical education or treating the indigent, and they suggest the plausibility of increasing this role even further. In this way, the VA may be, as I have contended, a *vehicle* for change in the free-enterprise American system.

HEALTH CARE AS A PRIVATE GOOD VERSUS A PUBLIC GOOD

There is a final difference between the VA and other nationalized health care systems and the American system. That is the important divergence in notions of who is ultimately responsible for the health care of a people. In the VA and in all the other advanced, industrial democracies, there is a widely shared belief that health care is a social, public responsibility. Just as with roads and bridges, postal services, and national defense, health care constitutes a policy domain in which the collective good calls for government intervention. This is so because free markets in health care have been historically incapable of providing public goods. This in turn hinges, of course, upon the belief that all members of society have some right to an adequate level of care regardless of market position, that is, that health care is a public not a private good.

The VA was founded upon the belief that all veterans deserve care, and although how one defines eligibility as a veteran has changed over time, as Wolcott and Smith show, the overriding principle of social duty to citizens (that is, veterans) still holds, rather than the principle of ability to pay. The health systems of Japan, Canada, France, Britain, Germany, Italy, and every other OECD country increasingly have embodied the principle of social responsibility to citizens since the turn of the century. The postwar period is particularly marked in this regard. In all these reference systems, health care has come to be regarded as a public good.

This suggests that until there is a consensus among American citizens that health care is a public good rather than a private one—not just a business-government elite consensus that it costs too much—reform modeled after elements of the VA or other reference systems will remain ad hoc, chaotic, poorly coordinated, incremental rather than comprehensive, and slow. That is, while there will be many reforms, they may not end up constituting a solid structure but rather a poorly designed fragile one. If so, the newly emerging consensus of business and government leaders based upon the effects of the fiscal imperative—that we must reform because the cost is too high—*will* in the end curb the autonomy and incomes of providers. But it will not necessarily improve access to the American system for those large numbers of citizens who have heretofore been excluded.

NOTES

1. I take this label from Milton I. Roemer (1977). In using it, I certainly do not mean to suggest that none of the American health care system is publicly financed or publicly administered. Yet compared with all of America's counterparts in the Organization for Economic Cooperation and Development (OECD), the health system in the United States is the only one clearly dominated by private delivery and private financing (see fig. 1).

2. The dollar amount is the estimate of the United States Commerce Department for 1990. Others statistics confirm, or even worsen, this portrait. For example, in 1990 total spending on health care increased by 11.9 percent. One survey also showed that the annual cost of employee health benefits to the businesses offering them increased by 17.1 percent between 1989 and 1990. The average cost—*to the firm*—rose to a total of $3,217 *per worker* (*New York Times*, January 29, 1991).

3. This generalization clearly does not hold in the same way for developing countries.

4. Or indeed, even, in our own "front yard," as Margaret P. Battin has suggested in her discussion.

REFERENCES

Derber, Charles, ed. (1982). *Professionals as Workers: Mental Labor in Advanced Capitalism*. Boston: G. K. Hall.
Evans, Robert G. (1986). "The Spurious Dilemma: Reconciling Medical Progress and Cost Control," *Health Matrix* 1 no. 4: 25–34.
Roemer, Milton I. (1977). *Comparative National Policies on Health Care*. New York: Marcel Dekker.

Wilsford, David. (1990a). "Expertise versus Cost: The Triumph of the Fiscal Imperative over Professional Autonomy." Paper presented at the Seventh International Conference of Europeanists, Washington, D.C., March 1990.

————. (1990b). "The Fiscal Imperative in Health Care: Responses in Seven Countries to Increased Demand and Scarcer Resources." Paper presented at the Second World Congress on Health Economics, University of Zurich, Switzerland, September 10–14, 1990.

————. (1991). *Doctors and the State: The Politics of Health Care in France and the United States*. Durham, N.C.: Duke University Press.

PART IV

Ethics and the Design of National Health Care

Health Care in a National Health Program: A Fundamental Right

Kenneth N. Buchi, M.D., and
Bruce M. Landesman

Do or should Americans have a right to health care or some appropriate level of it? To explore this difficult and complex question, we must say something about rights and ways to justify them; about considerations which favor a right to health care; about what level and kind of care the right may involve; and about what can be said against such a right. We believe that a right to a decent level of health care should be recognized and enacted in public policy.

RIGHTS

Health Care as a Claim Right

To say that people have a right to have or do something implies that whether they have it or not, or do it or not, is *their choice*; it is up to them. They have a legitimate and strong claim to choose to have or to do. Some rights are best described as "liberties." A person may choose to do something, but others do not necessarily have to allow him or her to do it. For example, a basketball player is "at liberty" to score a basket but the opponent does not have to permit this. Other rights—those we will focus on—are stronger; they are not mere liberties but are claim rights. This means that if a person has such a right, others have a correlative obligation or duty not to interfere. When a basketball player is awarded a foul shot, those on the opposing team may not try to block it—they have a duty to let the player shoot. Our most important legal and constitutional rights are claim rights. I have a right to free speech, which means that neither private parties nor the government may stop my speech.

Health Care as a Positive Right

The right to health care we have in mind, then, is a claim right, a right which is also the basis of duties in others. What are the duties? To answer this, we must distinguish between negative and positive rights. A right is a negative right when the correlative duties of others are duties of noninterference only. Thus my right of free speech is a negative right if the only duty others have with respect to that right is to nót interfere with my attempts to speak, to leave me alone to speak as I choose. It is not difficult to respect negative rights. All one has to do is leave other people alone and mind one's own business. Negative rights—to life, to liberty, to the acquisition of property—have historically played a large role in the American political tradition.

Positive rights, on the other hand, require more than noninterference. They require aid; they require that one help others obtain what they have a right to. My right to life is a negative right if not killing me is all that others must do to respect it. But if they must come to my aid when I am in danger of dying, by providing or paying to provide needed health care, then my right is a positive right. Positive rights are sometimes called welfare rights, for they involve positive contributions to the welfare of others. It is not enough simply to leave people alone; one must also help them when they are unable to help themselves.

The social enforcement of both negative and positive rights is expensive, but that of positive rights is usually more expensive. To protect an individual's negative rights, for example, to free speech or security of property, a police force, courts, and prisons are required to deter those who would invade these rights. It is also important for the state to restrain its own tendency to violate negative rights. All this is not cheap, as we know from the cost of the judiciary and the correction system. But though expensive, negative rights are less costly to maintain than positive rights, which require both programs to provide the help mandated by the right and agencies to administer these programs. Since such programs and agencies are funded from tax revenues, they are in reality transfer payments from those who have much to those with little. For this reason, such programs and the positive rights they secure are less popular in the United States than negative rights and the judicial institutions they require.

It is safe to say that the right to health care as a negative right is recognized in this country as part of one's general right to liberty. If you choose to seek medical help and have the money or insurance to pay for it, no one may stop you. The current issue has to do with health care as a positive right—not only something which people can claim as their due but something which society must provide to those unable to secure it by themselves. The obligation of citizens correlative to this right is that they provide the tax revenues to fund the needed programs. It is this right and set of correlative obligations that we will examine.

Health Care as an Inherent Moral Right

Before concluding this discussion of the nature of rights, it is important that we distinguish legal from moral rights. A right is a legal right when it exists as a matter of law and is enforced by the judicial authorities. A right is a moral right when it exists as a matter of moral principle, when moral reflection and argumentation are the grounds for its validity. A society may fail to give legal recognition to moral rights, as happens in regimes which either deny or do not protect what are generally accepted to be basic human rights. When we argue for a right to health care, we are arguing *both* for health care as a moral right and for its recognition as a legal right.

Within the domain of legally recognized rights one can distinguish those rights which exist prior to policies which secure them, and those which are the creatures of and dependent on policy. Suppose that a policy is thought desirable and enacted into law—for example, the practice of allowing elderly persons to pay only half-fare for public transportation. Once this law is enacted, senior citizens have a valid legal entitlement, a legal right, to pay half-fare for travel. There is, however, no fundamental moral right which existed prior to the enactment of the policy that made its passage morally mandatory. The policy is "a good idea," a desirable way to promote the common good, but not a mandatory demand of justice. The right is therefore the effect of the policy and comes into being only when it is enacted. Such a right is a *conventional* right.

Consider, on the other hand, a right to nondiscrimination in matters of public education. *Brown v. Board of Education* recognized and secured this right, but it seems reasonable to propose that the right preceded Brown. It existed not solely as a result of the policy or practice Brown announced but as the basic *reason* for that legal decision. Let's call such legal rights, which are based on prior moral right, *inherent* rights. The right to health care we wish to defend is an inherent right.

Rights and Self-Respect

Our final general point about rights is that when one has a right to something, one can "stand up and demand it as one's due." One need not beg for it or convince others of its desirability on a case-by-case basis. Receiving the aid to which one has a right is a different thing from receiving aid that has been gratuitously offered as a matter of charity. For this reason, it has been suggested that having rights is importantly connected with self-respect and social status.[1] To be a rights-holder with regard to certain things is to have a social recognition which promotes one's sense of worth and equality with others. A right is thus desirable not only for what is received through its exercise but also for its further effects on securing respect and status.

JUSTIFYING RIGHTS

Claims that people have certain rights require justification. Rights have typically been justified three different ways. The first holds that certain rights are natural and self-evident—basic propositions whose truth everyone is compelled to admit and which require no further defense. The Declaration of Independence invokes such a view when it holds as "self-evident" the truths "that all men are created equal [and] endowed by their creator with . . . inalienable rights" to life, liberty, and the pursuit of happiness. The problem with claims to self-evidence is that people may differ in what they accept as self-evident, and this view provides no grounds for adjudicating among conflicting claims. Further, and more important, there must surely be some reasons why certain things are legitimately demanded as rights and others are not. But this view is silent here.

The second theory remedies this by basing the recognition of rights on their tendency to promote general human well-being. On this *utilitarian* basis, rights are not simply self-evident but are justified by their consequences, their results. Since rights to health care meet urgent human needs, there is reason to think that the recognition of such rights might well be utility-maximizing. But there is a well-known problem of appeals to utility which weakens this argumentative ground. Utilitarian justification relies on the total quantity of human happiness or welfare that a particular system or policy produces, and it chooses that alternative which produces the greatest

---

[1]For a discussion of this idea, see Joel Feinberg, "The Nature and Value of Rights," *Journal of Value Inquiry* 4 (1970): 243–57.

total amount. The net happiness of each person is added together to achieve a sum total; it is this sum which plays the justificatory role. Utilitarianism is thus not directly concerned with the *distribution* of welfare among people. The distribution matters only insofar as it affects the general total. A system of unequal rights could receive utilitarian preference over equal rights if the improved welfare of those with greater rights under the system outweighs the losses of those with lesser rights such that the total benefit is greater than what a system of equality produces. To defend a right of *equal* access to health care, the utilitarian perspective is inadequate.

The third perspective is, unlike utilitarianism, inherently distributive. Its basic idea is that there are certain individual human interests which are of such fundamental importance to the ability to lead a decent life that *each* and *every* individual person should be able to satisfy those interests. This distributive perspective involves four elements, as follows:

1. First is the claim that people have fundamental interests such as the need for food, shelter, and clothing.

2. Second is the claim that it is a good and desirable thing that people are able to satisfy these fundamental interests. People are happier and lead better lives when they can do so, and it is difficult to deny that this is better than the frustration of such interests.[2]

3. Third is the idea that *if anyone is able to have these interests met, all should be able to do so.* This is an explicitly egalitarian premise, requiring that such interests be satisfied for each and every person, if they are satisfied for any. This differentiates this view from utilitarianism in requiring the satisfaction of the interests and well-being of *each* and *every* individual, not the highest sum total. It is concerned with the human welfare of *each*, not the general welfare of *all*.

4. Fourth, there is the idea that the only way to secure each and every one's fundamental interests is by attributing to individuals both moral and legal rights to the satisfaction of those interests and/or to the means necessary for their satisfaction. To accept these interests as rights makes their satisfaction a matter of particular moral urgency. Such fundamental interests need special defense against two strong opponents: the reality of the social and economic system, which results in some people being unable to satisfy these interests through

---

[2]This perspective shares with utilitarianism both the idea that it is a good thing to promote human well-being and the grounding of rights not on self-evident truths but in fundamental interests.

their own efforts, and the legislative enactment of social and economic policies that promote the general welfare at the expense of the
poor—for example, by cutting taxes to promote the well-being of the
middle classes and the affluent at the expense of social services for
those unable to afford them. A socially recognized claim of right
counters both tendencies. It underlies a demand that society act
positively to correct the vagaries of economic fortune and directs
legislation to give priority to the fundamental interests of the least
fortunate.[3]

THE RIGHT TO HEALTH CARE AS A RIGHT TO AN ADEQUATE LEVEL OF CARE

While using this scheme to justify a right to health care, we want to
make clear that the right to health care we wish to defend and put on
a secure basis is not the right to any care anybody might want but *a
right to an adequate or basic or decent level of care*. Many people in our
society are unable to secure even this level of care.[4] How has this come
about? Historically, physicians have been a primary source of health
care, and in the past were able and willing to meet the need for health
care as a positive right by directly providing uncompensated care to
those unable to pay for it. This was, and in many cases still is, a well-
accepted and widely practiced obligation of the medical profession.
The delivery of health care, however, has changed dramatically
during the past thirty years, and physicians are no longer the sole
caregivers. Physicians personally account for only 20 percent of
actual care delivery. The remainder, although to varying degrees
directed by or influenced by physicians, is actually delivered by
hospitals, nursing homes, extended-care facilities, home health agencies, and a multitude of other health care organizations and individuals. In many instances, the care delivered by these other entities is
directed or influenced by third-party payers (insurance, business,
and government) as much as by physicians, or even more so.

    Along with the shift in control of health care from physicians to
third-party organizations has come a corresponding change in the
perception of physicians and other health care professionals about

---

[3]This way of seeing rights and justice as giving special emphasis to the needs of the
least fortunate is firmly defended by John Rawls in his well-known work *A Theory of Justice*
(Cambridge, Mass.: Harvard University Press, 1971).

[4]For a chilling description of this, see "Health Problems of Inner City Poor Reach
Crisis Point," *New York Times*, December 24, 1990.

their profession(s) and their professional ethics. Many physicians have accepted the premise that health care is a business. Medicine is now operated as a business by large health care corporations managed by highly paid administrators (many of whom are also physicians), and by solo- or small group-practice physicians/small businessmen. The ethics of medicine require that "a physician shall be dedicated to providing competent medical service with compassion and respect for human dignity."[5] The ethics of business are less grounded in respect for human dignity and more concerned with financial survival and success.

This poses a difficulty, in that physicians appropriately recognize that guaranteeing a positive right to health care imposes a specific obligation to be sure that care is provided. When the question then arises concerning on whom the obligation falls to provide that care, the answer is muddled because both practical and financial limits preclude physicians from providing it all, and the "business" managers of health care delivery can provide it only as long as their ability to generate profits and continue operations is not threatened. The best way out of this dilemma is a societal consensus that the obligation to provide the degree of health care for which there is a right should be borne by society in general, including physicians and health care managers, through funding by the government.

But how much health care should government underwrite for all? Given the ever-inherent limitation of financial resources, for example, it is difficult to say that everyone should have an equal right to every expensive health technologic procedure, such as an organ transplant or magnetic resonance imaging scans, when by so doing the resources used in those cases would then not be available to provide more basic or less costly care to a greater number of people. The resolution of this problem is that there should be an "adequate level" or "basic level" of health care to which everyone has a right. Health care services which exceed this basic level would then be distributed as they currently are, on the negative-rights basis that those who are able to afford or provide additional services for themselves will purchase them.

How should this basic level of care be defined? There have been many attempts by interested groups to provide such a definition. These range in scope and underlying motivations from the "ideal" defined in the Organizational Charter of the World Health Organiza-

---

[5]*Principles of Medical Ethics* (Chicago: American Medical Association, 1980).

recently adopted by the
ch defines the maximum
funded with a set amount
also the Basic Benefits
oadly based input by the
People;[7] and perhaps the
developed by the state of
equitably.[8]

evel of care might be to
rovide *needed* care to all
and define the *need* by
to match this responsibility
with availa   rces. Criteria for provision would in a
sense be soc   on of who are most in need of societal
resources, and thus who (or what services) would represent a less
urgent use of those resources. The criteria might also be agreed-
upon equivalent *needs*. The criteria could be many potential factors.
Age or potential longevity could be used, for example, basing decisions on the presumed length of life prolonged in an individual case
per unit of resource spent. Various attempts have been made to
quantify these factors under such terminology as "Quality-Adjusted
Life Years."[9]

An adequate level of health care might also be defined as that
which can maximize individual well-being and opportunity to the
extent that available resources would allow. Relative individual and
societal benefits of the health care service could be incorporated
(that is, greater weight placed on immunizations, which benefit the
individual *and* the society in general). Such a definition does not limit
choices to *all* needed care, or *all* available care but would allow
flexibility. What is considered "adequate" could change as additional
knowledge develops concerning outcomes or opportunity, or as
societal resources available for health care change. The underlying

[6]American Medical Association Board of Trustees, *AMA's Minimum Benefits Plan*,
Report Y (Chicago: American Medical Association, June 1990).

[7]Health Policy Agenda for the American People, *Basic Benefits Package*. Ad Hoc
Committee on Basic Benefits (Governor Scott M. Matheson, Chair), June 1988.

[8]"Oregon Puts Bold Health Plan on Ice," *Science* 249 (1990): 468–71.

[9]J. LaPuma and E. F. Lawlor, "Quality-adjusted Life Years: Ethical Implications for
Physicians and Policy Makers," *Journal of the American Medical Association* (hereafter *JAMA*)
263 (1990): 2917–21.

consensus that an adequate level of health care should be provided would still remain.

We want to reemphasize that we do not wish to define exactly what an appropriate "adequate" level of health care should be. Quite the contrary, since much of the debate and effort which has historically tried to do so has thus far only impaired the development of a consensus that *any* level of health care is an inherent right. The attitudes of many segments of society (or their representatives) have instead been that unless a basic amount of health care can be defined and agreed upon in advance, they are not willing to accept the responsibility for providing it. We thus reemphasize that our goal is to justify that the inherent right to health care exists. If society can agree that a right to health care exists, then the tone of the ongoing debate changes significantly. It is no longer necessary to struggle with defining specifically that one health care service is a right and another is not (in an endless succession of such services) before being able to agree that there is a right to *any* such service. Rather, the debate can more appropriately and likely more effectively focus on determining whether a particular service improves individual (or societal) well-being or opportunity, and thus can be considered within the overall health care framework as part of "adequate" care. In the case of expensive technology, the debate can also focus on whether the potential for individual well-being or opportunity provided by the service or procedure justifies the expense enough to be considered adequate, or does it, in fact, fall into a realm of "heroic" care. These debates would also be able to change with changing resources and knowledge, while still focusing on whether, considering that change in resource or knowledge, the health care item should still be "adequate" or not.

Similar uncertainties about an adequate level of provision have characterized the public education system without disturbing the consensus which has long existed that education is a fundamental right which society has the obligation to provide for all its members. In actual practice, the amount of public education provided, and the identification of which members of society it will be provided for, have varied (and continue to do so) in response to societal resources and to changing interpretations of need. Most states currently agree that public education must be provided to all children from first through twelfth grades. Some also include kindergarten, based both on a societal recognition of its importance and on available resources. In the early years of our country's history, secondary education was not felt to be as necessary a right, and thus was not always provided at taxpayers' expense. It has only been in recent decades that the "right" to an adequate level of education has been extended to the developmentally or physically disabled segments of our society, through federal statutes developed by consensus as societal attitudes and resources change. Some states have even recognized a societal responsibility to provide higher education by allowing tuition-free college attendance for in-state residents, as California did through the 1970s. Many states still recognize that responsibility by having lower tuition levels for state residents attending state-supported colleges and universities; but as societal resources have diminished, even in-state residents have had to assume some of the financial burden.

Nevertheless, throughout all these changes in scope, the fundamental consensus has always remained: society has an obligation to provide an education for its members. Few will argue against this premise, although debate will always continue on what the current level of provision for that obligation should be.

JUSTIFYING A RIGHT TO AN ADEQUATE LEVEL OF HEALTH CARE

We return now to an attempt to justify a right to a basic level of care, using the "distributive/utilitarian" scheme discussed earlier. There are strong and persuasive arguments favoring the right to a basic level of care which we believe are generally accepted and not highly controversial. Objections to the right to health care tend to be based on counterarguments; that is, they do not reject the arguments *favoring* the right, but hold, instead, that there are reasons *against* it which are stronger and more weighty. We will therefore dwell only briefly on the reasons favoring such a right and spend the bulk of our time refuting the major counterarguments.

The first strand of our framework for justifying rights involves the claim that people have certain interests whose satisfaction is necessary for them to lead minimally good lives. Defining such interests can be done "subjectively," by identifying interests whose satisfaction is necessary for people to reach a tolerable level of happiness or contentment. Or it can be done "objectively" by reference to what an ideal of the good life [or lives] for humans requires.[10] In either case, it is likely that life itself, adequate nutrition, shelter, the minimizing of pain and suffering, and self-determination will all be considered elements of the good life. Health care thus also becomes an element of the good life, since it is an essential means to achieve or maintain these basic interests. Briefly, health care does or can do the following: save life, restore complete health, bring a person to as healthy a state as is physically possible, prevent ill health, relieve pain, suffering, and distress, restore or secure opportunities, and provide information necessary for exercising informed choice.[11] All these things meet fundamental interests and so it makes sense to think that health care will be an urgent good in any plausible theory of the good life. Of course, not all health care meets such urgent needs. Some forms of therapy, such as some cosmetic surgery, satisfy wants, not needs. That does not vitiate the case for the urgency of much health care. It simply again emphasizes that we must better distinguish what health care can do and secure a right to that "adequate" level of care which meets the most urgent or accepted needs.

Given that health care meets such essential interests, it is also clear—in accord with the second strand of our framework—that widening access to health care will promote the general welfare. But we argue that access to adequate care should be provided to all as a matter of right. This requires appeal to the egalitarian distributive premise that people should be treated equally with regard to basic health care. *Every* individual should be able to secure an adequate level of care. Although a full-scale defense of this egalitarian claim is beyond the scope of this essay, we point out that equality is a deeply held value in our political system. Although it can mean different things, surely most would agree that with respect to the means necessary for meeting our most urgent interests, inequality is acceptable only if there are morally important differences between people that justify the inequality. The most familiar and persuasive reason for inequality is that people *merit* or *deserve* different goods on the

---

[10]For an astute discussion of these alternatives, see T. M. Scanlon, "Preference and Urgency," *Journal of Philosophy*, 72 (1975): 655–69.

[11]For a discussion of what health care does for us, see the President's Commission for the Study of Ethical Problems in Medicine and Biomedical and Behavioral Research, *Securing Access to Care* (Washington, D.C.: Government Printing Office, 1983). For a view which stresses opportunity see Norman Daniels, *Just Health Care* (Cambridge: Cambridge University Press, 1985) especially chapters 1–3.

basis of positive personal achievements or on the basis of wrongs they have intentionally committed. Thus, high salaries may be rationalized on the basis of superior social contributions, and punishments on the basis of voluntary criminal acts. But surely, with regard to basic health care, the inability of the bulk of those who are unable to secure it by their own efforts is *no fault of their own.* They have not committed a crime or been otherwise irresponsible in such a way that they are no longer deserving of health care. They are simply poor. Thus, the most plausible grounds for inequality do not apply here, and justice seems to demand universal access to this basic good. It seems plausible, further, that the only way such access can be secured is by a legally recognized right to a basic level of care.[12]

Much of what we have argued may seem obvious. But, if so, why is a right to a basic level of care resisted as much as it is in this country? We suggest three reasons for the popular resistance to such a right. The first is a concern about government inefficiency. If government is authorized to secure basic care for all, it will do this inefficiently and ineffectively. Government bureaucracies will grow and red tape will multiply. Tax money will be wasted. Better not to recognize a right to basic health care than increase government ineptitude. These claims, it must be said, are empirical claims, claims about the facts. They may or may not be true and they may be more true in some contexts then in others. They do not vitiate the idea of a universal right to basic health care, but they warn us of the difficulty of developing effective institutions to secure that right. But the right survives this critique.

We would also argue that the economic costs of *not* providing adequate health care may already be a greater burden on society than the costs of providing such care. Evidence is continuing to accumulate, for example, that infants and children are paying a large part of the human costs for inadequate health care. Newborns who are uninsured are more likely to be of low birth weight and malnourished than those who are insured and are consequently more likely to have such adverse outcomes as prolonged hospital stays (including stays in intensive care units), transfer to specialized facilities, and deaths.[13] If the poor and uninsured child is able to overcome or survive its increased likelihood of perinatal morbidity and mortality, it still

---

[12]See the final paragraph of the section "Justifying Rights," above, for reasons why this interest needs to be recognized as a right.

[13]P. Braveman et al. "Adverse Outcomes and Lack of Health Insurance among Newborns in an Eight-County area of California, 1982 to 1986," *New England Journal of Medicine* (hereafter *NEJM*) 321 (1989): 508–13.

must face an increased risk for childhood trauma, accidental poisonings, tuberculosis, learning disability, mental illness and alcoholism, nutritional deficiency, lead poisoning, anemia, and other chronic illnesses and handicaps.[14]

Many of these problems will require ongoing, acute care as the child grows to adulthood, not just in the health care area specifically but also in education or other social systems. More important, when one recognizes that nearly 40 percent of the estimated thirty to thirty-seven million uninsured Americans are children, the economic consequences of diminished or lost productivity over lifetimes of lost opportunity become tremendous. We suggest that the investment early on in adequate health care will pay returns in later years of improved productivity in the overall society, which more than justifies the initial economic commitments.

The second and perhaps most fundamental reason for resistance to a right to a basic level of care rests on the individualism inherent in American political culture. A right to health care for all can be secured only by transfer payments from some groups to others through taxation. But to many, this transfer violates people's basic property rights, rights to earn what they can through their own efforts and to use what they earn as they please. This objection, then, is on the grounds of liberty. Those who are taxed to provide access to care for others are having their freedom violated, a freedom which must take precedence over the equality demanded by an equal right to care. This libertarian-type argument is, we believe, very persuasive to many Americans who resist a right to a basic level of care; it is a premise implicit in their resistance.

One response to this argument is that the appeal to equality in favor of such a right is more important than the liberty it takes away. But this raises the complex question of the worth of liberty versus that of equality, a question we cannot adequately address here. A more direct objection is, however, possible. A law that prohibits people from doing something imposes a *restriction* on their liberty. If this restriction is unjustified, there is a *violation* of liberty. Not all restrictions are violations. In most countries, for example, driving on the left side of the road is not permitted. This is a restriction that few would see as a violation. Even those most zealous about liberty agree that many other restrictions are not violations; for example, restrictions against injury, force, fraud, and theft do not violate liberty.

---

[14]D. M. Berwich and H. H. Hiatt, "Who Pays?" (Editorial), *NEJM* 321 (1989): 541–42.

Whether a restriction is a violation depends on whether the restriction is reasonable. The contention that transfer payments to underwrite health care for those who cannot provide it for themselves is a violation of liberty, as opposed to a reasonable restriction of it, requires argument. Merely *saying* that such redistribution violates liberty is *not* providing an adequate argument.[15] On the surface, it does not seem unreasonable to restrict the ability of the members of a society to use their earned income on things they want but do not need in order to fulfill the basic and urgent needs of those too poor to do so for themselves. The appeal to liberty per se does not refute the claim that this is a reasonable and just social aim.

One may respond, however, by arguing that the reasonableness of such a transfer does not show that it is morally required or permissible. A rich person will not act unreasonably if he or she donates half of his or her wealth to a charitable cause, but it does not appear that he or she, morally, *must* do so. Analogously, it might be reasonable and nice if those who can afford basic health care provide it (through taxes) for those who cannot, but must they do so? This question—and its implied negative answer—makes sense only on the assumption that people have a strong claim to their own income, so that transferring some part of it to others is morally problematic. People are typically taken to have this strong claim because they have earned their income through their own efforts, through hard work and the development and effective use of their talents. In other words, people are responsible for their abilities and therefore *deserve* the rewards they bring; and this desert, furthermore, is the basis of their right not to have their wealth "taken" (or even "stolen") to help others, unless there is a morally weighty reason to do so, such as the protection of everyone's security.

This picture of human endeavor raises very complex and fundamental issues of political theory which we cannot do justice to in this space. We simply point out that the picture is problematic because of the highly individualistic idea that people can claim sole responsibility for their efforts and abilities, and thus sole title to the reward these bring. In contrast, an individual's success is often highly dependent on their community and its structure of social and economic institutions. A person could not "strike it rich" through his or her develop-

---

[15]Readers familiar with Robert Nozick, *Anarchy, State, and Utopia* (New York: Basic Books, 1974), will rightfully see this criticism as directed at a libertarian theory such as his.

ment and use of talents were it not for the willingness of others to cooperate in the legal, economic, and social institutions which make such rewards possible. Furthermore, one's ability to develop his or her talents depends a good deal on educational support heavily subsidized by the public, and often on family and social circumstances over which a person has had no control. There are also elements of sheer luck frequently involved in how one fares. One is born with the capacity to develop certain talents and not others, and over this one has no choice. Further, and more important for our argument, whether one's talents will be rewarded in the society one happens to be born into is also a matter of chance—frail economic entrepreneurs, for example, would probably not be at the head of the pack in Homeric Greece. And, last but not least, our tastes and values, thoughts and preferences, aims and efforts, are heavily influenced by our society. We are social and interdependent members of communities, heavily dependent on the restraint and efforts of others for our own well-being and social and economic position. From this perspective the idea that much of what we earn results from good fortune and is best used to meet the most basic needs of those in our community who have lost out in this lottery is compelling. Americans may well resist recognizing a right to health care because they resist this community perspective, but in our view, interdependence cannot be justly denied, nor can the implication that justice requires ensuring that everyone's basic needs are met through universal access to health care.

The third reason for resistance to a right to health care has to do with an important feature of positive rights. Negative rights can be respected by leaving people alone. But positive rights require providing people with some good. In a market economy, however, the typical way people come to possess most goods is through earning income through work and buying them. The recognition of a positive right, then, implies giving people certain goods for free. With regard to health care, it means that everyone should be given such care without having to do anything by way of labor to earn it. That this goes against the American grain is obvious. And that is why negative rights are so much more respectable. They do not mean giving people things they have not earned but simply leaving them alone.

This understanding of positive rights, however, is mistaken. Suppose we wanted to guarantee everyone a decent standard of living. The most efficient and natural way to do this would be to have a set of social and economic institutions in which everyone has an opportunity to get a job and earn enough income to live up to that standard. In other words, we can ensure people's positive rights by making it possible for them to earn the wherewithal they need if only they choose to put in a reasonable effort.[16] The problem occurs when those institutions fail to provide every individual with that opportunity. Then some people, through no fault of their own, cannot provide for themselves. It is in this case *and only in this case* that concern for positive rights mandates help. So respect for positive rights does not mean giving people "something for nothing." It means helping those who need help because they cannot help themselves. It means, in other words, benevolence and being a good Samaritan. What we might call the "free-riding" objection is unpersuasive.

THE CONSTITUTIONAL STATUS OF A RIGHT TO HEALTH CARE

At the time of the drafting of the United States Constitution, and during most of the two centuries since, there has been neither a legal nor constitutional presumption that a right to a minimum level of health care services exists. Such a right has not been considered to be an inherent right, and thus is not part of the seventeenth-century political and legal philosophy on which the United States Constitution was based.

One of the widespread movements to establish a nationwide health care system occurred in the mid-1960s. During this time, much discussion was devoted to the concept of a right to a minimal level of health care services, which ultimately led to the establishment of the Medicare program to provide health care for the elderly, and the Medicaid program to provide health care to the poor. Despite that progress, however, there has been very little in the way of litigation or court action which would address the concept of a *legal* right or a *constitutional* right to a minimal level of health care, even to the current time.

The justices of the Supreme Court have held in two separate cases that state and federal legislatures are not obligated to fund abortion services for indigent or poor women.[17] These rulings support current

---

[16]This is argued by James W. Nickel, *Making Sense of Human Rights* (Berkeley: University of California Press, 1987).

[17]*Maher v. Roe*, 432 U.S. 464, 1977; *Harris v. McRae*, 448 U.S. 297 (1980).

federal law, which denies Medicaid funding to states for abortion services except in the case of a life-threatening pregnancy.[18] In an additional decision of the Supreme Court, however, Justice Thurgood Marshall made the observation that access to medical care of a nonemergency nature was a basic necessity of life for the poor, equivalent to general welfare assistance.[19]

These decisions served as the foundation for perhaps the most important case heard by the Supreme Court; in that case the plaintiffs forced a direct examination of the issue of a basic entitlement to health care services by bringing suit against a county government under federal civil rights statutes. A patient had experienced severe abdominal pain during her fourth month of pregnancy. She contacted her physician, who instructed her to meet him at the hospital. The patient then dialed the emergency number for ambulance service (provided by the county) and was taken by the ambulance to another hospital, where the county had a contractual arrangement, despite her protestations that she needed to see her own physician at her own hospital. At the hospital where she was taken, there was a long delay before she was seen. After finally being evaluated, she was then transferred to the original hospital where her primary physician was still waiting for her, but by this time it was essentially too late. She was well into premature labor and subsequently delivered a stillborn premature infant.

The woman's attorneys argued that the patient had a constitutional right to medical services provided by her own physician at her own hospital, and the county had interfered with that right by taking her to a different hospital. The United States Court of Appeals for the Eleventh Circuit ultimately ruled, with extensive background justification, that municipalities have no constitutional obligation to provide even the most basic protective services; not only health care, but also police, fire protection, and sanitation. The only exception seen by the Court of Appeals occurs when the municipality has entered into a "special relationship" with the person or persons involved, which results in that person being placed under a substantial degree of forced confinement or in custody of the municipality. Thus, this case established that persons who are in jail or prison, or in police custody in a courthouse or a hospital, are guaranteed basic levels of health care. Everyone else is not. The key element defined by

---

[18]"Hyde Amendment," Public Law no. 96–123, sec. 109.

[19]*Memorial Hospital v. Maricopa County*, 415 U.S. 250 (1974).

the court was whether or not there is present "the exercise of coercion, dominion, or restraint."[20]

Two other special groups must be recognized; no legal or constitutional precedent for their right to health care exists, but there appears to be substantial societal consensus that they do or should have such a right. These two groups are military-service veterans, for whom there is a nationwide system of health care, and pregnant females and infants. In the ongoing discussions concerning the establishment or existence of a right to health care, consideration of a constitutional amendment to guarantee such a right must be made. There is precedent for this in constitutions of other Western hemisphere nations.[21] Such an action would surely serve as a means to focus societal consensus to determine if there is indeed agreement over whether this right truly exists. If successful, such an amendment would then again focus the debate (now through court interpretations) on what specifically should constitute "adequate" health care.

CONCLUSION

The shift over the last three decades from medicine as a profession, controlled and practiced by physicians, to medicine as a business, controlled by businessmen (many of whom are also physicians), insurers, and government, has been accompanied by a major change in how medical care is delivered, in how that care is paid for, and in who may have access to that care. It has also been accompanied by a rapidly increasing reliance on high-cost technology, which then generates further expectations and costs by allowing less room for human fallibility in delivering care.

Unfortunately, there is little sympathy or flexibility within a business and high-technology framework for the poor and the disadvantaged. A growing segment of our society have thus been denied access not only to the high-cost health care system but to even a minimal level of care. We have argued that it is time for us as a society to recognize that a right to basic health care exists and that society has an obligation to secure that right. We must refocus our debate not on *whether* health care should be provided to all society members but rather on what the adequate level of health care should be and how we can prioritize our needs and our resources to provide that level of care.

[20]*Wideman v. Shallowford Community Hospital, Inc.*, 826 F 2d 1030 (1987).
[21]W. J. Curran, "The Constitutional Right to Health Care," *NEJM* 320 (1989): 788–89.

Expectations and the Design of a Universal Health Care System

Leslie Pickering Francis

Both as providers and as patients, Americans expect a great deal from their health care system. Sometimes these expectations are met; sometimes they are disappointed. Many proposals for change in the funding and delivery of American health care are currently under discussion. These proposals for change have the potential to bring important changes with respect to expectations: to disappoint expectations that are currently met, to satisfy expectations that are frequently disappointed today, and to create new expectations. Depending on how changes are made in access to health care, expectations may be created, disappointed, shaped, and reshaped in different ways. The anticipated effects of such changes on expectations will surely affect political support for, or opposition to, the various proposals for health care reform. My aim in this essay, however, is to look behind the politics and to consider whether, and how, expectations should be addressed morally in the design of a universal health care system in the United States.

This is an essay about ethical issues raised by a set of proposals for change. Although I do not put the current situation at center stage, it is the ever-present setting against which proposed changes must ultimately be judged. Americans are increasingly confronting cutbacks in their health care funding. These cutbacks surely affect expectations, perhaps just as seriously and in some of the same ways as the proposals for universal health care. For example, as current health care benefits are eroded or curtailed, employees who have relied upon employer-provided health insurance for years may suddenly confront the termination of family coverage.

Even more devastating than reductions in benefits is the reality that somewhere between thirty million and forty million Americans have no apparent source of funding for health care. It may very well be that reductions in the very generous health care benefits that some Americans receive will be needed to extend even minimal access to care to others. This essay focuses on the impact of cutbacks, impacts largely felt by those who have been doing well under the current system. But it should not be read as an apologia for the middle class. Because complaints about reductions in benefits are highly significant politically, it is important to see what kind of moral significance, if any, they have, and how strong that significance is. It is also important to explore morally acceptable ways to accommodate or cushion disappointments when change takes place. In the end, however, the moral issues associated with change must be judged in comparison with the moral issues raised by the continually evolving backdrop of the current situation. This essay is only a part of the broader picture, the part which centers on change and disappointments.

EXPECTATIONS AND HEALTH CARE: SOME CENTRAL EXAMPLES

As I use the term, "expectations" are beliefs about the future upon which people rely in structuring their lives. Many different kinds of expectations are characteristic of contemporary American health care. I begin by describing some kinds of expectations that are of particular ethical relevance for the design of a universal health care system. Although the term "expectations" appears frequently in discussions of physician-patient relationships and of access to health care, there has been little systematic study of the actual expectations of either patients or physicians. These descriptions are thus to some extent speculative. I believe, however, that they are characteristic of the kinds of expectations that physicians and patients are likely to have about the health care system. For the purposes of this essay, they can be viewed as hypotheses that warrant empirical study. Even if they are inaccurate (though I think it is unlikely that they are too far wrong), the general points about expectations will remain.

Patients have a variety of expectations about their relationships with physicians.[1] These expectations frequently arise from experience within the health care system, for example, through particular provider-patient relationships of an ongoing and relatively long-standing nature. Patients might expect, for example, that they will be able to continue to receive treatment from the same provider, that they will be able to choose other providers, or that they will be able to seek referrals to specialists. At least some expectations of continued care find legal support in the doctrine that physicians may not abandon their patients.[2] It is important to note the extent to which these expectations are rooted in experience with the current system of health care in the United States; by comparison, in the United Kingdom, for example, patients generally do not expect to be able to shop around for other general practitioners or to seek specialist care on their own.[3]

Patients may also have expectations about the extent and nature of shared decision making within provider-patient relationships. As the doctrine of informed consent has gained wider currency, patients may expect to be informed about risks and alternatives to proposed care, and to be educated about the risks of not seeking care.[4] Patients who have gone to the trouble of executing advance directives about treatment or specifications about organ donation may expect that their wishes will be honored by providers and by family members.[5] At the same time, from a more traditional perspective, patients may expect caring and paternalism.[6] Possibly patients also expect confidentiality and undivided loyalty on the part of their health care providers.[7]

Patients are also likely to have expectations about what medical care will be provided and what that care can or cannot do for them. There are in American health law examples of expectations that are fostered and memorialized in written contracts: the plastic surgeon who promised a beautiful nose to an aspiring actress or the surgeon who promised an easy cure for a peptic ulcer.[8] More frequently, expectations about what care can do remain unarticulated premises in the provider-patient encounter. Commentators often note that Americans and the British have very different ideas about what medical care can achieve, particularly about the efficacy of technology.[9]

Expectations about available medical treatments and likely outcomes come from a potpourri of sources: popular culture, gossip, women's magazines, self-help books, and other mass media. They also come from the medical profession itself, as new interventions such as coronary bypass surgery or, now, balloon angioplasty are heralded publicly as dramatic improvements in care. Expectations also come secondhand, as patients share information about what their different doctors have told them. The movement toward practice standards and consensus conferences, now largely motivated by concerns about quality and cost, may, as it becomes further developed and better known, extend patients' expectations still further with respect to the forms of care they receive and likely outcomes.[10]

Funding and access to medical services are the basis of another set of patients' expectations. Patients have expectations about the extent to which their care will be paid for by insurance or other sources. Examples of decisions made either explicitly or with background knowledge of the availability of medical services may include engaging in risky behavior—skiing, smoking, sky-diving—on the assumption that help will be available in the event of a bad outcome. To be sure, the availability of care may not be much of a factor to those who are highly risk acceptant—would many skiers *really* change their behavior if they *knew* treatment would be limited or unavailable for certain kinds of injuries?—but it may be more explicitly considered by those who are less risk acceptant. The willingness to take on or continue risky occupations may provide other examples, especially if the employer (or other insurers, including society) makes promises about the availability of care in the case of injury. Sometimes these promises are overtly contractual, as in examples of sports contracts that promise continued medical care for injured players. Sometimes, although there are contracts, they do not extend indefinitely into the future. An example would be workers who receive generous health insurance benefits on an annually contracted basis; they have no contractual right to receive the same generous benefits as part of their next deal, but they may well expect to do so or to experience only incremental reductions in available benefits. Generous health benefits are surely incentives to many peoples' choices of employers or even occupations. For example, both job security and the relative stability of health benefits are important incentives to enter employment in the public sector. Retirement benefits are another area where expectations play a role. Promises to continue to pay health insurance premiums have been used as inducements for early retirement; a recently litigated issue has been the extent to which these promises can be modified in light of rising insurance costs.[11]

Some of the most poignant examples of the importance of expectations about economic access to care come from pregnancy and neonatology. An older couple may undertake a pregnancy in the belief that amniocentesis, genetic screening, and abortion are available and covered by their health insurance. A high-risk mother may get pregnant with the understanding that she and her infant are fully covered by insurance. The availability of resources for continued care and support is often an issue raised in discussions of aggressive treatment of seriously compromised infants, although it is not regarded as relevant by the "Baby Doe" regulations.[12]

Physicians too have expectations about the structure of their relationships with patients. These expectations are formed largely in training and in practice. Some physicians may expect to be largely in control of the relation with patients; others may expect to function with the patient as partner.[13] There may well be generational differences here. Some physicians may expect little beyond pay from patients in return for continuing the caregiving relationship; others may not even expect pay from some patients. Some physicians may expect compliance from patients and the ability to dismiss or refer patients with whom they have difficulty working.[14] Physicians' expectations may also include important aspects of the working conditions they will face: the ability to arrange call, the difficulties of running a small business, or the ability to maintain an independent practice with privileges at several hospitals. There may also be expectations about the extent to which the physician-patient relationship will be insulated from financial and other third-party pressures. In other practice settings, the expectation may be that treatment decisions are increasingly dictated by managerial policy.[15] In this and other ways, the intrusion of third-party judgments into physicians' decisions about patient care may be perceived as disrupting physicians' expectations about trust and independent judgment. At least part of physicians' resentment of the increase in malpractice litigation and of the need to justify care to third-party payers may stem from the extent to which physicians feel that their judgment has come under fire in ways that are both unexpected and undeserved.

Like patients, physicians also may have expectations about what medical care can accomplish. These expectations may be rooted in technology but may outstrip what technology is available.[16] As far as I can discover, there has been little systematic study of the extent to which physicians' expectations are congruent with those of their patients.

Physicians surely also have expectations about likely income levels. These expectations may have affected choices about practice specialties. Primary-care specialists in general have lower projected incomes than surgical specialists; recent controversy about calculating physician reimbursement under Medicare by means of a resource "relative-value scale" reflected reactions to the possibility of changes in this balance.[17] Expectations about long-range income may have been translated into significant decisions: where to live, what kind of house to buy, how many children to have, where to send children to school, whether to assume that one's spouse will work, what kind of retirement planning to establish. Income expectations may also drive work patterns and in turn expectations about colleagues' performance: the seventy-hour week and the 6:00 A.M. breakfast meeting are part of the pressures of contemporary medicine, pressures increasingly questioned by critics.

My contention is not that all, or even any, of these expectations have moral weight. Indeed, there are no doubt major conflicts among some of these expectations; not all of them can be realized consistently. Frustration with changes in the current system of American medical care may well reflect some of these conflicts; even affluent doctors and affluent patients cannot get all that they have come to expect. My starting point for discussion is instead that changes in our system of delivering and funding health care will both affect existing expectations and create new ones. A universal health care system, depending on how it is designed, may affect different expectations in different ways. Of course, if we continue with the current system and if pressures to control costs continue to increase, we may also find that expectations are affected. We thus need to consider the extent to which any of the present expectations of physicians and patients do matter morally, in order to see whether they should be taken into account in the design or implementation of changes in our system of health care. We also need to consider what moral questions are raised by new expectations that might be generated by a changed system. These are large issues and I can only begin to investigate them here.

WHY DO EXPECTATIONS MATTER MORALLY?

This section presents a brief account of why expectations might matter morally. Expectations are related to autonomy, in that part of what is involved in treating people as autonomous is seeing them as capable of choosing and planning, helping to ensure the context in which they can choose and plan, and respecting those choices and plans which they undertake. If expectations are ignored altogether, people will not have minimally stable contexts within which to plan, or minimal assurance that their plans will be taken seriously. This does not mean that all expectations matter, or that expectations matter conclusively in determining what we ought to do. As Robert Nozick pointed out in *Anarchy, State, and Utopia*, wishing does not make it morally so; my expectations are not a trap that ensnares you whatever you do.[18] Expectations do not and should not redefine underlying realities. Nonetheless, if we are to take people seriously as choosers and planners, it is important to consider whether expectations matter morally under some circumstances, and why they do.

Here are some features of expectations that are relevant to how we view them morally. First of all, expectations are based on beliefs about the future ("base beliefs"). To the extent that base beliefs are unreasonable, that counts against giving expectations moral weight. People should not be encouraged to build their houses on quicksand and then be rewarded when they do. Base beliefs might be unreasonable because they are known or suspected to be false, or because they are known to be without the kind of support that might reasonably be called upon in favor of that type of belief. A belief in the efficacy of a therapeutic modality that has either no or highly suspect scientific support would be an example of an unreasonable base belief.

One of the most difficult problems here is that the reasonableness of beliefs is relative to context. The reasonableness of a belief rests on the support that is available to a given person at a given time, rather than on the inherent truth or falsity of the belief. Thus if well-designed studies have confirmed the efficacy of a therapy, it is reasonable for physicians to believe that the therapy is efficacious. If there are no confirming studies, or if new studies question earlier findings, these beliefs about efficacy diminish in reasonableness. Lay beliefs about the efficacy of therapy may be reasonable if they have been based on efforts to seek out appropriate expert advice—advice that may or may not in itself be reasonable.

Encouragement more generally is a second feature that counts in favor of giving expectations some moral weight. Without the acknowledgment that it is sometimes reasonable to rely on encouragement, much planning would be undercut. Encouragement includes overtly promising or leading someone on, but it also reaches to the failure to disabuse someone of beliefs in situations in which a disclaimer would ordinarily be expected. For example, an employer can encourage an employee to believe that her employment will not be affected by her expensive health needs by reassuring her outright that she "will always have a job as long as he's in charge." But it is equally encouraging for the employer to fail to tell her that her job is in jeopardy in situations in which these concerns would normally be articulated, for example, in a review of the utilization of employee benefits that is specifically directed to issues of overutilization and its burdens for the employer.

Like the reasonableness of belief, the reasonableness of reliance is context-related. Encouragement matters particularly when it comes from a privileged source such as an employer, a source on which it is reasonable to rely with respect to the matter in question. We rely on experts when they recommend courses of action, employers when they make assurances of job security, and family members when they say they will help carry out our wishes. In addition to the source, other features of the situation may also contribute to the reasonableness of reliance. The longer the encouragement persists, the more reasonable the reliance. Diversity of sources may also be a factor; some of the expectations about health care that I have described above are encouraged by a wide range of different sources, often cumulatively: individual physicians, organizations of physicians, Office of Technology Assessment reports, employers, insurance companies, the Department of Health and Human Services or state health departments, the Center for Disease Control, gossip among neighbors, the popular press, and dozens more. Complex issues of moral responsibility and legal liability lurk here. Should encouragers ever be viewed as morally responsible for the disappointment of the expectations they foster? If so, should responsibility be limited to primary encouragers or should others who have played supporting roles be called upon when the question is satisfying encouraged expectations? Should encouragement be the basis for legal liability, only in the context of antecedent legal obligations, for example, those created by statutory duties, the employer-employee relationship, or the provider-patient relationship? Or should reliance interests more broadly be the basis of legal liability and, if so, where should limits be drawn? Is there an argument for assigning the government a special role with respect to encouragement, when expectations are generated from a wide range of sources, or are in effect culturally generated? Emergency room care is an example of a policy area in which some of these alternatives have been explored. The initial common-law view was that there was no legal duty to treat emergency patients unless an underlying contractual relationship had been established.[19] This view has been gradually eroded by holdings that the hospital has undertaken to provide care by minimally examining the patient, or even by indicating that it provides emergency services.[20] Most recently, the federal government has imposed a duty to provide stabilizing emergency care on all hospitals receiving federal reimbursement.[21]

Another feature that counts in favor of according expectations moral weight is their connection to the fabric of an individual's life, to the individual's sense of who she is and what her aims are. Expectations that are central to the fabric of an individual's life, to her conception of identity and purpose, are likely to be both deeply felt and especially important to the realization of plans. Physicians' expectations of being able to deliver good-quality medical care, and of being able to act with integrity in the interests of their patients, are examples of expectations that are important to their conceptions of who they are.

To this point, I have ignored the connection between expectations and an underlying theory of moral rights or justice.[22] Some expectations are generated under conditions of justice; others under conditions of injustice. The expectations of white South Africans about the continued protection of apartheid or the property expectations of a slave owner might be examples of expectations that are generated under conditions of such injustice, and with such understanding of and complicity in that injustice, that they bear no moral force whatsoever. But it does not follow that we should give no moral weight to any expectations that are generated under conditions of imperfect justice. On the other hand, the injustice of a background situation may diminish the moral weight of the expectations it generates, just as the justice of a background situation may provide moral support for the expectations that it generates. Moreover, the desirability of correcting injustice and moving toward a more just state of affairs is an argument for overriding expectations that stand in the way.

Nonetheless, some expectations that arise under conditions of less than perfect justice give rise to some of the most difficult moral dilemmas we have.[23] Consider some examples in which there are moral arguments that support satisfying the expectations but that are relatively weak in comparison to other moral considerations. An example might be health care benefits that have been promised in exchange for early retirement, when keeping that promise conflicts with keeping promises to other workers or investing in expensive pollution-control equipment. Here, the promise provides a moral argument for the expectation; the expectation is probably also reasonable, encouraged, and relatively important to the individual's well-being, particularly if he or she is not yet eligible for Medicare or has health needs that are not well covered by Medicare. On the other hand, the retirement promises may have been improvident or far more generous than was justifiable on the basis of considerations of justice such as the employee's contributions or fairness to other generations of employees. This kind of dilemma has occurred fairly frequently in troubled, "rust-belt" industries, where the employer claims that it is impossible to continue to honor promises to retirees and to remain economically viable. In some cases, retiree health benefits have been terminated entirely, pushing employees who are not yet eligible for Medicare into the ranks of the uninsured. An argument for universal health care is that it is a compromise solution to this dilemma. Retirees are not dependent on their former employers for health care benefits, although they may get less generous benefits under a universal system than they had originally been promised.

Another example of the moral complexity of expectations in contexts of injustice might be a young adult with expensive, chronic health needs, including anticipated eventual transplant surgery. His wealthy parents have been able to meet his needs to date, and plan also to pay for the transplant. Yet there are questions about the justice of the underlying distribution of wealth or about the parents' manner of acquiring their wealth. A "one-tiered" system of universal health care, which did not pay for the transplant at issue because it had determined that other needs such as prenatal care were more pressing, and which did not allow for the private purchase of additional care, would disappoint this expectation. There is a real moral conflict here. On the one hand, the expectation may be long-standing, encouraged, crucial to survival, and based on a conception of parental obligations. It may have played a role in the young man's plans about his future—for example, what kind of life span and capacities he has expected to enjoy. The expectations of a funded transplant may have seemed reasonable under the current mixture of American health policy. On the other hand, it might not have been reasonable for the young man to expect social policy to continue to permit him to be the recipient of his parents' largesse. And there are certainly arguments of justice both against allowing people to continue to benefit from certain forms of unjust wealth distribution and against a health care system that permits wide differences between what is publicly funded and what can be purchased privately. These more general considerations of justice may outweigh the patient's expectations that his parents will be allowed to pay for continued care. To see how evenly balanced the dilemma is, compare this scenario with one in which organs are sold to the highest bidder, and the young man expects to have a very good chance of getting an organ because his parents are very wealthy indeed. In this situation, the considerations of justice are surely strong enough to outweigh the young man's expectations. Or, consider another scenario in which the young man's *parents* were suddenly to tell him that they would not pay for the transplant because they had decided their money would be better spent on a charitable contribution to prenatal care. Here, additional moral support is lent to the young man's expectations, if parents have moral obligations to support their adult children who are in medical need.[24] His parents may also have encouraged him in very direct ways and there may have been no reason whatsoever for him to have guessed they were likely to change their minds about paying for his care. Although the reasons of abstract justice that favor prenatal care are just as strong as they were in the argument about the allocation of resources by society, there are no special reasons to think that the parents have obligations to ensure good prenatal care. But there are reasons to think that the parents have obligations to care for their son, and so in this case we might conclude that the son's expectations override the more general concern for social justice.

Even if there are arguments to be made that it would be morally problematic to disappoint certain expectations, it does not follow that we are locked in, morally, to the status quo. The need for change might be important enough to override the disappointed expectations. But the expectations might still bear some moral weight in how we shape the change. For example, in introducing a system of universal health insurance, we might consider phasing the changes in gradually, grandfathering certain existing claims, or allowing a parallel voluntary system to continue. We might also consider the possibility of compensating those who will be especially dislocated by the change; for example, employees of health insurance companies might be offered alternative employment or retraining if the United States moves to a single-payer system of universal health care. Moreover, an understanding of when expectations may bear moral weight is helpful in the design of social policies that will themselves predictably create new expectations.

To summarize, reasonableness, encouragement, longevity, integrity, and an underlying theory of rights and justice all provide support for the recognition of expectations. This account of expectations has necessarily been very brief, but it will serve as a basis for some comparative judgments about the impact on expectations of several of the current proposals for universal health care in the United States.

UNIVERSAL HEALTH CARE AND EXPECTATIONS

The many proposals for universal health care in the United States are likely to affect expectations in different ways. Two kinds of proposals, the employment-based and Canadian models, have garnered particular attention.[25] Employment-based models rely primarily on employer-provided insurance, expanded to include risk pools for the currently uninsured and uninsurable. The example of this approach considered here is the consumer-choice plan proposed by Alain Enthoven and Richard Kronick. The Canadian model incorporates provincial negotiation and payment for health care. The example used as a prototype of this approach is the physicians' plan, developed by David Himmelstein and others.

The consumer-choice plan proposed by Enthoven and Kronick is incrementalist in design. Their proposal is specifically tailored to minimize disruption and to respond to consumer and provider preferences.[26] It uses current employer-provided health plans as a basis; employers would be required to offer all full-time employees a choice of plans including the basic benefits package specified in the Health Maintenance Organization (HMO) Act, with deductibles of no more than $250 (in 1988 dollars). Employers would be required to contribute at least 80 percent of the costs of basic coverage; employees who wished to could buy more extensive coverage, using after-tax dollars. Employers would also be required to pay an 8 percent payroll tax on uninsured (part-time) workers to help fund subsidized coverage for uncovered workers. States then would be encouraged to create "public sponsor" agencies to negotiate a choice of health insurance plans for anyone not covered by employer-provided insurance. Just like employers, the public sponsor would subsidize coverage at 80 percent of the cost of an average basic plan; additional subsidies would be available for those within 150 percent of the poverty level. The public sponsor could also serve as broker for small employers otherwise unable to obtain affordable insurance plans for their employees. This scheme is designed to encourage cost-effective, managed-care plans. To that extent, the plan would affect physicians' income and practice patterns. It is also designed to encourage people to buy coverage. Enthoven and Kronick do not say explicitly that care would be unfunded for the stubbornly imprudent uninsured. If those who do not purchase insurance receive care anyway, however, incentives would be created for the relatively well to opt out of purchasing insurance.[27]

The Enthoven-Kronick proposal may have a number of effects on expectations, only some of which they mention explicitly. Fee-for-service and single-specialty practices would be likely to diminish or disappear.[28] Managed care itself might affect the autonomy with which physicians practice more than Enthoven and Kronick discuss, particularly if significant cost savings became necessary. Enthoven and Kronick think there would be a happy congruence between successful managed-care plans and physician satisfaction. But if cost control and physicians' judgments about optimal (or even only good) practice conflicted with each other, as they have been alleged to do in some HMOs,the happy congruence will be put to the test.[29]

Patients, too, might have diminished choice in a managed-care plan. At a minimum, they would be more limited in choice of provider than under a traditional insurance program such as Blue Cross. Perhaps more important, many employees have been used to plans that cover more than the basic coverage listed in the HMO Act. There are some extremely significant limits on what is considered "basic" care under the HMO Act. Mental-health care is the most notable; it is limited to "short-term (not to exceed twenty visits), outpatient evaluative and crisis intervention mental health services."[30] Home health services are included as basic, but long-term care is not.[31] Rehabilitative care and physical therapy are limited to short-term interventions that the HMO determines can be expected to result in improvement of the patient's condition within two months.[32] No home-use durable medical equipment, such as surgical beds or wheelchairs, is included in the basic package.[33] No outpatient prescriptions are included, surely a significant expense for anyone in need of medication for a chronic condition such as hypertension.[34] Care that the secretary of the Department of Health and Human Services (HHS) determines is infrequent, unusual, and not necessary for the protection of individual health is also excluded; and so are organ transplants that were not considered standard care as of April 15, 1985.[35] These are certainly impressive limitations on what is considered to be basic care. To be sure, they may be limits that are peculiar to the HMO Act. Nevertheless, what is not peculiar to the HMO Act, but is central to the Enthoven-Kronick proposal, is the linkage between cost control and limitations on the kinds of care to be provided.[36] Moreover, in the Enthoven-Kronick plan, while employees would continue to be able to purchase insurance packages that included more than the basic package, they would have to do so under less favorable conditions than presently, with their own after-tax dollars. There thus would be a clear incentive for those who do not expect to need mental-health, rehabilitative, or other expensive, nonbasic services to select the cheaper, managed-care plans, thus potentially driving up the costs of the additional plans still further because risks would not be spread as widely.[37] To be sure, mental-health and long-term care are often not included in current care plans, but those with the more generous plans would find themselves facing the choice between cutbacks or the more expensive options. In short, if the cost-saving incentives the Enthoven-Kronick proposal seeks to create are likely to drive managed-care plans to coverage that includes basic care only, the result will be a gradual phase down in what well-insured people are now used to receiving, particularly in the mental-health area but in other areas as well.[38]

Employment-based plans may also have a substantial effect on employment patterns and wages. Enthoven and Kronick predict that increases in health insurance costs or payroll taxes are likely to result in a decline in wages, particularly for part-time workers affected by the 8 percent payroll tax. There also may be a decline in willingness to hire low-skill, minimum-wage workers, since the 8 percent payroll tax in effect represents an 8 percent increase in the minimum wage. Another concern is the effect of required employment-based insurance on the job security of employees with expensive health needs. Currently employers in most states have the alternative of buying a less expensive health insurance plan which excludes certain high-cost services, or discontinuing employee health insurance altogether.[39] These options would be eliminated under the Enthoven-Kronick proposal, although for small employers the elimination would be countered by the opportunity to seek coverage through the risk pool of the public sponsor. Thus some firms, particularly those who do not qualify for or do not want to participate in the public sponsor pool, may be inclined to ease out into the public sponsor pool—that is, fire—those workers whose health benefits have proved most expensive. Job mobility is another issue for employment-based plans if firms are discouraged from hiring workers with potentially expensive health care needs.[40] To be sure, mobility may be difficult for these employees today, since if they change jobs and thus health insurance, they may find themselves with coverage that excludes their preexisting conditions. Enthoven and Kronick believe that these effects of requiring employment-based insurance are likely to be relatively minimal and offset by the increased access to health care.[41]

Although a full discussion of employment policy is beyond the scope of this essay, I am concerned that Enthoven and Kronick dismiss these risks fairly easily. Moreover, proposals for universal health care that are not based on employment—for example, proposals that cast the government as the sole purchaser of health care—do not pose these risks to jobs and employment mobility.

Enthoven and Kronick believe that plans that are not employment-based, such as plans based on the Canadian model, are not easily importable into the United States. Their chief concerns are the radical changes the Canadian model would require and the unlikelihood that American public policy would engage in meaningful cost control, driven as it is by interest-group pressures.[42] A group of physicians led by David Himmelstein, however, are more optimistic about the potential the Canadian model holds for the United States. These are the basic features of the Himmelstein plan, which the authors propose as a first step in developing a Canadian plan for the United States and suggest should be worked out through a series of state demonstration projects.[43] First, public coverage would be extended universally for all medically necessary services, including mental-health services and long-term care. Expert and community boards in each state would determine which services were considered ineffective or unnecessary under that state's program. Expanded technology assessment and cost-effectiveness scrutiny would be relied upon to control costs, rather than methods such as co-payments that impose the burden largely on patients. As in Canada, hospitals would each year negotiate a lump-sum payment for operating expenses with the national health program payment board in place in each state. Capital expansion would be negotiated separately and could not be funded from the operating budget. Physicians could choose fee-for-service practice, practice in an HMO, or salaried hospital-based practice. Those reimbursed on a fee-for-service basis could not double bill patients for covered services (although they could bill in full for uncovered services) or include charges for costly in-office capital facilities in reimbursement. The HMOs would be reimbursed on a capitation (per person) basis, again not including capital facilities. The program would be funded by a tax on employers roughly equal to what is now paid for employee health benefits (with a credit for continuing obligations) and from a tax on individuals roughly equal to current out-of-pocket expenditures for health care.

The drafters of the Himmelstein plan anticipate that importing the Canadian model would actually increase physicians' autonomy.

Under the Canadian model, physicians would continue to have a choice of practice settings. They would not be constrained by a myriad of insurance regulations in making therapeutic choices about patient care. Pressures to skimp on care to allow capital investment would be reduced. The drafters also anticipate stability and predictability of hospital income, as well as a gradual phase-out of the for-profit sector of the hospital industry. They anticipate that capital investment decisions would be largely responsive to community needs. On the patients' side, the Himmelstein group also anticipates increased autonomy; patients would continue to be able to choose providers freely, and would have more choices available as access to care improves. The losses under the scheme would fall mainly on insurance companies, because the introduction of a public payer would replace their primary role in the health insurance market.

As it is described, the Himmelstein plan does not anticipate any major disappointment of expectations on the part of either physicians or patients. It is hoped that the plan would continue existing levels of autonomy and existing levels of care for those who already have care, would expand care to others, and would deal with issues of new development and investment through community democracy. If these hopes were unrealized, and they are impressively ambitious, where would expectations most likely be disappointed?[44] The drafters of the plan—largely physicians—apparently see the risks to the physicians' autonomy of practice and clinical judgment as more serious than the risks posed by the introduction of cost-control measures imposed by community choice. Thus as a central cost-control strategy, they propose community-determined limits on payment for new capital facilities. Similarly, cost control is achieved in Canada largely by delays in public authorization of payment for new forms of expensive, technologically intensive care. In Canada, these forms of care are either not introduced, or are introduced more slowly, with some variation among geographical areas.[45] Predictions about what would happen if the Canadian model were imported to the United States must remain somewhat speculative because there are significant differences between the two countries; and the Himmelstein group's proposal may contain features that other Canadian-prototypes would not. Nonetheless, it is fair to say that the Himmelstein proposal is optimistic and does not focus clearly on the likelihood that it would be unable to achieve all that it set out to do. If the proposal does prove overly optimistic, it is designed to disappoint expectations about the introduction of new forms of care, rather than expectations of autonomy and access within the system.

Just as employment-based plans may have broader social consequences, so surely would the introduction of the Canadian model. The chief losers under the plan would be insurance companies, their employees, and those who have invested in them. Although my focus here is the expectations of patients and physicians, these other dislocations also warrant moral analysis.

To summarize to this point, the employment-based and Canadian proposals for universal health care are likely to affect different sets of provider and patient expectations. Expectations that the physician-patient relationship would remain largely insulated from pressures to manage care or control costs are more likely to be disappointed under employment-based, managed-care plans like the Enthoven-Kronick proposal. So are expectations of continued access to particular kinds of care, particularly mental-health care or rehabilitative services. These risks to the autonomy of both provider and patient are explicitly contemplated by Enthoven and Kronick. But they may also arise under the Himmelstein or other Canadian-prototype proposals, if it proves necessary to move beyond limits on new capital investment to control costs. Expectations about what medical care can do, and that there is always something new to try when standard treatment modalities have failed, are more likely to be disappointed with the importation of the Canadian model. These expectations of access to new forms of technology, surely at risk under the Himmelstein plan and other Canadian prototypes, may also be unsatisfied under the Enthoven-Kronick plan if they are not considered part of basic care. The Himmelstein plan also contemplates a shift in physician reimbursement toward primary-care specialties, and thus a shift in expectations as well. Finally, the availability of employment and job security is a more general policy question posed by employment-based plans. The effect on the insurance industry is a more general question raised by proposals based on the Canadian experience.

Now, to what extent are these differing effects on expectations morally problematic? What I will say here is preliminary and speculative. Nonetheless, the issues raised by expectations are morally and politically important enough to the design of universal health care— as well as to other issues of policy-making in situations of imperfect justice—to warrant bringing them out into the open, even at the risk of seeming partially wrong.

Let me begin by comparing physicians' expectations about their abilities to exercise professional judgment with their expectations about income levels. The moral nature of the physician's role—as patient advocate, as gatekeeper, or as something else—is much discussed. My analysis here is directed to the issue of expectations which arises if physicians who have expected to play one role—say, patient advocate—are gently or not so gently shifted into a different role—say, rationer. There are several reasons why expectations about professional roles are morally serious. The anticipated ability to practice a profession in a certain way may have played an important role in initial career choices to enter medicine. When these decisions were made, expectations about the nature of professional life may have been reasonable. Loyalty to patients has been a central premise of the practice of medicine since the earliest discussions of medical ethics. These expectations have been encouraged both within medicine, in how medicine is taught, and in society more generally—for, example in popular writing by and about physicians. They may be a crucial part of physicians' understandings of what their own professional integrity means and of patients' understandings of how their doctors will behave. Finally, expectations about roles may be bolstered by our underlying account of the moral nature of the physician's role. To the extent that arguments from expectations are strengthened by underlying moral justification of what is expected, physicians' expectations about loyalty are correspondingly strengthened by the view that physicians are morally bound to be the agents of their patients.

The importance of this connection to moral justification can be underlined by comparing some other expectations physicians may have about their professional roles, such as the expectation that their judgment will remain insulated from outside examination—"second-guessing"—including quality review. This expectation has been encouraged by some images of glamorous medicine. But it is not supported by an underlying moral theory of the profession; good care in the interests of patients may well be fostered by rigorous peer review. Nor is it based on well-supported beliefs about the long-standing nature of the profession. So the case for the moral significance of physicians' expectations about loyalty is much stronger. Another less defensible example might be physicians' expectations about the structure of their work load. Many physicians may have entered medicine and chosen specialties with the expectation that they would have readily controllable demands on their time—no night calls or emergency-room duty, for example. The recent Omnibus Budget Reconciliation Act, strengthening the obligations of emergency rooms and imposing penalties on physicians for noncompliance, has the potential to threaten these expectations.[46] But once again, the case for these expectations is not very strong; it is not reasonable to expect that favorable practice patterns will remain unchanged, and the expectations are undercut by ethical arguments about the duty to provide care.

Now, compare physicians' expectations about high levels of income with their expectations about the ability to exercise independent judgment on behalf of patients. Consider a careful career planner who selected medicine, and even a particular medical specialty, because of its projected income level. While this physician may have believed reasonably that physicians' incomes would remain relatively high compared with other occupations, it is less clear that the physician had any reasonable foundation for believing that medicine would remain disproportionately highly paid or that the chosen specialty would remain one of the most lucrative. There may have been some sources of encouragement—for example, from those already in the specialization, or funding patterns set by current governmental reimbursement policy. But it would not have been reasonable to construe either of these as reassurance that things would not change. Professionals today generally are struggling with the realization that it is not reasonable to assume that the world will be unchanging, and that chosen occupations will remain frozen in time, in success, or in prestige. Nor are very high incomes integral to conceptions of identity and purpose in the same way that enjoyment of work and pride in excellence generally are, although there may be a few counterexamples who fundamentally define themselves in terms of maximizing what they earn. Finally, no one has the right to earn the income that some physicians might even have reasonably projected they were likely to earn at the time they entered professional training. Indeed, it is surely arguable that the very high income levels enjoyed by many professionals are unjust.

Moreover, this hypothetical income-maximizing physician surely overrepresents many physicians' expectations about earnings. Expectations of very high income are quite different from expectations of relative affluence. It does seem reasonable for physicians entering medical school, even today, to believe that they will lead lives of relative affluence. They are encouraged in this belief, not least by the expense of medical-school tuition and their ready access to debt.

Most of them will have taken out student loans and made various other important life choices—marriage, childbearing, mortgage debt, retirement investments—based on assumptions of relative affluence. Any restructuring of the medical profession so radical that it made it difficult for physicians to lead such relatively affluent lives, that changed their whole conceptions of what kinds of opportunities would be available to them and their families, would be a more serious matter from the point of view of expectations. This is an illustration of the kind of difficulty posed by doing moral theory in conditions of partial injustice. Even if we believe there is a background argument that the current structure of professional earnings is unjust, there are moral reasons that count against immediately and completely changing the structure without giving some attention to the expectations it has engendered. This is not to say that physicians' incomes must remain untouched at their current level, but it is to say that changes should not entirely ignore expectations about life-style. And there are many ways to introduce changes while taking some of these expectations into account. An example would be forgiving educational debt in exchange for participation at lower income levels in one of the versions of a universal health care system discussed above.

On the physicians' side, we might therefore conclude that expectations about professional integrity carry the most moral weight. Expectations about a relatively affluent life-style carry some moral weight, at least in terms of suggesting we consider gradualism and accommodation when changes are introduced. Specific expectations about high income levels or of comparative income levels for different specialties are not morally significant. To the extent that the Canadian prototypes are more protective of physician integrity than other proposals for universal health care, they are thus morally preferable from the point of view of physicians' expectations.

On the side of patients' expectations, the desire to be able to exercise autonomy may have affected the kinds of care settings patients have sought for themselves. So may the desire to receive certain kinds of care. These care settings may in turn have engendered expectations. Expectations both of autonomy and of caring are relatively important morally. They may be reasonable and long-standing. They may have been encouraged by the patient's care setting and access to that setting. They are likely to be connected to the patient's sense of self-definition. Finally, they are each connected to important moral themes about the practice of medicine, and receive important support from that connection. On the other hand, some patient expectations about individualized kinds of care may be increasingly unrealistic in light of shrinking resources. To the extent that either the employment-based or the Canadian models are likely to affect current choices or ongoing care, this is cause for moral discussion. Once again, a possible conclusion to draw is the need to phase in or cushion the impact of change.

Patients also have expectations about access to care. These expectations too may have been reasonable and encouraged by many sources, including employer promises of insurance, the conduct of physicians, or long-standing social policy. Like expectations about the structure of the physician-patient relationship, expectations of access may also acquire moral importance because of their connection to underlying moral imperatives, in this case the linkage between care and health or functioning. To the extent that managed-care plans seem more likely to disappoint patient expectations about access to certain forms of care and continued autonomy, they are less desirable than plans based on the Canadian model of universal insurance.

Finally, the American expectation that medical care can bring results, especially technologically intensive care, will no doubt be in for disappointment under any of the proposals for universal health care. All the plans seek cost savings as the trade-off for expanding coverage. The favorite source of cost savings is expensive, low-efficacy care. Eliminating such cost-ineffective care seems relatively painless. But it will take away some of those straws at which people grasp, the sense that there is always something to be done or something new to be tried. The more gradual phase-in of new technology of the sort found in Canada, moreover, may delay even the introduction of some highly beneficial forms of care. On the one hand, we might argue that this disappointment of expectations is not a serious problem morally, because these expectations are largely based on irrational beliefs and perhaps are flatly unsatisfiable. But patients may well have been reasonably encouraged to hold such beliefs. Sometimes the new forms of care may indeed be medically useful. Perhaps the best compromise is a gradual testing of the efficacy of various therapeutic modalities, many of which are used without clear empirical support today, and a phase-out of those that are of limited efficacy. This could be coupled with rigorous but expeditious evaluation of proposed new therapies. I suspect, however, that disappointments about new discoveries will be something of a political problem, that pressures will continue to be placed on the system, and that American attitudes here will not change easily.

Thus, consideration of expectations suggests a priority of concerns, with access to expected kinds of care being of serious concern, along with physicians' abilities to pursue their careers with integrity and patients' expectations of autonomy, caring, and fidelity. Ironically, however, the real problem of expectations in American health care is posed by the expectations that cost a great deal but do not matter morally—that health care can conquer death, if we only try hard enough.

NOTES

1. One study that attempts to correlate patient expectations with patient satisfaction is Feletti, Firman, and Sanson-Fisher, "Patient Satisfaction with Primary-Care Consultations," *Journal of Behavioral Medicine* 9 (1986): 389–99.

2. E.g., *Ricks v. Budge*, 64 P.2d 208 (Utah 1937).

3. See, e.g., Thomas Halper, *The Misfortunes of Others: End Stage Renal Disease in the United Kingdom* (Cambridge: Cambridge University Press, 1989), esp. chap. 3.

4. Legal obligations now accompany some of these expectations. See, e.g., *Canterbury v. Spence*, 464 F.2d 772 (D.C. Cir., 1972) (reasonable patient standard of informed consent); *Truman v. Thomas*, 611 P.2d 902 (Cal. 1980) (right of informed refusal requires disclosure of the risks of forgoing care). There are many discussions of the significance of these changes in the law of informed consent; for the suggestion that physicians should clarify expectations about informed consent, see Green, "Minimizing Malpractice Risks by Role Clarification," *Annals of Internal Medicine*, August 1, 1988, pp. 234–41.

5. State statutes governing the creation of advance directives may provide that it is unprofessional conduct to fail to honor a directive; see, e.g., Utah Code Ann. § 75-2-1112(3).

6. Franz Ingelfinger, "Arrogance," *New England Journal of Medicine* (hereafter *NEJM*) 303 (1980): 1507–11, laments the ways in which a medical ethic of autonomy appears to brush aside expectations of being cared for.

7. Arguments that professionals have obligations of confidentiality frequently presume that clients will not feel free to seek fully effective advice unless confidentiality is assured. A classic example of this view about confidentiality is Monroe Freedman, "Professional Responsibility of the Criminal Defense Lawyer: The Three Hardest Questions," *Michigan Law Review* 64 (1966): 1469–84. There appear to be no controlled studies, however, that have assessed the importance of confidentiality to consulta-

tion, in either law or medicine. For a defense of confidentiality that does not presume clients' expectations, see Landesman, "Confidentiality and the Lawyer-Client Relationship," in David Luban, ed., *The Good Lawyer: Lawyers' Roles and Lawyers' Ethics* (Totowa, N.J.: Rowman and Allanheld (1984), pp. 191–213.

8. *Sullivan v. O'Connor*, 296 N.E.2d 183 (Mass. 1973). *Guilmet v. Campbell*, 188 N.W.2d 601 (Mich. 1971).

9. Halper, *The Misfortunes of Others*; Rudolf Klein, *The Politics of the National Health Service* (London: Longman Group, 1983). One very interesting longitudinal study of five family practices in London suggests that patients both expected more than they got (only 57 percent of those who had expected physical examinations actually received them) and got more than they expected (48 percent of those who had not expected prescriptions were given them) (Margot Jefferys and Hessie Sachs, *Rethinking General Practice: Dilemmas in Primary Medical Care* [London: Tavistock Publications, 1983], p. 287).

10. For discussion of practice standards, see, e.g., Pierce, "The Development of Anesthesia Guidelines and Standards," *Quality Review Bulletin* 16 (1990): 61–64; Robinson, "Medical Practice Standards: HCFA Joins the Fray," *Hospitals* 62 (1988): 18. For discussion of consensus conferences, see, e.g., Wortman, Vinokur and Sechrest, "Do Consensus Conferences Work? A Process Evaluation of the NIH Consensus Development Program," *Journal of Health Politics, Policy and Law* (hereafter *JHPPL*) 13 (1988): 469–98; Kosecoff, Kanouse, Rogers, McCloskey, Winslow, and Brook, "Effects of the NIH Consensus Development Program on Physician Practice," *Journal of the American Medical Association* (hereafter *JAMA*) 258 (1987): 2708–13.

11. See, e.g., *Musto v. American General Corp.*, 861 F.2d 897 (6th Cir. 1988); Kress, "Benefit Vesting in Employee Health Plans," *Tort and Insurance Law Journal* 24 (1988): 88–117.

12. The "Baby Doe" regulations are at 45 C.F.R. § 1340.15 (1990).

13. Jay Katz's study of communication between doctors and their patients, *The Silent World of Doctor and Patient* (New York: Free Press, 1984), is as much about physicians' expectations as it is about the expectations of patients.

14. American physicians can terminate relationships with their patients provided they give the patients notice that is adequate enough to allow them to seek alternative care. E.g., *Payton v. Weaver*, 182 Cal. Rptr. 225 (Cal. App. 1982). It is more difficult in the United Kingdom for physicians to rearrange care for their patients; one study of family-practice physicians in London suggests that a reasonable share of referrals to specialists occur because general practitioners cannot "fire" patients but need relief from some patients whom they find difficult, recalcitrant, or unresponsive (Jefferys and Sachs, *Rethinking General Practice*, p. 53).

15. For a discussion of the possibility that public or corporate policy might constrain physician behavior, see, e.g., Paul Campbell and Nancy M.

Kane, "Physician-Management Relationships at HCA: A Case Study," *JHPPL* 15 (1990): 591–605.

16. A pathbreaking sociological study of physicians' expectations about care is Renée Fox and J. P. Swazey, *The Courage to Fail* (Chicago: University of Chicago Press, 1974). Jay Katz's *The Silent World* also describes the difficulty physicians have in admitting uncertainty, even to themselves.

17. See, e.g., Hsiao et al., "Estimating Physicians' Work for a Resource-Based Relative-Value Scale," *NEJM* 319 (1988): 835; *JAMA* 260 (1988): 2347–2444 (a set of articles setting out the controversy).

18. Robert Nozick, *Anarchy, State and Utopia* (New York: Basic Books, 1974).

19. *Campbell v. Mincey*, 413 F. Supp. 16 (D. Miss. 1975), aff'd., 542 F.2d 573 (6th Cir. 1976); *Hurley v. Eddingfield*, 50 N.E. 1058 (Ind. 1901).

20. *O'Neill v. Montefiore Hospital*, 202 N.Y.S.2d 436 (N.Y. App. 1960); *Guerrero v. Copper Queen Hospital*, 537 P.2d 1329 (Ariz. 1975).

21. 42 U.S.C. § 1395dd (1990).

22. This point was suggested to me by Allen Buchanan.

23. Rawls calls this "partial compliance" theory (John Rawls, *A Theory of Justice* [Cambridge: Harvard University Press, 1971]).

24. There has been a great deal of recent discussion about the moral significance of special relationships. See, for example, Thomas Nagel, *The View from Nowhere* (Princeton: Princeton University Press, 1986), esp. chap. 9. But there has been little discussion about the interrelationships between special relationships and expectations.

25. For full discussion of the various types of plans under consideration, see Robert P. Huefner, "Designing a Health Care System: Considering the Need to Know," this volume.

26. Alain Enthoven and Richard Kronick, "A Consumer-Choice Health Plan for the 1990s," part 1, *NEJM* 320 (1989): 29–37; "A Consumer-Choice Health Plan for the 1990s," part 2, *NEJM* 320 (1989): 94–101.

27. The expectations created by a practice of providing care for the improvident might themselves be a new source of moral claims. Unless Enthoven and Kronick are prepared to insist that everyone purchase care, they will face an unappealing choice between watching the improvident suffer the consequences of going without care and creating the incentives and expectations associated with a practice of bailing people out. This dilemma illustrates how a policy can create new expectations, which themselves raise moral issues.

28. Enthoven and Kronick, "Consumer-Choice Health Plan," part 2, p. 96.

29. See, e.g., Gina Kolata, "Being Thorough Can Be Costly—to the Doctor," *New York Times*, March 20, 1986, p. E6.

30. 42 U.S.C. § 300e-1(1)(D). The federal regulations specify that no other mental-health services are to be included as basic, beyond these acute outpatient services (42 C.F.R. § 417.101[d][2] [1989]).

31. 42 U.S.C. § 300e-1(1).

32. 42 C.F.R. § 417.101(a)(2)(i) (1989).

33. 42 C.F.R. § 4l7.101(d)(15) (1989).

34. 42 C.F.R. § 417.101(d)(4) (1989).

35. 42 U.S.C. § 300e(1). This statutory presumption against the inclusion of new forms of organ transplantation was originally intended to last for only three years (Public Law no. 99–660, § 812, 100 Stat. 3801 [1986]). But in 1988, Congress deleted the time limitation; HMOs are not required to include in basic care any organ transplants that were not recognized as standard care as of April 15, 1985. Public Law no. 100–517, 102 Stat. 1579 (1988). The intention was to put HMOs on an equal footing with other health care plans that are not required to include organ transplants; see 1988 U.S. Code, *Congressional and Administration News*, p. 3235.

36. See Huefner, this volume. Huefner argues that these trade-offs should be made with public awareness and discussion.

37. See, e.g., Hellinger, "Perspectives on Enthoven's Consumer Choice Health Plan," *Inquiry* 19 (1982): 199.

38. Of course, this phasedown is quite likely happening to some extent anyway, as employers seek to cut the costs of their health insurance programs. Nevertheless, it is likely to be accentuated under the Enthoven-Kronick plan and, in any event, there would also be a shift in the ability of employees to purchase additional care with pre-tax dollars.

39. Marjorie M. Kress, "Benefit Vesting in Employee Health Plans," *Tort and Insurance Law Journal* 24 (1988): 88–117.

40. Swartz, "Why Requiring Employers to Provide Health Insurance Is a Bad Idea," *JHPPL* 151 (1990): 779–92.

41. Enthoven and Kronick, "Consumer-Choice Health Plan," part 2, p. 97.

42. Ibid., p. 100.

43. David V. Himmelstein, et al., "A National Health Program for the United States: A Physicians' Proposal," *NEJM* 320 (1989): 102–8.

44. Surely, there will be empirical debate over whether expanding the range of health care coverage will require cutting back elsewhere. Daniel I. Wikler, for example, argues that administrative cost savings of a single, universal insurance system would be sufficient to offset the costs of bringing everyone into the system. I am not equipped to judge whether Wikler's claims are anywhere near likely to be true. The American College of Physicians estimates that the approximate costs of health care administration in 1989 were $110 billion ("Access to Health Care," *Annals of Internal Medicine* 112 [1990]: 641–61). If all these costs were saved under a universal system of health care, surely an unrealistic assumption, this would free up $2,973 for health care spending on each of the thirty-seven million uninsured in the United States. This may be more than generous enough, since estimates of the appropriate premium for basic single coverage seem to be about $1,400/year. See, for example, Enthoven and Kronick, "Consumer-Choice Health Plan," part 1. On the other hand, it allows nothing for administrative costs (which may be fairly high if there are limits on what

care is funded) or for others who are currently underinsured. Even if Wikler is correct about the possibility of administrative cost savings, there are a variety of ways in which changes could be structured that would still affect expectations—about autonomy, for example—in different ways.

45. See the essay by John G. Francis, this volume.

46. 42 U.S.C. § 1395dd (1990).

Public and Private Responsibilities in the U.S. Health Care System

Allen Buchanan*

THE EXPERIENCE OF ETHICAL CONFLICT IN THE PRIVATE SECTOR

Some private health care insurers report that they are experiencing conflicts between what they take to be their ethical obligations and the pressures of escalating competition and cost-containment strategies. Among the questions they are asking themselves are these.

1. Is it ethically permissible to charge higher premiums or to deny coverage to individuals who presently have or have had a specific disease or who test positive for a high probability of some disease (e.g., those who are HIV positive or those whom genetic testing or screening indicates are at high risk for certain diseases)?
2. Is it ethically permissible for the insurer to limit payment to care received from providers selected by the insurer in order to reduce the insurer's costs?

Some provider-insurers are asking similar questions about the scope and limits of their ethical responsibilities. Should health maintenance organizations (HMOs) continue their traditional commitment to "comprehensive coverage" for all subscribers even if this means that fewer potential subscribers will be able to afford to join the plan? Should the organization depart from its traditional "first-dollar coverage" philosophy and introduce substantial co-payments or deductibles to reduce costs?

---

*This essay is a revision of one prepared for a Blue Cross/Blue Shield project on the ethics of insurance. I am indebted to the following individuals for their valuable comments on an earlier draft of this essay: Norman Daniels, Albert Jonsen, and Paul Menzel.

Similarly, administrators of private health care provider organizations also report that they are increasingly grappling with ethical dilemmas that arise because of competition and cost-containment pressures.[1] Now that the use of diagnosis-related groups (DRGs) has reduced the surplus revenues from Medicare hospital payments and private insurers are much more careful about which services and procedures they will reimburse, hospitals find it much more difficult to "cross-subsidize" uninsured patients. Is it, therefore, ethically permissible for a hospital to target its marketing strategies only to insured patients or simply to adopt a policy of not admitting the uninsured (except where law requires emergency treatment regardless of ability to pay)?[2]

It is tempting to plunge immediately into these ethical issues, but before doing so there is a prior puzzle to be solved: Why are these private organizations—these business concerns—exercising themselves over these issues in the first place? What assumptions about the ethical obligations or responsibilities of their organizations must they be making for it even to be possible for them to experience these ethical conflicts?

OBLIGATIONS CONCERNING ACCESS

It is important to understand that the ethical problems listed are not the familiar ones that virtually any large corporation faces and which are grist for the mill of the emerging discipline of business ethics— the standard dilemmas concerning truth telling, exploiting the misfortune or ignorance of competitors (or customers), whistle-blowing, and all the rest.[3] Instead, the chief ethical issue common to these concerns of private insurers and providers is something quite different. It is the question of the scope and limits of the ethical responsibilities these organizations have to help solve or at least not to worsen the problem of access to health care in the United States.

Even to pose this question is to assume or at least strongly to suggest that such private organizations do have some ethical obligations concerning access. Indeed, unless members of these organizations made this assumption, they would not experience the ethical conflicts in question. It is this assumption that we should first probe. There are two distinct ways in which an obligation to help people secure access might be understood, but neither of them by itself implies that private health care insurers or providers have any special obligations concerning access.

The first focuses upon the potential recipient of care and assumes that all citizens have a moral right to health care, the sort of right which has as its correlative an obligation on the part of someone to provide health care to those who have the right. The most plausible arguments for such a right, however, imply that the correlative obligation falls upon society as a whole, not upon some particular organizations within society.[4] If any institution or agency can be said to be ultimately responsible for seeing that this societal obligation is met it would have to be the state, not any particular organization. And in American society it is both customary and reasonable to assume that the federal government has the ultimate responsibility for seeing that societal obligations are met. The federal government alone, because of its taxation powers, is equipped to provide adequate resources for securing all citizens' rights to health care and to do so in such a way that the burden of providing these resources is distributed fairly in society, with no segment of society bearing a disproportionate share of the costs of fulfilling what is a societal obligation.[5]

The second way of understanding the assumption that there is an obligation (on someone's part) to provide access to health care focuses not primarily upon the individual who is the recipient of care but upon various benefits to society at large of having a healthy citizenry—a more productive work force, a sturdy army to preserve national security, and so on. It is generally thought that this way of conceiving of the obligation to provide access to health care rather than any assumption that access to health care is a fundamental individual moral right, provided the ideological underpinnings of the first modern health and social welfare programs in Western Europe. The obligation to provide access to health care, then, is based upon the need for the social goods derived from a healthy populace, and the ultimate responsibility for seeing that the obligation is met rests again with the state as the entity that is authorized to ensure that important social goods are achieved. Whether or not any private organizations have obligations to provide access to health care cannot be inferred from the assumption that an individual has a moral right to health care or that public health is an important social good. Much more must be said about what the division of responsibility is (or ought to be) before any determinate claims about obligations can be warranted.

What is common to both approaches is the assumption that the obligation to provide access to health care is primarily a *societal* obligation rather than an individual obligation or one that falls primarily on particular private organizations or entities within society. The President's Commission on medical ethics summarized the chief reasons for regarding this obligation as societal. "Securing equitable access is a societal rather than a merely private or individual responsibility for several reasons. First, while health is of special importance for human beings, health care—especially scientific health care—is a social product requiring the skills and efforts of many individuals; it is not something that individuals can provide for themselves solely through their own efforts."[6]

Second, because the need for health care is both unevenly distributed among persons and highly unpredictable and because the cost of securing care may be great, few individuals could secure adequate care without relying on some social mechanism for sharing costs. Third, if persons generally deserved their health conditions or if the need for health care were fully within the individual's control, the fact that some lack adequate care would not be viewed as an inequity. But differences in health status, and hence differences in health care needs, are largely undeserved because they are, for the most part, not within the individual's control.[7]

Still, even if the primary obligation to provide adequate access to care falls on society as a whole, this does not mean that particular social entities and individuals have no obligations regarding access. Although a distinction must be made between society and government as one institution within society, in a system such as that of the United States the central, or federal, government has a special responsibility for ensuring that basic societal obligations are met, for reasons already noted. In particular, the federal government alone has the authority and the resources to devise and enforce an effective and coordinated societal effort to ensure access. Moreover, whereas modern pluralistic societies are composed of many communities, each with its own collective obligations, the federal government alone can serve as the ultimate agent for meeting collective obligations that transcend the boundaries of various communities within society.

The nature and extent of governmental activity required to ensure that the societal obligation is met will vary depending on the particular circumstances, resources, and ethical and political traditions of the society in question. Thus "the recognition of a collective or societal obligation does not [itself] imply that government should be the only or even the primary institution involved in the complex enterprise of making health care available."[8]

ALTERNATIVE SCHEMES FOR SECURING ACCESS

There are four different ways in which the federal government might discharge its responsibility for seeing that the societal obligation to provide access to health care is met. Each constitutes a different division of responsibilities among organizations and institutions within society.

1. Government provision of an adequate level of health care for all: a national health service, with health care professionals serving as direct employees of the government.
2. Government funding of care with private provision: national health insurance—that is, a single insurer, the federal government—which allows individuals to choose among private providers; or insurance vouchers supplied by the federal government, which individuals can use to purchase insurance from whichever private insurer they choose.
3. Mixed system: some government provision of care and/or funding of privately provided care, along with private insurance and private provision (the current U.S. system, which includes the VA CHAMPUS [the government health care program for families of active military personnel], Medicaid, Medicare, a large number of private insurers and private providers, as well as some private charitable institutions).

In the fourth system the government would have to do nothing positive to discharge its responsibility to see that the societal obligation is met:

4. Purely private system: adequate access to care achieved for all through a combination of private insurance markets and private provision, supplemented by private charity.

Current policy debates about access to health care as well as the ethical conflicts experienced by private insurers and providers assume that this fourth approach would not be adequate and I will proceed in this discusssion upon that assumption as well. (It is worth pausing for a moment to reflect, however, upon whether the assumption that a purely private system will not suffice reflects skepticism about the extent of the charitable impulse, appreciation of the difficulties of coordinating charitable efforts in an efficient way so as to fill the gaps left by market provision, or an uneasy suspicion that there really is no social consensus that individuals do have a moral right to health care).[9] The present U.S. health care system is, of course, of the third type, but in almost any interpretation of what an adequate level of care is, this system is not providing it for everyone. Estimates vary, but there is a broad consensus among health care researchers that at least thirty-five million Americans have no private health care insurance and are not eligible for any government programs, including Medicare, Medicaid, VA, and CHAMPUS. Perhaps another fifteen million or more have private insurance whose benefits fall below what would count as an "adequate level of care" in any reasonable interpretation of that rather vague concept.[10]

TWO CONTRASTING MODELS OF THE ROLE OF PRIVATE ORGANIZATIONS IN A MIXED SYSTEM

There are two quite different ways in which ethical responsibilities for access could be distributed in a mixed system. First, the federal government could itself assume full responsibility for filling in any gaps left by the combined operations of the private insurance market and private charity. In other words, the scope of government provision and/or funding of care or of private insurance would be determined by the size of the gap between an adequate level of care for all and the care provided through private insurance and charity. According to this arrangement, neither private insurers nor private providers (nor private insurers/providers such as HMOs) have any obligations to help ensure access to an adequate level of care for all. They will, presumably, have obligations to pay taxes, and some portion of their taxes will be used by the federal government to see that the gap between the level of care provided by the private sector and an adequate level of care for all is closed, but in this respect they will be indistinguishable from other taxpayers. Private insurers and providers, in this model, are simply businesses like any other. They have no more of an obligation to provide access to care to those who cannot purchase insurance coverage or pay directly than automobile dealers are obligated to give cars to the poor or grocers are obligated to hand out free food.[11]

If such private organizations could be said to have obligations concerning access at all, they are obligations only in a very loose sense, what moral philosophers call imperfect duties or duties of charity. These are not specific obligations to provide some determinate level of aid to any particular needy persons, but rather simply a duty to do something to benefit some of the less fortunate.[12] The standard form of an imperfect duty or charitable obligation is as follows: one ought to help (some) persons in need (in some way or other), so long as one can do so without "excessive cost" to oneself. The looseness of their obligations strongly affects the possibility of ethical appraisal of the organizations' practices. They cannot be judged deficient if they fail to provide any particular kind or level of aid to any particular potential recipient, and it is not appropriate for society to hold them accountable, by public censure or through legal penalties or regulative actions.

The second way of conceiving of the obligations in a mixed system has quite different implications for the ethical status of private insurers and providers. The idea is that private insurers and providers have special obligations, just as the government has its own obligations. The extent of the government's obligations is limited by the extent of the obligations of private organizations. In the first model, any gap in access signals a failure on the part of the government, since its obligation is simply to fill whatever gap is left by the operation of the competitive market plus charity. In the second model, a gap in access need not signal a failure on the government's part. Instead, the fault may lie with private insurers or providers who have not fulfilled the special obligations that are assigned to them in the overall social division of responsibility. There are various ways in which such special obligations might be assigned. As in the case of the Hill-Burton Act, private organizations might receive public resources (in outright grants or subsidized loans) in exchange for discharging certain obligations to improve access. Alternatively, tax exemptions or other tax incentives may be granted in exchange for organizational policies that improve access. Finally, the government (federal or state) may unilaterally impose obligations on certain institutions or types of organizations, as in all-payers schemes that require all licensed insurers in a particular jurisdiction to share the burden of insuring some of those who could not afford insurance on terms the market offers or as in taxes on hospital revenues to create a fund for the medically indigent. For ease of reference let us call the first conception of a mixed system the "governmental responsibility conception" and the second the "shared responsibility conception." The difference between these two ways of conceiving of how the job of providing equitable access gets done in a mixed system is crucial. Once the difference is clearly articulated it becomes evident how ambiguous appeal to cooperative private sector/public sector solutions to the access problem is, and what a handy tool of obfuscation this ambiguity supplies to the federal government for rationalizing its failure to discharge its fundamental responsibility for ensuring that the societal obligation to provide equitable access to all is actually met. It is all too easy for the federal government to divert attention from its failure to fulfill its distinctive responsibility to ensure that the societal obligation is met by suggesting that private entities should do more. The common slogan that health care in the United States is provided by the combined efforts of the public and private sectors, then, is descriptively true but tends to obscure the ethical issues. Unless the division of responsibility is more clearly specified, it is simply not possible to evaluate the ethical behavior of actors within the system.

Under the governmental responsibility system it will not be possible to say that a particular private organization is not fulfilling any particular obligation—at most it will be possible to say that this or that organization is ungenerous or uncharitable or "ought to do more," just as we might say this of an individual who did little or nothing to help the needy. But nothing of substance can be said about how much more should be done or precisely what should be done by this or that actor, since all of the "duties" that they have will be imperfect or indeterminate, duties of charity. Nor will it be possible to say that this or that organization is not doing its fair share, since there will be no basis for ascertaining what a fair share is. The very notion of a fair share, at least as far as it can serve as the basis for determinate ethical appraisals, has sense only where there is an integrated, systematic assignment of specific responsibilities. And where no determinate sense can be given to the notion of a fair share, no organization can rightly be publicly censured or penalized for failing to do its fair share. In a mixed system of the governmental responsibility type, then, the "ethical obligations" of private insurers or providers are a matter of private morality, the corporate analog of the question of conscience which an individual may pose herself when she asks whether her charitable contributions are adequate.

This last statement admits, however, of one important qualification. Some private organizations have imposed upon themselves and their members certain specific obligations, or, perhaps more precisely, have voluntarily taken on certain special commitments through their collective choices. The "constitution" of a particular HMO or of a private insurer such as the Blue Cross/Blue Shield system could be understood as including a self-imposed special obligation of a very general and somewhat abstract sort—a self-chosen mission of providing "affordable, comprehensive coverage," for example.[13] By such an organization's "constitution" I mean, not necessarily a written, explicit document, but rather something that is to be constructed from certain documents and from authoritative interpretations and elaborations of them as well as the long-standing patterns of official behavior of the organization in question. In the process of its development, such an organization may translate these rather abstract mission statements or ideals into more concrete, self-imposed obligations. To the extent that these obligations are self-imposed and flow from the organization's own interpretation of its self-chosen mission, they may be modified or even repudiated through appropriate processes within the organization. This places a severe limitation on the appropriateness of public ethical appraisal of the organization's behavior, in effect removing the possibility of society holding the organization accountable for failing to live up to these obligations (unless, of course, their doing so happens to violate contractual obligations or involves illegalities).[14]

COST CONTAINMENT AND COMPETITION IN MIXED SYSTEMS

In an effort to curb rising health care expenditures, the federal government, as well as a number of health policy analysts, has advocated increasing competition.[15] But when the governmental-responsibility type of mixed system is subjected to serious competitive pressures, altruism becomes more costly for any particular organization and the scope of its imperfect duties shrinks. Unless a particular organization has assurance that its competitors are making commensurate transfers of resources to the needy, it risks putting itself at a competitive disadvantage by shaping its policies so as to improve access. But its imperfect duty—the only "duty" concerning access it has in a governmental-responsibility mixed system (unless it happens to choose to impose on itself some special, determinate obligation)—is only a duty to render aid *if this does not involve excessive costs* to the organization itself. And as competition increases, the cost of being charitable rises.

Even if every private organization in such a system sincerely desires to do something substantial to ameliorate the access problem, each may find it not only rational but ethically permissible to reduce its contributions to coping with the access problem. Purely voluntary agreements among organizations in the private sector are not likely to solve this problem for two reasons. First, it may be very difficult to achieve a consensus among all potential competitors as to the level of contribution for each that would put none at a competitive disadvantage. For one thing, they may lack the institutional mechanisms and authority structures for creating such a consensus. But second, and more important, as long as the agreement is purely voluntary there will be an incentive to defect either because one hopes thereby to gain a competitive advantage or because one fears that someone else will do so and that this will damage one's own competitive position. Let us call this the "shrinking imperfect duty phenomenon." In sum, as competition raises the costs of altruism, the threshold at which a private organization's efforts to improve access begin to involve "excessive costs" lowers, and the scope of its imperfect duty shrinks. Purely voluntary efforts to avoid the shrinking imperfect duty phenomenon are likely to be of limited value.

At present the U.S. government not only permits but encourages increasing competition in health care (as a means of reducing costs), while at the same time abdicating more and more of its responsibility for ensuring access and attempting to justify this policy by emphasizing the role of the private sector in achieving adequate access. The result is likely to continue to be a widening access gap, as the government's contribution and the level of charity that it is reasonable to expect from private organizations both shrink. In general, the strategy of containing costs by increasing competition in the private sector makes sense only if one or the other of three circumstances obtain. (1) A governmental-responsibility type mixed system is utilized and the government is willing and able to fill the widening access gap that will result from the shrinking scope of private imperfect duties (as ever smaller contributions tend toward "excessive costs"). (2) A shared-responsibility type mixed system is successfully implemented so that each organization's specific obligations are fairly assigned and in such a way that no organization is thereby put at a competitive disadvantage, and these obligations are adequately enforced by the government. (3) A governmental-responsibility type system is utilized but private organizations develop arrangements for binding agreements among themselves so as to ensure that all will do their part and so as to eliminate the incentive to be a free rider, thus avoiding the shrinking imperfect duty phenomenon. For example, private (i.e., nongovernmental) providers or insurers might make a multilateral contract with each other to divide among themselves the burden of ensuring access for some or all of those individuals who are not covered by government programs and who cannot afford private insurance at market rates. If such contracts were deemed legally valid, then the ordinary mechanisms of contract law would provide enforcement to overcome the problems of purely voluntary agreements mentioned above. There would be no need for the government to specify and assign special obligations to private sector organizations and to enforce them.

As a way of coping with the access problem, the third approach suffers from serious limitations. I have already noted that private organizations may lack collective decision-making and authority structures. Yet these may be indispensable for creating a consensus as to what a fair division of responsibility for access among private organizations would consist of. Unless such a consensus can be gained, no multilateral contract will be made and the shrinking imperfect duty problem will not be averted. The larger the number of parties to the attempt to work out such contracts and the more diverse and conflicting their interests, the slimmer the prospects will be for achieving the needed consensus. Further, while smaller-scale, local arrangements are more likely to succeed in gaining sufficient consensus to create multilateral contracts that will assign specific special obligations to private organizations, merely local efforts are of limited efficacy as a response to the access problem for two reasons. First, the result is likely to be an uncoordinated patchwork of local arrangements with redundancies here and gaps there. Second, small-scale arrangements are prone to instability. A new provider or insurer that comes on the scene will not be a party to the multilateral contract, and its presence will give those who are an incentive to defect from the agreement or let it lapse. Indeed the inability to control entrance into local markets will be a barrier to achieving an agreement in the first place, since local organizations will not wish to make themselves vulnerable to newcomers who will not be under the constraints of an agreement and who will consequently enjoy a competitive advantage. Finally, and perhaps most important, if, as I have suggested, the obligation to provide adequate access is a societal obligation, then a fair division of responsibility for achieving adequate access must be all-inclusive, society-wide, not merely local. Merely local efforts have in fact been rightly criticized on grounds of fairness. For example, in some states "all-payer schemes" have been instituted requiring all health care insurers to contribute to a fund for the medically indigent. Critics of all-payer schemes point out that these arrangements improve access for the poor by, in effect, placing a special tax on one segment of the population, the insured sick. The general problem is that merely local efforts are unlikely to be coordinated in such a way that a fair overall division of responsibility across institutions and organizations is achieved. Instead, local arrangements are likely to shift the burden of securing adequate access onto others in ad hoc ways. The implementation of the second way of conceiving of obligations concerning access in a mixed system, the shared responsibility model, then, encounters serious difficulties. An appreciation of these difficulties might well lead private organizations to opt for a governmental-responsibility type of system, if they had the choice.

THE OBLIGATIONS OF PRIVATE INSURERS AND PROVIDERS UNDER EXISTING CONDITIONS

The current U.S. health care system is much closer to a governmental-responsibility type of mixed system than a shared-responsibility type. Neither social consensus nor federal law provides a clear and systematic, much less fair, distribution of determinate obligations for securing access among private-sector institutions and organizations. Tax laws provide exemptions or other advantages to health care providers or insurers that are legally classified as not-for-profit, and the justification of these privileges is that of a pro quid pro: these organizations are thought of as earning the advantages in question in virtue of providing a public benefit, a contribution to the fulfillment of the societal obligation to provide adequate access for all. There are, however, two serious defects in these arrangements. First, the nature of the pro quid pro ensures that we have no reason to believe that what the private organization contributes and what it receives are even roughly equivalent, much less that this is the most efficient way of eliciting private contributions to fulfilling the societal obligation. Second, these are isolated instances, developed in an ad hoc way, not integral elements of a systematic, fair division of responsibilities.

Given the assumption that providing access to health care is a societal obligation and that the responsibility for seeing that this obligation is met rests ultimately with the federal government, the federal government can be faulted for failing *either* to specify, assign, and enforce a fair division of responsibilities among private organizations *or* to do an adequate job of filling in the gaps in access left by the private sector. But what, then, are the obligations of private insurers and private providers under these imperfect conditions?

Apart from any special pro quid pro arrangements and special, self-imposed commitments (which they may revise if they wish), private insurers and private providers have no determinate obligations to help provide access to an adequate level of health care to all. They are at most obligated only in the loose and indeterminate way in which individuals are said to have imperfect duties of charity. In neither case is the obligation sufficiently determinate to justify society or the state holding these private organizations accountable.

It can be argued, however, that at least the larger and more powerful private provider and insurer organizations do have an important higher-order obligation: an obligation to take a leadership role in exerting pressure upon the federal government to fulfill its basic responsibility in one of two ways, either by implementing an effective governmental responsibility system and discharging the responsibility of filling gaps in access left by the private sector or by creating an effective shared-responsibility system in which the obligations of private organizations will be sufficiently determinate so as to justify holding them accountable. If, as may well be the case at present, the prospects for succeeding in getting the federal government to fulfill its basic responsibility are dim, then major private insurers have an obligation to work together to develop arrangements to share among themselves some of the burdens of providing access that the federal government has failed to bear, just as private citizens are obligated to try to coordinate their efforts to aid the needy in the absence of adequate state-directed welfare programs. Because of the special problems created by increasing competition and cost-containment pressures in health care, there may be a greater need for larger-scale coordination and cooperation and for developing private enforcement mechanisms (such as reliance on multilateral contracts) in the case of private health care organizations than is generally the case with individuals who seek to fulfill imperfect duties of charity. Although, as I have already indicated, such private-sector efforts to create a determinate structure of obligations and to overcome free-rider and assurance problems are fraught with difficulties, they may for the forseeable future be the best alternative available. This obligation to help create a system that more effectively addresses the access problem is not, of course, absolute or unconditional. But it seems clear that at least many of the more powerful private insurers and providers could afford to expend significant efforts toward this end without incurring such costs as to undermine their competitive positions. My suggestion is that the effort currently wasted on trying to ascertain the scope and content of specific obligations which do not in fact exist or in attempts to point the finger of blame at other organizations for not doing "their fair share" when no real sense can be given to this notion, should be directed toward developing a system in which obligations are determinate and substantive moral appraisal and social accountability are possible.

NOTES

1. For discussions of ethical issues arising from the new emphasis on competition, see "Money, Medicine, and Markets," ed. Baruch A. Brody, *Journal of Medicine and Philosophy* 12 (February 1987): 1–99.

2. See Dan W. Brock and Allen Buchanan, "Ethical Issues in For-Profit Health Care," in *For-Profit Enterprise in Health Care*, ed. Bradford M. Gray (Washington, D.C.: National Academy Press), l986, pp. 224–49.

3. See Tom L. Beauchamp and Norman E. Bowie, eds., *Ethical Theory and Business*, 2d ed. (Englewood Cliffs, N.J.: Prentice-Hall, 1983).

4. Norman Daniels, *Just Health Care* (Cambridge: Cambridge University Press, 1985), pp. 11–17 and 114–39.

5. Brock and Buchanan, "Ethical Issues in For-Profit Health Care," pp. 227–28.

6. President's Commission for the Study of Ethical Problems in Medicine and Biomedical and Behavioral Research, *Securing Access to Health Care*, vol. 1: *Report* (Washington, D.C.: Government Printing Office, 1983), p. 14.

7. Ibid., p. 23.

8. Ibid., pp. 22–23.

9. Allen Buchanan, "Competition, Charity, and the Right to Health Care," *The Restraint of Liberty*, ed. Thomas Attig et al. (Bowling Green, Ohio: Bowling Green State University, Applied Philosophy Program, 1985), pp. 129–43.

10. Gray, *For-Profit Enterprise in Health Care*, pp. 97–99. Pamela J. Farley, "Who Are the Uninsured?" *Milbank Quarterly*, 63, no. 3 (1985): 476–503. For a discussion of the difficulty of specifying an adequate level of care, see President's Commission, *Securing Access to Health Care*, pp. 35–43.

11. It might be thought that the public subsidies for health care research and medical education would generate special obligations for providers. For a refutation of this claim see Brock and Buchanan, "Ethical Issues in For-Profit Health Care," pp. 228–29.

12. For an analysis of the concept of charity and of distinctions between justice and charity, see Allen Buchanan, "Justice and Charity," *Ethics* 97, no. 3 (1987): 558–75.

13. In the case of the Blue Cross/Blue Shield system the prominence of a self-imposed ethical mission may be explained by the fact that the founders of the organization emerged from a physician-dominated hospital environment in which professionals acknowledged a duty to serve the

needy even at some cost to themselves. (Odin W. Andersen, *Blue Cross since 1929: Accountability and the Public Trust* [Cambridge, Mass.: Ballinger, 1975], pp. 20–21, 29, 40–41, 104–5).

14. Even self-imposed ethical duties, however, are not wholly immune to ethical criticism. For example, a charitable organization might rightly be criticized for having racist policies. This point is due to Norman Daniels.

15. Perhaps the most widely discussed version of the competitive approach is Alain Enthoven's Consumer-Choice Health Plan, described in Alain Enthoven, *Health Plan: The Only Practical Solution to the Soaring Cost of Medical Care* (Reading, Mass.: Addison-Wesley, 1980).

Designing a Health Care System: Considering the Need to Know

Robert P. Huefner

Proposals for national health care are a moving and changing target: stampede-like in their numbers and speed of passing; chameleon-like in changing their concerns and perspectives. To gain some fix on the matter, I will try, in the following five brief and admittedly rough analyses, to contribute some understanding of what the important policy choices are and what ethical discussions might especially help inform these choices.

In the first two analyses I provide background by looking at aspects of feasibility and acceptability which should, or will, shape proposals for change. The first analysis deals with structural problems in the present system; the second analysis, with the political context. These two analyses provide background for a third analysis, in which I review and classify significant approaches which have been recently tried or proposed. The fourth analysis builds upon this review: I inventory significant program choices and take a closer look at the value questions inherent in the various choices. All four analyses then provide the basis for the last and most speculative analysis, in which I attempt to identify those program decisions and related ethical considerations most important to the nature and success of a national health program.

PROGRAM FEASIBILITY

Health policy is commonly divided into three aspects or concerns: cost, quality, and access; there are fundamental flaws in how the present system deals with each of these. If new programs are to be feasible, that is, if they are to do more good than harm, they must address these flaws.

Cost

The health care system includes neither the market mechanisms (cost-conscious consumers, reasonably informed buyers, etc.) nor the regulatory machinery (rate setting, control of supply, etc.) necessary to manage health care costs. While public debate argues over whether a market or a regulatory approach is better, public policy wallows in uncertainty and neither approach is put in place to correct this fifty-year flaw. The uncertainty of public policy is further aggravated by the rapid transitions to vertical integration, managed care, and entrepreneurism among providers.

While either a market or a regulatory approach could work, if made clear and reasonably complete, future efforts to deal with the cost problem are more likely to combine market and regulatory approaches. The combined approach could manage costs if it was organized by a coherent design and directed by coordinated administration: results hard to achieve in any event and nearly impossible until ideological polemics are replaced with an honest admission that a combination is acceptable and sought. The proposal by Enthoven and Kronick (see the list of proposals in a later section) is an attempt to fashion an effective mix of public programs and regulation to encourage further vertical integration and managed care in the private sector in order to establish market mechanisms for cost consciousness, and to help ensure that all or most persons have access to this private care. This mix is an example of a reasonable combination, using competition to control cost (and perhaps quality) and regulation to shape the nature of the competition and to ensure reasonable access. Any combination must decide the following questions:

1. How will the market be structured to assure competition and effective bargaining? For example, will the providers be organized to include primary and specialized care under central management? Will they be vertically integrated to include the physician, hospital, and insurance functions under central management? Will the buyers be organized in some form, as in various proposals for all-payers systems such as the UNY-Care proposal (see the list of proposals)? Whatever the desired competitive structure, how will this structure be encouraged by public programs, tax or other incentives, or regulation? How will the competition affect fairness, relate short-term to long-term cost-effectiveness, respect

privacy, offer choice, deal with personal responsibility, and value life and the quality of life?
2. How will regulation (of employers, insurers, and consumers) attempt to ensure basic coverage? Will the result be fair and efficient?

If the first set of questions is looked at too narrowly in terms of cost reduction, the choices made will violate other legitimate interests such as quality, autonomy, and privacy. This raises a particular concern for process: that choices be made through deliberations which discover and publicly share the trade-offs. It also suggests a special concern for the standards of professional ethics: to what extent can these standards be depended upon to balance the pressures for cost containment, and how will the proposed new structures undermine or strengthen these standards?

Inherent in the second set of questions is the acceptance in a "basic" plan of the need to ration health care and of the fact that there are multiple tiers and that some limit has been placed upon the value of a comfortable and productive life and of life itself. There are rationing, multiple tiers, and limits on the value of life in the present fragmented and incomplete system. But explicitly accepting rationing can be argued as dangerous because the very recognition makes it easier to excuse inadequate care. This, in effect, says that deception, of self and others, may be safer. The counterargument presumes that the best protection is to be found in accurate acknowledgment of the situation and open assessments of options. In either case, and for the choice between them, the issues of truthfulness become especially important to explore.

Quality

The consumer depends, nearly entirely, upon trust in others to measure and ensure the quality of health care. There are only limited audits to ensure that the trust is well placed, and increasingly there are questions of whether such trust is well placed when the delivery system and its incentives focus upon cost management. The quality assurance problem has two aspects. First, the providers have carried nearly the entire responsiblity for the quality of care. While the health care system in the United States enjoys high respect for its quality, it is not perfect: there are conflicts of interest and there are substantial fears that the restructuring of the market will increase the conflicts of interest—to jeopardize seriously the future capacity of the internal control upon which the system now depends. Second, quality has been assessed primarily on the basis of facilities and of the qualifications and processes of the providers, with limited attention to outcomes. Correcting these problems raises two questions which health care professionals and systems have been slow to address:

1. Who, beyond the providers themselves, will share in the responsibility for quality assurance and what will be their roles? This question grows from a concern about the extent to which quality can be ensured by trusting the providers, for whom there may be conflicts of interest, real or perceived. The resolution of the concern raises related considerations of the ethical standards of the professions and of the relative values to be placed upon life versus quality of life when evaluating quality of care.

2. What criteria and data will be used in quality assurance? This question emerges from a concern about the extent to which quality can be ensured by trusting generally accepted standards for facilities, staffing, and procedures. Increased attention to outcomes and to healthiness is an attempt to address this concern and is forcing more careful attention to questions of who should have what data, who should have formal responsibilities for assessing the implications of the data, and what criteria and values regarding life and quality of life should guide the data collection and assessment.

Those who have the most at stake, the patients, are poorly equipped and poorly positioned to make the assessments, while those with technical understanding, the providers, are in positions increasingly suspect for conflict of interest and in any event may not share the patient's perspectives on the values of life and its quality. A structuring of the provider and payer system to build a technically qualified but independent assessor might help. So could more attention to the standards of professional ethics. And so could concern for the issues of truth telling—for example, more fully informing the payer and patient of the performance of providers and of the probable outcomes of procedures.

The second question, about criteria and data, has even more to do with truth telling. Given that information about quality of care can never be complete, what is the best approximation of the truth (in terms of being reasonably complete, usable, and fair) and how can that be more accurately shared? Concerns about the collection and use of data also bring up privacy issues which condition conclusions about truth telling.

Access

The feasibility of extending accessibility is made difficult, even desperate, because 5 percent of the population account for 50% of the costs in any given year, and because insurers have some capacity to predict who will be in that 5 percent.[1] The basic structure of the present insurance market is fundamentally flawed: it rewards insurers for avoiding coverage of persons needing health care. Community rating (insurance rates based upon average costs of covering all subscribers within a geographic market) and open enrollment (the ability of a person to shift from one insurance carrier to another) are means to avoid this problem. But the trend is in the other direction. There is increasing use of experience rating (setting insurance rates for particular employers or groups on the basis of past and predicted costs for only that group), and those persons with health problems are offered impossibly expensive policies or simply refused coverage.

There are two solutions: (1) comprehensive public (national or state) health insurance or (2) radical reform of insurance regulation to require community rating and open enrollment. The choice between these two approaches raises important and difficult questions of values. But more crucial ethical questions are whether and how to make a public case against the present structure. Again we face truth telling: how certainly do we know that the insurers' rewards for not insuring those most needing insurance is the fundamental flaw, and what is our responsibility for understanding the seriousness of this flaw and/or for sharing our understanding?

Answering these questions about cost, quality, and access will be complicated, and will take time. Many answers will be made by legislators and bureaucrats in specialized subcommittees and agencies, not in full public view and perhaps without careful consideration of ethical issues. But the results will be felt by the public. Ultimate program success will in large part depend upon the confidence, whether justified or not, which the public gains or loses in the persons (physicians, politicians, and others, usually acting as groups) and in the processes making and implementing the decisions.

POLITICAL ACCEPTABILITY

It helps, in understanding which choices and value questions are most important, to ask the following questions: Which choices in designing a health care program are most important in political terms, that is, which decisions will be most important in achieving political acceptability? Which issues will be the focus of the public debate and the legislative processes outlining the structural organization and administrative procedures of a national health program? When, where, and how will the basic decisions about a national health program be made?

For most of the century-long debate about a national health program, the central political issue concerned control: to what extent should the government, rather than private providers, control health care? But the dramatic increase in costs during the past quarter-century has changed the situation; high costs made the question of Who pays? the central political issue, pushing the question Who controls? into the background. The primary players are more willing to relinquish some control in order to find the means to pay the costs and are less concerned with ideological purity in issues of the market versus government.[2] The now-central political issue of who pays puts the focus upon questions of fairness, including what constitutes a fair distribution of benefits (what will be covered) and what process is fair for deciding distributions of both costs and benefits.

This last concern for process is a concern about democratic processes and the checks on these processes—a concern about the powers and protections provided majorities and minorities, as in James Madison's discussion of factions in the *Federalist Papers,* particularly in "Number Ten." The constitutional framework of the United States reflects preferences for slow change, for multiple points of access to introduce proposals, and for numerous veto points to thwart or slow changes seen as threatening by any one of the nation's innumerable minorities or majorities. These preferences are institutionalized through the fragmented government built upon the separation of powers within each unit of government and the sharing of power (legal and political) across levels of government. This fragmentation, particularly between levels of government, establishes political economics which do much to shape and constrain health care policy.

In its present situation, the federal government is crippled in its ability to extend access to health care. In part its disability came through self-destruction: financial irresponsibility creating debilitating deficits. The resulting financial constraint is aggravated by the present economy and international situation. The other part of the disability is political timidity, aggravated by the debacle of the 1988 Medicare Catastrophic Coverage Act and by campaign professionals and strategies which institutionalize a preference for victory over governance.

The role the states can be expected to play is shaped and limited by the federal system, which positions the state governments to be better at promoting economic advantage than at supporting the needy through income redistribution.[3] Economic development rewards a state with increased revenues and rewards its leaders with political popularity. Effective management of the cost and quality of health care generates economic advantage to a state because it is important to employers and employees. This natural interest matches a special state capacity in health care: states are the governments with the best opportunities to connect with the rest of the health care community because most health care institutions and activities (medical associations, hospital associations, practitioner licensing, insurance regulation, public health, etc.) are organized on a state basis.

On the other hand, state-level action to ensure access to health care is difficult because it requires income redistribution. States compete for economic development, and a state which extends access to health care may be doubly penalized in this competition. States compete through low costs (taxes; personnel costs, including health benefits; etc.) and high-quality services (transportation, education, etc.) to business and its most valued employees. The cost of extending health care access is high. It puts the state at a disadvantage by increasing taxes and/or drawing funds from services important to economic development. In addition, the state which improves coverage will risk attracting those not covered in other states, further undermining its competitive position. Besides these difficulties in extending access, the states are limited by a number of federal policies, such as the pervasive incentive in federal tax law to cover not just extraordinary expenses, but even the very first dollar of health care costs and ERISA's 1974 prohibition on state regulation of about half the health care insurance plans.[4]

It seems reasonable for the federal government to assume basic responsibility for access and to focus state attention upon cost management and quality assurance. This is, in fact, the allocation of responsibilities in Canada. But in the United States the states are pressed to extend access, filling the void left by the federal incapacity, and the federal government has been taking the most important initiatives to manage costs and ensure quality. Why does this division of responsibility not better match state and federal roles to their respective advantages?

Cost and Quality

The federal government's initiatives regarding costs (e.g., first the regulation of capital expenditures through certificates of need [CONS], and then prospective hospital payments according to diagnosis-related groups [DRGS], and now rate setting for physician fees, based upon a resource-based relative-value scale [RBRVS]) have been driven by the same cost pressures which are crippling its efforts to expand access. The federal government's initiatives regarding quality (e.g., peer review organizations [PROS] to monitor the appropriateness of procedures and the Health Care Financing Administration's publication of hospital mortality data) have been aimed at complementing (protecting) its initiatives to manage costs. The federal government will continue these efforts as long as health care costs continue to increase and the federal fisc is dangerously strained.

Some states have taken initiatives regarding cost and quality; nearly all the federal programs either picked up programs developed in the states or built upon the experience of related state experiments. Yet most states have lagged behind the federal initiatives, in spite of the fact that states, as public/private communities, are the fields in which the contests and cooperation between health interests can, perhaps must, be shaped—and in spite of the fact that state governments, usually through their governors, often act as leaders of their public and private communities. The complexity of the health care problems, in political, economic, and organizational terms, has not encouraged politicians to stake their careers on these issues. Health policy has looked like political quicksand, not pay dirt.

Whether the states will assume more initiative, and even begin wresting leadership from the federal government, depends upon whether the leaders and their publics give more credit and priority to success with these problems. The fact that the National Governors' Association made health policy its first priority for 1990–91 suggests that such a change may take place.[5] It is yet to be seen whether the states will develop the capacity to innovate successfully and to share quickly and accurately their experiences so that health care cost and quality can be better managed either by themselves or by the decentralized administrators of a national program.

Access

In terms of the problems of access to health care, the present financial and political limitations of the federal government make it unlikely that a truly comprehensive federal program will be adopted in the near future, in spite of the current general dissatisfaction being expressed by government and industry as well as by physicians and the general public—and in spite of the preference U.S. citizens have expressed for a comprehensive system such as Canada's.[6]

Extending access to health care is income redistribution, and therefore a particular problem for state governments because it increases taxes and/or reduces expenditures on services which attract and sustain economic development. The federal government is in the better position to accomplish income redistribution. Yet as long as the federal government fails to ensure access to health care, the political leadership of at least some states will either have enough concern or feel enough pressure to make some attempts to address this need. The fact is that most of the recent initiatives to extend access have been state initiatives or federal mandates for state actions. This situation is likely to continue until there is a national program for comprehensive coverage.

While the health policy debate focuses upon the question of who shall pay, it may produce an ironic result. The efforts of employers, the federal government, and the states to avoid the costs prompts them to try pushing costs, especially cost increases, upon each other. The desperate avoidance of the costs is evidence of the difficulty of finding funding to fulfill the present expectations of consumers and of providers. But it may increase these expectations, as each potential payer encourages the public to go to another trough, suggesting that there is water there. The more desperate the efforts to shed costs, the less realistic will be the presumed and stated expectations of the abilities of others to carry the costs. This could produce an increasingly inaccurate debate, which in the long run undermines trust in both systems—the health care and the political. A primary concern for future discussion deserves to be the importance of accurate portrayals of the present condition, of its future without change, and of proposed adjustments.

The related question of fairness, regarding what procedures and services will not be covered, is (understandably, from a political perspective) being avoided by many policy proposals. Because questions of fairness involve increased costs and reduced benefits for some, they are not attractive political decisions. But ultimately they will be forced upon the agenda, either by public rebellion or by political leadership (as has been attempted in Oregon), because political nondecision-making allows obvious and disputed inequities to become too common and too large. This again raises the importance of careful, and public, consideration of the criteria by which fairness may be assessed and of the processes by which the distribution of benefits and burdens might then be allocated.

Incremental Changes Most Likely

These analyses and speculations suggest answers to the questions of when, where, and how the political decisions might be made. The likely situation for the coming decade is a confused mix of state and federal roles. Although there could be a dramatic program initiative at the federal level before the turn of the century, it is more likely that programs will develop in fits and starts, with financial pressures prompting both federal and state action to manage costs and with much of the initiative on access taken, surprisingly, at the state level. A revolution as dramatic as comprehensive national health insurance probably requires substantial national debate and legitimation, of the sort which occurs when an issue is a major topic and determinant of a presidential campaign. Perhaps this could happen in 1992. Or the problems of peace, debt, and recession could recede by 1996, to leave room then for such a debate. But more likely are incremental adjustments and state experiments whose successes and failures build the foundation for major restructuring at the end of this decade or in the next.

The answers are not quite as clear regarding a second set of questions, which concern motive. Will the program be an effort to address all three aspects of health care (cost, quality, and access), or will it target one of them? What will be the relative emphasis upon each of these three aspects? For the reasons of complexity already discussed, the developments are likely to be concerned with and affect all three aspects but without being comprehensive or well balanced. Quality will receive the least attention, until its neglect results in substantial new fears about the health care system. A comprehensive solution may come well after major restructuring.

In any event, the reduction of problems will be complicated, will be a series of related steps and learning experiences, and will take place over a long time. Actions today will determine the trust which various parties will have in each other tomorrow, and therefore the ease with which future understanding is shared and future adjustments are made.

PROPOSED APPROACHES

There are so many and such varied health care reform proposals that a complete inventory is impossible and a reasonable categorization very difficult .[7] This analysis addresses the thirty "proposals" summarized in the list which follows. These represent the major proposals and the range of proposals now being used or being given the most serious attention. All these proposals were made in the past two decades; most in the past five years. Some, particularly those of the 1970s and early 1980s, have been enacted as federal and/or state law and thus tested to some degree. But most are untested, some being rather specific proposals which are developed in more or less detail and others being only guidelines or concerns set forth to guide the design or selection of specific programs. Each entry begins with the name or sponsor of the proposal in abbreviated form.

Thirty Frequently Discussed Proposals

AM.ACAD.PED. (1990).[8] Universal Access to Health Care for Children and Pregnant Women is a proposal of the American Academy of Pediatrics to ensure the coverage of children through age twenty-one and pregnant women. It establishes a standard benefit package to be provided either through employer benefit plans or new state insurance funds financed by taxes on employers not offering the coverage, by individual premiums, and by transfer of Medicaid funds so, as under Medicare, there is not a separate program for the poor. Coverage may not exclude pre-existing conditions and shall include preventive care, without cost sharing, and primary and major medical care, with cost sharing.

AM.COL.PHYS. (1990).[9] Universal Access to Health Care in America is a policy guide (not a specific proposal) by the American College of Physicians. It calls for a "comprehensive and coordinated program to

assure access on a nationwide basis (which) in the near term ...
should build on ... existing health care financing mechanisms (but)
in the longer term (should give) careful consideration (to) a nationwide financing mechanism." It points in the direction of national
health insurance and differs significantly from the American Medical
Association's (AMA's) calls for adjustments and expansions which
"preserve the strengths of our current system."

AM.HOS.ASSOC. (1991).[10] "National Health Care Strategy: A Starting Point for Debate" is the American Hospital Association's latest
suggestion for national health care reform. It seeks universal coverage through expansion of Medicare and Medicaid and mandated
expansion of the employer-based system.

AM.MED.ASSOC. (1990).[11] Health Access America builds upon the
AMA's 1989 "Report Q" and the Health Policy Agenda for the American People (see below). It calls for Medicaid expansion and uniformity, required coverage of employees and families, tax incentives, state
risk pools, and practice parameters. While the proposal includes
concerns about costs, it is primarily prompted by concerns about
access and argues for expanded access even at higher total costs.

AM.NURS.ASSOC. (1991).[12] Nursing's Agenda for Health Care
Reform recommends that the federal government define a "standard
package" of essential health care benefits to be provided by public
and private sources. It emphasizes primary care, managed care,
public health and preventative care, and delivery of care at the
workplace, schools, and other community settings. It suggests insurance reform which may include community rating.

CALLAHAN (1987). The Limits of Medical Progress is not a specific
proposal, but Daniel Callahan is one of several analysts who accept—
in Callahan's case strongly argues for—the need to ration health care
and wrestle with the questions of what criteria are appropriate for
such rationing.[13]

CON (1974). In certificate of need programs, state governments
regulate capital expenditures for health care facilities and equipment. The first such program was established in New York in 1964.
This approach was mandated across the country by the National
Health Planning and Development Act of 1974. The mandate was
dropped in 1983. The 1974 act established planning and regulatory
Health Systems Agencies (HSAs) in each state, replacing the planning
agencies established by the 1966 health planning legislation and
providing stronger regulatory sanctions than those established two
years earlier in section 1122 of the Social Security Act amendments.[14]

CONNECTICUT (1990).[15] The Health Care Access Commission is an agency established along with a series of programs by the state and the insurance industry to build the capacity of private insurance (a less expensive basic benefits policy, reform of small-group insurance, etc.) and Medicaid (Medicaid expansion, subsidized Medicaid buy-in, etc.) to extend access for medical care.

DRGs (1983). Diagnosis-related groups is Medicare's prospective payment system (PPS) for hospitals, mandated by Social Security Act amendments in 1983. This PPS is frequently supported as a market approach: it encourages cost consciousness. But if the government, as a major purchaser, unilaterally establishes the payments, it is rate regulation.

ENTHOVEN (1978 and 1989).[16] Consumer-Choice Health Plan, outlined by Alain Enthoven and Richard Kronick in January 1989, and building upon earlier Enthoven proposals of 1978, provides that everyone not covered by Medicare or Medicaid be enabled to acquire affordable coverage either through their employer or a "public sponsor." It uses a strategy of "managed competition" in which competing health plans manage health care services under contract with "informed" large employers or public sponsors. It includes a notion of "efficiency" which is achieved "when the marginal dollar spent on health care produces the same value to society as the marginal dollar spent on education, defense, personal consumption, or other uses."

FAMILIES USA (1990).[17] *To the Rescue*, a report issued in November 1990 by the Families USA Foundation, suggests that state rate regulation could trim 2 percent off the rate of medical inflation each year (saving $245.7 billion per year by the year 2000) and that single-payer systems could reduce insurance administration costs 12 percent by reducing them from existing levels which are as high as 40 percent and presumed to average 15 percent, to the 2.7 percent of Medicare and Medicaid (saving $52.8 billion per year by 2000); either of these savings would be more than enough to fund the estimated $24.3 billion per year cost of coverage for the uninsured.

HAWAII (1989).[18] The State Health Insurance Program (SHIP) makes insurance available to all state residents at income-adjusted and community rates. It builds upon Hawaii's 1974 Prepaid Health Care Act, which mandates that most employers provide health insurance to their workers.

HEALTHPOLICYAGENDA (1987).[19] *The Health Policy Agenda for the American People*, prepared by a "blue ribbon" panel formed by a coalition of 172 organizations with key sponsorship by the American Medical Association, made a comprehensive review of the health care system. Initiated in 1982, reporting 195 recommendations in 1987, and continuing some studies thereafter (including a Medicaid report in 1989), the effort appears to be a response to the cost concerns but addresses quality and access as well. The recommendations refine the present systems, including expansion and reforms of Medicaid; they do not set forth a comprehensive plan for a new national program.

HERITAGE FOUNDATION (1989).[20] The National Health System for America Plan, proposed by the Heritage Foundation, involves a major restructuring of tax preferences to eliminate the relatively unlimited tax exemption for employer-paid health insurance and replace it with a set of income-adjusted tax preferences encouraging cost-effective major medical insurance and helping cover out-of-pocket costs of health care. It mandates all households to carry basic health insurance. The proposal is concerned with cost management as well as with access, but its tax changes and mandated insurance perhaps have more dramatic impact upon the latter.

HIAA (1988).[21] The Health Insurance Association of America proposes to solve the access problem through reforms which preserve private insurance. These are to end state mandates, develop low-cost plans for basic coverage, extend tax preferences, establish risk pools, and extend Medicaid.

HIMMELSTEIN (1989).[22] Physicians for a National Health Program set forth a proposal prepared by Himmelstein, Woolhandler, and others patterned after the Canadian system. Building upon Himmelstein's and Woolhandler's earlier criticism of the costs of administering health insurance in the United States, the proposal replaces private insurance with a single public plan. It includes annual lump-sum budgets for each hospital and nursing home, negotiated fees for physicians, and appropriations for capital expenditures.

HMOs (1973). Health maintenance organizations provide care on the basis of a annual per-capita fee, thus combining the roles of insurance carrier and health care provider. The concept is old, at least as early as 1721 in North America (Dr. William Douglas of Boston accepted fee-for-service or "five pounds per annum sick or well"), and became well known through the Kaiser-Permanente plan on the West Coast during World War II. The Health Maintenance Organization Act of 1973 made HMOs a major element of national health policy, when the Nixon administration and Congress saw HMOs as a market mechanism for cost management.[23]

KENNEDY/WAXMAN (1987). The Basic Health Benefits for All Americans Act (by Senator Edward Kennedy, [D., Mass.], and Congressman Henry Waxman, [D., Calif.] introduced in the 101st Congress, 1989) carries forward adjusted versions of the bills introduced in 1987 in the 100th Congress. These bills mark a pragmatic shift away from Senator Kennedy's two-decade press for national health insurance and toward a public/private mix, to a bill which he hopes is more politically and fiscally acceptable. The bills mandate employment-based insurance for basic health services but require less coverage for small employers. They establish insurance pools and provide federal/state coverage for the unemployed poor. They ban exclusions based upon health status or pre-existing conditions. They rely upon public action, both in expanding public programs and in further requirements made of employers, though there is some expectation that by concentrating purchasing power there would be a major shift in market forces, which could better control costs.[24] Parts of the Kennedy/Waxman and of the Pepper Commission (see below) proposals were carried forward and further developed as the "Health America" proposal announced June 5, 1991 by Democratic Senators George Mitchell, Edward Kennedy, Don Riegle, and Jay Rockefeller.

MASSACHUSETTS (1988).[25] The Act to Make Health Security Available to All Citizens of the Commonwealth and to Improve Hospital Financing declares that access "to basic health care services is a natural, essential, and unalienable right" and creates a Department of Medical Security to contract with health plans in order to make affordable health insurance coverage (with benefits "which typically are included in employer-sponsored health benefit plans") available to small employers and individuals. The act establishes a "play-or-pay" tax on all employers of six or more workers, beginning in 1992. It extends the regulation of hospital rates and financial support for hospitals providing uncompensated care and care for Medicare patients. Implementation is faltering and the act itself is in political trouble.

MCCLURE (1986). Walter McClure, Chairman of the Center for Policy Studies in Minneapolis, proposes a "Buy-Right" plan to manage costs through competitive pressures brought about by focusing the consumer's attention upon a search for quality. He argues that groups of consumers in a given health care market, represented by employers or others, should demand that providers be regularly measured for quality, using risk-adjustment measures such as those developed for hospitals. He argues that not until consumers are enabled to focus upon quality will there be creative and constructive competition by the providers. He argues that once such competition is established it will improve management of both quality and cost.[26]

MORTALITY DATA (1986). Hospital Mortality Data based upon Medicare claims have been released for several years by the Health Care Financing (HCFA) Administration in the U.S. Department of Health and Human Services. These data are hospital and disease specific and have prompted special attention to those hospitals showing statistically significant higher mortality rates.[27]

NACOMHEALTHCTRS (1990).[28] Access 2000, proposed by the National Association of Community Health Centers, calls for public and private financing of community and migrant health centers throughout the nation—to serve every county. It comes closer to direct government provision of basic care than do the other proposals reviewed here but still does not create a government health service as does the Veterans Administration (now Department of Veterans Affairs—VA) hospital system. It might be classified as an incremental expansion of present programs, but it proposes a five- to tenfold increase over the next decade and would represent a major shift in the institutional setting of health care services.

NAOFSOC.WORK (1991).[29] The National Association of Social Workers also recommends a system similar to Canada's, established under federal law and administered by the states. It recommends financing through income and payroll taxes and coverage of acute, long-term, mental health, and dental care.

NAT.LEADER.COMM. (1989).[30] The National Leadership Commission on Health Care, chaired by former congressman Paul Rogers (D., Fla.) and former governor Robert Ray (R., Iowa), builds upon existing employer insurance, charging premiums to employers and individuals without coverage as a mechanism to encourage broader coverage and to fund an insurance pool (UNiversal ACcess: UNAC) which would be federally financed but state administered. The pool would be a prudent purchaser by negotiating contracts with providers. The plan looks to quality controls to maintain costs and proposes an annual budget of $500 million for research on clinical effectiveness. The plan relies primarily on private insurance, but with a substantial public safety net (UNAC) to provide universal access.

OREGON (1987).[31] Oregon Basic Health Services Act, passed in 1989 as a follow-up to a 1987 decision that ended Medicaid funding for most organ transplants, expands Medicaid coverage to all persons with income equal to or less than 100 percent of the federal poverty level, establishes a process by which procedures to be covered will be listed according to priority and cost to the state, and limits future state appropriations decisions to deciding how far down the list of priorities to provide funding (thus eliminating the options of changing the priorities, of changing eligibility, or of changing reimbursement rates). Companion acts establish a risk pool and require that employer-provided insurance cover at least the procedures provided by the Medicaid program. The program is particularly identified with Dr. John Kitzhaber, president of the Oregon senate when the program was developed and adopted. It builds upon an earlier project, Oregon Health Decisions, which promoted public discussion of health care priorities. The list of priorities was announced May 2, 1990, widely criticized, quickly assigned to reconsideration, re-released in substantially revised form February 20, 1991, and then submitted to the U.S. Dept. of Health and Human Services for the Medicaid waivers necessary for implementation.

OUTCOMES RESEARCH (1988). The Medical Treatment Effectiveness Program and Clinical Guidelines, coordinated by the Agency for Health Care Policy and Research (AHCPR) of the Public Health Service in the U.S. Department of Health and Human Services, builds upon a long history (Ernest Codman's "End Result System" in 1910, John Williamson's health accounting in 1971, and D. D. Rutstein's "sentinel events" in 1976) and a recent surge of interest in using outcomes to guide medical practice. New interest was stimulated by John Wennberg's findings of dramatic variations in frequency of procedures in his small-area variations research. William Roper gave outcomes research top priority as HCFA's Medical Treatment Effectiveness Initiative in 1988, an initiative which was implemented by the establishment of the AHCPR (by the OBRA of 1989, see RBRVS, below), which replaced the National Center for Health Services Research and Health Care Technology Assessment, giving the new agency an expanded budget and a special focus upon outcomes research. While this research measures quality, it initially—as in the case of the PROS—grew from cost concerns: to reduce procedures which are unnecessary or not cost-effective. The research and guidelines could be components of market or regulatory approaches, but have been initiated with presumptions of voluntary use of the guidelines. The approach must face issues of the relative weighting of conflicting values (life, quality of life, cost, etc.) and of the rigidity of the weighting across individuals and over time (outcomes research could improve the opportunities for flexibility in care, through informed patient decision making, as in Wennberg's efforts toward a "shared decision-making procedure").[32]

PEPPER COMMISSION (1990). The Bipartisan Commission on Comprehensive Health Care is the "Pepper Commission," established because of the persistent pressure of Representative Pepper (D., Florida) before his death, and chaired by Senator John D. Rockefeller 4th (D., W. Va.), which reported March 2, 1990. By an 8 to 7 vote it supported a $43.4 billion ($23.4 billion federal, $16 billion employers, and $4 billion employee contributions) health insurance program mandating universal coverage. By an 11 to 4 vote it supported a $42.8 billion (all federal) expansion of nursing-home coverage to three months for the severely disabled of all ages, which would require less spend-down (to $30,000 of assets for individuals and $60,000 for couples) for eligibility for Medicaid-type assistance. Its recommendations include the federalization and expansion of Medicaid, establishment of a minimum benefits package, requirements that employers provide insurance, and requirements for community ratings. The recommendations do not specify sources of funding.[33]

PROs (1972). Peer Review Organizations were originally developed as Experimental Medical Care Review Organizations (EMCROS) on a voluntary and pilot basis beginning in 1968, then required as Professional Standards Review Organizations (PSROS) to review Medicare hospitalizations by the Bennett Amendment of 1972, and subsequently reformed to their present structure and purpose. While the PROs look at both cost and quality, and are sometimes publicly described as quality-review organizations, the impetus behind the review is cost more than quality.[34]

RBRVS (1989).[35] The Resource-Based Relative-Value Scale, incorporated in the Omnibus Budget Reconciliation Act (OBRA) of 1989, bases payment of Medicare physicians' claims upon the relative value of each procedure in terms of work, practice expenses, and costs of malpractice insurance. This presumably shifts payments in favor of primary-care procedures and away from specialized procedures. It is to be implemented in phases from 1992 through 1996. The scale was suggested by William Hsiao of Harvard in 1979. Representative Henry Waxman recommended the 1986 establishment of the Physicians Payment Review Commission to consider such a payment system. The 1989 OBRA also restricts balance billing, provides that there shall be target rates of growth in physician expenditures for

Medicare, and establishes the Agency for Health Care Policy and Research (see above under Outcomes Research).

REINHARDT (1990).[36] The Corrosive Effects of American Health Insurance is a prediction, not a definite proposal. It is based upon Uwe Reinhardt's severe criticism of the present insurance market structure, which encourages, or even forces, insurers to avoid those persons most needing help. He outlines options for universal access and then suggests that probably the most acceptable and workable approach would include open enrollments, community ratings, and a system of regional associations of payers negotiating with regional associations of providers, much like the German system. This would establish in each region an all-payer system to ensure more equity in the costs of coverage available to all.

RELMAN (1990).[37] "Reforming the Health Care System" is a proposal put forth by Arnold Relman, as editor of the *New England Journal of Medicine*, building upon his long-time and frequently expressed concerns about conflicts of interest in health care delivery and his concerns about enthusiasms for formal rationing of care. He proposes that all insurance subsidized by employers and government be contracts for prepaid health care (e.g., HMOs), in a manner similar to the Enthoven-Kronick plan. Traditional health insurance, which pays for procedures and allows more choice in providers, could be purchased by those who could afford it and chose to do so. This creates a two-tiered system but, he argues, it constitutes reforms (of the insurance market and of the way medicine is practiced) which are required in order to achieve necessary cost consciousness and shifts toward primary care. His proposal calls for a substantially expanded national program of assessment and accountability and for a control of, or escape from, medical entrepreneurialism. His proposal might be classified as being primarily concerned with costs (as is the similar Enthoven-Kronick proposal) or with access (for the same reasons the National Leadership Commission proposal and the Hawaii plan are so classified), but for this analysis it is classified as a reform emphasizing quality, because Relman shows a particular concern that the revolution in health care delivery, though it may be much needed, puts quality seriously at risk.

UNY-CARE (1990).[38] The Universal New York Health Care proposal is for the state to act as the paying agent for all health insurance, public and private. It would establish a basic minimum coverage for all insurance, would require community rating and open enrollment, would subsidize the premiums for those with low income, would require employers to "play or pay," and would establish the state as the single payer in order to reduce administrative costs and to enhance bargaining positions in negotiations with providers.

Classification by Structural Theory

Three classification schemes reveal three different aspects of the current debate. The first classification compares (a) the structural theory (i.e., an analysis of health care systems in terms of a market, public regulation—as for utilities, or direct delivery of public services) upon which a particular approach is based with (b) the health care concern (i.e. cost, quality, or access) to which the proposal gives the most certain attention (table 1).

This classification scheme has problems in that any serious proposal must deal with all three concerns of cost, quality, and access. The classification is done largely on the basis of probable result, but usually reflects the presumed primary motivation of the proposal; Families USA is a clear exception: its motivation appears to be access but its structure joins it too certainly with other cost-driven proposals. In fact, many proposals are difficult to force fit to the classification scheme: for instance, McClure's proposal, emphasizing quality measures, does so to stimulate competition and thereby cost consciousness; it might as easily be placed in a cost as a quality cell. The classification difficulties also result in proposals with similar structural components being in different categories: for instance, both New York's UNY-Care proposal and Reinhardt's prediction are systems in which all claims are paid by a "single-payer" agency instead of the present multiplicity of public and private payers; but UNY-Care is particularly focused upon cost savings (though to extend access) and a major new governmental agency and role, while Reinhardt is particularly concerned about the dysfunctional incentives to limit access under the present structure of the insurance market and may be implemented through private or quasi-governmental associations. Proposals which have persisted over time may be put forth for somewhat different purposes at different times: the Enthoven proposal was initially responding to the concerns for cost management but now is argued with equal force to answer concerns about access.

Distinctions according to structural theory are equally difficult. The programs of Hawaii, the National Leadership Commission, and Enthoven all intend to encourage more cost-effective competition and all include regulatory requirements that employers "play or pay," that is, provide health insurance or help finance an alternative insurance program available to persons not covered under employer plans. Relative emphasis upon regulation and competition and other

Table 1. Proposals for a National Health Program, by Theory of Reform

Structural Theory of Reform	Chief Health Care Concern		
	Cost	Quality	Access
COMPETITION			
Typical provisions	Charge comparisons	Quality comparisons	Encouragement of, or mandated, private coverage
	Patient sharing of costs	Prohibitions of conflicts of interest	More public coverage
	Practice guidelines		
	Prospective payments		
Specific proposals	HMOs (1973)	Mortality Data (1986)	Nat. Leader. Comm. (1989)
	Health Policy Agenda (1987)	McClure (1986)	Heritage Foundation (1989)
	Outcomes Research (1988)	Relman (1990)	Connecticut (1990)
	Enthoven (1978 and 1989)		Am.Med.Assoc. (1990)
			HIAA (1991)
			Am.Hos.Assoc. (1991)
			Am.Nurs.Assoc. (1991)
PUBLIC UTILITY			
Typical provisions	Regulated investments, charges, & prospective payments		Community rating
	Practice guidelines with review		More public coverage
	Rationing		Mandated private coverage
			Regulated pricing
Specific proposals	PROs (1972)		Kennedy-Waxman (1987)
	CON (1974)		Massachusetts (1988)
	DRGs (1983)		Hawaii (1989)
	Callahan (1987)		Am.Acad.Ped. (1990)
	RBRVS (1989)		Pepper Commission (1990)
	Oregon (1987)		Reinhardt (1990)

Continued on next page

Table 1—Continued

GOVERNMENT PROGRAMS		
Typical provisions	Public agency pays all claims	Universal public health insurance Public, or primarily public, funded providers
Specific proposals	UNY-Care (1990) Families USA (1990)	Himmelstein (1989) Am.Col.Phys. (1990) NAComHealthCtrs (1990) NAofSoc.Work. (1991)

Note: See the list of proposals in the text for the full names of the specific proposals.

aspects of the programs must be used to force each into a competition or public-utility cell of the classification matrix. Since all three of these programs establish public agencies to provide the alternative insurance program, they might also be placed in the government programs cells. In sum, the classification along either axis of the matrix often is rather arbitrary.

In spite of its difficulties, this first classification scheme has value. The structural categories are often used in public debate. The very difficulties encountered in using them to classify actual proposals is helpful, by showing the lack of pure cases, a point that is important in understanding the proposals and in dealing with simplistic and ideological perspectives.

The categories of structural theories also help reveal the range of perspectives by which the situation is being viewed, while the classification of the significant proposals according to these theories suggest the important options by which the health care system might be changed to reflect these perspectives. For example, various approaches to the public-utility model emphasize various regulations, some concerned with who is eligible, some with what services are covered, and some with what amounts will be paid for a particular procedure. The several approaches to competition show a number of options concerned with improving the market: increasing available information (about charges, but perhaps, more importantly, about outcomes) to encourage competition, structuring provider systems to reward cost consciousness, and sharing costs with consumers to encourage cost consciousness.

The classification of the proposals reveals several ways to control costs and the values which are at issue in choosing from among these approaches. Four basic controls are represented in the proposals: (1) to ration types of care, which tends to relate to the public-utility cell—as in the Oregon proposal, (2) to control utilization, which tends to relate to the competitive cell—as in HMOs, (3) to eliminate major indirect costs such as administrative and legal (malpractice suits), which may tend to relate to the government program cell—as in UNY-Care, and (4) to regulate the price paid for a particular procedure, which tends to relate to the public-utility cell—as in DRGs and RBRVs. These four controls are in addition to a fifth approach: to restrict enrollees by number or type—as in the present private and public insurance systems—which is an approach outside the matrix of reform proposals. To the extent that one control is successful, it reduces the pressures to apply the other controls, which may help explain who supports which approach and may reveal potential conflicts of interests in the proposals. For example, might providers as a group find relative advantage in rationing as opposed to rate regulation?

A very uncertain, somewhat ironic, conclusion regarding the choices in how to finance universal coverage is hinted at by the three access cells. The proposals which would have government institutions replace private institutions (proposals in the access/government-programs cell) tend to argue that public-service delivery will realize efficiencies not to be had in the present private system, efficiencies great enough to cover most or all of the extra costs of universal coverage. The proposals for more regulatory approaches (access/public-utility cell) tend to look to expanded financial support from both governments and employers. So do most programs in the remaining cell (access/competition) although the Heritage Foundation proposal is a clear exception. Thus as proposals move to more emphasis on the private market they also tend to increase the financial burdens given government to cover expansions in total costs.

Another value of the classification system is that by forcing proposals of the past two decades into the matrix they trace a path revealing how concerns have shifted through time. The early 1970s produced a surge of interest in new public programs for cost management (e.g., the beginnings of the PROs and CONs) and for access (e.g., proposed Family Health Insurance Program—not included in this inventory because it was never adopted). The middle and late 1970s and early 1980s narrowed the focus to a more exclusive concern about cost management: first encouraging market corrections (e.g., HMOs to increase providers' cost consciousness) and then expanding public roles (e.g., prospective payments using DRGs). Proposals of the last half-decade show renewed concern for access, usually combining mandated, private, employee health benefits and expanded public coverage. Now attention may be shifting to the questions of subsystem structures, particularly to concern about the shift in health insurance from community rating to experience rating. This shows a progression from the earlier, and more simplistic, generalizations about competition or regulation across the whole delivery system. It also opens up new options which may prove not only more feasible in technical terms but also more acceptable in political terms.

The classification suggests that some perspectives have received only limited attention. Most obvious is the paucity of attention to quality assurance. Yet the proposals falling into the quality cells are mostly recent, perhaps representing a new turn in the path through the matrix. Comparing these and other proposals in the matrix raise the question of who should be responsible for quality assurance. Relman's proposal has the purpose of sustaining and extending the responsibility of the providers, while the HCFA mortality data and McClure hope to extend significant responsibilities to providers, and perhaps to payers. The Enthoven proposal, shown in the cost/competition cell, clearly extends responsibility to the payer. The approach of the National Association of Community Health Centers could shift substantial responsibility to government.

Another cell with relatively few proposals is that focusing on cost and using government to deliver health care. A more complete inventory, including the unsuccessful as well as the applied proposals of the 1970s, might fill in this cell. Proponents of the 1970s proposals to substantially increase the population covered by government insurance argued that the increased role would enhance the government's bargaining position in managing costs.

Classification by Primary Direction of Reform

A second system of classification is presented in table 2. It changes just one dimension of the matrix, replacing the alternative structural theories about reform (competition, public-utility regulation, or government programs) with alternative targets of reform (broaden

Table 2. Proposals for a National Health Program, by Proposed Solution

Primary Direction of Reform	Chief Health Care Concern		
	Cost	Quality	Access
Broader insurance coverage	Health Policy Agenda (1987)		Kennedy-Waxman (1987) Massachusetts (1988) Nat. Leader. Comm. (1989) Hawaii (1989) Connecticut (1990) Am.Med.Assoc. (1990) Pepper Commission (1990) Am.Acad.Ped. (1990) HIAA (1991) Am.Nurs.Assoc. (1991) Am.Hos.Assoc. (1991)
Change in payers' roles and incentives	Callahan (1987) Oregon (1987) RBRVS (1989) Enthoven (1978 and 1989) UNY-Care (1990) Families USA (1990)		Reinhardt (1990) Himmelstein (1989) Am.Col.Phys. (1990) NAofSoc.Work.(1991)
Change in providers' power and incentives	PROs (1972) HMOs (1973) CON (1974) DRGs (1983) Outcomes Research (1988)	Mortality Data (1986) McClure (1986) Relman (1990)	NAComHealthCtrs (1990)
Change in consumers' desires and incentives			Heritage Foundation (1990)

insurance coverage, adjust payers' roles and incentives, adjust providers' power and incentives, or adjust consumers' desires and incentives). Again, most proposals cross lines, making the assignments a matter of judgment and hence open to dispute.

Compared with the first classification, this classification reveals a less certain path through time: an ambivalence between tinkering with the present system (by broadening insurance coverage) and adjusting a variety of fundamental incentives and controls for the various participants (providers, payers, and consumers) in the system. Perhaps this better reveals the political ambivalence, and hence difficulty, of the situation. It makes quite certain the point that the debate is complicated and confused. Not only is there ambivalence between tinkering and expansion on the one hand and fundamental reform on the other, there also are the differing emphases on cost and access and upon payers, providers, and consumers. This surely reflects significant differences in values and interests as well as a limited ability for any single acceptable reform to deal with the whole range of concerns and roles. The picture offered by this classification is one which again suggests that change is likely to be partial, uneven, and unpredictable.

This approach to classification shows several interesting groupings. The access proposals tend to be proposals to broaden insurance coverage. The exceptions probably present the more innovative suggestions; they come from outside the mainline political and special-interest processes. The proposals primarily concerned with cost management focus upon changing the incentives of payers and of providers; there is relatively less concern for cost control in proposals to broaden insurance coverage without changing the market structure, and there apparently is little hope for cost control by focusing on the consumer's role. The nearly empty row of cells concerning consumer incentives suggests that this last point can be stated more broadly: there is relatively little expectation that consumers can play the major role in dealing with quality, access, or costs.

Consolidations of Classifications: Seven Approaches

A third classification combines the previous two and adds an additional categorization. In table 3 the structural theory of reform (competition, public utility, or government programs) seen in table 1 is contrasted with the primary direction of reform (broader coverage, payer incentives, provider incentives, or consumer incentives) in table 2. The chief health care concerns (access, cost, or quality), which were the categories common to the two previous tables, now become footnotes to each reform proposal.

An additional categorization in the new table identifies who carries responsibility for ensuring that all persons have access to

Table 3. Proposals for a National Health Program:
A Summary Categorization

Primary Direction of Reform	Competition	Public Utility	Government Programs
Broader coverage	HealthPolicyAgenda (C,g) HIAA (A,b) Connecticut (A,g) Am.Med.Assoc.(A,n) Nat.Leader. Comm. (A,b) Am.Hos.Assoc. (A,b) Am.Nurs.Assoc. (A,n)	Kennedy-Waxman (A,b) Massachusetts (A,b) Hawaii (A,b) Am.Acad.Ped. (A,n) Pepper Commission (A,b)	
Payer incentives	Enthoven (C,b)	Callahan (C,n) RBRVS (C,n) Oregon (C,n) Reinhardt (A,b)	UNY-Care (C,b) Himmelstein (A,g) Am.Col.Phys. (A,g) NAofSoc.Work. (A,g) Families USA (C,g)
Provider incentives	HMOs (C,n) Outcomes Research (C,n) Mortality Data (Q,n) McClure (Q,n) Relman (Q,b)	PROs (C,n) CON (C,n) DRGs (C,n)	NAComHealthCtrs. (A,g)
Consumer incentives	Heritage Foundation (A,g)		

Note: Capital letters in parentheses refer to the chief health care concern: A = access; C = cost; Q = quality. Lowercase letters in parentheses refer to responsibility for access: b = business and government; g = government; n = neither.

health care, irrespective of economic circumstances or health status, the issue raised by Allen Buchanan. In a mixed economy, as in the United States, the responsibility to ensure that there are no significant holes in coverage could be jointly carried by the private and public sectors through laws which might require such private responsibilities as open enrollments by insurance carriers or coverage of all employees. An alternative is for government to carry the full responsibility, allowing private insurers to be involved only when and how they choose to do so for traditional business purposes. The third possibility is that no one carries this responsibility; this is the present

situation. The way the footnotes referring to this choice are distributed on table 3 reflects the fact that proposals which focus upon
access are more likely to establish clear responsibility for ensuring
access. If dates are again inserted in this table, the distribution shows
a trend over time: the more recent proposals more frequently
establish responsibility to ensure the availability of health care to all
persons.

   The three tables reveal the complexity of the situation: a wealth
of alternatives but proposal-overload for policymakers. In spite of
the confusion of this complexity, the third table offers a basis for
grouping the proposals, suggesting four general types and three
interesting and unique proposals which do not fit these general
types. These may be summarized as follows:

1. *Ensured access through incremental additions to present system.* The
   largest group of proposals, including most of the recent proposals, fall into this group; and most of this group fit into the cells
   which broaden coverage. These proposals tend to come from
   provider groups, national political leadership, and states. Those
   with stronger ties to insurance (Connecticut) and traditional
   medicine (Am.Med.Assoc.) are in the competition cell, while those
   from political leadership (Kennedy-Waxman; Massachusetts) in
   the public-utility cell. The NAComm.HealthCtrs. proposal, in the
   government-programs provider incentive cell, might also be in
   this group. Most of these proposals designate responsibility for
   ensuring that care is available to all persons, some dividing the
   responsibility between the public and private sectors and some
   giving it to government alone.
2. *The Canadian approach.* These are recent proposals, seeking administrative efficiencies to finance coverage for all persons. They show
   up in the government programs/payer incentive cell because they
   involve a major or complete shift to government underwriting
   (Himmelstein) and/or administration (UNY-Care) of insurance
   coverage. They do assign responsibility for ensuring access to
   health care.
3. *Government allocations of fees and/or care.* These are of two types which
   usually are not joined: those which replace the market with rate
   setting (DRGs) and those which ration care (Oregon). They show up
   in the payer incentives row under "public utility" (not including
   Reinhardt) and in the provider-incentive row under "competition" and "public utility" (not including Mortality Data, McClure,

and Relman). Few of these proposals make specific assignments of responsibility for ensuring access to health care.

4. *Focus on quality.* This small group attempts to introduce quality as a (the) chief concern in a competitive environment, and hence as a (the) chief incentive for providers. They are in other respects a diverse group (Mortality Data, McClure, Relman).

5. *Carefully articulated market.* Enthoven, in the competition/payer-incentives cell, develops the specifics of a market approach, for which so many others have argued without being specific. Since all the proposals in group 4, "Focus on quality," presume a market, the Enthoven proposal might be related to any one of them; Relman specifically suggests such a tie. The Enthoven proposal also restructures provider incentives, but deserves to be distinguished (as is done in tables 2 and 3) from other proposals which restructure provider incentives since Enthoven includes the crucial, though often overlooked promotion of "informed" payers. If health care is too complex for the individual consumer to make well-informed choices about cost and quality, how is the consumer's interest to be represented? The Enthoven proposal is one of the few to seriously address this matter.

6. *Individual responsibility.* This is the Heritage Foundation's adjustment of incentives, which includes major revision of tax laws (competition/consumer incentives).

7. *The German approach.* Reinhardt (public utility/payer incentives), finding the structure of the insurance market irreparably flawed, suggests that the German system of decentralized bargaining between payers and providers offers the alternative which best fits the U.S. culture and situation.

Speculations about Acceptability, Feasibility, and Approaches

The political scientist Edward E. Banfield, who particularly drew the contrast between program feasibility and political acceptability, opined (a) that public policy proposals concerning urban affairs may be feasible or acceptable but rarely are both; (b) that when faced with a problem, the U.S. style of politics urges action: to "do something"; (c) that because political acceptability trumps program feasibility, the results of urban public policy are likely to aggravate, not reduce, problems.[39] With this warning, let's explore the feasibility and acceptability of the seven approaches, beginning with the question of political acceptability.

The federal government, being fiscally incapacitated and politically timorous, is unlikely to make revolutionary reforms before the late nineties or the twenty-first century. Adoption of the Canadian approach (no. 3, above) requires more leadership than is likely to be applied in the near future. The Enthoven (no. 5), Heritage (no. 6), and German (no. 7) approaches are only slightly less revolutionary, and probably still too revolutionary to be realized soon. The fact that most recent proposals are incremental additions to the present system (no. 1) is a reflection of the limited political opportunities in the near future. Perhaps the pressure to do something will be strong enough to break one of the incremental proposals loose during this decade. There are two relatively likely federal actions. The first is continued expansion of its role in allocations of fees and care (no. 3), primarily for purposes of cost management. This influences the entire health care delivery system because of the now-dominant role of the federal government as the payer for health care services. The second is continued experimentation with quality measures (no. 4), again prompted by concerns about cost.

State governments, being constrained by the federal law and operating in a competitive environment in which businesses and people easily migrate across state lines, are not likely, or do not have the authority, to adopt comprehensive solutions such as those of the Canadian (no. 3), Enthoven (no. 5), Heritage (no. 6), or German (no. 7) approaches. This leaves the states to make partial efforts at these approaches, such as UNY-Care, and with the same approaches most likely at the federal level: incremental additions (no. 1), government allocations of fees or care (no. 3), and a focus on quality (no. 4). Individual state governments (but not all fifty states) are more likely than the federal government to be aggressive and creative in pursuing these approaches in the near future.

Thus the next five years could see continued development of federal programs to regulate fees and guide care; substantial additions to present programs in some states to enhance access; and innovations in some states to regulate fees, ration care, assess and ensure quality, and restructure health insurance. The federal steps will not solve the access problem, and may aggravate it by increasing the financial pressures on providers and insurers and hence the incentive to avoid persons most needing health care. Individual states may embark upon experiments which show promise for broader application. Successful state programs to contain costs are likely to be most quickly emulated by other states and the federal government. Successes in the ensurance of quality also will be watched with interest, but they are more likely to carry political or economic burdens which make diffusion slower. State programs to ensure comprehensive access are as likely to come from unstudied promises as from carefully conceived strategies. In either case they will be prompted by the growing problems of access, yet will be modest in eventual result: if poorly conceived they are likely to run into surprising costs, forcing retrenchments; if carefully developed, conservatism is likely to limit coverage and choices substantially. The states may be able to make some progress, particularly in cost management and quality assurance, yet comprehensive solutions will prove to be beyond the grasp of most states.

Combining the tests of acceptability and feasibility gives a picture of 1997 as a year in which state and federal governments are still seeking new solutions. Although there may have been some promising innovations at one or both levels, the failure to achieve a comprehensive solution will produce a more certain pressure for federal action. Will the result be an increasingly furious series of incremental federal adjustments? The political tasks of supporting so many adjustments could exceed those of comprehensive reform, and the ultimate success of such incrementalism is more vulnerable to delay or sabotage by established organizations and interests inclined to frustrate implementation. Revolutionary change might then be as likely as continued adjustment. If so, it might be prompted by either a crisis or political leadership. It is not clear which is the more likely to bring a well-reasoned approach.

AN INVENTORY OF CHOICES IN DESIGNING AND ADMINISTERING A HEALTH CARE PROGRAM

Drawing distinctions between the proposals suggests three categories of policy choices important in designing and operating a national health program. The first choices are concerned with what is to be covered. These choices are particularly revealed by the regulatory approaches to managing costs and extending access, and by comparing most proposals with the present multi-tiered, exclusionary, and geographically differentiated systems.

The second choices deal with financing the care. They are most evident in the approaches put forth in attempting to find a politically acceptable and economically feasible means to extend access. They also represent choices of who shall control the health care systems.

The third choices concern the administration of the program. They deal with questions of public versus private roles, type of provider system, and such supporting programs as medical research and reforms in the legal environment. They show up particularly in the attempts to manage costs and the newer interests in quality. These choices have proven difficult to decide because their implications are complex and difficult to predict and because they too generate political concerns and conflicts over control.

These three categories of choices are used to identify the value issues which will be important in making the choices (tables 5–7). The value issues (table 4) form a basis for considering the choices presented in tables 5 through 7. While the choices in each table raise a wide range of questions about values, a fundamental value issue, or theme, can be drawn from each of the three categories of choice.

What Is to Be Covered?

The first category of program choices, that is, what is covered (table 5), is addressed each year in nearly every state when Medicaid programs are adjusted to changing budgetary constraints and public pressures. The table suggests values at issue in each of the four dimensions (i.e., eligibility, procedures, utilization, and payments) of these choices, showing that the choices involve a broad range of value issues. Because there are so many issues, the task of informing the debate through discussion of the value issues is daunting indeed, even though most of these issues already are being seriously addressed.

Two issues show up especially frequently, are important to each of the four aspects of the choices concerned with coverage, and intuitively seem central to such choices. These are the questions of rights and of fairness. The debate over these questions is often poorly framed as simply a question of rights, sometimes of the rights of the provider as well as of the patient. The special opportunity for the exploration of values in this case is to bring clarity to the public discussion, through careful consideration of whether there are various forms of rights, how rights might be usefully defined, and what processes appropriately establish and adjust rights. In what sense do "entitlements" become rights? Is health care an appropriate arena in which to develop entitlements, from either public programs or private contracts (i.e., insurance policies), which adjust with income (e.g., co-payments increasing with income), in order to provide a more specific approach to fairness and also more uniform and universal incentives for cost consciousness?

The matter of rights needs clarity not just to give precision to policy analysis which might be performed by policy specialists but, more important, to preserve and build the public's trust in the health care systems and in the political systems by defining and using language in a way that understanding is matched to reality. In other

Table 4. Value Issues of a Health Care System

Issue	Concerns
ACCOUNTABILITY	
Patient	Life-style (reporting it, managing it, paying its costs)
Provider	Quality care (assessing it, reporting it, ensuring it)
	Promised results at promised costs (financial and quality-of-life costs)
	Truth telling regarding choices, and prognoses (as opposed to paternalism)
Payer	Coverage of promised or reasonably expected entitlements (in terms of financial capacity and willingness to pay)
AUTONOMY	
Patient	Choice of care, to reflect patient's own values regarding life, quality of life, and life-style
	Choice of caregiver to reflect patient's preferences of caregiver personality, location, etc.
Provider	Freedom from demands by patients (ability to choose patients)
	Freedom from restrictions imposed by payers (ability to choose treatments)
	Freedom from restrictions on scope of activity
COMPASSION (including its relationship to fairness and utility)	Establishment of priorities of procedures (e.g., priority given to treatment of identifiable patient over prevention for statistical beneficiaries).
	Differentiation between groups (e.g., veterans and addicts)
	Preservation of entitlements to care in spite of personal choices (e.g., unhealthy life-style, inadequate insurance)
CONFLICTS OF INTEREST	
Provider	Personal financial rewards vs. patient interests in managed health care (underserving) or traditional care (overprescribing)
	Personal comfort, privacy, and control vs. patient understanding and control of choices
Payer	Cost vs. quality of care
	Short-term costs (this payer's responsibility) vs. long-term costs (perhaps others' responsibility)
Patient	Personal health and convenience vs. reasonable expectations of entitlements and responsibility for personal action

Continued on next page

Table 4—Continued

EQUALITY	
Care	Group specification (all groups or by income, by locations such as states or nations, by age, etc).
	Type of measurement (overall outcome, specific procedures, etc.)
Cost	Co-payments (equality vs. income adjusted)
	Premium costs
	Tax support (type, extent)
FAIRNESS, IN	Existence of multiple tiers of treatment
DISTRIBUTION	Exclusions based upon personal life-style or choices
OF CARE AND	Patient's portion of payments for care
COSTS	Distribution of costs for the insurer's portion of payments for care
	Geographic differences in care and financing
PRIVACY	
Patient	Health records
	Life-style
Provider	Finances
	Treatments and outcomes
RIGHTS TO	Degree (absolutely, only if promised, qualified by some
HEALTH CARE	measure of society's medical or financial capacity, etc.)
	Circumstances (by prognosis, life-style, ability to pay, etc.)
	Quantity
TRUTHFULNESS	Accuracy (in words and in real understanding)
	Promises of access,
	Political processes,
	Health care contracts
	Completeness of explanations
	Options
	Probable outcomes
UTILITY TO THE	Positive contributions to cost management (as in improve-
COMMUNITY	ment of cost-effectiveness), quality of life (as in improve-
	ment of life-style), and equitable access (as in enlargement
	of the community's acceptance of responsibility for an
	equitable health care system)—the contributions to each
	aspect of health care (cost, quality, and access) being
	weighed against the associated contributions and costs to
	the other two aspects
	Trade-offs between expenditures (of financial, administra-
	tive, political, and other resources) for health care and for
	other valued goods, services, and aspects of the society

words, a broader and clearer understanding of rights will demand and facilitate truth telling in two important and somewhat independent spheres. The first is the relationships between patient, provider, and payer and is concerned with the trust each has in the others when decisions are made about appropriateness of care. Misunderstandings as to what the patient has a right to expect will undermine these trusts. The second sphere is the political process and is concerned with the respect or cynicism with which the public views its government. Public expectations are frustrated, and respect diminished, by confusions over what can be expected and by disparities between expectations and performance.

Who Is to Pay and How Is Pay to Be Administered?

The second category of choice, how to pay for health care costs (table 6), has become the primary political issue. It contains three important elements: (1) Who pays? (2) Who administers the payment system? (3) What determines the rate at which providers are paid? While all aspects concern financing, they also do much to determine system control. Thus, while the question of who pays has replaced the question of who controls as the central issue of political debate, they

Table 5. Coverage of the Health Program

Choice	Specific Decisions	Value Questions
Eligibility	Whether coverage is universal or only for subgroups (by age, locations, income, etc.) Whether there are different plans for different subgroups Do choices in plans reflect willingness and/or ability to pay	Whether tiers of care are prohibited by *rights, fairness,* or *utility* (shared benefits mean shared concerns for adequacy) Whether tiers are justified by *utility* (some ages or skills more important), *autonomy* (to decide relative value of types of care) or *compassion* (veterans, not addicts)
Procedures	How broadly health care is defined (mental health, nursing home, home health care, health education, exercise, etc.) Within the broad categories, what care is covered (transplants, cosmetic surgery, etc.) If multiple plans, whether those persons covered may choose from optional forms having the same actuarial costs	Whether priorities are justified by *utility* (cost-effectiveness in regard to lives saved or quality of life), *compassion* (identifiable beneficiaries vs. prevention); personal *accountability* (for not using seatbelts; for costs likely to be shifted to others if not covered by major medical) Whether exclusions are prohibited by *rights, fairness, compassion, privacy* (life-style) Whether choices are required for *autonomy* (individual values concerning care and risks)

Continued on next page

Table 5—Continued

Utilization	Whether covered procedures are paid for (by government or insurance) whenever performed, or is reimbursement subject to review	Whether review impinges upon patient *rights*
	If subject to review, who does the review, with how much discretion, with what professional perspective, and having what financial incentives	Whether review hurts or helps *fairness* in the distribution of care and of costs
	Whether educational efforts attempt to control utilization	Whether review minimizes *conflicts of interest* on the part of the reviewer
		How review impinges upon reasonable *autonomy* on the part of patients and providers
		Whether concerns for *truth telling* shape the nature of the educational efforts
Payment	Whether there is full payment	When partial payments are prohibited by *rights, fairness*
	Whether payment is based upon income	How co-payments should be guided by *fairness, equality* of absolute burden, equality of relative burden (e.g., for consistent cost management incentives)
	Whether payment is determined by charges, costs, bidding or prospectively established (negotiated?) rates	
	Whether balance billing is allowed	Whether balance billing is contrary to or supported by *rights* of and *fairness* to patient, payer, or provider

are much the same question. The change that has taken place is that now the players are asking each other to take more, rather than less of the responsibility. Yet it can be quite reasonably presumed from the specific decisions listed in table 6 that the old debate over control remains alive and will not only be a major force in shaping the details of a national health program, but by influencing the administration of these policies will show up again in attempts to reshape whatever policies are adopted.

For these financing issues, there is an obvious central question of values, which is fairness. No amount of analysis is likely to achieve a common national perspective on the fair distribution of the benefits and costs of a national health care program. Good discussion, however, can show the flaws of simplistic, thoughtless, and self-contradictory proposals. It also can refine reasonable proposals and more accurately describe the choices between these proposals. While national consensus cannot be expected, careful discussion might enlarge the portions of the choices for which there is more common agreement.

Table 6. Choice of Payer and Administration of Pay

Choice	Specific Decisions	Value Questions
Sources of finance	What premium is paid by the consumer and whether it is scaled according to cost or means What coverage is the responsibility of the private sector (insurers and employers) and what is that of the public (and of which levels of government) Whether the employers' share is based on number of employees, employer's payroll, or employer's income The revenue source for the government's share	Whether burdens should be distributed according to *fairness* (equality, means, use of care, life-style, residence in high-cost location) or *utility* (incentives for life-style, cost management) Whether equality is required by *fairness*; *rights*; *privacy* (life-style)
Type of Administration (of Payment System)	Whether there are multiple or single payers (government or private) for a particular region Whether administration is centralized or decentralized (to states? to federal regions?) If decentralized, what program discretion is delegated to the local level?	How structural choices should be guided by *fairness*; *utility* (efficiency); *autonomy* (choice by patient or provider within the region or across regions—in choosing place of residence or business) Whether uniform financing is required by *rights*; justified by *fairness*
Basis of Payments	Whether institutions are financed through service fees or annual budgets Whether professional fees are negotiated or regulated Whether payments are made by procedure or per capita	How financing arrangements should be guided by *autonomy* (patient, physician, hospital, or payer); by *fairness* How fees should further *utility* (encouraging cost-effective treatments); *equality* (provider income, patient access); provider *autonomy* (as party to negotiations)

For the issues of control which lurk behind these matters of finance, there are questions of autonomy, rights, and privacy. These, along with utility, are important values which create an environment of issues within which the questions of fairness deserve to be considered. But they should not be allowed to take attention away from the questions of fairness. It may be that the relative import of the interests of the providers, as opposed to those of the consumers, in health policy will be reflected in the extent to which the concerns for fairness are swamped, rather than refined, by questions of autonomy, rights, and privacy.

How Is the Program to Be Administered?

The third category of choices, how shall a program be administered (table 7), also is organized around three subelements: (1) How is health care delivered? (2) How is health care evaluated? (3) How are complementary programs structured and administered? Their import is substantial, both in terms of the attention they attract (e.g., the concerns about malpractice) and of the real significance of their impact upon the costs and outcomes of the health care system (e.g., the question of how quality shall be assessed and assured remains at the fringes of the public debate but may be a core problem by the turn of the century).

The complexity of the choices raises an equally complex set of issues about values. It is this complexity which establishes a theme for these choices, a theme which hardly occurs in the listing itself: how trust will be established and protected when complexity forces a high degree of dependence upon expertise regarding health care and public policy. This echoes the concern about truth telling raised in the discussion of coverage, the first category of choices (table 2).

The more complex a choice, the more important is communication between those having various expertise and points of view (patient and physician, legislator and scientist). The more complex a choice, the more likely the decision making will be incremental, allowing the testing of waters and the use of experience to refine programs (the treatment of a developing disease, the development of programs to ensure quality). The more complex the situation, the more necessary is delegation of decision making from generalists to specialists (primary-care provider to surgical specialist; Congress to National Institutes of Health). Communication, the long-term evolution of programs, and the delegation of responsibilities all depend upon trust. Whether in the personal relationships between patient and provider, or the political world of public policy, trust—especially over the long term—depends upon truth telling.

SPECULATIONS, FROM A BROAD PERSPECTIVE, ABOUT THE IMPORTANT CHOICES

The above analyses put forth a broad range of ethical issues that deserve to be addressed in designing a health program. But they also

Table 7. Administration of the Health Program

Choice	Specific Decisions	Value Questions
Management	Whether providers are public or private agents Whether programs administered at the national or regional (state? federal region?) level How far is the shift from individual and group providers to larger, vertically integrated, organizations What choices are offered in selecting providers, with what price constraints What restrictions are placed upon providers' financial interest in ancillary services What processes and standards are priorities of care set when resources (funds, organs, etc.) are limited	How organizational structures should reflect concerns for *autonomy* (of provider, patient); *utility* (quality through size or incentives); *equality* How *conflicts of interest* should be identified and restricted How scarce resources should be allocated according to *fairness* (ability to pay); *utility* (cost-effectiveness, life-style)
Evaluation	Who (providers, payers, patients) ensures (by what process and having what sanctions) quality of care What information will be available, to whom, to assess quality	Whether the sharing of information is justified or prohibited, with whom, by *utility* (improve quality); *autonomy* (basis for choice); *privacy*; *truthfulness* (probable outcomes)
Complementary Programs	What emphasis and direction will be given practice guidelines What emphasis and direction will be given reforms in the legal environment (antitrust and malpractice) What emphasis and direction will be given disease prevention and health promotion (education, economic incentives, regulation, environmental controls from air quality to passive restraints in cars) What emphasis and direction will be given medical research How the roles of various provider professions, and their interactions, will be adjusted	How practice guidelines should will foster or inhibit *autonomy, truthfulness, accountability* When disease prevention violates or facilitates *autonomy, privacy, truthfulness, fairness* How the allocation of resources to or by complementary programs is justified by *fairness* (research to aid present vs. future generations); *utility* (prevention vs. treatment) How the relative treatment of professions is justified by *fairness* (tradition, equality); *utility* (contribution, market)

suggest some priorities for the exploration of values and consideration of choices by showing some issues to be particularly crucial to the future public policy of health care.

To suggest priorities as to which value issues especially deserve consideration may seem to be of dubious usefulness. First, it is difficult to predict which program choices will be the primary subjects of debate when decisions finally are made, even if they are made immediately. It is more difficult to predict the issues if decisions are postponed to the future. Even more difficult to predict is whether the choices will be made sooner rather than later. Thus any analysis based upon such a prediction is likely to be found wanting when political dynamics suddenly determine the time for decision. This argues for considerations which cover the broad field of value issues important to health care.

Still, there is enough reason to focus. There are issues which are especially likely to be central whenever program choices are made, and therefore should not be missed. By using the present situation (the situation which we best understand) to guide priorities, we focus our analysis on questions important if decisions are made now. Future analysis can move toward other choices as such choices become more central to the debate, as analysis moves in time with the debate. Some issues have such import that they justify an attempt to insert them into the policy debate whether or not they relate to the choices which are being raised by the politics of the times.

While the preceding analyses suggest that prudence requires further refinement of thinking about most potential issues, they point to three issues especially deserving of substantial and immediate consideration: (1) the claims to rights to health care, (2) the criteria for considering fairness in the distribution of care and costs, and (3) the meaning of and the need to tell the truth in both the delivery of health care and the policy process.

What Are the Rights to Health Care?

This issue is important in itself but also, in practical politics, joins together the other two priority issues of distributive justice and truth telling. There is, and probably will be, a multitiered system. Should there be a deliberate and publicly explicit multitiered system? In political debate we avoid the question, and through such deceit we confuse the issue, build unwarranted and damaging expectations, and generate cynicism about both health care and politics. On the other hand, will a frank admission become a tool to escape compassion: will it make discrepancies in access more acceptable and allow us to shrug off social responsibility (if we decide we ought to have such) to narrow the discrepancies which result from the uneven distribution of relative advantages and disadvantages among individuals of the society?

Until a persuasive argument is made to the contrary, the public policy debate ought to admit to and give major attention to the existing multitiered system—given a presumptive favoring of truth telling, which seems reasonable. Similarly, the public policy debate ought to admit to and give major attention to the tiers which are explicit or implicit in proposed reforms. To spotlight rights will give precision and credibility to the policy debate, and also may be the best protection against the risks that the existing discrepancies, once admitted, will become too easily acceptable. More forthright discussion of the multitiered systems could enlarge public policy options, which now are restricted by an unreasonable expectation that accepts the limits of technology but not those of economics in providing effective health care.

Studies of rights therefore should address the concern about what discrepancies are least acceptable and about the gaining and sustaining of commitment to correct such discrepancies. Continued development of definitions, rationales, and criteria regarding rights should seek to build the foundation for realistic debate and for the understanding upon which to build the societal consensus and commitments necessary in order to draw and hold a line that ensures a reasonably equitable package of basic services.

What Is Fair in the Distribution of Care and Costs?

Who pays and what is provided to whom? These issues are central to the policy debate, although much of the public may not be aware of nor party to their discussion; the public policy forum often involves only a small fraction of the general public. These issues are the questions of distributive justice and make fairness a priority question. They inevitably become entwined with deeper questions of justice, such as the motives behind the allocation. They go beyond the boundaries of the health care system itself: is the present allocation motivated more by concerns about the risk of being blamed for death than concerns about death itself, so that society more quickly utilizes the technology of scanners to avoid liability than that of seat belts to avoid death and injury? The questions of fairness also raise questions about the standards of democratic processes, particularly as they conflict with conclusions drawn from a consideration of distributive justice: for example, are the interests of those who are less powerful being fairly protected? Thus while the consideration of fairness is a large and useful question in and of itself, it also sets the groundwork for a range of related issues, from the motivations to the processes of policy-making.

Fairness in spending for health care is a large question because the spending is so large. The more than six hundred billion dollars now spent on health care each year is about the amount the nation spends on defense and education combined. It constitutes one of the greatest pools of resources yet allocated in human history. It is large enough that questions of fairness go beyond how health care itself is allocated to consider whether this is the right proportion of the community's resources to go to health care, as opposed to education, economic development, consumer consumption, and so on. It is large enough that it deserves to be placed in the even larger perspective of the amounts allocated to health care for U.S. citizens versus the amounts available for residents of other parts of the world, for health care and for other purposes. While the task of weighing health care expenditures just in the context of U.S. domestic expenditures is challenge enough for the present, this task becomes the basis for dealing with the broader concerns by building the connections to national and international budgeting, which themselves address the broader issues of relative value and fairness.

There is clear necessity to address fairness. Especially helpful will be analyses identifying how specific policy and administrative choices could affect the distribution of benefits and costs, and syntheses of these analyses to suggest the choices which will be most important to various conceptions of distributive justice. More difficult, yet also helpful, will be analyses of how these key choices are likely to pit various conceptions of fairness against probable political forces.

What Are Appropriate Expectations of Truth Telling in Health Care?

The third priority issue, about truth telling, is raised as a primary concern because of the complexity of the medical and public policy choices to be made. The concerns for truth telling arose repeatedly in the analyses of political acceptability and technical feasibility, doing so in two distinct contexts. The first dealt with the operation of a health program, particularly the ability of the patient to make reasoned choices. While in this first context the concerns for truth telling give special attention to what and how information should be given the patient, the concerns also are important to payers and providers and depend upon the truthfulness of the provider, the payer, and even the patient (the patient's responsibilities for informing provider and payer of conditions and circumstances). Perhaps one of the most important long-range effects of the changes now occurring in the delivery of health care is found in the questions being raised of the provider's responsibility to inform the patient, and its relationship to the extent and reliability of professional standards of ethics, given the growth of entrepreneurial incentives and cost-management pressures operating on the providers. Also, and probably equally significant, are the questions about the responsibilities of business and public policy. How might businesses and governments share or hide information and how might they support or undermine professional standards by which providers share accurate information? What are their responsibilities to reveal the risks and conflicts which the patient faces?

This moves the issue of truth telling to encompass the question of who is responsible for quality assessment and assurance to a particularly complex mix of the ethical issues of professional standards, personal responsibility and expectations, privacy, and choice regarding procedure and provider. This question inevitably is raised by the changes taking place in the delivery of care and attention to costs, but it is on the outer edge of public discussion. Because of its central importance to health, it must be clearly addressed, whether or not it is naturally on the agenda. It will be on the agenda if breakdowns in the changing system are broadly experienced, yet the ultimate public demand for better assessment and reporting of quality could come too late to protect the public interest effectively.

What Are Appropriate Expectations of Truth Telling in Health Care Policy?

The second context in which truth telling arises is in how the public and private programs are structured and adopted, particularly the accuracy of understanding about the entitlements being considered or created and about the costs and risks involved. For example, will the various payers succumb to the temptations to avoid costs or hard choices by misrepresenting the capacity of others to carry greater financial burdens? As in the previous context of health care itself, the concern is not just with outcome but with long-term trust in the systems (medical, governmental, and business) as well. This concern for truth telling and trust substantially increases the burdens being placed upon health care policy: to protect not just health but confidence in the social structure. We expect health care to address both the ends (health care outcome) and the means (truthfulness).

Truthfulness is especially important because of the complexity of the transition taking place in health care and the complexity of the policy-making process. The magnitude of the transition increases fears and mistrust because of the unknowns the transition represents. The complexity makes it impossible for any single person or institution to understand or fully manage the situation and makes it highly unlikely that there will be a one-step solution. Each step in the process will be substantially influenced by the trust which has been built or eroded in previous steps.

To achieve truthfulness may mean, or require, revolutions in both politics and professions: revolutions which already are under way to escape paternalism by either doctors or leaders. Or perhaps the needed truthfulness can be acquired by cultivating the strains of integrity which have always been pursued by the best of the providers and public leaders. In either case, particularly crucial choices are those which determine how truthfully the health care program is sold and managed.

NOTES

1. M. L. Berk, A. C. Monheit, and M. M. Hagen, "How the U. S. Spent Its Health Care Dollar: 1929–80," *Health Affairs* 7 (Fall 1988): 46–60.

2. Julie Kosterlitz, "Softening Resistance," *National Journal* 23 (January 1, 1991): 64–68.

3. Scott M. Matheson, "The States' Roles and Responsibilities for Providing Universal and Affordable Health Care to the American People," in *Providing Universal and Affordable Health Care: The Richard and Hinda Rosenthal Lectures* (Washington, D.C.: Institute of Medicine, 1989). See also Paul E. Peterson, *City Limits* (Chicago: University of Chicago Press, 1981).

4. The prohibition was included in the Employee Retirement Income Security Act of 1974 (ERISA).

5. Booth Gardner, *Prescription for a Healthy America* (Washington, D.C.: National Governors' Association, 1990).

6. Therese Droste, "Will Employers Accept a National Health Plan?" *Hospitals* 63 (May 20, 1989): 81; Lawrence K. Altman and Elisabeth Rosenthal, "Changes in Medicine Bring Pain to Healing Profession," *New York Times*, Sunday, February 18, 1990, sec. A; Lisa Belkin, "Many in Medicine Are Calling Rules a Professional Malaise," *New York Times*, February 19, 1990; and Gina Kolata, "Wariness Is Replacing the Trust between Physician and Patient," *New York Times*, February, 20, 1990; Robert J. Blendon, "Three Systems: A Comparative Survey," *Health Management Quarterly*, First Quarter, 1989, pp. 2–10.

7. Earlier articles which looked at the range of proposals being offered include Stacey T. Cyphert and James E. Rohrer, "A National Medical Care Program: Review and Synthesis of Past Proposals," *Journal of Public Health Policy*, 9 (Winter 1988): 456–72; and E. Richard Brown, "Principles for a National Health Program: A Framework for Analysis and Development," *Milbank Quarterly*, 66, no. 4 (1988): 573–617. A recent review of many of the proposals considered here, as well as some others, is the entire issue of *Journal of the American Medical Association* (hereafter *JAMA*) 265 (May 15, 1991): 19.

8. Lewin/ICF, "American Academy of Pediatrics Proposal for Universal Access to Health Care for Children and Pregnant Women, Draft," American Academy of Pediatrics, Elk Grove Village, Ill., April 30, 1990.

9. American College of Physicians, "Access to Health Care," *Annals of Internal Medicine* 112 (May 1, 1990): 642–61.

10. American Hospital Association, "National Health Strategy: A Starting Point for Debate," (Chicago: American Hospital Association, 1991).

11. American Medical Association, "Health Access America," February 1990. Also see "Report: Q (I-89): Covering the Uninsured," proposal approved at the AMA House of Delegates, December 1989.

12. American Nurses Association, "Nursing's Agenda for Health Care Reform (Washington, D.C.: American Nurses Association, 1991).

13. Daniel Callahan, *What Kind of Life: The Limits of Medical Progress* (New York: Simon and Schuster, 1990); Daniel Callahan, *Setting Limits: Health Care in an Aging Society* (New York: Simon and Schuster, 1987). Also see Richard D. Lamm, "The Brave New World of Health Care," University of Denver, 1990; John F. Kilner, *Who Lives? Who Dies? Ethical Criteria in Patient Selection*, (New Haven: Yale University Press, 1990); Robert H. Blank, *Rationing Medicine* (New York: Columbia University Press, 1988); H. I. Aaron and W. B. Schwartz, *The Painful Prescription: Rationing Hospital Care* (Washington, D.C.: Brookings Institution, 1984); President's Commission for the Study of Ethical Problems in Medicine and Biomedical and Behavioral Research, *Securing Access to Health Care* (Washington, D.C.: Government Printing Office, 1983); R. W. Evans, "Health Care Technology and the Inevitability of Resource Allocation and Rationing Decisions," *JAMA* 249 (1983): 2208–19.

14. Keith J. Mueller, "Federal Programs to Expire: The Case of Health Planning," *Public Administration Review* 48 (May/June, 1988): 719–25.

15. Connecticut Public Act Number 90–134.

16. Alain Enthoven and Richard Kronick, "A Consumer-Choice Health Plan for the 1990s," in two parts, *New England Journal of Medicine* (hereafter *NEJM*) 320 (January 5, 1989): 29–37 and 320 (January 12, 1989): 94–101; Alain C. Enthoven, *Theory and Practice of Managed Competition in Health Care Finance* (New York: Elsevier, 1988), efficiency quote on p. 11; Alain Enthoven, "Cutting Cost without Cutting the Quality of Care," *NEJM* 298 (June 1, 1978) :1229–38; Alain Enthoven, "Consumer-Choice Health Plan," *NEJM*, 298 (March 23 and 30, 1978): 650–58, 709–20.

17. Families USA Foundation, *To the Rescue: Toward Solving America's Health Cost Crisis* (Washington, D.C.: Families USA Foundation, 1990; Families USA Foundation, *Emergency! Rising Health Costs in America* (Washington, D.C.: Families USA Foundation, 1990).

18. Chapters 393 and 431N Hawaii Revised Statutes; State of Hawaii Department of Health, "Interim Report to the Legislature, State Health Insurance Program," Honolulu, October 1989; State of Hawaii Department of Health, "Progress Report to Hawaii Legislature, State Health Insurance Program," Honolulu, March 1990; State of Hawaii Department of Health, "State Health Insurance Program Quarterly Report: June, 1990–August, 1990," Honolulu.

19. Health Policy Agenda Steering Committee, *The Health Policy Agenda for the American People* (Chicago: The Health Policy Agenda for the American People, 1987). See also Health Policy Agenda Steering Committee, "Health Policy Agenda for the American People," *JAMA* 257 (1987): 1199–1210; J. R. Tallon, Jr., "A Health Policy Agenda Proposal for Including the Poor," *JAMA* 261 (1989): 1044; Health Policy Agenda for the American People, Ad Hoc Committee on Medicaid, *Including the Poor*, February 1989; Kenneth E. Thorpe and Joanna E. Siegel, "Covering the Uninsured: Interactions among Public and Private Sector Strategies," *JAMA* 262 (October 20, 1989): 2114–18; Gilbert Welch, "Health Care Tickets for the Uninsured," *NEJM* 321 (November 2, 1989): 1261–64; James R. Tallon, Jr., "Including the Poor: Recommendations for Medicaid Reform," *in* Health Policy Agenda for the American People, *Innovative Partnerships for Affordable Health Care* (Washington, D.C.: National Governors Association, 1990).

20. S. M. Butler and E. F. Haislmaier, eds., *A National Health System for America* (Washington, D.C.: Heritage Foundation, 1989).

21. Health Insurance Association of America, *Health Care Financing for All Americans* (Washington, D.C.: Health Insurance Association of America, 1991).

22. David U. Himmelstein and Steffie Woolhandler et al., "A National Health Program for the United States," *NEJM* 320 (January 12, 1989): 102–8; Steffie Woolhandler and David Himmelstein, "A National Health Program: Northern Lights at the End of the Tunnel," *JAMA* 262 (October 20, 1989): 2136–37; Steffie Woolhandler and David U. Himmelstein, "Resolving the Cost/Access Conflict," *Journal for General Internal Medicine* (January/February 1989), pp. 54–60; Steffie Woolhandler and David U. Himmelstein, "Cost

without Benefit: Administrative Waste in U.S. Health Care," *NEJM* 314 (February 13, 1986): 441–45.

23. Florence A. Wilson and Duncan Neuhauser, *Health Services in the United States* (Cambridge; Mass.: Ballinger, 1987), pp.112–17, 206–9.

24. "Kennedy, Waxman Introduce Insurance-for-all Proposal," *Congressional Quarterly*, April 15, 1989, pp. 826–27; "Senate Labor OKs Mandated-Benefits Measure," *Congressional Quarterly*, February 20, 1988, pp. 363–67.

25. Commonwealth of Massachusetts, "An Act to Make Health Security Available to All Citizens of the Commonwealth and to Improve Hospital Financing," chapter 23 of the acts of 1988; Alan Sager, Peter Hiam, and Deborah Socolar, "Promise and Performance: First Monitoring Report," Access and Affordability Monitoring Project, Boston University School of Public Health, Boston, April 9, 1989; Alan Sager and Deborah Socolar, "Fact Sheet No. 2," Access and Affordability Monitoring Project, Boston University School of Public Health, Boston, August 30, 1989; Alan Sager and Deborah Socolar, "Hospital Expenses: Massachusetts vs. United States," Access and Affordability Monitoring Project, Boston University School of Public Health, Boston, September 11, 1990.

26. "Who Should Measure HMO Quality?" *American Medical News,* 29 (October 10, 1986): 2, 49; Paul J. Kenkel, "Seeking a Rational System: Consultant Urges Purchasers to 'Buy Right,'" *Modern Health Care* 18 (November 4, 1988): 64.

27. Two recent articles exploring this use of hospital mortality data are: Arthur J. Hartz, Henry Krakauer, Evelyn M. Kuhn, Mark Young, Steven J. Jacobson, Greer Gay, Larry Muenz, Myron Katzoff, R. Clifton Bailey, and Alfred A. Rimm, "Hospital Characteristics and Mortality Rates," *NEJM* 321 (December 21, 1989): 1720–25; Rolla Edward Park, Robert H. Brook, Jacqueline Kosecoff, Jean Keesey, Lisa Rubenstein, Emmett Keeler, Katherine L. Kahn, William H. Rogers, and Mark R. Chassin, "Explaining Variations in Hospital Death Rates," *JAMA* 264 (July 25, 1990): 484–90.

28. National Association of Community Health Centers, "Access 2000, Concept Paper, Draft," Washington D.C., 1990.

29. National Association of Social Workers, "National Health Care Proposal," Silver Springs, Maryland, 1991.

30. National Leadership Commission on Health Care, *For the Health of a Nation* (Ann Arbor, Michigan: Health Administration Press, 1989). See also "Broad Plans to Revise Health Insurance Offered," *Congressional Quarterly*, February 4, 1989, p. 221; and Arnold S. Relman, "The National Leadership Commission's Health Care Plan," *NEJM* 320 (February 2, 1989): 314.

31. Senate bills 27 (basic health services), 534 (insurance pool), and 935 (minimum benefits for employee coverage), 65th Oregon Legislative Assembly (1989); "Oregon Puts Bold Health Plan on Ice," *Science* 249 (August 3, 1990): 468–71; John Kitzhaber, "Oregon Plan Can Heal an Ailing System," Thomas Mason and Theresa Julnes, "Oregon's List a Deadly Prescription," and others' views, *Healthweek*, May 21, 1990, pp. 18–22.

32. *Health Services Research* 25 (December 1990): 691–824 (full issue

devoted to the AHCPR program and related efforts); "Cookbook Medicine," *National Journal* 23 (March 9, 1991): 574–77; S. Reverby, "Stealing the Golden Eggs: Ernest Amory Codman and the Science and Management of Medicine," *Bulletin of the History of Medicine* 55 (Summer 1981): 156–71; J. W. Williamson, "Evaluating Quality of Patient Care; A Strategy Relating Outcome and Process Assessment," *JAMA* 218 (October 25, 1971): 564–69; D. D. Rutstein, William Berenberg, Thomas Chalmers, Charles E. Child, 3rd, Alfred Fishman, Edward B. Perrin, "Measuring the Quality of Medical Care: A Clinical Method," *NEJM* 294 (March 11, 1976): 582–88; J. Wennberg and A. Gittelsohn, "Small Area Variations in Health Care Delivery," *Science* 182 (December 14, 1973): 1102–8; W. L. Roper, W. Winkenwerder, G. M. Hackbarth, and H. Krakauer, "Effectiveness in Health Care: An Initiative to Evaluate and Improve Medical Practice," *NEJM* 319 (November 3, 1988): 1197–1202; John E. Wennberg, "On the Status of the Prostate Disease Assessment Team," *Health Services Research* 25 (December 1990): 709–16.

33. The Pepper Commission, *A Call for Action* (Washington, D.C.: Government Printing Office, 1990); Martin Tolchin, "Panel Says Broad Health Care Would Cost $86 Billion a Year," *New York Times*, March 3, 1990.

34. P. E. Dans, J. P. Weiner, and S. E. Otter, "Peer Review Organizations: Promises and Pitfalls," *NEJM* 313 (October 31, 1985): 1131–37.

35. Department of Health and Human Services, Health Care Finance Agency, *Report to Congress: Medicare Physician Payment*, HCFA publication number 03287 (Washington, D.C.: Government Printing Office, 1989); John K. Inglehart, "The New Law on Medicare's Payment to Physicians," *NEJM* 322 (April 26, 1990): 1247–52; John K. Inglehart, "The Recommendations of the Physician Payment Review Commission," *NEJM* 320 (April 17, 1989): 1156–60; William C. Hsio, Peter Braun, Douwe Yntema, and Edmund R. Becker, "Estimating Physicians' Work for a Resource-Based Relative-Value Scale," *NEJM* 319 (September 29, 1988): 835–41.

36. Uwe E. Reinhardt, "Bringing Out the Worst in People: The Corrosive Effects of American Health Insurance" (Paper presented at the National Governors' Association Conference, "Innovative Partnerships for Affordable Health Care," Washington. D.C., September 23, 1990; Uwe E. Reinhardt, "Toward a Fail-Safe Health-Insurance System," *Wall Street Journal*, January 11, 1989.

37. Arnold S. Relman, "Reforming the Health Care System," *NEJM* 323 (October 4, 1990): 991–92; Arnold S. Relman, "The Trouble with Rationing," *NEJM* 323 (September 27, 1990): 911–13; Arnold S. Relman, "Assessment and Accountability: The Third Revolution in Medical Care," *NEJM* 319 (November 3, 1988): 1220–22; Arnold S. Relman, "The New Medical-Industrial Complex," *NEJM* 303 (1980): 963–70. Regarding concerns about conflicts of interest, also see "Warm Bodies: Doctor-Owned Labs Earn Lavish Profits in a Captive Market," *Wall Street Journal*, March 1, 1989; "Warm Bodies: Hospitals That Need Patients Pay Bounties for Doctors' Referrals," *Wall Street Journal*, February 27, 1989.

38. New York State Department of Health, "Universal New York Health

Care: UNY-Care: A Proposal, Revision I," Albany, May 10, 1990; Dan E. Beauchamp and Ronald L. Rouse, "Universal New York Health Care," *NEJM* 323 (September 6, 1990): 640–44.

39. Edward E. Banfield, *The Unheavenly City* (Boston: Little, Brown, 1970), chap. 11.

A National Health Program: Would Implementation Be the Problem?

Frank J. Thompson

In April 1991, roughly twenty-five years after the passage of Medicaid and Medicare, the lead story on the front page of the Sunday *New York Times* asserted:

> Long a growing worry of the poor, medical expenses and health insurance are now a source of mounting anxiety for millions of middle-class Americans—healthy or sick, insured or not.... As the nation's medical costs soar, more and more people are being squeezed financially or abandoned altogether by insurers. Their fears, and the vaguer disquiet of many well-insured people ... are becoming important new forces for change in the nation's health system.[1]

It is problematic whether these forces and the media attention they generate will give birth to a public program ensuring universal access to medical care. American politics has long provided barren soil for the flowering of such initiatives. The massive deficits and conservative politics of the 1980s and 1990s have further eroded prospects for bold new policies.

Still, the mounting concerns of the middle class about medical insurance could in time allow advocates of a national health program to create or use a policy window to launch major reform. For this and other reasons, it behooves us to be sensitive to the important and complex ethical issues a national health program would pose. Some of these ethical concerns revolve around the rights and duties of individuals (e.g., physicians) in their dealing with others (e.g., patients) given a certain setting or situation. Other issues, of greater concern here, involve the moral quality of the collective practice of health care.[2] Ultimately this collective ethical problem focuses on achieving some difficult-to-calibrate balance among access, quality, and cost in the medical sector. The essays by Leslie P. Francis,

"Expectations and the Design of a Universal Health Care System,"
and Robert P. Huefner, "Designing a Health Care System: Considering the Need to Know," beam light on the factors involved in promoting this delicate balance through a national health program.

As valuable as their contributions are, however, we need to
recognize a topic that they do not very explicitly address—the
problem of policy implementation and evolution. This problem as
well as others raised by Francis and by Huefner intersect with claims
about "American exceptionalism." Assertions about exceptionalism
typically run something like the following: It's all well and good to
talk about the lessons of Canada, Germany, or some other country for
a national health program in the United States, but these lessons will
probably not transfer because we have a very distinctive political
tradition—one built on fear of government in general and of centralized power in particular. This political culture, the claim continues,
combines an emphasis on individualism with the separation of
powers, federalism, weak political parties, and other forces to frag-
ment, even pulverize, power in the United States, and the currents
unleashed by these political factors make it difficult to gain approval
for and implement a national health program that makes sense
morally.

If the moral consequences of a national health program are to be
dissected, the challenge of American exceptionalism, especially as it
pertains to policy implementation and evolution, must be joined.
Prior to this, however, certain issues raised by Francis and Huefner
deserve attention.

DESIGN AND EXPECTATIONS

Francis and Huefner constructively rivet attention on different
facets of developing and implementing a national health plan. Huefner provides a useful top-down view of policy design. He understands
that flawed policy hypotheses can thwart the most diligent and astute
efforts to implement a program successfully. His nearly encyclopedic
coverage of current proposals for a national health program provides
a conceptual anchor for comparative analysis of different policy
options. For her part, Francis supplements Huefner's broad review
with analysis of two major contending models—the Enthoven-
Kronick plan, with its emphasis on employer-based health coverage
and managed competition, and the Himmelstein proposal (or Physi-

cians for a National Health Program), which espouses a model similar to the Canadian system. More fundamentally, however, Francis reminds us of a critical bottom line—the way in which a program will shape expectations about medical care and whether these expectations will be morally satisfying.

Among the many insights yielded by Francis and Huefner, three in particular struck me. These involve the potential contribution of the states, the role of "truth telling" in any government effort to launch and implement a program, and the risk that dashed expectations arising from a comprehensive health program will breed dissatisfaction with medical care institutions and government.

During the 1980s, the more imaginative policy initiatives to deal with problems of the medically uninsured came from the states rather than Washington. Governor Dukakis's Massachusetts program captured much attention. In New York, the Department of Health under the direction of Dr. David Axelrod carefully crafted a plan for Universal New York Health Care (UNY-Care).[3] Proposals to ensure comprehensive health insurance coverage also made it to the policy agendas of several other states.

Huefner, however, provides a sobering and accurate assessment of these developments. He understands that the pressures that drive states to be concerned with economic development make it extremely unlikely that even the most progressive states will move one-by-one to launch and sustain comprehensive health programs. States that adopt such plans risk dysfunctional migration. Generous public health insurance programs may on the margins persuade lower-income groups to come to or remain in a state.[4] Of greater importance, the higher taxes that may well be needed to support such a program may dim the attractiveness of a state to business or higher-income groups. Generous states thereby risk a pattern of people and firms voting with their feet in a way that erodes the state's tax base at the same time that the demand for state-subsidized medical coverage grows.

To avoid this dynamic, the federal government must play the dominant role in any national health program. Through a mix of greater federal funding and mandates that all states implement a program along similar lines (e.g., the same basic-service package), Washington can help remove health insurance coverage from the bid-down dynamics of interstate economic competition. As both the Enthoven-Kronick and Himmelstein proposals suggest, states can

effectively shoulder pivotal responsibilities for implementing a comprehensive health program, but only if the federal government
substantially subsidizes and structures the initiative.

In addition to clarifying the limits to the state role in fostering a
national health program, Huefner stresses the importance of "truth
telling." He calls for elucidating the concept of a "right to health care"
not just to facilitate precision in policy analysis but to sustain and
enhance the public's trust in the medical care and political systems.
Without clarification of this and other matters, we risk a politics of
deceit that can confuse the debate, build unwarranted and damaging
expectations, and generate cynicism about both health care and
politics. He asserts that attaining truthfulness may require "revolutions" in both politics and the professions.

Few would doubt the legitimacy of Huefner's concern. Truth
telling will often be the handmaiden of trust—an element essential to
both politics and the health arena. However, the pursuit of truth
telling is complex both empirically and morally. Uncertainty
presents one set of problems. While social scientists know much
about health care policy, any national health program is bound to
yield some unanticipated outcomes. The best efforts at telling the
truth will probably be somewhat off target. This can breed dissatisfaction and skepticism even in the face of the highest ethical conduct by
those who attempt to assess and shape health policy. To compound
problems, the language of public discourse condones only so much
probabilistic reasoning, especially in a fragmented political system
where oversell is usually needed to get action. The passage of a sound
national health program may well require supporters to paint a
rosier picture of its virtues than strict adherence to truth telling
implies.

Beyond this issue, ambiguity (as distinct from deceit or lying) at
times has positive functions. The concept of a "right to health care"
serves as a condensational symbol reaffirming an important value in
the political culture. Explicit consideration of its operational meaning or the trade-offs it entails is not always better. The more explicit
we become the more we risk conflict and the harder it will be to keep
coalitions supporting guaranteed health care together. In this regard, it bears repeating that much of political life is about symbolic
affirmation of particular moral orders and desirable ends—not
about hard-edged instrumental, cost-benefit analysis.[5] Philosophers
can contribute much by explicating the concept of a right to health,
but policy debate and action will probably not benefit from preoccu-

pation with the issue. Backers of national health programs face enough difficulties coalescing without forcing them to agree on first principles.

Truth telling must also confront the problem of the language of understanding in a democracy. The contemporary administrative state, or "bureaucratic democracy," faces the dilemma that its vocabulary is often technical and obscure.[6] How can one communicate basic truths about achieving a balance among cost, access, and quality in health care that great masses of the citizenry can understand? Experts and policymakers essentially face the challenge of translating their message across cultures; in this regard their relationships with the popular media become critical. Currently, reporters who take health care issues seriously run the risk of MEGOS—My Eyes Glaze Over Stories.[7] The desire to avoid MEGOS generally leads to the pursuit of the colorful, dramatic, and simple, which in turn can easily fuel a misallocation of public attention in the health care arena. Hence, the quest for truth telling about health care policy must wrestle with how *USA Today* and CNN can contribute to the process.

Whatever the complexities of truth telling, Huefner is right to emphasize its importance in designing and implementing a national health program. The degree to which truth telling occurs and is understood by the citizenry may markedly affect expectations about the health care system and government.

Here, Francis's analysis lays a sturdy foundation. She appropriately asks what expectations will be dashed once a national health program emerges. In this vein the surveys of Louis Harris and associates clarify that having a national health plan does not guarantee public satisfaction with the medical system or government. Their ten-nation survey found that 89 percent of American respondents believed that the health care system required either fundamental change or complete rebuilding. But in eight of nine other countries, all of which have national health programs, a majority expressed the same sentiment (albeit by smaller margins).[8] Only in Canada did most respondents express basic satisfaction with their medical care system.

As Francis suggests, dissatisfaction could spring from such sources as more limited access to certain less essential care and from delays in the introduction of beneficial technologies. More fundamentally, the Harris ten-nation survey found a relationship between lower levels of health care spending per capita and public dissatisfaction *among countries with national health programs* (Sweden being the

primary exception).[9] Constrained budgets under a national health
program can crimp the physical and human resource capacity of the
medical sector, and fuel the discontent Francis describes.

Whatever the exact source of dashed expectations, it is critical to
remember that almost any policy solution, including a national
health program, will generate a new set of problems and dissatisfac-
tions. The point is to get a better set of problems to work on than we
currently have. Once approved, a national health program seems
likely to move concerns about deficiencies in the health care system
to more satisfying moral ground (e.g., worries about marginal threats
to quality or insufficient innovation rather than large numbers of
people with inadequate access to care). Still, the degree to which we
move toward a more optimal balance in terms of quality, access, and
cost depends upon the implementation and evolution of the program. In this regard, issues of American exceptionalism surface.

IMPLEMENTATION AND EVOLUTION

The American political system is in many respects all anchor and no
sail. Its fragmentation of power and its political culture help account
for why the United States stands alone among advanced industrialized democracies in having no national health program. In the event
policymakers adopt a comprehensive program, the elements of
American exceptionalism will also come home to roost in the implementation process. The politics generated after the program
becomes law will be as important as the politics leading to its
adoption. Implementation will trigger certain political dynamics
and pressures which in turn will shape the evolution of national
health policy.

All the comprehensive health plans, even those like the
Enthoven-Kronick proposal, which rely heavily on private employers,
require government administrative agencies to do something. Significant discretion over major decisions affecting cost, access, and
quality will be left to implementing agents involved in interpreting
the authorizing legislation and carrying out the program. This does
not mean that civil servants will be enormously powerful. To the
contrary, they will come under heavy pressure from interest groups,
Congress, the courts, the White House, competing administrative
agencies, the media and at times popular sentiment in exercising
discretion and supervising implementing agents outside government
(e.g., hospitals). But whatever the influences on them, their actions

will do much to shape who gets what, when, where, and how from a national health program. Those concerned with the moral dimensions of policy can ignore the implementation process only at great peril.

Students of American exceptionalism often portray implementation as the Achilles heel of government action. For instance, a recent comparison of the political context of health policy in industrialized democracies by James Morone points to a "devaluation of good administration" in the United States. He believes that "the recruitment patterns, social standing, and reward structures of public service all reflect this bias. The general reluctance to develop competent public administration has been particularly disabling for health care policies."[10] In a similar vein, Harvey Sapolsky suggests that one of the most formidable barriers to cost control in the health arena is "our tradition of limiting the administrative capacity of government." He observes that "we work hard to make government service unattractive."[11]

Advocates of particular national health programs have not hesitated to use claims about limited government capacity to bolster the case for the policies they espouse. In discussing the virtues of their consumer-choice health plan vis-à-vis a plan modeled after the Canadian system, Enthoven and Kronick argue:

> Serious questions can be raised about the capability of the American federal and state governments to manage the whole health care system with a tolerable level of competence. The Canadians have a parliamentary system that is less vulnerable than our own to the pressures of special-interest groups. They have a stronger tradition of civil service. And the provinces operate on a similar scale and with much more cultural homogeneity than many of our larger states.[12]

These views need to be taken seriously. The 1980s witnessed growing concern about the deterioration of the basic administrative infrastructure of the federal government. In part as a response, Paul Volcker agreed to chair a National Commission on the Public Service (the Volcker Commission). Initiated in 1987 with funding from major private foundations, the commission issued recommendations in early 1989 to counter what it saw as a "quiet crisis" in American government.[13] While the Volcker Commission has had a positive impact, questions about the adequacy of governmental capacity persist.

In recognizing the capacity problem, however, we should not fall prey to crippling and undue pessimism. Given halfway plausible policies, the administrative apparatus of government often proves more than adequate in implementing them. The panoply of health programs launched in this country, from the Veterans Administration medical system to Medicare, can boast of impressive achievements.

Ultimately, issues of administrative capacity comprise only one piece of the concern with implementation and policy evolution. Proposals for national health programs need to be scrutinized in terms of the critical choices they will leave for program implementors and the constellation of political pressures likely to bear on officials at these decision sites. Such analysis can heighten sensitivity to how a national program will affect the delicate balance among cost, access, and quality and thereby generate pressure for change in policy.

Two examples make the need to focus on implementation and evolution more vivid. Consider Francis's concerns about the limits to the basic care package found in the Enthoven-Kronick proposal. An implementation perspective asks whether the forces unleashed after the plan goes into effect would tend to generate pressure to expand, diminish, or stabilize that service package. Limits to space prohibit in-depth analysis of possible scenarios, but one can readily sketch two possibilities. Under the Enthoven-Kronick proposal, the costs of health care remain spread among many payers thereby reducing the incentive for any one of them to curtail actions that boost aggregate national expenditures on medical care. Overall, this dispersion of payers could weaken resistance to pressure from patients and providers to expand the basic service package over time. Policy evolution might tilt toward more generous coverage. Alternatively, one can conjure up a scenario where the Enthoven-Kronick plan (despite tax disincentives) spawns a flourishing market in supplementary, privately purchased health insurance much as medigap policies fill lacunae left by Medicare. To the degree that the more affluent secure such policies, support for expanding the basic service package may well recede. Rising health care costs could even stoke political dynamics that cause the package to erode.

One can also employ implementation analysis to assess more fundamental evolutionary claims made by Enthoven and Kronick themselves.

> A system that was publicly administered in large part might evolve from our mixed proposal if the public sponsors could work effectively, causing large numbers of employers to choose to arrange coverage for

their employees through them. Thus, those who would prefer to see a model that was financed and administered publicly might view our incremental proposal as one step in an evolutionary process toward public sponsorship on behalf of those who would not be better served by private-sector sponsors. If all but the largest employers chose to contract for coverage through a public sponsor, many disadvantages of the employment-based system would be alleviated.[14]

What implementation scenario must prevail for this evolution to occur? Given certain economic and political factors, is this scenario at all likely? Both questions deserve systematic, politically astute analysis.

These sketches only scratch the surface but they illustrate the importance of contemplating implementation scenarios and their effects on the evolution of a national health program. Obviously, projections about implementation and evolution associated with different proposals for a national health program must recognize uncertainty. Predictions often go awry. But we know enough about policy and implementation dynamics to shun agnosticism.

In sum, Francis and Huefner advance understanding of the challenges involved in creating ethically sound, comprehensive policies for health care in the United States. Any such consideration must confront issues raised by American exceptionalism, including the forces that make it difficult to implement programs effectively. But while we should heed the alarm bells of exceptionalism, they should not foster resignation or defeatism. American political culture and institutions do not make public administration easy, but they do not make it impossible. Government agencies at times demonstrate great ingenuity in implementing health programs. A national health initiative need not flounder on the shoals of defective implementation and dysfunctional policy evolution, but avoiding that prospect requires that we pay attention to implementation issues at the outset.

NOTES

1. Tamar Lewin, "High Medical Costs Hurt Growing Numbers in U.S.," *New York Times*, April 28, 1991.

2. Amy Gutmann and Dennis Thompson, eds., *Ethics and Politics: Cases and Comments* (Chicago: Nelson-Hall, 1984).

3. Dan E. Beauchamp and Ronald L. Rouse, "Universal New York Health Care: A Single-Payer Strategy Linking Cost Control and Universal Access," *New England Journal of Medicine* (hereafter *NEJM*) 323 (September 6, 1990): 640–44.

4. Studies of migration in response to welfare benefits and taxes pose complex methodological issues. Additional research is needed. For recent findings in support of migration theory, see Paul E. Peterson and Mark Rom, "American Federalism, Welfare Policy, and Residential Choices," *American Political Science Review* 83 (September 1989): 711–28.

5. See especially James G. March and Johan P. Olsen, *Rediscovering Institutions: The Organizational Basis of Politics* (New York: Free Press, 1989).

6. The term is from Douglas Yates, *Bureaucratic Democracy* (Cambridge, Mass.: Harvard University Press, 1982).

7. Charles C. Mann, "The Prose (and Poetry) of Mario M. Cuomo," *Atlantic Monthly*, December, 1990, p. 104.

8. Robert J. Blendon, Robert Leitman, Ian Morrison, and Karen Donelan, "Satisfaction with Health Systems in Ten Nations," *Health Affairs* 9 (September 1990): 185–92.

9. Ibid., p. 189. The United States spent the most per capita and had the lowest level of satisfaction with the system.

10. James A. Morone, "American Political Culture and the Search for Lessons from Abroad," *Journal of Health Politics, Policy and Law* 15 (Spring 1990): 133.

11. Harvey M. Sapolsky, "Prospective Payment in Perspective," in Lawrence D. Brown, ed., *Health Policy in Transition* (Durham, N.C.: Duke University Press, 1987), pp. 71–72.

12. Alain Enthoven and Richard Kronick, "A Consumer-Choice Health Plan for the 1990s," *NEJM* 320 (January 12, 1989): 100.

13. National Commission on the Public Service, *Leadership for America: Rebuilding the Public Service, the Report* (Washington, D.C.: National Commission on the Public Service, 1989).

14. Enthoven and Kronick, "Consumer-Choice Health Plan," p. 98.

PART V

Providers and Patients under National Health Care

Dying in 559 Beds: Efficiency, "Best Buys," and the Ethics of Standardization in National Health Care

*Margaret P. Battin**

In *The Notebooks of Malte Laurids Brigge*, the "heavy, difficult book" begun in Rome during the winter of 1903–4 and not finished until 1910 in Paris, Rilke employs a series of rapid, jolting impressions to express his pervasive concern with death and his distress about the institutional character of death among the poor. To convey an image of poverty, he describes the worn furniture of a cheap rented room: "if I were not poor I would rent another room with furniture not so worn out, not so full of former occupants, as the furniture here. At first it really cost me an effort to lean my head on this arm-chair; for there is a certain greasy-grey hollow in its green covering, into which all heads seem to fit."[1] To portray the nature of dying in medical institutions for the poor, he describes the Hôtel-Dieu, the hospital for the poor, across the plaza from the Cathedral of Paris: "This excellent hôtel is very ancient. Even in King Clovis' time people died in it in a number of beds. Now they are dying there in 559 beds. Factory-like, of course. Where production is so enormous an individual death is not so nicely carried out; but then that doesn't matter. It is quantity that counts."[2] And to describe the actual medical course of dying among the poor and sometimes even the rich, he creates the notion of what might be called the "official" death for a given disease, that is, its standard or most likely outcome: "the wish to have a death of one's own is growing ever rarer. . . . One dies just as it comes; one dies the death that belongs to the disease one has, for since one has come to know all diseases, one knows, too, that the different lethal

*For their comments, I would like to thank Larry Brown, Paul Menzel, Dan Brock, Allen Buchanan, and participants in the Seventh Utah Conference on Ethics and Health, January 17–18, 1991, where an earlier version of this essay was originally presented.

terminations belong to the diseases and not to the people; and the sick person has so to speak nothing to do."[3]

In this short essay I'd like to take Rilke's rather enigmatic, impressionist descriptions seriously, not just to discover what it is that disturbs him about the medical character of dying among the turn-of-the-century European poor, but to see what this extraordinary poet's intuitions might tell us about turn-of-the-next-century national health care. What troubles Rilke most, I think, is what we might call the prospect of *standardization:* the tendency of a system to treat people under its control in a uniform, regulated, unindividualized way—robbing them, Rilke hints, of the capacity to function fully as persons. The poor are the immediate victims, since they are economically powerless to resist; but even the rich can be co-opted by expectations in medicine which have the same standardizing and hence dehumanizing effect.

The prospect of standardization is, in Rilke's view, associated with large numbers and severe cost pressures: the poor are "dying in 559 beds" in a dismally equipped hospital funded only by charity. But it is this association of numbers and costs that invites us to consider the relevance of Rilke's concerns for contemporary national health care systems: after all, national health systems involve both very large numbers and very severe cost pressures. Nor is there any way to relieve either of these pressures: by definition, a national health system involves the largest possible numbers, since everyone is to be eligible for care; and, as in any health system, a national health system is continuously subject to increasing cost pressures for which there is no natural solution. Since there is always need for more rapid and effective cure of disease, for better ways of controlling chronic conditions, for more reliable relief of pain with fewer side effects, and for more effective preventive efforts, and since there are always more patients who would benefit from these developments, there will always be cost pressures associated with providing better health care. Furthermore, since all patients eventually die, there is no natural bound to the resources in labor or technology which could be used to try to ease or postpone this event.

EFFICIENCY IN NATIONAL HEALTH CARE

In the face of very large numbers and continuing cost pressures, a national health system will have, at least in principle, a predictable goal: the development of greater efficiency (also often called cost-effectiveness[4]) in the treatment and cure of disease and in the control of chronic conditions. It will continuously work to restructure its practices, including its medical practices, so as to achieve cure or control for less money. The early symptoms of this tendency are already apparent, in the current transitional medical climate, in the so-called "outcomes revolution,"[5] evident in some sectors of U.S. medicine and followed with interest by many European observers. This reorientation of treatment evaluation practices seeks to change medicine's conservative reliance on conventional patterns of practice to direct inspection of the results obtained from specific procedures, that is, it looks not so much at whether the procedures physicians employ conform to a standard of practice as at what results these procedures actually get. As outcomes are correlated with procedures, it is then possible to formulate efficient, cost-effective practice guidelines for the profession. For example, the federal Agency for Health Care Policy and Research has already begun the development of practice guidelines for six common conditions—angina pectoris, benign prostatic hypertrophy, gallstones, arthritis of the hip, conditions of the uterus, and low back pain—which now occasion treatment amounting to more than half of inpatient surgery.[6] The effort here, at least in principle, is to identify those procedures which are effective in treatment, discarding those which are not; to identify criteria under which they should be performed; and to stipulate ways of measuring morbidity and mortality that will realistically reflect the effectiveness of the procedure given a specific severity of illness—or, in short, to identify the most effective way to cure or control these disease conditions, which can then be correlated with cost considerations.

A similar though unnamed emphasis on outcomes has long been at work in the development of associated practices such as preventative guidelines and early diagnosis programs, including screening programs, prophylactic care, instruction in self-help, genetic counseling, and so on. Here, it is assumed that prevention or early identification of a disease offers a more efficient way of controlling or curing it than medical intervention could provide at a later point in the expected course of the disease. The impulse behind these programs might be described as akin to the concerns to be expected in a national health program, inasmuch as the effort is to save money, as well as human costs, for the population as a whole. To be sure, some authors have pointed out that screening and early-risk-identification programs can prove more expensive because they identify disease which then requires treatment but which would otherwise go untreated;[7] partisan bickering then begins when it is observed that money to be expended in prevention programs in a non-national system comes out of different pockets from those that would realize the savings. Nevertheless, in a well-designed national system, this need not be so,[8] and it remains the case that such programs are in general both more humane and more efficient—if not initially cheaper—ways of responding to disease.

Thus it appears that both the development of practice guidelines and the development of prevention and risk-identification programs have in common that feature which Rilke suggests is the root of the problem of dehumanization in medicine: they invite "standardization." After all, practice guidelines have the effect of stipulating to the physician how a given disease condition is to be managed; prevention and risk-identification programs initially treat all subjects uniformly, subjecting them to the same screening procedures, and then feed those identified as positive risks into the health care system for treatment under its practice guidelines. Both thus increase the likelihood that all patients with a given condition will be treated in a uniform, "standardized" way. To be sure, similar developments may also occur in market-based, non-national health care organizations; nevertheless, the distinctive problem of standardization will be most acute in a national health system for which efficiency in care is the principal objective.

Of course, to suggest that a national health system would predictably make efficiency in cure or control of disease its central objective is in certain ways an ideal view: it assumes that the system's administrators and professionals, including physicians, are not functioning primarily from greed or other ulterior motives, that the system is well run and efficiently administered, that the development of bureaucracy within the system is not so complete as to take on self-perpetuating characteristics, and that other distortions have not corrupted the system. It overlooks the bells and whistles a national health system might have to add, perhaps at the cost of other efficient care, in order to maintain political support.[9] It also assumes that available funds are limited and that, as we have seen, health needs are never fully satisfied. But these conditions aside, a well-run national health system should nevertheless be more likely than a commercial health system to promote efficiency in providing health care. Were it not the case that the various factors involved are much too complex to admit such simplistic comparisons, it would be tempting to point out that the substantially better health status of the populations of the major industrialized nations with national health care systems than that of U.S. citizens suggests just such results: these populations, it would seem, get more efficient health care: care that is as good or better than that in the United States at substantially less cost.

Well-run, competitive, commercial health care systems also seek to be efficient, of course, but they seek to be efficient in ways that enhance their own profitability. For example, providers are likely to try to increase their market share in providing a particular service—whether or not the service is actually effective in curing or controlling disease. Providers, at least those who are not also payers, have less incentive to seek effective care than to expand the quantity of care provided, especially when the patient has little way of determining whether the care is necessary, since care is the source of their profit; this is the familiar phenomenon of overtreatment, a phenomenon directly addressed by federal controls such as DRGs. Other strategies, such as offering amenities and advertising directly to patients, represent additional techniques for stimulating demand for services in a profit-motivated system. In contrast, payers in a profit-motivated system, unlike providers, seek to limit their obligations as a way of enhancing their profits; this strategy is currently most evident in the insurance industry's attempt to move away from community rating, in which all insurees within a geographic region are assumed to pose the same risk, to a refusal to cover specific individuals and members of high-risk groups. But a national health system, though both provider and payer, will pursue neither of these strategies; it cannot seek to increase market share by overtreatment, since there are no competitors from whom to take away business; and it cannot seek to exclude high-risk individuals, since it is mandated to cover everyone. It is therefore forced to seek efficiency in providing the services it is required to give to all, since under limited funding there is no other way for it to function.

Thus, the essential features of a national health system, and those features which encourage it to strive for "health-targeted" efficiency in providing care, are the mandate to provide care under a limited resource pool for very large numbers—everybody—and a lack of competitors in doing so. These features will be especially pronounced in a well-run national provider system under which physicians and other providers are employees of the state; but they will also characterize a national insurance system in which reimbursement schedules are tight and explicit enough to control physician and other provider autonomy by limiting options for practice. In either form of national system, if physician and other provider activity is controlled by practice guidelines which have been developed on the basis of demonstrated effectiveness in achieving specific outcomes, and if, furthermore, the system is mandated to provide care for all, there will be no internal incentive to provide more care in general or more care for some people than is needed. While there will still be pressures to exclude some types of treatment, there can be no pressures to exclude individuals or high-risk groups. In general, neither overtreatment nor risk-exclusion will be favored. To be sure, we already notice some of these altered trends in our current transitional system: quelling overtreatment is already a goal in some components of U.S. health care, including federal and state programs like Medicaid and Medicare, the VA, and large health maintenance organizations which, operating almost like mini-national health systems, are their own payers as well as providers. Resisting exclusion is also becoming a goal, at least in some states—for instance, in those attempting to expand Medicaid coverage or to develop insurance pools for persons deemed uninsurable by commercial firms.

EFFICIENCY AND "BEST BUYS"

If health-targeted efficiency is predictably to be the central goal in a national health system, as distinct from the profit-targeted efficiency to be expected in competitive commercial systems, it is essential to explore what forms health-targeted efficiency might take and to consider whether these forms of efficiency would give rise to the kind of standardization and consequent dehumanization against which Rilke warns. In the absence of corrupting features, we can expect a national health system to be a system in which cost pressures operate to influence the formulation of practice guidelines, and in which the least expensive way of achieving the best outcomes will be designated as the standard regulating all medical care. Leaving aside for the moment the scientific and research difficulties of measuring out-comes and developing practice guidelines, as well as the administra-tive difficulties of promoting universal use of them, one way a national health system's tendency to favor health-targeted efficiency might take shape is in selecting not the *best* way to cure or control disease but the most efficient, cost-effective way to do so. A national health system operating under substantial cost pressures might thus employ—to use the term *Consumer Reports* made famous—not the best procedures for curing illness, but the "best buy" in procedures for doing so. Examples of best buys in procedures, as distinguished from the best procedures for treating the same conditions, include a number of modalities which are markedly cheaper than their "best" counterparts but still give nearly as good results. These might include, for example, the use of hydrochlorothiazide instead of ace inhibitors for hypertension; the use of medical rather than surgical methods of treating appendicitis; the use of traditional rather than low-osmolality contrast mediums in radiologic imaging; the use of cheaper, nonprescription niacin instead of the prescription drug cholestyramine in controlling serum cholesterol; the use of medical rather than surgical methods of treating coronary heart disease; reliance on nonrepair rather than reconstruction in ACL-MCL ligament knee injuries; medical rather than surgical methods of treating ulcers; and the use of aspirin in place of nonsteroidal antiinflammatory drugs or NSAIDs. Perhaps the most visible controversy over best versus best-buy options has been that involving the thrombolytic agents TPA and streptokinase for use following myocardial infarction (MI): despite the results of the major Gissi-2 and Isis-3 studies concluding that the two drugs are of equal efficacy in saving the lives of heart-attack patients, some physicians continue to insist that although streptokinase, at as little as $76 a dose, may be a best buy, the $2,200-per-dose TPA is nevertheless best.

Traditionally, considerations of the effectiveness of a procedure have in principle been given greater weight in the United States than considerations of cost: this is why the United States has developed a medical system providing care that, while very, very good, is also very, very expensive: its medical system has been providing first-class care, at least for some people, and has not, until recently, worried much about the price. It has insisted on the best, not on best buys. The prospect of a national health system seeking full efficiency in providing care for all but operating under budget limitations, however, forces us to consider whether it ought to turn to best buys in medicine rather than the traditional best in order to make ends meet.

To be sure, what counts as a best buy is a function of the amount of resources available, following the intuitive notion that a best buy is the best item of its kind one can get for the money one has available. If resources are not very limited the best buy will be nearly as good as the best; under greater scarcity, however, the difference between them will be pronounced. In either case, a national health system

relying on fully demonstrated cost-effective best-buy practice guidelines or standards of practice for all medical and associated services
would provide, in theory at least, the most benefits for the least cost
for all persons. This would provide an alternative way of putting into
practice the notion of "decent minimum": access to all services for all
persons, but services of lesser efficacy.

Developing practice guidelines or standards of practice based
either on best or on best-buy treatments is itself a form of standardization: such guidelines attempt to describe and put into practice a
uniform way of providing care for each disease condition, thus
producing results for each patient which are uniformly effective to
the same degree. In general, by codifying and regularizing uniform
ways of treating specific conditions, well-developed practice guidelines benefit all patients with such conditions except the few statistical outliers—that is, patients who would have responded better to
some less orthodox form of treatment. But a carefully developed
practice guideline will have few if any such patients and, more
important, it will be impossible to predict which individuals they are;
for if it were possible to predict which patients would respond better
to some other form of treatment, this fact would call for the development of a new practice guideline for this specific subgroup. Thus,
practice guidelines are, in principle, maximally effective. Of course,
in real life, under any system, practice guidelines in some contentious
areas of medicine are likely to be adopted not just on the basis of
unequivocal, exhaustive reporting of clinical experience and impec-
cable scientific research but on the basis of political pressures from
various groups partial on less-than-scientific grounds to one form of
treatment or another. Then too, the development of practice guidelines presents other problems—most notably, the problems of how
such guidelines can be challenged, if accepted practice is uniform
and there is no way short of formal, controlled trials to gather
contrary findings; whether the disincentives for challenging guidelines would stifle clinical progress in medicine; whether they would
provide too easy a target for litigation; as well as the problem
mentioned earlier of ensuring universal compliance.[10] Furthermore,
there are continuing problems about measuring the efficacy of
treatment, about weighing the value of various objectives (e.g., pain
control versus rehabilitation), and about weighing nonmedical factors such as the value of privacy or confidentiality. Yet these problems
do not outweigh the overwhelming utility of efficient practice guidelines in a cost-pressured system. In contrast to a market system in

which some patients get precisely the treatment they need but other patients are undertreated, overtreated, treated inappropriately, or not treated at all, depending on what incentives affect the physicians who provide their care, a system based on practice guidelines— uniform throughout the medical system, and universally observed— would provide the most efficient care for all patients.

But, of course, the development of "best-buy" practice guidelines under cost constraints involves standardization at a lower level of effectiveness than when "best" guidelines are used. Discussion of disparate levels of care in medicine is already familiar talk in pro- posals for two-tiered health care systems, but the conjecture here about what a national health program would favor is different. It considers an alternative form of two-tiered national health system, one which relies for cost savings neither on excluding individuals from treatment (as would be prohibited in a national health system in any case) nor on excluding certain conditions or procedures, such as transplants (a form of tiering which invites political pressure from advocacy groups for patients with specific diseases), but which instead establishes two (or perhaps more) sets of practice guidelines to be employed depending on whether the patient is receiving publicly funded or privately paid care. Of course, two-tiered systems provide little protection against erosion of the lower tier; if overall funding for a public system is meager, the gap between highest- quality-possible care and most-efficient-given-the-budget-limita- tions care (that is, between best and best-buy care) could be quite large indeed, even though all persons would be eligible for care. Nevertheless, this form of a two-tiered system, under which best-buy care would be provided for the publicly funded and best care for those who could cover the additional cost, is demonstrably more just than other forms of public/private tiering (if any tiered system can be said to be just), since it imposes the liabilities of less adequate, lower- tier care equally on all publicly funded persons rather than, as in an exclusion system, on some few individuals from that group.

RILKE'S PARADOX? BEST AND BEST-BUY SYSTEMS

Is it possible that a gap of this sort is the real problem which Rilke's concerns with standardization would have us address, though of course there were no practice guidelines in turn-of-the-century France? The Hôtel-Dieu, committed to providing for all the poor with limited charitable resources, would no doubt have had to practice a crude kind of cost-efficiency, of which standardization of practice would have been an earmark. Perhaps it is this standardization that Rilke observes: "They are dying in 559 beds," he writes, "factory-like, of course." He continues this ironic industrial metaphor: "Where production is so enormous an individual death is not so nicely carried out; but then that doesn't matter. It is quantity that counts." Of course, Rilke might be objecting simply to the medicalization of death generally or to a kind of crude regimentation in medicine that pays little real attention to outcomes or the results of health care—that is, to either socially or medically callous warehousing of the dying—but his argument is still more interesting if we assume that the Hôtel-Dieu is doing the best it can to treat its patients' illnesses and that the standardization Rilke is objecting to involves practices as efficient as possible given the medical science of the time. Whether or not this is what Rilke saw, it is what Rilke lets us see.

Yet what we see is paradox. If we look closely at Rilke's concerns, we see that the issue of standardization in medical care is much more complex than we might at first expect, and that even his images of illness and poverty do not support any general rejection of standardization or the apparent claim that it dehumanizes people. Consider, for instance, his image for the depersonalized condition of the poor: if he were not poor he would rent another room, he says, and describes the effort it has cost him to lean his head on the armchair in the room he currently occupies. The armchair has a greasy-gray hollow into which all heads seem to fit—the heads of the previous, equally poor and transitory occupants of this shabby room. Not all of these occupants have been of the same physical size, but they have all been obliged to accommodate themselves to the same green armchair and it is the fact that persons are forced by circumstances to accommodate themselves to a standardized item neither chosen by them nor suited to them that is the basis of Rilke's complaint. But is it a complaint that would also apply to an efficient national health system based on best-buy standards of practice, even one stretched by an inadequately funded attempt to provide health care for all to the point where its "decent minimum," as stipulated by its lower-tier standards, is set quite low? To be sure, complaints about standardization, uniformity, and regimentation are a staple of naive objection to social-welfare systems generally; but Rilke's objection is much more subtle in its comment on the special nature of health care.

After all, Rilke's argument against standardization initially appears altogether inadequate in the health care context. Indeed, it does not even work for the furniture of rooming houses. However dispiriting a thing it may be, an item of furniture like the green armchair in his room is remarkably efficient. Given cost pressures so severe that an armchair appropriately adapted to each new occupant cannot be provided, this unappealing green chair manages to accommodate everyone: "all heads seem to fit." It would of course be preferable for each individual to live in a better-equipped room with furniture of his or her own; but for the poor, it is this shabby room or nowhere at all. And it is this chair, used by all the previous down-and-out tenants, or no chair at all. Given no possibility of expanding the pool of resources available in this situation, the green armchair actually serves its purpose remarkably well: "all heads seem to fit."

Analogously, in health care, it is preferable to receive "standardized" lower-tier health care, including treatment stipulated in standards of practice and in mass prevention and identification programs, than to receive no care at all. Better to fit one's head into the greasy-gray hollow in the green armchair than to sit on the floor. Of course, one might idealistically spurn the armchair, preferring to camp on the floor, but the analogy does not work in medicine: unless one rejects health care altogether or some components of it for extraneous reasons (for example, on religious grounds, on the basis of fears about specific procedures, or on the basis of differing values about risk) or because the risk of iatrogenic complication is high, some health care is better than none at all. After all, the consequence of no treatment may be dysfunction, pain, or death, and it is never rational to prefer these to probable cure or restoration of function, except perhaps on outside grounds.

Thus, in a cost-pressured national health system, one may imagine a two-tiered system with dual practice guidelines. In such a system, for example, appendicitis patients in the lower tier, who would be treated medically rather than surgically, might have a slightly greater chance of dying than those in the upper tier, but nobody would risk the substantially greater chance of dying that exclusion from treatment altogether would entail. Patients in the lower tier would use niacin rather than cholestyramine, but they would still be getting medical supervision of their cholesterol levels. Knee patients in the lower tier could expect conservative treatment of their ACL-MCL injuries, and while this would leave them unable to play certain sports and risk some instability, they could still function fairly well in most activities. Patients getting medical rather than surgical treatment of their ulcers would do nearly as well; and in all these circumstances, no patient would risk being entirely excluded from treatment. Although patients undergoing radiologic contrast studies would get traditional rather than low-osmolality contrast mediums and would therefore be at greater risk of anaphylactic reactions, no patient would be denied necessary diagnostic procedures. And whether or not TPA might eventually prove to have some therapeutic advantage over streptokinase, lower-tier patients would get streptokinase, while upper-tier patients (or their physicians) might be permitted a choice; yet all heart attack patients would receive effective thrombolytic therapy.[11] Of course, a two-tiered system risks allowing a substantial gap to develop between the upper and the lower tiers; on the other hand, if, as in Canada, the system prohibited a second tier (as I believe justice ultimately requires), political pressures would operate to keep the level of the single tier as high as possible. In either case, however, incentives characterizing a system under cost pressures, without competition, mandating care for all, would—if it were a system attentive enough to the requirements of justice to reject exclusion practices that impose unequal liabilities on persons—encourage the development of practice standards for maximally efficient health-targeted care. Thus, whether a national health system is a single-tiered or two-tiered one (or perhaps has multiple tiers), standardization is not the disadvantage a cursory reading of Rilke or inspection of our own stereotypes might seem to suggest but is, on the contrary, the mechanism of its principal advantage. Of course, "standardization" does not mean utter uniformity in every detail of medical practice, and it does not require routinized interactions, inflexible schedules, physicians with indistinguishable smiles and identical bedside manners, or examining rooms all painted the same color. It refers only to adoption of the most effective practice where differences in practice make demonstrable differences in outcome, and it requires only the discarding of demonstrably ineffective, less effective, or damaging ways of doing things. Variety can flourish, but not uselessness or harmfulness, and because uselessness and harmfulness do not flourish, such a system provides the most effective care for all. Tied to considerations of cost, such a system would provide the most efficient care under cost-limiting constraints. This, I have argued, would most likely be the case, barring other corruptions, in a national health system that is noncompetitive but cost pressured and mandated to provide care for all.

But it would be hasty to conclude that Rilke's intuitions are simply wrong and that there is no moral problem raised by the prospect of standardization—even by the prospect of the sort of thoroughgoing standardization one might expect from a genuinely efficient national health system. Rilke describes dying at the Hôtel-Dieu as "factory-like," a situation where "production is enormous" and it is "quantity that counts." But if it is "factory-like" that all items of a kind are treated in the same way, and if "production is enormous" means that everyone gets what he or she needs, then there is no moral problem here. Quantity *does* count: that is the whole point of national health systems, to ensure that everyone gets the health care he or she needs.

Yet there is something else to notice about Rilke's observations: they are focused on a specific kind of health care, and the point he has to make has special application in this setting. What the patients in the 559 beds of the Hôtel-Dieu are doing is *dying*: this is a hospital for incurables, for terminal cases, as distinct from the Maison d'Accouchement, the obstetric hospital, and the Val-de-Grace, the military hospital, down the street. The division of these hospitals in Rilke's turn-of-the-century Paris reflects a distinction central in his observations: there is something different about dying, and it is in dying as distinct from other medical events that the moral problems raised by standardization arise. It is not just that Rilke is obsessed with the notion of death—as not only Rilke but the Existentialists influenced by him would also be—but that he sees that there is something different from other medical situations about this process.

EFFICIENCY IN DYING

What, then, is disturbing about the "factory-like production" of deaths in the 559 beds of the Hôtel-Dieu? No one cares anymore for a "finely-finished death," Rilke laments. "No one. Even the rich, who could after all afford this luxury of dying in full detail, are beginning to be careless and indifferent; the wish to have a death of one's own is growing ever rarer."[12] But if our account of efficiency in medical care is correct, surely the "factory-like production" of deaths would not raise any moral problem, unless of course it were accompanied by callousness, abuse, or cruelty—peripheral institutional problems which are not part of our focus here.

But this brings us to the central problem: the very notions of "standards of practice" and "practice guidelines" cannot function in the same way in dying as they do for the treatment of other medical conditions, because these are concepts that make central reference to the medical outcome to be attained. The procedure or medical treatment to be designated as standard in a practice guideline for a given condition is the one which is most effective in producing cure or control of the condition within the limits of resources available: it is the most efficient, cost-effective manner of producing a given outcome. But the sense in which death is the "outcome" of medical treatment is a very different one from the one associated with measurements of efficacy in standards of practice, as, for instance, cure of appendicitis is the outcome of appendectomy or control of kidney failure is the outcome of dialysis. Unlike cure or the control of a chronic condition, death is not the *objective* of medical treatment and not the outcome in terms of which efficacy can be measured. Medical treatment does not aim at death; medical treatment aims at cure or the control of a condition, and death occurs only if it fails rather than succeeds. Thus, there can be no such thing as an "efficient" or "cost-effective" way of dying, since, except in the specific final procedure of euthanasia, death cannot be the objective of treatment. Even in the hospice care provided to terminally ill patients, death is not the objective, although it is the expected, unresisted outcome; on the contrary, the objective, to use the rhetoric associated with this important movement, is the fullest, best possible living of the last moments of life. If death were the objective, either in ordinary medical care or in hospice care, efficient dying would be that which gets the process over with in the shortest and hence cheapest possible time—but this is what few patients or physicians would regard as ideal and what no national health or similar system ought to encourage. This is not to encourage the prolongation of life, but it is not to encourage arbitrarily abrupt termination of life either. Cheap, rapid dying may be a personal goal for some patients but ought not be imposed as an institutional or societal one.

But if there can be no such thing as "efficient dying," there can be no standards of practice for dying either, even when the dying is expected to follow the usual pattern of a predictable downhill course in a familiar fatal disease—advanced colon cancer, for instance, or kidney failure or lung disease. At best, one could string together a series of procedures, each governed by its own practice guidelines, for the events or medical episodes along the way of this downhill course—for example, a procedure to relieve tumor pressure on a nerve, therapy for congestive heart failure, treatment to relieve respiratory distress—but this is to view dying as a series of isolated, discrete events and to miss, as it were, the forest for the trees. If dying is seen as an integral process, not just as a series of interconnected medical failures, understanding it in the terms appropriate to other areas of medicine cannot fully succeed. There is no best buy in dying, though there may be best buys in specific sorts of symptom relief; there is no standard, efficient pattern that dying ought to follow. This is not to romanticize dying but only to remark that viewing it in the way appropriate to other medical conditions is to cut off from view what we most ought to see: it is a circumstance in which efficiency is beside the point.

It might be suggested that Rilke's overwhelming concern with death raises only a tangential issue in medicine. But this is hardly so, especially given the cost-related issues that fuel pressures for national health care. After all, according to the various figures so frequently cited in discussions of health care's high cost, an immense proportion of health care dollars are spent in the last month, two months, or half-year of life. Of course, the last month, two months, or half-year of life can be identified only retrospectively, and not all patients were "dying" during those periods. Nevertheless, in a society in which approximately three of every four deaths occur as a result of degenerative disease (cancer, heart disease, stroke, liver, kidney and other organ failure, AIDS, neurological diseases, etc.) and deaths from acute, rapidly fatal parasitic and infectious diseases and trauma are comparatively few, the issue of how dying is to take place in a cost-pressured, efficiency-oriented system, as a just national health system must be, is no trivial matter and cannot remain of peripheral interest only.

In Rilke's view, most systems—not only that of charity care for the poor of Paris at the Hôtel-Dieu but also Europe's private sanatoria for the wealthy—do function in effect by imposing standardized practices even in terminal cases. "One dies the death that belongs to the disease one has," Rilke remarks, "for since one has come to know all diseases, one knows, too, that the different lethal terminations belong to the diseases and not to the people; and the sick person has so to speak nothing to do." This is what I've called the notion of the "official" death, and it is what one might expect were standards of practice formulated to govern the whole scope of that series of medical events characteristic of specific downhill, terminal courses.

It is this standardization in dying that Rilke sees as particularly dehumanizing; he writes, sarcastically, "In sanatoria, where people die so willingly and with so much gratitude to doctors and nurses, they die from one of the deaths attached to the institution; that is favorably regarded."[14]

Of course, one might argue that the objective of medical care in dying is the achievement of the longest life possible consistent with the least suffering; thus, there is a "standard of practice" in the broader sense even for dying. Indeed, this seems to be the assumption of contemporary terminal care: there is a course deemed to be the easiest, which the patient can be expected and encouraged to follow. But Rilke—and here it is difficult and important to be sensitive to his intuition—would regard this as an imposition of values where, because there is no objective goal for medical care, there is no legitimate basis for doing so. While some dying patients might regard a terminal period weighing maximized life against minimized pain as preferable, others might prefer it some other way. As an illustration, Rilke creates the extraordinary character Chamberlain Christoph Detlev Brigge, whose death was "two months long and so loud that it could be heard as far off as the manor farm."[15] To be sure, Rilke romanticizes a vigorous, rebellious, almost athletic dying—a value judgment there is no need for us to accept—but what he thus succeeds in pointing out is that there is no reason at all why everyone should die in the same way. Such contemporary devices as Living Wills may seem to protect individual choice, but they are not very robust: in general, advance directives mean only that one's course through the standard progression of dying can be interrupted after one is no longer competent, typically quite late in the game. The wish to have "a death of one's own" ought to be recognized, indeed admired, Rilke insists, and in this he is clearly right, since because it is not like other medical processes there is no compelling reason for it to be any one, uniform way. Indeed, diversity may be the best protection against manipulation and abuse. It is precisely the having of "a death of one's own," however, that the standardization of practice, clearly so efficient and beneficial in other areas of medicine, would preclude. Being treated for appendicitis or hypertension or ulcers or ACL-MCL knee injuries or myocardial infarction "factory-like" in 559 beds (assuming the personal character of the care provided is humane, not literally factory-like, and the institutional environment reasonably pleasant) would present no moral problem, because treating these conditions in the most efficient way would increase all 559 patients' chances of cure, especially where no patients risk nontreatment. But dying is different, and it is not morally appropriate for a system governed by principles of efficiency to impose a standard expectation of how this final period of an individual's life should play itself out. Perhaps it is appropriate for a society to reassess its communal expectations about the nature of old age and medical responses to dying, as Daniel Callahan would recommend,[16] but it is not the role of a single, sole-provider system in effect to decide or enforce this.

A national health care system may certainly be greeted with enthusiasm on many grounds (and I strongly support its adoption in the United States), but—especially where very large proportions of its resources are at stake—it may also pose substantial moral problems. I think these risks are greatest in matters of dying. Of course, competitive, for-profit health care systems also pose moral risks concerning dying, though these risks will differ as a function of the different incentives under which these various systems operate. A particular risk in competitive, free-market systems is a function of incentives to increase the quantity and technical quality of care performed: this may take the form of lengthening the process of dying so as to be able to provide more care, a practice which has been the focus of much public sentiment against the "prolongation" of dying. I think the risks in dying we can expect to see posed under a national health care system will be less damaging to individual welfare than those we are now subject to in our current health care environment, even in the more complex real world than the idealized version considered here, but that does not mean we can pretend there are none. Nor is it the case that the ethical issues a national health care system will generate, for all its advantages, will be limited to the matter of dying, but they will be particularly conspicuous in this difficult area.

NOTES

1. Rainer Maria Rilke, *The Notebooks of Malte Laurids Brigge* (New York: Norton, 1964), p. 49.
2. Ibid., p. 17.
3. Ibid., pp. 17–18, punctuation slightly altered.
4. While it is equivalent to the sense in which I will be using the term "efficient," I will generally avoid the term "cost-effective" because it is so frequently misapplied and misunderstood. For instance, "cost-effective" is variously used to mean "cost saving," "effective," "cost saving, with an equal

(or better) outcome," and "having an additional benefit worth the additional cost" (see Peter Doubilet, Milton C. Weinstein, and Barbara J. McNeil, "Use and Misuse of the Term 'Cost Effective' in Medicine," *New England Journal of Medicine* [hereafter *NEJM*] 314 [January 23, 1986]: 253–55).

5. Arnold S. Relman, M.D., "Assessment and Accountability: The Third Revolution in Medical Care," *NEJM* 319 (November 3, 1988): 1220–22.

6. John E. Wennberg, "Outcomes Research, Cost Containment, and the Fear of Health Care Rationing," *NEJM* 323 (October 25, 1990): 1202.

7. See, e.g., Louise B. Russell, *Is Prevention Better than Cure?* Studies in Social Economics (Washington, D.C.: Brookings Institution, 1986).

8. On why national and non-national systems are different, see Norman Daniels, "Why Saying No to Patients in the United States Is So Hard," *NEJM* 314 (May 22, 1986): 138–83.

9. Robert P. Huefner points out this risk.

10. On the problem of litigation, see Paul M. Ellwood, M.D., "Outcomes Management: A Technology of Patient Experience," Shattuck Lecture, *NEJM* 318 (June 9, 1988): 1555. On universal compliance, see Jonathan Lomas et al., "Do Practice Guidelines Guide Practice?" *NEJM* 321 (November 9, 1989): 1306–11.

11. On the discussion of these last two examples in one Canadian province, see Adam L. Linton and C. David Naylor, "Organized Medicine and the Assessment of Technology: Lessons from Ontario," *NEJM* 323 (November 22, 1990): 1463–67.

12. Rilke, *Notebooks*, p. 17.

13. S. Jay Olshansky and A. Brian Ault, "The Fourth Stage of the Epidemiologic Transition: The Age of Delayed Degenerative Diseases," in Timothy M. Smeeding et al., eds., *Should Medical Care Be Rationed by Age?* (Totowa, N.J.: Rowman & Littlefield, 1987), p. 17.

14. Rilke, *Notebooks*, p. 18.

15. Ibid.

16. Daniel Callahan, *Setting Limits: Medical Goals in an Aging Society* (New York: Simon and Schuster, 1987), and his subsequent *What Kind of Life?*

Loyalty Conflicts and the Quality of the Doctor-Patient Relationship in the Context of Managed Health Care

Leonard J. Haas and Peter C. Appleby

This essay is an exploration of one aspect of the doctor-patient relationship, the loyalty of the provider to the consumer, in the context of recent and forthcoming innovations in health care financing. In a health care environment which now seems to favor contractual relations over personal attachments (Morreim, 1989; Svarstad, 1976), the evocation of loyalty as a virtue may seem as quaint and irrelevant as the suggestion that the professions should once again be regarded as vocations or sacred callings, rather than mere jobs or occupations. Indeed, as one of our critics recently suggested, loyalty may nowadays appear not to be a virtue at all in creatures who can walk on two feet, but only in those who are sentimentally regarded as humanity's best friends. Yet we will argue on empirical as well as ethical grounds that this apparently archaic quality of character and human interactions is both urgently needed and pragmatically feasible in the practice of modern medicine, its importance increasing as structural changes in our delivery systems threaten more and more to depersonalize and thus dehumanize the delivery of health care. We consider the possible consequences of further erosion of the quality of the doctor-patient relationship and examine the proposition that new health care arrangements necessarily damage its quality by lowering trust and increasing cynicism.

We begin with the assumption that changes in the financing of health care, dictated by the need to increase access and to control escalating costs, have contributed to the perception that physicians are no longer as committed to their patients as they once were (Belkin, 1990). Anecdotal evidence suggests that with the advent of actuarially managed health care, doctors are feeling deprived of professional autonomy and control over their own work and are increasingly inclined to encounter their patients as adversaries, burdens, complications in their professional lives, and customers (Kolata, 1990). More and more patients, facing the starkness, complexity, and impersonality of large clinics and hospitals, seem to regard their physicians as mercenaries, price gougers, impersonal technicians, and interchangeable purveyors of unintelligibly specialized services (Press, 1984). And suspicions on both sides are intensified by the general awareness of bureaucratic absurdities, astronomical malpractice awards, outlandish fees, and exponentially increasing insurance premiums (Kolata 1990; "Special Report," 1986). Thus, for many, the prospect of a nationwide system of health care delivery threatens Orwellian depersonalization in a domain where individual commitments and attachments have traditionally mattered a great deal. We may have felt some regret when the local grocery store was put out of business by the supermarket chain, and many of us are distressed by the absorption of family farms into huge agribusinesses. But we are frightened by the advent of corporate health care, because it threatens to leave us without personally involved caregivers when we need them most. The question with which we attempt to grapple in this essay is whether or not it is the case that the features of emerging health care arrangements which tend to reduce physician autonomy necessarily lead to reduced caring and loyalty to patients.

Now, it may never have been the case that physician-patient loyalties stemmed from entirely high-minded motives on either side. In the fee-for-service and Blue Cross eras, doctors certainly had self-interested reasons for maintaining contact with and control over their patients, pursuing aggressive courses of testing and treatment. And equally clearly, patients had compelling motives for exhibiting loyalty to practitioners who were, from their points of view, the only acts in town. But however that may have been, even if the ever-faithful family doctor was little more than a figment of Norman Rockwell's imagination, provider-to-client fidelity, real or perceived, has always been and continues to be a crucial element of effective treatment (Balint, 1968; Kleinman, Eisenberg, and Goode, 1978). Thus, efforts to mitigate its erosion must be included in any realistic plans to expand access and control costs by way of managed care or large-scale insurance programs.

THE NATURE OF PROFESSIONAL LOYALTY

As we will use the term, loyalty is centrally a matter of faithfulness to others and reliability in fulfilling obligations of duty, trust, and affection. For the most part, we will ignore the abstract loyalties to states, guilds, or other transcendent entities; instead, we will concentrate on the duties of fidelity, devotion, and constancy, which derive primarily, though not exclusively, from the particular moral attachments created by such relationships as kinship, collegiality, or voluntarily established dependencies. Our models of loyalty will thus be the friendships of Aristotle's *Ethics*, rather than the morally suspect guardianships of Plato's *Republic*. And presuming that the relations between professionals and their clients are essentially fiduciary in character, we will see the physician's allegiances to her patients as involving reliable candor and straightforwardness and a durable commitment to the promotion of their best interests, even at some cost to herself.

In contemporary codes of professional ethics, the duty of loyalty is often expressed negatively in prohibitions against the abandonment of clients or patients (Windt et al. 1981, app. 2). But we will move beyond this minimalist notion, seeing practitioners who present themselves voluntarily for service in clinics or hospitals as undertaking the full array of positive obligations implicit in the establishment of a relationship of trust. A doctor's office is not a used-car lot, and "caveat emptor" must not be the rule of the day for health care provision, even in the rare circumstance of the well-informed consumer. Professionals in general and physicians in particular enjoy high social standing and generous remuneration, in large part because they are routinely expected to be reliable sources of dispassionate advice, competent treatment, and empathic concern. Thus, their allegiances to clients and patients include the duty not to abandon but much more as well. Once a provider-client relationship has been established, the practitioner becomes "my doctor" or "my therapist" in the eyes of the patient, and for the duration of the sequence of treatment (and often beyond it), the client rightly expects steady support, care, and advocacy from the provider (Roter and Hall, 1989).

It might be argued that these expectations are unrealistic in the current situation and that the way to preserve the integrity of the health care system and improve its efficiency would be to adopt a contract model for doctor-patient relations, instituting clear-cut rules governing what is to be expected from the provider and the client in each course of treatment, with these rules being subject to negotiated modification as each interaction develops. If this model were to achieve general acceptance, it would eliminate many of the most troublesome questions about loyalties in the same way that well-drafted real-estate contracts prevent controversies between buyers and sellers. Patients would not need to rely on the ill-defined goodwill and fidelity of their doctors; physicians would not be plagued by doubts about the adequacy of their own moral positions; and everyone would know how things were going at each stage of the transaction.

But this suggestion overlooks the irreducible disparity in power between professionals and their clients. It is true, of course, that providers and patients (or their surrogates) should have clear understandings of the commitments they make to one another, and that progress in treatment should be discussed as openly and freely as circumstances allow. For the most part, however, people seek professional help, especially medical care, precisely because they are in situations of relative weakness and ignorance. The patient is sick and the doctor is not. Patients do not know how to cope with their disorders and the doctor does. And these facts by themselves create an inequality of power which would hopelessly handicap nearly any consumer who undertook to bargain with a knowledgeable provider. Even the current and much-needed emphases on patient autonomy and informed consent create significant difficulties for many participants in the health care system (Price, 1984). So the proposal that the consumers of services should become contractors seems extremely implausible.

Nor, we suppose, would most practitioners care to engage in detailed contractual negotiations with prospective clients even if it were feasible as a practical matter to do so. Medical professionals are socialized to perceive themselves as caregivers and healers, as the providers of highly valued services, working with their patients on the basis of respect and trust (Bayles, 1981; Coombs, 1978, chaps. 1, 2). So if, as we have suggested, bureaucratic intrusions are a major current source of trouble in provider-patient relations, surely the introduction of still more formalities and an even more litigious atmosphere could not be perceived as an improvement.

In the end, physician-patient relationships are ineluctably personal in character, much more like Aristotelian friendships among

unequals than agreements between dispassionate and equally qualified sellers and buyers. One might imagine a world in which medical
interactions were purely technical and mechanical, requiring no
more affective involvements than visits to vending machines or self-
service markets. But, as long as medicine continues to be as much an
art as it is a science, there is no viable alternative to the fiduciary
model for practitioner-client relations (Thomasina, 1983). The
patient must be able to trust and rely upon his doctor, and the
physician must be able to demonstrate her concern and commitment
without undue regard for contractual formalities. Thus, loyalty as a
durable and conspicuous character trait or disposition must remain
among the central virtues of medical practitioners.

CONFLICTS AMONG LOYALTIES

Like everyone else, of course, physicians encounter conflicting
demands upon their loyalties. The fact, for example, that each
provider works with many patients necessarily restricts the amount
of time, attention, and emotional energy available for each, and it
requires that practitioners perform triage functions fairly regularly.
That is, the needs of individual patients can force the practitioner to
curtail her work with some in order to deal effectively with others.
And when particular treatment strategies prove ineffective, or when
patients are systematically uncooperative, providers' loyalties may be
overridden by obligations to terminate relationships with individual
clients, with steps being taken to arrange for the provision of needed
care by others (see, for example, American Psychological Association,
1990). Limitations of these well-understood kinds can pose difficult
problems in the organization of professional practices, especially in
large clinics and hospitals, but they are not peculiar to the field of
medicine, and they raise no special ethical issues for health care
providers.

For our purposes, much more challenging and interesting conflicts among loyalties are generated by the economic changes which
have introduced an ever-expanding array of managerial controls into
all kinds of medical relationships and are transforming more and
more solo and small-group practitioners into employees of large
organizations (see Windt et al., 1981, chap. 3). Where we once had, at
least theoretically, a simple dyadic relation between doctor and
patient, with relatively minor complexities of the sorts mentioned in
the previous paragraph, we now have insurance administrators,

government authorities, case managers, and other "gatekeepers" complicating the picture in alarming ways. And when diagnosis-related group (DRG) regulations require that patients be discharged prematurely from hospitals, with their doctors feeling impelled to tell them that they are really well enough to go home; when psychiatric therapy is abbreviated by the limitations of insurance coverage; and when costly treatment must be withheld because it is officially classified as experimental, physician-patient allegiances can be strained to the breaking point by conditions beyond the direct control of either participant. In effect, there are now many "stakeholders" (Mirvis and Seashore, 1979) in most medical transactions, and the trick is to sort out the legitimate claims in such a way as to preserve the primacy of the doctor-patient bond.

There is some truth in the idea that whoever pays the piper is (morally) entitled to call the tune. And it may be fairly conceded that physicians who enter voluntary agreements with health maintenance organizations, hospitals, or government agencies thereby undertake serious obligations of loyalty to their contract holders or employers. Thus, it can be argued that if a doctor chooses to work for the Veterans Administration (now the Department of Veterans Affairs) or the state mental hospital, she undertakes the duty to play by the rules of her institution, faithfully carrying out its policies and not seeking to evade the restrictions imposed by its administrators or the government. And if this means limiting her commitments to individual patients, that might simply be a hard fact of her professional life for the duration of her employment.

But this view overlooks the fact that the contractual relations between health care providers and clinics, hospitals, insurance companies, and government agencies are not altogether voluntary now, and are becoming less voluntary as time passes. In theory, it might be true that physicians and therapists can still design their own practices, avoiding bureaucratic entanglements and confining their attention to unencumbered clienteles. But in reality, there are fewer and fewer available opportunities to pursue such independent careers; and for most practitioners, moves in this direction would mean both professional isolation and economic disaster. Medical practice is inevitably becoming more and more thoroughly corporate and institutionalized because of the interdependencies of the specialties of modern care, as well as the exigencies of financing and cost containment. And this means that, while there is still some latitude in available choices among potential employers and practice arrangements, it is not a matter of free choice that the practitioner will become involved in a tangle of institutional restrictions and regulations somewhere. If she chooses to practice medicine at all, she will be thus encumbered now, and more so in the future, if proposed national health care arrangements take effect.

Practitioners, of course, tend to experience these encumbrances as thoroughly unwelcome restrictions on professional autonomy, forcing them to subordinate their clinical judgments and sometimes the well-being of their patients to institutional rules. And, not surprisingly, these feelings of external domination precipitate "reactance" responses (Taylor, 1968) among people who are socialized to a high degree of self-respect and independence of mind. Covertly or overtly, they resist attempts to restrict their freedom by engaging in such practices as "hoarding" and "poaching" equipment, facilities, and services (Morreim, 1989). They may also develop cynical and resentful attitudes toward the patients whose helpless presence forces them through so much bureaucratic hurdle-jumping. And, ironically, the more they attempt to circumvent the system, the more the system reacts by increasing the complexity and specificity of its rules.

We see no way out of this self-perpetuating conflict other than to increase the involvement of practitioners in the formulation of health care policy and in its administration, thereby increasing their sense of ownership in the institutions for which they work. They need to participate in decisions about cost containment and limitations on services so they can know that their concerns have been heard, so they can be fully aware of the reasons for restrictive policies, and so they can present the realities of their own practices forthrightly to their patients. They must recognize that all employer-employee relationships involve external constraints upon individual discretion and that such relationships are the wave of the future across the entire array of professional occupations (see Windt et al. (1981), 33, pp. 229–46). But they can also be helped to see that well-designed, reasonable, and fair limitations on the range of their choices do not unduly restrict their autonomy and thus need not compromise their professional integrity.

On the other hand, practitioners' ownership in institutional and government policies must not be allowed to transform medical caregivers into bureaucratic gatekeepers, abandoning their commitments to their clients in response to structural exigencies. The balance we need is not one which makes mindless Platonic guardians of our doctors at the expense of their patients' well-being. Our view is rather that, like other professionals, physicians can learn to balance the claims of the various stakeholders in their work without losing their sense of autonomy, and without giving up the primacy of their loyalties to individual clients. And our claim is that the maintenance of these loyalties is essential to the provision of effective and humane health care.

THE NEED FOR LOYALTY TO PATIENTS

Although the existing data on the health effects of such medical "intangibles" as hope, caring, and authentic communication are still subject to debate (Blum, 1985; Roter and Hall, 1989), it seems beyond serious controversy that high patient morale is an important contributor to successful outcomes (House, Landis, and Umberson, 1988) and that patient morale in turn is highly dependent upon the patient's perception of his relations with the people who are providing his care (Blum, 1985; House, Landis, and Umberson, 1988; Roter and Hall, 1989). The placebo effect, for example, is a widely recognized example of the curative power of confidence in treatment (Berblinger, 1963; Clyne, 1985). And Jerome Frank (1981) has shown that, at least for mental-health problems, faith in the provider, and faith on the part of the provider that she is doing the best that can be done for her patient, are common factors in effective treatment. The mobilization of the patient's optimism, "will to live," sense of control, and willingness to care about himself are key ingredients in both prevention and treatment (Blum, 1985; Frank 1981; House, Landis, and Umberson, 1988). And, in our view, the provider's success in activating these dispositions in her patients is a direct result of her ability to inspire their confidence and trust in her competence, caring attitude, and consistent interest in positive outcomes (Svarstad, 1976; Waitzkin, 1984). It is also a direct result of the doctor's ability to set aside her own frustrations with the bureaucratic intrusions and seemingly arbitrary constraints placed on her professional discretion and to focus on the needs of the patient. Balint (1968) has well described the need for physicians to examine this "displacement" of problems onto patients and has suggested methods to bring these issues to the surface and prevent them from contaminating the treatment.

When doctors feel no commitment to their patients, treatment becomes impersonal, mechanical, and technical, rather than caring and restorative. And when patients believe that their doctors are not seriously interested in their well-being, they become cynical and pessimistic about their treatment and their chances of success and thereby significantly reduce both their own inclination to comply with medical advice and the probability of favorable results from the therapies they undertake (Svarstad, 1976). Admittedly, some patients may have sufficient resources outside the clinic or hospital, such as actively supportive families, to compensate for nonchalant attitudes on the part of medical professionals (House, Landis, and Umberson, 1988); and others may have internal strength adequate to the task of overcoming their doctors' lack of commitment. Our abilities to survive or benefit from impersonal treatment are clearly matters of great individual variation. But if we start from the idea that most of us seek medical help because we are in weakened conditions of one sort or another, surely it will be obvious that finding or developing a caring relationship with a provider will and should be among our highest priorities. All the scientific and technical competence in the world may be of no use to us if it is not deployed by someone who cares enough about our individual situations to guide us attentively and thoughtfully through our courses of treatment. If we do not have substantial reason for believing that our doctors care about us individually, we will be disinclined to take their opinions seriously and much less likely than we might be otherwise to feel confident about our prospects and to follow their advice (Davis, 1969 and 1971).

Cynically, it might be argued that what is really required is not that the doctor *be* loyal to her patient, but only that the patient needs to perceive her as, or think that she is, loyal. For our present purpose, however, this is a distinction without a difference. People are often quite skillful at detecting insincerity in gestures of concern and friendship (Ekman and Freisen, 1977), so it would be a substantial undertaking to feign unfelt allegiances throughout a medical practice. But we will offer no conjectures about the possibility of success in such an enterprise. Our concern is with the behavioral and (sincere or pretended) attitudinal gestures from which people gain the confidence they need in their health care providers. Stated differently, the physician's felt or expressed loyalty may be necessary but not sufficient to ensure the perception by the patient that the doctor is "there for him."

In traditional views of medicine, tokens of physician-patient loyalty were such actions as the doctor's willingness to make house calls, to provide reliable coverage when the primary provider was unavailable, to take whatever steps were necessary to ensure the patient's return to health, and to accept sliding fees, or no fees at all, according to the patient's ability to pay (Kitzhaber, 1988). At least in gilded memory, these, along with the physician's long-standing and intimate knowledge of the patient and his family, were the evidences by virtue of which people felt secure in their interactions with doctors and confident that they were receiving the best available care. But these tokens are largely no longer available. Generally speaking, house calls and personalized surrogate coverage are practical impossibilities. Cost shifting can no longer be carried out by individual practitioners, though of course it is and must be continued institutionally. And, for the most part, even family practitioners cannot be expected to develop social relations with the dozens of patients they see each day, let alone their relatives. Thus, it seems clear that other ways of displaying loyalty must be developed to accord with the realities of modern practice. We will conclude with some suggestions.

PRESERVING DOCTOR-PATIENT LOYALTIES

It seems inevitable now that physicians, like lawyers and almost all other professionals, will have to adjust to major structural changes in the worlds of their work. The day of the solo practice and the small clinical partnership has ended (Altman and Rosenthal, 1990). One way or another, the new world of medicine will be corporate, rather than individualistic in character. And the expectations on both sides of the doctor-patient dyad must change. Patients will need to abandon their aging dreams about doctors coming to their homes in the middle of the night and forgetting to send bills. And physicians must adopt more realistic views about their roles as team players in medical care, about the limits of their individual autonomy and professional discretion, and, very likely, about their economic prospects as well (Belkin, 1990).

But these developments need not be seen as a tragedy on either side. Our current problems, after all, are very largely products of our successes. If modern technological medicine were not so obviously beneficial, we would not now be concerned about making it available to everyone through vast insurance plans. And, if the extent of medical knowledge had not increased so dramatically in the past half century, no one would be worried about the psychological effects of moving patients through long series of brief encounters with special-

ists and technicians. The trick, of course, is to "rehumanize" the
system while increasing its efficiency.

We believe that patient confidence in any particular level of
health care could be greatly increased if people clearly understood
the range and limitations of the services they were being offered. This
means that where rationing of one kind or another is required, the
expression "all that can be done" should be explained in sufficient
specific detail to prevent the creation of unrealistic hopes and
expectations. If DRG regulations limit stays in hospital beds, that fact
should be explained forthrightly and, whenever possible, well in
advance of discharge. And if a payment system will not cover long-
term dialysis, no effort should be made to disguise that limitation.
Patients are much less likely to distrust their doctors and much more
likely to appreciate the care they receive, if they are able to compre-
hend the constraints under which their providers are operating. In
this connection, the contract model considered earlier has some
merit, since it recognizes the potential for avoiding disappointment
and conflict in the clear articulation of what can and cannot be
accomplished.

A closer inspection of the situation faced by a physician deciding
whether to be forthright about the constraints on his or her actions
reveals that the most comfortable choice is to dissemble. This is
because to be straightforward runs the risk that the patient will ask
the physician to be an advocate, and to attempt to change the rules
(since "doctor's orders" are supposed to carry some powerful weight).
This means that the physician must either admit to the patient that
he has limited power, time, or interest in changing matters, or
actually expend effort and time in attempting to make an exception
for this patient. Preventing the patient from making such a demand
on her doctor is an understandable, if not praiseworthy, tactic likely
to be used by a harried physician.

Physicians can improve the situation, and not incidentally relieve
themselves of enormous emotional burdens, by recognizing that they
are not individually responsible for the well-being of their patients,
that they too must work within the constraints of a system which is
struggling to achieve a more just distribution of care, and that it is a
Utopian dream to aspire to do "all that can be done" absolutely. In
this regard, their moral position is not unlike that of professors in
large public universities who constantly encounter more students
with more educational needs than they can hope to meet in anything
like ideal pedagogical circumstances. In both cases, the only viable

resolution is that we try to do the best we can under existing conditions. And once these conditions are well understood, the chances for successful outcomes are enormously increased.

Still, it is undeniable that for an educator socialized and prepared to enlighten the elite, such an experience can lower job satisfaction, just as the reduction in anticipated autonomy lowers the morale of physicians socialized and prepared to make independent decisions. Prospective physicians should be helped to prepare themselves for these coming circumstances, possibly through education designed to foster more of a team approach to health care, or possibly through professional education that helps the physician to appreciate that promotion of health and cure of disease must be considered in terms of entities larger than the individual patient. In other words, we might consider training future physicians to appreciate their obligation to the larger public good.

Beyond constructive changes in the training and socialization of doctors, however, is the recognition that innovations in health care delivery and financing have interpersonal effects. Whatever they may do to improve access and lower costs, these innovations can make structural changes in the doctor-patient relationship. In this essay we have alluded to the patient's increased difficulty in freely choosing a doctor, which may lead to the perception that doctors are more interchangeable than formerly; the pressure on doctors to spend less time with patients; and the increasingly powerful role of third-party gatekeepers. Health care financing arrangements should be carefully examined for their structural influences on the medical encounter, and we propose that administrators and medical educators work together both toward arrangements that do not sacrifice caring and other important curative elements in the medical encounter and toward improvements in medical training that counteract the expectable effects of increased management. For example, there are ways of establishing deeply appreciated personal commitments in relatively brief clinical encounters (Frankel, 1983). Hospital nurses know a great deal about this, and their counsel would be well worth seeking. Small gestures such as physical touching, a few minutes of nonmedical conversation, or the occasional unscheduled call or visit can establish the bonds needed for successful medical care. If the understandings we urge can be achieved, these gestures, combined with technically efficient treatment modalities, could do much to restore (or establish) that aspect of healing that stems from the sense that we are in the caring hands of *our* doctors.

REFERENCES

Altman, L. K., and L. Rosenthal (1990). "Doctors in Distress: Changes in Medicine Bring Pain to Healing Profession (Part I)." *New York Times*, February 18.

American Psychological Association. (1990). *Ethical Principles of Psychologists*. Washington, D.C.: American Psychological Association.

Balint, M. (1968). *The Doctor, His Patient, and the Illness*, 2d ed. London: Pitman.

Bayles, M. (1981). *Professional Ethics*. Belmont, Calif.: Wadsworth.

Belkin, L. (1990). "Doctors in Distress: Many in Medicine Are Calling Rules a Professional Malaise (Part II)." *New York Times*, February 19.

Berblinger, K. W. (1963). "The Physician, Patient, and Pill." *Psychosomatics* 4:265.

Blum, L. H. (1985). "Beyond Medicine: Healing Power in the Doctor-Patient Relationship." *Psychological Reports* 57:399–427.

Clyne, M. B. (1985). "The Doctor as a Placebo." *Stress Medicine* 1:37–40.

Coombs, R. H. (1978). *Mastering Medicine: Professional Socialization in Medical School*. New York: Free Press.

Davis, M. (1969). "Variations in Patients' Compliance with Doctors' Advice: An Empirical Analysis of Patterns of Communication." *American Journal of Public Health* 58:274–88.

————. (1971). "Variation in Patients' Compliance with Doctors' Orders: Medical Practice and Doctor-Patient Interaction." *Psychiatry Med.* 2:31–54.

Ekman, P., and W. Freisen. (1977). *Unmasking the Face*. Monterey, Calif.: Brooks/Cole.

Frank, J. (1981). *Persuasion and Healing*. Rev. ed. New York: Basic Books.

Frankel, R. M. (1983). "Talking in Interviews." In G. Psathas, ed., *Interaction Competence*. New York: Irvington.

House, J. S., K. R. Landis, and D. Umberson. (1988). "Social Relationships and Health." *Science* 241:540–45.

Kitzhaber, J. (1988). "Uncompensated Care: The Threat and the Challenge." *Western Journal of Medicine* 148 (June): 711–16.

Kleinman, A., L. Eisenberg, and B. Goode. (1978). "Culture, Illness, and Care: Clinical Lessons from Anthropological and Cross-cultural Research." *Annals of Internal Medicine* 88:251–58.

Kolata, G. (1990). "Doctors in Distress: Wariness Is Replacing Trust between Physician and Patient (Part III)." *New York Times*, February 20.

McKinlay, J. B. and J. Arches. (1985). "Towards the Proletarianization of Physicians." *Journal of Health Services* 15:161–95.

Mirvis, P. and S. Seashore. (1979). "Being Ethical in Organizational Research." *American Psychologist* 34:766–80.

Morreim, H. (1989). "Strategies in Cost Containment." *Hastings Center Report* 15:76–85.

Press, I. (1984). "The Predisposition to File Claims: The Patient's Perspective." *Law, Medicine, and Health Care* 12:53–62.

Price, L. (1984). "Art, Science, Faith, and Medicine: The Implications of the Placebo Effect." *Sociology of Health and Illness: A Journal of Medical Sociology* 6:61–73.

Roter, D. L., and L. A. Hall. (1989). "Studies of Doctor/Patient Interaction." *Annual Review of Public Health* 10:163–80.

"Special Report: The Professional Liability Crisis." (1986). *New England Journal of Medicine* 315:1105–8.

Svarstad, B. (1976). "Physician/Patient Communication and Patient Conformity with Medical Advice. In D. Mechanic, ed., *The Growth of Bureaucratic Medicine*. New York: Wiley.

Taylor, D. (1968). "The Theory of Reactance." In A. Cartwright and A. Zander, eds., *Social Psychology*. New York: Wiley.

Thomasma, D. C. (1983). Limitation of the Autonomy Model for the Doctor-Patient Relationship. *Pharos*, Spring, 2–5.

Waitzkin, H. (1984). "Doctor-Patient Communication: Clinical Implications of Social Scientific Research." *Journal of the American Medical Association* 252:2441–46.

Windt, P., P. C. Appleby, M. P. Battin, L. P. Francis, and B. M. Landesman, eds. (1981). *Ethical Issues in the Professions*. Engelwood Cliffs, N.J.: Prentice-Hall.

National Health Care, Patient Trust, and Physician Loyalty

Dan W. Brock

The organization and financing of health care is undergoing fundamental changes. A central force driving many of these changes is financial pressure to control increases in health care costs. Some results of these changes are already upon us, such as a variety of forms of prepaid and managed care, while other possible outcomes are further into the future, such as some form of national health program. The essays of Margaret P. Battin and of Leonard J. Haas and Peter C. Appleby in this volume explore related worries about the consequences of these changes in health care financing and organization for patients' trust in their physicians and physicians' loyalty to their patients. I shall use this occasion of commenting on their essays to press further the concerns expressed in them. Since the sources of their respective worries are quite distinct, however, my comments will address each essay in turn.

Battin argues, quite correctly I believe, that a national health program would be subject to continual pressures to deliver health care more efficiently to the patients it serves. This should have the desirable effect of eliminating many of the perverse incentives for overtreatment still common in fee-for-service medicine. These cost pressures would also increase the already intense interest in effectiveness research designed to improve, or in some cases just to create, data about outcomes of treatments for common medical conditions. And this new data, together with continuing cost pressures, would lead to increasing standardization of treatment of patients with common medical conditions. The program would seek to identify not the best treatment, as has traditional medicine, but what she calls the "best buy" treatment. Since almost certainly there would be no prohibition on parallel private care outside of the program for those willing and able to pay for it, a two- or multitiered system would result. Battin is surely correct, however, that even "ill-fitting" standardized care for the now uninsured would be an improvement over no care at all.

Battin argues that this standardization is especially problematic in the care of dying patients where practice guidelines make less sense, since there is no common medical outcome sought for dying patients as there may be for those with prostate disease or an inflamed appendix. The problem for standardization, however, cuts more deeply than Battin suggests, across all of medicine, not just the care of dying patients.

Battin takes standardization for cost-effectiveness to be a special problem for dying patients because there is no common medical goal on the basis of which a cost-effective treatment could be identified and standardized. But it seems to me a mistake to hold that there is no goal in the treatment of dying patients against which treatments could be measured for cost-effectiveness. Euthanasia is *not* the cost-effective treatment for most dying patients, because their goal is not to die as soon as possible. Most dying patients, though of course not all, wish to have many treatments that extend their lives, as long as those treatments do not so reduce their quality of life that they then find it worse than no further life at all. Virtually all dying patients wish to have their pain treated, though not always minimized if that would leave them unable to interact with others, and to be kept comfortable and have their dignity maintained as much as possible. The precise content of the goals of particular dying patients varies, depending on their values, concerns, and medical condition. But it is not true that because they are dying, there are no medical goals for treatment.

Now, this does not mean that standardization of treatment for dying patients on a best-buy basis is ethically unproblematic. Such standardization for different patient conditions is ethically problematic in general, not just for dying patients. To see why this is so, we need to recall one central respect in which ideals of the physician/patient relationship have changed in recent decades, and what the basis of that change has been. It is a commonplace of medical ethics that the ideal for physician/patient relations has shifted over the last several decades from an authoritarian or paternalist ideal that lodged decisional authority with the physician to an ideal of shared decision making with essential roles for both physician and patient.[1]

[1] President's Commission for the Study of Ethical Problems in Medicine and Biomedical and Behavioral Research, *Making Health Care Decisions* (Washington, D.C.: Government Printing Office, 1982).

What are the grounds of this new, expanded role for patients? One ground is the recognition that the goal of promoting the patient's well-being with treatment requires the input of the patient's values to determine which treatment alternative best promotes that patient's well-being. This is so for at least two reasons: first, it is increasingly the case that there is more than one medically acceptable mode of treatment for a particular condition, no one of which is best for all patients; second, the seemingly objective treatment goals of promoting health and preserving life are ultimately in service of the patient's well-being, but a particular patient's well-being depends significantly on the particular aims, values, and preferences of that patient. The second ground for patient participation in shared decision making is respecting patient self-determination—the interest of ordinary persons in making significant decisions about their lives for themselves and according to their own values. Together, these two grounds imply that increasingly often a patient's particular aims and values must be taken into account to determine which treatment is best for that particular patient, and that the patient's treatment choice must be respected.

This point does not hold just for unusual patients or unusual patient conditions. One of the leading proponents of outcomes research, John Wennberg, noted about his research on treatment of prostate disease: "Perhaps the most important conclusion so far is that for individual patients with benign prostatic hypertrophy, rational choices among treatments depend on attitudes about risks and benefits—on how patients view their predicaments."[2] Thus, shared decision making implies greater individualization of treatment, not greater standardization. If Battin is correct that a national health program under cost-constraint pressures would seek to standardize treatments by providing efficient "best-buy" treatments, in doing so it would come into deep conflict with the individualization of treatment at the heart of the ideal of shared decision making and with its requirement of informed consent. Providing the patient with full information about all possible treatment alternatives is a part of securing the patient's fully informed consent to treatment. But it would be difficult for physicians to provide, and perhaps unreasonable to expect them to provide, that information if non-best-buy treatments were not in fact available under the program. Henry J.

---

[2]John Wennberg, "Outcomes Research, Cost Containment, and the Fear of Health Care Rationing," *New England Journal of Medicine* 323 (1990): 1202–4.

Aaron and William B. Schwartz observed this difficulty among British physicians dealing with patients beyond the age at which renal dialysis was generally available. The physicians tended to tell these patients that there was nothing more that could be done for them.[3] Most patients probably understood this to mean there was no medical treatment for their condition, though the truth was that social policy did not make available a possible treatment. Full informed consent about all medically possible treatment alternatives would be difficult to maintain in the face of the limited availability of non-best-buy treatments.

I do not conclude that we should oppose a national health program—on the contrary, I believe there is no higher ethical priority in United States health policy than to secure universal access to health care. But I believe we must be attentive to not losing the hard-won gains in patient participation in decisions about their health care and in the greater seriousness with which the requirement of informed consent is now often taken, both of which would be under pressure from a program seeking efficient best-buy health care. Shared decision making and informed consent would require some limitations on the standardization of care in the service of controlling costs. It is worth adding that we will face this problem in coming years even if we do not get a national program. The intense cost-containment pressures already present in our current heterogeneous health care financing and delivery system, together with the increased standardization of treatment that effectiveness research will make possible, will put pressure on patient participation and informed consent with or without a national health program.

Haas and Appleby pursue a different but related strain on the physician/patient relationship from new forms of health care organization and financing. As was true of standardization, the loyalty conflicts and the erosion of patients' trust with which they are concerned will increasingly arise whether or not we get a national health program. In their essay they explore these conflicts in the context of managed care, not a national program, but I will assume the conflicts will increasingly arise under either form of organization and financing. The conflicts they focus on are between these new forms of organization and financing and the traditional loyalty and commitment of physicians to their patients. Haas and Appleby

---

[3]Henry J. Aaron and William B. Schwartz, *The Painful Prescription: Rationing Hospital Care* (Washington, D.C.: Brookings Institution, 1984), pp. 36–37.

argue, in my view quite correctly, that inequalities between most patients and their physicians in medical knowledge, training, and expertise, together with the fear, anxiety, and regression common in seriously ill patients, give patients good reason to want to be able to place their care in the hands of physicians whom they can trust to provide them with all needed treatment. It would be a mistake for defenders of shared decision making to deny these facts or the consequent importance of physician loyalty to their patients' needs and interests. Moreover, patients' belief in their physicians' commitment to care for them appears to have significant therapeutic benefits for patients. When physicians have new conflicts of interest, however, either under managed care or in a national health program, from incentives to limit costs by providing best-buy instead of best treatment, this loyalty is seriously threatened.

How then can this important loyalty of physicians to their patients, and patients' trust in that loyalty, be protected? One suggestion of Haas and Appleby is for physicians to become increasingly involved in health care policy and administration to increase their "sense of ownership in the institutions for which they work." But this has the danger of only exacerbating the problem as physicians come more to take the perspective of their institution and employer and come to be more alienated from their patients. Haas and Appleby also suggest small informal ways in which personal, caring relations can be maintained such as physical touching and "a few minutes of nonmedical conversation." While these personal gestures are no doubt desirable, I believe it is doubtful they can have a major role in securing patient trust in the face of the forces dividing physicians' and patients' interests.

The decade of the 1990s is likely to see a fundamental transformation in physicians' and patients' expectations about the care that will be provided for patients. That transformation, which has already begun, will not come easily and will be a major source of strain on physician loyalty and patient trust. I will continue to use Battin's distinction between best care and best-buy care as a shorthand to signal the shift in expectations with which I am concerned. Many, probably most, American physicians continue to believe that they ought to be able to provide their patients with the best, not merely the best-buy, care for their condition. This is not to ignore that many physicans already now practice in institutional settings, such as HMOs and managed-care plans, in which there are strong incentives to limit costs by providing less than the best care. But the professional standard of care remains largely set by the norms and incentives of traditional fee-for-service practice with insured patients in which physicians believe that they should do everything of positive expected benefit for their patients, without regard for cost. "Defensive medicine," in response to worries about legal liability for malpractice, reinforces this norm. In practice, of course, this ideal has often not been pushed to its full limit, and diagnostic or therapeutic measures of very high cost and very low benefit for the patient have often been omitted. But the ideal and norm for many physicians remains the best, not best-buy, care for their patients.

The expectations of many patients too are still that they should receive the best, not best-buy, care when they are ill. While most of the public is, no doubt, well aware of concerns and efforts to limit health care costs, widespread public expectations remain from days when health insurance often had few limits, co-payments or deductibles, and so patients could expect any care that might be of benefit with little worry about its costs. As third-party payers both limit what they will pay for and shift more costs to patients, patients will increasingly be forced to be more cost conscious and to shift their expectations from best care toward best-buy care. While this cost consciousness may come relatively easily when people are paying for health insurance or health care, it will be especially difficult when patients are seriously ill and then quite naturally want the best care possible.

These changes in expectations of physicians and patients about the standard of care which they should be able to provide or receive will not come easily, though I believe they are to a significant degree inevitable and on the whole desirable. What might be called an increased "economic realism" about health care is needed by both physicians and patients. But during the coming period of significant transformation of these expectations, it will be difficult for physicians to be fully open and honest with their patients about what potentially beneficial diagnostic or therapeutic measures are not available because they are too costly. The example I cited earlier from Aaron and Schwartz of how British physicians often fail to deal openly with patients who cannot be offered dialysis for their renal disease illustrates this difficulty. Physician openness about these limits will only be made more difficult by the ambivalence of patients about accepting these limits. I have no doubts that Haas and Appleby are correct about the importance of preserving physician loyalty and patient trust. But the transformation needed in the expectations of physicians about the care which they should be able to provide and of patients about the care which they should receive will make doing so even more difficult than Haas and Appleby suggest.

Contributors

PETER C. APPLEBY

Peter C. Appleby, Ph.D., is Professor and Chair of the Department of Philosophy at the University of Utah. He received his doctorate from the University of Texas at Austin, where he specialized in the philosophy of religion. For the past ten years, he has been working in professional ethics, especially in the ethics of mental health care. He is currently a nonpsychologist member of the Ethics Committee of the American Psychological Association.

MARGARET P. BATTIN

Margaret P. Battin, Ph.D., is Professor of Philosophy and Adjunct Professor of Internal Medicine at the University of Utah. She holds an M.F.A. in Fiction Writing as well as a doctorate in Philosophy, both from the University of California at Irvine. She has authored, edited, or coedited eight books, among them a study of philosophical issues in suicide, an edition of John Donne's treatise *Biathanatos,* a collection on age-rationing of medical care, a casebook in aesthetics, a text on professional ethics, and a study of ethical issues in organized religion. In recent years, she has been engaged in research on active euthanasia and assisted suicide in Holland and Germany.

HAROLD BAUMAN

Harold Bauman, Ph.D., Associate Professor, has been teaching the History of Science and the History of Medicine at the University of

Utah since 1965. His areas of research interest are medicine in Prussia, 1790–1820, and American surgery, 1890–1940.

DAN W. BROCK

Dan W. Brock, Ph.D., is Professor of Philosophy and of Human Values in Medicine at Brown University. He served in 1981 as Staff Philosopher on the president's Commission for the Study of Ethical Problems in Medicine and Biomedical and Behavioral Research. He is the author (with Allen E. Buchanan) of *Deciding for Others: The Ethics of Surrogate Decision Making*, published in 1989 by Cambridge University Press, and has published many papers in ethics and biomedical ethics.

LAWRENCE BROWN

Lawrence Brown, Ph.D., who previously served on the faculty of the University of Michigan and the staff of The Brookings Institution, is now Professor and Head of the Division of Health Policy and Management in the School of Public Health at Columbia University. Editor of the *Journal of Health Politics, Policy and Law* from 1984 to 1989, he writes on competitive and regulatory issues in health policy and on the politics of health care policy making. He is currently (with Catherine McLaughlin) evaluating the Robert Wood Johnson Foundation's Community Programs for Affordable Health Care and their Program for the Medically Uninsured.

ALLEN BUCHANAN

Allen Buchanan, Ph.D., is Professor of Philosophy at the University of Arizona and is the author of numerous articles in political philosophy, ethical theory, and bioethics as well as the following books: *Marx and Justice: The Radical Critique of Liberalism* (1982); *Ethics, Efficiency, and the Market* (1985); *Deciding for Others* (with Dan Brock) (1989); and *Secession: The Morality of Political Discourse from Fort Sumter to Lithuania and Quebec*.

KENNETH N. BUCHI, M.D.

Kenneth N. Buchi, M.D., is an Associate Professor in the Department of Medicine at the University of Utah School of Medicine. He practices at the University Hospital, with active clinical and research interests in interventional gastrointestinal endoscopy, laser ablation or palliation of bowel cancers, hemostasis of bleeding ulcers and other bleeding lesions, and treatment of bile duct stones, strictures, or tumors. He is also interested in health policy issues and is active in both the Utah and American Medical Associations.

SUZANNE DANDOY, M.D.

Suzanne Dandoy, M.D., is Executive Director of the Utah Department of Health. Her medical and public health degrees are from UCLA, with specialty training in epidemiology and preventive medicine. Prior to her current position, she was Professor of Health Administration at Arizona State University. She is Chair of the Editorial Board of the *American Journal of Public Health* and President of the American College of Preventive Medicine.

PAUL J. FELDSTEIN

Paul J. Feldstein, Ph.D., has served as Professor and FHP Foundation Distinguished Chair in Health Care Management at the Graduate School of Management, University of California, Irvine, since 1987. He has served at the University of Michigan as Professor in both the Department of Economics and the School of Public Health and as Director of the Division of Research at the American Hospital Association. He received his Ph.D. from the University of Chicago in 1961. His most recent book is *The Politics of Health Legislation: An Economic Perspective.* Professor Feldstein's current research interests concern the reasons for the rapid increase in health insurance premiums and an examination of the effect of insurance company cost-containment programs, such as utilization review, on health insurance premiums and employee use of services.

JOHN G. FRANCIS

John G. Francis, Ph.D., is Professor of Political Science at the University of Utah. His field is comparative public policy, particularly in the fields of environment and health. He is currently completing a book on comparative regulation to be published by Blackwell's.

LESLIE FRANCIS

Leslie Francis, Ph.D., J.D., is Professor of Law, Associate Professor of Philosophy, and Adjunct Associate Professor of Internal Medicine at the University of Utah. She is currently at work on a book entitled *Legitimate Expectations*. Her fields in philosophy include philosophy of law and bioethics.

LEONARD J. HAAS

Leonard J. Haas, Ph.D., is a clinical psychologist and Associate Professor in the Department of Family and Preventive Medicine at the University of Utah School of Medicine. He received his Ph.D. from the University of Colorado. A former member of the Ethics Committee of the American Psychological Association, he is a current member of its Board of Professional Affairs. He is coauthor (with J. Malouf) of *Keeping Up the Good Work: A Practitioner's Guide to Mental Health Ethics*, and has published a number of journal articles in professional ethics.

J. WILLIAM HOLLINGSWORTH, M.D.

J. William Hollingsworth, M.D., was Chief of Medicine at West Haven, Connecticut, Veterans Administration Medical Center in the 1950s and held the same position at the San Diego, California, VA Medical Center from 1978 until retirement in 1991. In between, he was on the Yale faculty and was Chairman of the Department of Medicine at the University of Kentucky in Lexington.

ROBERT P. HUEFNER

Robert P. Huefner, D.B.A., holds a doctorate in business administration from Harvard University and is currently the FHP Professor of Political Science at the University of Utah. He has contributed to the *Public Administration Review*, the *National Tax Journal*, and various studies and books concerned with questions of finance and leadership in public policy. He received the National Governors' Association's Eighth Annual Award for Distinguished Service.

BRUCE M. LANDESMAN

Bruce M. Landesman, Ph.D., is an Associate Professor of Philosophy at the University of Utah. His specialties are political philosophy, ethics, and applied ethics. He has published articles on the nature of justice and on lawyer-client confidentiality, and is an editor of the anthology *Ethical Issues in the Professions.*

ALAN R. NELSON, M.D.

Alan R. Nelson, M.D., is a past President of the American Medical Association. Currently a member of the Institute of Medicine, he is the President Elect of the World Medical Association. Dr. Nelson's awards include that of Distinguished Internist, American Society of Internal Medicine, in 1989.

CHARLES B. SMITH, M.D.

Charles B. Smith, M.D., graduated from Harvard Medical School and was trained in medicine and infectious diseases at the Boston City Hospital. He was the Chief of the Division of Infectious Diseases at the University of Utah during the 1970s, and for the past ten years served as Chief of the Medical Service of the Salt Lake Veterans Administration Medical Center. This year he moved to Seattle to become Associate Dean of the Medical School and Chief of the Medical Staff at the Seattle VA Medical Center. His research interests are in the areas of assessment and management of quality health care.

FRANK J. THOMPSON

Frank J. Thompson, Ph.D., is Dean of the School of Public Affairs and Professor of Public Administration, Political Science, and Public Health at the State University of New York, Albany. He is the author of *Health Policy and the Bureaucracy: Politics and Implementation* with MIT Press as well as other books and articles. He was a Public Administration Fellow with the U.S. Public Health Service and subsequently served as consultant to that agency.

NORMAN WAITZMAN

Norman Waitzman, Ph.D., is an assistant professor in the economics department at the University of Utah. He is on leave during the 1990–91 academic year, coauthoring a book on physician supply and working on several other health services research projects at the

University of California, Berkeley, and the University of California, San Francisco.

DAVID WILSFORD

David Wilsford, Ph.D., is currently Assistant Professor of International Affairs at the Georgia Institute of Technology. His research focuses on the industrial and social policies of advanced industrial democracies, especially Western Europe and Japan. His book, *Doctors and the State* (1991), was published by Duke University Press. He is working on a second book about health policies in the OECD Group of Seven, *The Fiscal Imperative in Health Care*, which will compare the United States and France to Canada, the United Kingdom, Germany, Italy, and Japan.

MARK W. WOLCOTT, M.D.

Mark W. Wolcott, M.D., graduated from the University of Lehigh and did undergraduate work at University of Pennsylvania. He trained in General and Cardiothoracic Surgery. Dr. Wolcott has served as Chief of Surgical Research at the Veterans Administration and as Chief of Staff, Veterans Administration Medical Center, Salt Lake City, Utah. Recently, Dr. Wolcott was the Assistant Chief Medical Director for Clinical Affairs, Washington, D.C., and now serves as Chief of Surgery, VA Medical Center, Salt Lake City, Utah.

Index

Aaron, Henry J., 10, 152, 169, 347–48, 350
Abortion, 12, 206–7
Acceptability, political, 256–61, 279–81
Access
  classification of proposals, 276–78
  cost containment and competition in mixed systems, 243–46
  cross-country comparison of statutory, 122–24
  ethics and justification for national health systems, 80–82
  ethics and private sector, 236–38
  failures of U.S. health policy, 129, 244
  feasibility of health care proposals, 255
  federal government and alternative schemes for securing, 239–40
  increasing concern with, 140
  inequities in U.S., 102, 169, 176, 208
  patient expectations, 212, 229
  political acceptability of proposals, 259–60
  private sector role in mixed systems, 240–43
  private sector obligations under existing conditions, 246–48
  universal and cost, 75–76
  Veterans Affairs services, 143, 153–57, 163–64, 180
Access 2000, 266

Accreditation, 149
Act to Make Health Security Available to All Citizens. . . , 265
Administration
  Canadian and U.S. costs compared, 53, 54
  cost containment strategies, 23–24
  cost savings of universal system, 233–34n.44
  government and capacity problem, 307–8
  inventory of choices in health care program design, 281–88
  program choices, 288
  Veterans Affairs health care system and costs, 148, 156
  waste and inefficiency, 121
Age. *See also* Elderly
  allocation of health care, 198
  informed consent and social policy, 348
  Medicare and national health insurance, 4
Agency for Health Care Policy and Research (AHCPR), 267, 315
Alcohol abuse, 165
Allocation. *See also* Rationing
  classification of proposals and government, 278–79
  ethical issues, 6–12
All-payer schemes, 245–46
American Academy of Pediatrics, 261
American Association for Labor Legislation, 31

Veterans Affairs health care system, 145–48, 156, 180
Egalitarianism, 6–7
Ehrenreich, Barbara, 29, 46
Eisenhower, Dwight D., 41
Elderly. *See also* Age
access to health care, 102
German health care system, 92
groups with concentrated interest in change, 62, 65
long-term care programs, 68
VA eligibility, 165
Elwood, Paul, 42
Embryo research, 12
Emergency room care, 216
Employers and employment. *See also* Business
employment-based health care models, 220–23, 225
fairness and national health programs, 16–17
groups with concentrated interest in change, 60–61
higher insurance costs among small business, 70n.1
tax incentives and health-insurance plans, 36, 68–69, 71n.10
Encouragement, 215–16
Enthoven, Alain, 44. *See also* Enthoven-Kronick plan
Enthoven-Kronick plan
acceptability and feasibility, 280
access, 140, 270
classification of proposal, 270–72, 274, 279
combination of market and regulatory approaches, 252
description of plan, 263
employment-based health care models, 220–23
expectations, 232n.27
government and administration, 307
implementation and evolution, 308–9
phasedown of insurance programs, 233n.38
state and federal government roles, 303–4
Equality, 201–2

d'Estaing, Valery Giscard, 95
Ethics. *See also* Morality.
access and private sector, 236–38
allocation, 6–12
conflicts in private sector, 235–6
contrasting models of private sector role in mixed system, 240–43
death and dying, 329, 346
fairness, 16–17
freedom of choice, 14–17
important choices in program design, 288, 290–94
justifications for introduction of national health systems, 80–85, 103–4
physicians and professional, 197
Progressive Era debate on national health program, 33
proposals for national health insurance, 3–6
social values, 12–14
Veterans Affairs health care system, 144–45, 152–53
Europe. *See also* specific country
comparison of health care systems, 79–80
politics compared to American, 89–90, 132
Euthanasia, 14, 346
Evans, Robert G., 178, 179
Evolution, 306–9
Exceptionalism, American political, 88–89, 302, 306
Excise tax, 66
Expectations
morality, 214–19
patients and physicians, 210–14, 349–51
program design, 302–6
proposals for change in American health care, 209–10, 220–30
Expenditures. *See also* Costs
failures of U.S. policy, 129
high level of in U.S. and rate of increase, 101, 186n.2
limits on providers, 67–68, 70
per capita in U.S., 86–87
as percent of GDP in U.S., 173
reasons for poor U.S. health performance, 110–13

adequate levels of health care, 196–
206
American political culture and
policy entitlements, 131
Constitution and status of health
care as, 206–8
coverage and program choices,
282–85
ethics and national health care,
81–82, 290–91
health care as, 191–94
justification of, 194–96
Rilke, Rainer Maria, 313, 321–25,
327–28
Risks, 212
Rockfeller, Jay, 265
Rockefeller, John D. IV, 29, 268
Rogers, Paul, 266
Roosevelt, Franklin Delano, 34–35
Roosevelt, Theodore, 31
Roper, William, 267
Rural locations, 15

Sandier, Simone, 114
Sanford, J. P., 148
Sapolsky, Harvey, 307
Schwartz, William B., 10, 152, 169,
348, 350
Schweiker, Richard, 44
Science, modern medicine, 176–77
Self-determination, 347
Self-evidence, 194
Self-interest, 52
Self-respect, 194
Sickness funds, 91–92, 93
Smith, Dr. Charles B., 146, 163, 166,
179–80, 185
Social Darwinism, 39
Socialized medicine, 38
Social needs, 10–12
Social responsibility, 185–86
Social Security
financing of Medicare, 57–58, 59
history of national health policy,
30, 33, 34
pressure to reduce taxes, 66
Socioeconomic status, 122–23
South Africa, 217
Soviet Union, 14
Staffing, Veterans Affairs health care
system,146, 156

Standardization, 314, 316, 320–25,
345–46
State governments. *See also* Politics
cost and quality initiatives, 258–59
groups with concentrated interest
in change, 65
Medicaid and cost control, 59, 60
Medicaid benefits and recipients,
75
prospects for action, 280–81, 303–
4
role in access to health care, 257–
58
State Health Insurance Program
(SHIP), 263
Sterilizations, 16
Stockman, David, 44
Structural theory, 270–74, 276–79
Structure, projected national health
system, 65–70
Sunshine, J., 149
Supreme Court, 54, 206–7
Surgery, cross-country comparison,
119, 120

Taxation
financing of national health proposals, 66
incentives to employer health
insurance plans, 36, 68–69,
71n.10
incentives to nonprofit organizations, 246
middle-class and employer-paid
health insurance, 63
Taylor, Glenn H., 37
Technology. *See also* Innovation;
Research
basic levels of health care, 197
Canadian health care model, 229
cost containment, 84
increasing costs of medical care,
70
increasing reliance on, 208
Thatcher, Margaret, 100–101
Thomas, Elbert, 37
Thurow, Lester C., 16
To the Rescue, 263
Transfer payments, 203, 204
Transplant, organ, 218–19
Truman, Harry S., 30, 37–41, 56